M000316666

DISCOURSES AND ESSAYS

Classic Reformed
Discourses and Essays

J.H. Merle D'Aubigne

Solid Ground Christian Books
Birmingham, Alabama USA

Solid Ground Christian Books
2090 Columbiana Rd, Suite 2000
Birmingham, AL 35216
205-443-0311
sgcb@charter.net
http://solid-ground-books.com

Classis Reformed Discourses and Essays

Jean Henri Merle D'Aubigne (1795-1876)

Taken from the 1846 edition by William Collins, Glasgow & London

Solid Ground Classic Reprints

First printing of new edition September 2005

Cover work by Borgo Design, Tuscaloosa, AL
Contact them at nelbrown@comcast.net

Cover image is of the Genevan Valley where D'Aubigne spent most of his life.

1-599250-18-7

INTRODUCTION.

IT may not be amiss to give the reader, in a few words, some account of the history and contents of this volume.

For several years the desire has been entertained and expressed, by many in this country, to have a volume in English of such of the occasional Essays and Discourses of Dr. MERLE D'AUBIGNE as are of a general nature; and three years ago the subscriber gave assurances to the public that the task of selection and translation would be undertaken by him, or under his auspices, at no distant day. But circumstances, which it is not necessary to state, for a long time prevented the accomplishment of this purpose. He is happy, however, to say that the work has at length been executed, and the result the reader will find in this volume, containing seventeen Discourses and Essays.

A few of these productions have at one time or another been translated into English, and published separately in England or in this country, and some in both, either in small volumes or in pamphlets. But the greater part are now given to the public for the first time, in an English translation.

Although it does not become me to say much about the manner in which the task has been executed, I think that I may safely assure the public that it has been performed with all reasonable fidelity. The meaning of the author has been conscientiously given, and, it is believed, with proper ease and clearness of expression. Doubtless a French idiom, or an approach to one, may be occasionally discovered; but these things, when they do not render the sense obscure, rather excite the attention and interest of the reader than otherwise, by breaking up the monotony of ordinary style.

All of these Discourses and Essays bear the impress of the same masterly mind which beams forth on every page of the author's inimitable History of the Great Reformation in the Sixteenth Century. The first six Discourses were delivered to a French church in Hamburg in Germany. The others were preached at Brussels in Geneva. Of the Essays, all but one were read in the last named city, at the openings of the sessions of the Theological Seminary, of which the author is the president.

The same simple, beautiful, and perfectly philosophical analysis runs through each of these productions. The same clear statement, the same rapid and effective mode of reasoning which characterizes the French mind; and the same resistless driving onward to a conclusion which often strikes and surprises us by the suddenness with which we are brought upon it. The formal and tedious syllogism does not suit the Gallic mind; it more befits the Anglo-Saxon, the Norman, and the German.

These Discourses are very different from our American sermons. No one can read a page of them without being struck with this fact. There is a vivacity and point in the style, a condensed and penetrating statement of the leading ideas, a rapid discussion of each topic, and an abrupt dismissal of it, which are unknown to our modes of thinking and writing. This very circumstance will render their perusal profitable, in no ordinary degree, to those among us whose office it is to preach the Gospel. At the same time they are such as cannot be read without advantage by the layman.

As to the Essays, it would be hard to find in any language an equal number that can be compared with them. Take, for instance, those on the Study of the History of Christianity, the nature and tendency of Puseyism,[1] the duty of the Church to confess Christ, Lutheranism and Calvinism, and the Miracles, or two Errors. Where shall we find the subjects there treated handled with such ability?

These Discourses and Essays possess one grand characteristic: that of a glorious baptism, if I may so express myself, into the spirit of the Reformation. This spirit pervades them all; but it is most manifest in the Essays. Of all men of this age, it may be safely said, Dr. Merle D'Aubigné is the most thoroughly imbued with the spirit of the Reformers. In fact, he hardly lives in the present era, though he does move bodily about among the men of our times. Sure I am, his mind, his heart, his whole spiritual man is, at least, as much conversant with the events and spirit of the age of the Reformers as with those of our day.

---

[1] Geneva and Oxford.

As to the author, I have been importuned to give some notice of him in this introduction. But it is not the place to say more than a few words.

Dr. Merle D'Aubigné,[1] though born in Geneva, is like many of the inhabitants of that "City of Refuge," of French origin.

His great-grand-father, John Louis Merle, emigrated, for the sake of his religion, from Nismes to Geneva, about the epoch of the revocation of the Edict of Nantes. His son, Francis Merle, in the year 1743, married Elizabeth D'Aubigné, a daughter of Baron George D'Aubigné, a Protestant nobleman who resided in that city, and who was a descendant of the celebrated Chevalier Theodore Agrippa D'Aubigné, whose memoirs have been recently published in this country;[2] a faithful but poorly rewarded adherent of Henry IV, a decided Protestant, a brave cavalier, a prolific author; the grand-father of Madame de Maintenon, mistress and wife of Louis XIV; and in his own age was exiled to Geneva for his religion by the ungrateful race for whose elevation to the throne of France he had spent twenty long years and more in the camp. It is from his paternal grand-mother that Dr. Merle derives the addition of *D'Aubigné* to his name.

The immediate progenitor of our author was *Aimé Robert Merle D'Aubigné*, born in 1755. He was the father of three sons, the eldest and the youngest of whom are respectable merchants in our country, one in New-York, the other in New-Orleans. The death of this excellent man was most deplorable; for he was murdered by the Austrians and Russians, near Zurich, in the autumn of 1799, as he was returning from a commercial mission to Constantinople and Vienna. Falling in with these infuriated troops, a day or two after the decisive defeat which the French under Massena had given them, he was inhumanly slain. He left a widow, who with faith and courage contended against adversity, brought up well her three sons, gave them all a liberal education in the city of their birth, lived to see them far advanced in their various careers, and died in peace on the 11th of January last, at an age exceeding four score.

[1] He received the degree of Doctor in Divinity from the college of New Jersey in 1838.   [2] Under the title of *The Huguenot Captain.*

Dr. Merle D'Aubigné was born in the year 1794; he is therefore in his 52nd year at present. He is a tall, erect, fine-looking man, of dark complexion, black eyes, and commanding mien. His health is by no means good; but his energy is indomitable. He has just published the fourth volume of his admirable History of the Reformation; to complete this work will require at least two if not three or four volumes more.

In the autumn of 1817 or 1818, our author, having completed his studies at the Academy or University of Geneva, went to Berlin, where he spent some time engaged in theological and historical pursuits under the guidance of the celebrated Neander, and other distinguished professors of the University in that city. On his way thither he visited the Castle of Wartburg, near Eisenach; and while standing in the room in which Luther spent almost a year as a sort of prisoner, the thought came into his mind to write the History of the Reformation. That thought soon became a settled purpose; it gave direction to all his subsequent feelings, studies, and aims.

From Berlin he went to Hamburg, where he preached for five years and more to a small French Protestant church. It was there he preached and published the first six sermons which are contained in this volume.

From Hamburg he removed to Brussels, where he preached to a Protestant church until the Revolution of September 1830, which severed Belgium from Holland. As he was a great favourite with the late king of Holland, who heard him with much regularity when he came to the Belgian capital of his kingdom, he was not likely to meet with favour from the revolutionary party. In fact he narrowly escaped death on that occasion. Returning to his native city soon afterward, he took up his abode there, and was appointed President of the new Theological Seminary which was founded by the Geneva Evangelical Society in the year following. There he has resided ever since.

With these remarks and notices, the volume which they are intended to introduce is commended to the favourable regards of the Christian public. R. BAIRD.

NEW YORK, April, 1846.

CONTENTS.

DISCOURSES.

DISCOURSE I.

EMMANUEL.

" Behold, a virgin shall be with child, and shall bring forth a son, and they
shall call his name Emmanuel, which being interpreted is, God with
us."—MATTHEW, i, 23.

THE union of man with God is the great work which true
religion was to accomplish. Any religion that has not
this object, and that does not provide the means necessary to
attain it, thereby becomes useless and vain. This union is
not designed to qualify us to reason concerning God, to define
his nature, to expatiate on all his attributes; this is not the
aim which true religion should have in view, whatever philosophers may think. Neither does it imply the paying of an
external homage to the Divine Being; approaching him with
genuflections, in processions, or through sacrifices; such is
not the aim which true religion should have in view, however
the vain superstitions of nations may have represented it. It
is not the discovery of certain principles which may be considered the expression of the Creator's will, nor their presen-
tation as rules of conduct to the creature; this is not the object
which true religion should have in view, though it is in this
that moralists deem its essence to consist. Some of these
things may follow, but it is with something else that we must
begin. A greater work must be accomplished—man must be
united to God. Of what value is all his learning, his worship,
or his morality, while he does not sincerely love Him whom
he ought to know, to adore, and to follow? Man is separated
from God: this is one of the fundamental truths of our history; one of the great explanatory principles of our nature;
one of those great facts to which the conscience of every man
testifies. In vain is man ignorant of the origin of this fact;

he knows and feels its existence; and whenever the wants of his soul are awakened, whenever he listens to that secret voice which sometimes speaks to remind him of the primitive nobility of his nature, he sighs for a union the want of which he then knows and feels. As a child is said to be separated from his father when he has revolted against him, has left his house, entertains wrong sentiments towards him, and delights in doing what he disapproves; so it must be said that man, in the state in which we know him, is separated from his God. And as such a child should first of all be reconciled and reunited to his father; so man should first of all be reconciled and reunited to his God. There can be no order, no justice, no peace, no happiness, while such a disunion exists. To effect this reunion is the object of Christianity. It is the work which God has had in view; and this day reveals [1] to us the means wherewith he sees fit to accomplish it. God has come into the world to reconcile us unto himself. The birth of Jesus Christ is the link which connects that which was separated. On that day Emmanuel was given to us; on that day this oracle of an ancient prophet, repeated by the Evangelist in the words of our text, was fulfilled : " Behold, a virgin shall be with child, and shall bring forth a son, and they shall call his name Emmanuel, which being interpreted is, God with us." That day was the epoch of the union of man with God. We will consider with you the principle of this union, namely, that God has been with us ; and the consequence of this principle, namely, that we should be with God. Thus, the principle and the consequence, GOD WITH US, and WE WITH GOD, will form the two divisions of this meditation.

And Thou who didst come in the flesh to reconcile unto thyself the fallen race of man, grant thy blessing upon the words of our lips; that, while displaying unto the minds of many what thou hast done, this day may become for them the day of an everlasting covenant with thee ! Amen.

GOD WITH US.

GOD has been with us. This, my brethren, is the great truth which we proclaim unto you; and perhaps it is a truth

---

[1] This discourse was delivered on Christmas.

entirely new to some who, though they may often have heard
it before, have never yet understood it. God has been with us.
In uttering these words we do not make use of figurative language, but we mean simply what we say. *God himself* became
flesh, and a *man* like ourselves. The day which we commemorate is that on which the Eternal Being humbled himself, and
appeared among men in the form of a child. Do these assertions seem extraordinary or inadmissible? We have the means
of proving them. We have not lightly advanced them; we
can dissipate the smallest doubt in the mind of any one who
still respects the infallible word of God.

In that Jesus of Nazareth, whose birth we commemorate
to-day, and who was crucified thirty-three years later, under
Pontius Pilate, dwelt all " the fulness of the Godhead." It
was not an angel, nor an archangel, nor any creature, who put
on human nature in the person of Jesus Christ, but it was *God*.
This, my brethren, is a fundamental and immovable truth,
which the word of God displays in all its splendour. We do
not wish to accumulate here all the quotations we might make
to prove it. One alone might suffice. A few ought to be
enough. Consider then, first, the words of our text: it were
difficult to find any more clear: " They shall call his name
Emmanuel, which being interpreted is, God with us." From
the Gospel according to Matthew, from which our text is taken,
turn, I pray you, to the Gospel according to John, and you will
see that it begins thus: " In the beginning was the Word, and
the Word was with God, and the Word was God. All things
were made by Him, and without him was not any thing made
that was made. And the Word was made flesh, and dwelt
among us, full of grace and truth." From the Gospel according to John, turn to the Epistle of Paul to the Romans, and
you will read these words: " Whose are the fathers, and of
whom, as concerning the flesh, Christ came, who is over all,
God blessed for ever." Pass on to the first Epistle to Timothy, and you will find this beautiful testimony: " Without
controversy, great is the mystery of godliness: God was manifest in the flesh, justified in the spirit, seen of angels, preached
unto the Gentiles, believed on in the world, received up into
glory." And conclude, if you please, with the first Epistle of
John, at the end of which you will read: " We are in him that

is true, even in his Son Jesus Christ. This is the true God and eternal life.'' Thus God has been manifested in the flesh; we can not believe in the word of God without believing in this truth.

But can not the very nature of the work which was to be accomplished make us feel beforehand that God himself would come, and would give to no other being so great a charge? It was indeed for no work of slight importance that he was manifested in the flesh. It was not to found some sect of philosophy; it was not to teach some precepts which he might have delivered unto men quite as well through one of his prophets. If he was with us, it was to save the human race which was lost; to restore life to the dead; to transport to heaven what had been the prey of hell. That was a greater work than all that had been done till then, and one which required nothing less than the immediate interposition of Divinity. Assuredly, to create beings was a wonderful work; but to save beings who already existed, and whose lot was everlasting misery, was a still more important and wonderful work. And since God had of himself executed the work of creation, why should he not of himself have accomplished that of redemption? Why would he have left to another the glory of saving the world, while he left to no other that of creating it? Assuredly, to preserve the life of the body, as God does daily by his providence, is a wonderful work; but to restore the life of the soul to those who had lost it, to make those who were dead unto God live unto him, was a still more important and wonderful work. And why should not God, who of himself performs the very smallest work necessary for the preservation of the body which perishes, come himself when the spirit, which can not perish, is to be restored to life? Why should he leave the care of these things to one of his servants? Ah! that was precisely the work which he was to fulfil *himself;* for it was emphatically the work of *charity.* I could perhaps imagine that he might have given to others the execution of the work of power at the day of creation; but he was himself to accomplish, at the day of redemption, the work of love. He might give to another his power, but not his mercy.

And who but God could perform this work? Who but he sufficed for the things which were to be the foundation of our eternal redemption? Sinful creatures were to be placed in possession of felicity and glory. But did the sovereign holiness of Him who weighs in his balance the least iniquity, allow him thus to raise sinful man? All the attributes of God must, in all his actions, be entirely satisfied, and fully manifested: you will find, on reflection, that in this consists all his perfection. But had he simply, by an act of his power, restored all sinful creatures to eternal happiness, would not this act, instead of displaying his holiness, have covered it with a thick cloud? He was therefore not content with raising up man, but at the same time he abased himself; he became like unto a servant, so that the humiliation of Divinity should justify the elevation of humanity, and that the same deed which revealed his mercy should also proclaim his holiness in the eyes of all creation. But if such are the means by which our redemption was to be effected, who but God could accomplish it? What being, by his abasement, could have justified the elevation of sinful humanity? Who, by his sufferings, could ever have deserved to receive, as a reward, the salvation of the whole guilty creation? Who has not yet so much to answer for as to make it impossible for him to enter the lists, to answer for sinful man? No creature could have come forward for such a purpose. The everlasting Word alone could do it. He alone was to become flesh.

He became flesh. He was with us, and like one of us. He endured all we endured. He dwelt among us, full of grace and truth. He was obedient even unto death. And those who were his friends bear witness that they beheld his glory, the glory as of the only-begotten of the Father.

God has been with us; and he is yet with us. After having dwelt here below in the flesh, as the Representative of the whole human race, to procure salvation for it, he is now here in the Spirit, as Prince and Protector, to give the possession of that eternal salvation to it. Such is the important meaning of these words: "If, when we were enemies, we were reconciled to God by the death of his Son, much more, being reconciled, we shall be saved by his life." Since Jesus Christ became flesh, God continually stoops down to the most wretched of his creatures. There is now nothing more that can separate God from man; our very sins can not repel him; on the contrary, it is on their account that he came.

Nevertheless, great as the position is which this truth occupies in the Christian revelation, we know that it encounters much unbelief in our hearts. We do not deceive ourselves, dear brethren; we do not suppose that it is sufficient for us to announce this truth from the pulpit, to have you believe it; and as we desire to preach to you not merely for the sake of form. but truly to lead your spirits captive unto the obedience of faith —as " I say these things, that ye might be saved," and as we value our words only in proportion to the conviction which they may carry with them in your minds, we ask you, What hinders you from believing, with sincere and firm faith, *without any doubt or restriction*, this great principle of our salvation?

Perhaps you may say, ' We can not understand how God can have become man to save men; consequently, we can not fully believe it?' You can not fully believe what you do not understand: this we grant you, my brethren; but that you can not understand this truth, we deny. On the contrary, we assert that no truth can be clearer to the comprehension. There is certainly one thing that you can not understand; that is, *the manner* in which God was united to man in Jesus; neither can you conceive the manner in which your soul is united to your body; yet this is a matter which more immediately concerns you. But the word of God does not require your belief in this point. It does not summon you to believe *how* the thing was done, but only *that it was done ;* and this the mind of even a child can understand. " The secret things belong unto the Lord our God; but those things which are revealed belong unto us and to our children." The manner in which God was united to Christ is a *secret* thing; it does not belong unto us. But that God was really in Christ is a *revealed* thing, and the most glorious of all revealed things; this, therefore, belongs to us and to our children, and nothing can excuse you from believing it.

' It is true,' you will perhaps reply, ' that God should have become man is, indeed, a clear and evident fact to my mind; but what a fact! How can it be consistent with the ideas which I form, and which I ought to form, of the greatness and majesty of God?' And do you think then, my dear brother, that the greatness of God is a greatness of ostentation, like that of the powerful of the earth? And do you think that his majesty consists in dwelling constantly in inaccessible palaces of glory, infinitely above the misery of creation? No! the greatness of God is a greatness of mercy. And in the fact that *God became man* this grandeur is revealed to me with such splendour as I can never describe. It is in the ignominy that God endured that I discern all his glory. If all beings had spent all ages in endeavouring to imagine some action by which God could manifest his love and consequently his greatness to the whole universe, I do not believe they could have discovered any thing to equal this, that *he became man to save us.*

But, at least, when I consider the smallness of this earth, the little space which it fills, the small number of the creatures of God who dwell upon it in comparison with all those who probably fill the universe, how can I conceive that *God, the great God,* should have become man for so small a thing? *So small a thing!* Perhaps the salvation of the human race is not of as slight importance in the sight of God as it is in yours, my dear brother. If a single soul is of more value than the whole world, what is the value of all the souls that shall have been saved here below? *So small a thing!* And is any thing *small* before God? Is any thing *great* before him? Are not all things equally small and great in the eyes of that Being who is *infinite?* You think it wonderful that God should have become man for our sakes, and you ask what he must have become for so many other worlds of which you are thinking? But since you choose to trouble your mind about such things, do you suppose he is not for those other worlds all that is necessary that he should be for them? Herein consists the greatness and universality of God's providence, that he is unto every one all that he needs to be. He supplies the wants of all beings according to their nature: those of the plants according to theirs; those of creatures endowed with life, but deprived of reason, according to theirs; for us it was necessary that he should become man, and he became man.

'But this is an idea which could never have entered into our minds; God *really* on earth! God *really* man! This is far beyond our understanding, and opens a new field to our thoughts.' But do you not perceive that it is positively necessary that an entirely new field should be opened to you? Do you suppose that you can possess immortal souls, yet always remain attached to the little things which engage your thoughts through life? Do you not feel that some capital and fruitful truth must

open to you the gates of a new system? Oh, immortal beings!
that which should astonish is, not that God has appeared in
the flesh to raise you up unto himself, but that you should not
feel the need of it! It is that you should be satisfied with the
things which now satisfy you; it is that you should not rise
toward him who stooped toward you. This assuredly is strange;
and *this* ought to be an almost inconceivable idea.

But if it be true that God came in the flesh, should not all
things be changed, in our hearts as well as in our lives? Is
there any thing on earth that ought to remain the same? It
is true, dear brethren; all things ought to change; we feel this,
and this is the very cause of our unbelief. We are unwilling
that God should come so near to us, because this proximity
would require a complete regeneration. Jesus himself declared
it in the days when he dwelt in the flesh. He knew our hearts
as he knew those of the Israelites who surrounded him, when
he said, "Men loved darkness rather than light, because their
deeds were evil." But even though such a change be the consequence of God's coming on earth, even though all things must
be made new, this truth is nevertheless immovable, and God
was nevertheless manifested in the flesh. Far more: this moral
revolution which must be the consequence of it is precisely the
most striking proof we can adduce in support of it. A fable
has no such effect. By means of the realities produced by
faith in this event, you will recognize the reality of the event
itself; falsehood has not been suffered to exert such power; and
that which builds up the kingdom of God on the earth can not
be an imposture proceeding from the gates of hell itself.

Thus, beloved brethren, notwithstanding all the subtleties of
our hearts, *God is with us*. This is the "great mystery of godliness" of which St. Paul speaks; this is the *rock* on which the
church of the Redeemer is built. *God is with us;* no human
sophistry can disturb this glorious principle of our faith. No
school of philosophers, no society of the learned, no assembly
of carnal men, could hinder God from coming into the world.
The earth is his property, and he came to visit that property.
In vain were the husbandmen unwilling to receive the beloved
Son; in vain would they cast him out of the vineyard; he has
been there, he is there still, and he will be there yet. No art
of human pride can efface the traces of God on earth. *He has*

been with us, "and we testify concerning him," and we declare it unto all, that all may hear, understand, and believe it.

WE WITH GOD.

BUT wherefore has he been with us, my brethren? Wherefore did he leave the eternal mansions of glory? It can not have been for a small matter that he did it.

God has been with you *that you might be with him.* Surely he came not hither merely to display his glory before our eyes. If you are not with God, you arrest with a wanton and audacious hand the work which he came to accomplish.

God has been with you. God has been on earth to save you; you should then attend to this, my dear brother; you should be deaf to all the voices which have hitherto bewildered you, and above all, seek to hear what that God who came in the flesh has to say unto you. You should turn away from all that the world lays before you, and direct your first researches to that which God brings you. You should feel the emptiness of all the works and enterprises that men accomplish, and perceive that God has come to accomplish the capital work, the supreme enterprise. In a word, *God has been with you ;* you should then be on his side, and choose your lot for eternity. A weight which arrests all vacillation has been thrown into the balance; all hesitation was at an end from the moment that God appeared in the flesh. And how could it be otherwise? The man who comes forward to perform any important work is soon surrounded by men attentive to his actions, who, if they can reap any advantage from it, will aid him in his undertaking. And shall God have come to begin a work in which none will join him? Shall he in vain stretch forth his hands all the day long to a rebellious people? In what, then, are you engaged? What retains you? God is here; the world has nothing to oppose to him. His work is stronger than all others. There is not a seduction in the world, there is not a sophism in your heart which must not fall in its nothingness before this simple truth : " God has been manifested in the flesh." With it we force you back into your last retreats; we summon you authoritatively to advance henceforth toward the path of truth and life. It will be the first step of your union with God.

But when once you have turned to God, what will you have still to do ? God has been on earth; you should profit by it in *being reconciled with him.* It was that you might find access unto him that God became man, and was with us. In heaven, even the angels, notwithstanding their purity, dare not turn their looks toward him. " The seraphim," the Scriptures say, " cover their faces with their wings and cry, Holy, Holy, Holy is the Lord God of hosts." But here below, the greatest sin- ner, when he has acknowledged his sin with tears, can come unto him boldly, as to a friend who has already pardoned him. He has made himself like one of us. He is willing to treat us as equals. Hasten, then, oh ! sinful men, to take advantage of this opportunity. If you delay, tremble lest you should find nothing but inexorable holiness in Him who now offers you mercy beyond all comprehension. Behold ! there is nothing in him that should terrify your hearts and justify your estrange- ment. He was born in a stable; he was laid in a manger; he did not " strive nor cry;" he does not break the bruised reed; he is meek and lowly of heart; sinners washed his feet with their tears, and he forgave them; his whole life was a continual invitation to those who were weary and heavy laden. There are no longer any obstacles to keep you far from him; there are none save *in yourselves,* and it is yours to remove them. Oh! make your peace with him while he is near unto you.

But to unite you with God it is not enough to be merely reconciled with him; you must also *give yourselves to him.* It is not to make peace with your rival, but to surrender yourselves to your Master. God has come on earth, like the woman seek- ing the piece of silver she had lost; her money must be recover- ed, that she may put it back in her treasure; to withhold it longer from her would be a sacrilegious theft. God has been with you; give yourselves back to him to whom you belong, and who came himself to seek you. All your weapons should be laid at the feet of him who has conquered you. Your revolt should have an end. You should indeed be bound by a chain, but a chain which comes from heaven. Had he sent one of his angels to seek you, even then your resistance would have been a crime; but by what name shall we call it since it was he him- self who came ? Which of your affections can you hold back from Him who gave *himself* to obtain them ? How shall you

dare to appear before his bar in heaven, if you retain on earth
that which cost him so much? Wander then no longer blindly,
constantly changing masters in the world. You have found
what you sought. To him you should belong.

God with you: you with God. You with God *throughout life.*
The piece of money will never leave the treasury in which it
has been replaced. The union between God and yourself should
be ever closer. It should exist not only in your faith, but also
in your life. By your walk it should be seen with whom you
are walking. You should follow his look. "God should dwell
in you: you should dwell in him."

God has been with you: oh, perfect law of justice and holiness!
This can supply the place of every other precept for you; you
need no other lawgiver. God has been with you. Think of
his *abasement*, and you will be ashamed of your pride. Think
of his *poverty*, and the love of riches will be extinguished in
your soul. Think of his *gentleness*, and anger will no more disturb your mind. Think of his *obedience*, and the desire of independence or dominion will be banished from your heart. Think
of his *charity*, and you will love all your brethren. Every
mental quality that appeared in him should become so entirely
your own that he would form as it were another being within
you. Let Emmanuel be your companion; let your life bear his
seal, and let every thing in it testify that *God is with you.*

But it is especially in the hour of danger that you may glory
in the fact that God is with you; then, especially, you ought
to be with God. It is when temptation approaches, when the
world would draw us away, when an evil destiny threatens us,
that this word, "God with us," has a peculiar meaning. So
long as we remain on earth we are on a field of battle, and we
advance through the close ranks of our enemies; the adversaries are powerful, their attacks are frequent, and we ourselves
are nothing. But *God is with us;* he has chosen our side; he
stands with us; what power shall we fear? On the cross he
overcame sin, Satan, and death; which of them can conquer
us now? He constantly surrounds with his power all who put
their trust in him. We can at all times go and seek from him
the victory that overcometh the world. He who came once in
all our woes will not refuse to visit us in the portion of woes
allotted to each of us. God has been on earth; the thing will

end well. "The Lord is the strength of my life; of whom shall I be afraid? Though a host should encamp against me, my heart shall not fear."

And if we say, *God is with us on earth,* can we not say with assurance, *we shall be with God in heaven?* We have already seen what "God manifested in the flesh" requires of you in the present time; should we not now examine what he promises you for the life to come? Can God have had any other object in appearing in our inheritance than to give us the possession of his own? Was not his object, in being with us during a human life, to cause us to be with him on high throughout an eternity? *We with God for ever!* This is the last and most glorious consequence of the great mystery of godliness. Yes, my brethren, let this mystery teach you the greatness of your destiny. Give up these vulgar ideas; throw off these earthly prejudices which render you worthless. Refuse not to receive and open these true patents of nobility which the Divine Being returned to you when he assumed your nature. This human nature of yours is the throne which God was pleased to choose. How great, then, are the purposes for which it may be reserved! God has been made flesh; since such a transformation has occurred, how great a transformation you can now hope for! And since God has become man, what, then, can man become! Neither angels nor principalities nor powers have the same titles of glory, the same pledges of greatness; for God did not assume their natures. God has been here below as our neighbour; let us not wonder, then, that he declares that we shall share all things with him; that his inheritance shall be ours; that his throne shall be ours; that if we *suffer* with him, we shall also be glorified together with him. Preserve in your hearts this glorious truth, O ye who believe in *God manifest in the flesh.* You can never be with God here below in as literal a sense as God has been with you; but if *God with you* has been a principle in this world, you with God will be a principle of heaven. There alone will be fulfilled the union of which this day speaks. Here below we follow the road; there we shall reach the goal. Here below we only make efforts; there the work will be accomplished. "Then cometh the end," says the apostle. "God will be all in all." It will be the last measure of our union with God

Lord! how is it with thy work, that work for which thou didst become a man here below? Oh! why are there still so many left behind? So many who believe not that thou hast dwelt with us! Lord! shall thy work remain imperfect? And when thy hand has raised the scaffold, shall the edifice remain unbuilt? O thou who didst come in the flesh, fulfil the purpose for which thou didst come! Let not our wicked unbelief neutralize the effect of thy manifestation! Call men unto thyself! Destroy the enmity which is in our hearts, *that all may be one!* Thou dost not lay the corner-stone of the building without erecting the building. We know and confess that the work which thou didst begin in Bethlehem is accomplishing in the world. That work goes on. The laying of the foundation of the heavenly Jerusalem is constantly advancing here below. All things are hastening on. " Thou art worthy to receive honour and glory and blessing."

But, my brethren, are we those " lively stones " of which Peter speaks, "who are built up a spiritual house of God"? You have seen, my brethren, that God has been with us, to accomplish on his part the work of our union; we should be with God, to accomplish it on ours. You know all; we have kept back nothing from you; you have been enabled to contemplate that work as it should be. But we ask you once more, Has that work been executed? Examine, my dear hearer, the state of your soul in this respect. Can you avoid looking upon this work as worthy of all your consideration? Can it be that, having heard the truth to-day, you will not think of being united with God? What, then, will occupy your attention? To what undertaking will you give up your time? If the things of which we have spoken to you to-day do not concern your eternal peace, what can there be besides that does concern it? Will you not remember that indifference has its bounds, and that the day is coming when we can no longer postpone the consideration of this subject? May that moment have arrived for you, my dear hearer! May this day be blessed to you, so that it may become the glorious epoch of your union with God; and that, in the same hour in which I have said, GOD WITH US, I may be able to say, YOU WITH GOD! Amen.

DISCOURSE II.

THE CROSS OF JESUS CHRIST.

" But God forbid that I should glory, save in the Cross of our Lord Jesus Christ."—GALATIANS, vi, 14.

MY brethren,—God did not choose to deprive man of all occasions of glorying. To glory is one of the most characteristic propensities of our nature. It is seen in every class of society, and in every portion of the human race. From the highest dignitary to the lowest beggar, from the enlightened and refined citizen to the savage in whose mind scarcely a spark of reason appears, all discover something in which they think they can glory. And in what do they glory? In foolish toys, of which they should rather be ashamed than proud. Oh! what a sad spectacle our vanity presents; and how evidently it shows that the human race has lost that in which it ought to glory; that " it has come short of the glory of God;" and that in this abject poverty it grasps eagerly at the first bauble it sees, as a substitute for the reality which it does not possess. Thus the inhabitant of a city, reduced to the most dreadful famine, seizes with avidity the loathsome food at the sight of which in common times he would sicken. God designed to give man something in which he could reasonably glory : He gave him " the Cross of Jesus Christ." " God forbid," says St. Paul in the words of our text, " that I should glory save in the Cross of our Lord Jesus Christ." And herein he utters a sentence of condemnation against all the delusive objects which we usually worship. He commands all men to cease their vain researches; and he commends the Cross of Jesus Christ as the only thing worthy of being gloried in eternally by every rational being. And when the apostle speaks of *the Cross*, do not suppose that he means that visible sign, the representation of which is frequently seen in many countries of Christendom, and which superstition has so greatly abused. He refers to the death of the Son of God, which in due time occurred, for the remission of our sins. But he uses this expression, *the Cross*, to remind us, by the remembrance of that punishment which was esteemed infamous among all nations, that this death in which he requires us to glory is full of humiliation, reproach, and shame, and is even accursed of God. Such, my brethren, is the *glory* of which God permits, nay commands you to boast. On this day was laid the only foundation of all greatness which humanity can claim. Never could man have had reason to glory had not that scene occurred on Golgotha eighteen centuries ago; had not that Jesus, who was dragged from Pilate to Herod, and from Herod back to Pilate, been crucified then; had he not been nailed to the tree, " a reproach of men, and despised of the people;" and had not the most fearful condemnation rested on the only innocent being that ever dwelt on earth. On that day the great battle was fought, the great victory achieved, which brought us honour and immortality. On that day our perpetual grant of nobility was inscribed in the Book of Life. " God forbid that I should glory save in the Cross of our Lord Jesus Christ."

This meditation will be devoted to the examination of the new *right of glorying* which has been granted to man. On this subject there are two opinions :—

One is the *apostle's opinion*, which we shall sustain.

The other is the *opinion of the world*, which we shall refute.

In other words, we shall first display the greatness of the Cross of Christ, and shall then examine your sentiments with regard to it. And when we shall have defended the truth and opposed error, we shall have accomplished our design.

And do thou, O Lord! fulfil the work which thou alone canst perform; for both the beginning and the end and all things are thine. Show us that the Cross of Jesus Christ is " the power of God and the wisdom of God." Amen.

THE APOSTLE'S OPINION.

We have observed, my brethren, that the apostle of the Gentiles holds up the Cross of Christ as the only thing in which he has a right to glory. And the first reason which led him to do

so was because he saw the character and glory of God fully
displayed in it.   It is true that St. Paul had been taught concerning God in his early years.   But the zeal which led him
so violently to persecute the disciples of the Nazarene before
his conversion is sufficient evidence of the nature of his knowledge of God.   But afterward the Cross of Jesus Christ was
revealed to him; it spoke of a God concerning whom he had
not been taught in the school of Gamaliel; and he gloried in
the gift of that wonderful knowledge.   Yes, my brethren, the
Cross is the only teacher that reveals the living God.   It matters not from what source we have drawn our knowledge; unless the Cross of Jesus Christ has instructed us, we have no
real acquaintance with God.   Without that Cross, even nature
and conscience speak in an unknown tongue; and that which
is most important for us to know is hidden from us.   Where
will you learn to know God's *holiness*, the absolute detestation
with which he looks upon sin, and of which he gives you so
serious a warning ?   Conscience will tell you something about
it.   But if you would form a correct idea of it, go to the Cross
of Jesus Christ.   See him who dwells in the fulness of the
Godhead nailed to that tree on account of sin, and because
iniquity exists on earth.   Will you ever have *vague* ideas of
God's holiness again ?   And will you ever think that God has
not given sufficiently striking tokens of it to the world ?   Where
will you learn to know the *love* of God, that infinite mercy which
must be the foundation of all your happiness ?   Nature will
tell you something about it.   But if you wish to hear it speak
with a power compared with which nature can only stammer,
go to the Cross of Jesus Christ.   See the beloved Son of the
Father humbling himself unto death, and nailed to the cross,
to the end that the world might have life.   Is not that an act
of love ?   "Scarcely for a righteous man will one die, yet per-
adventure for a good man some would even dare to die.   But
God commendeth his love toward us, in that while we were yet
sinners Christ died for us."   Where will you learn to know the
glory of God ?   Where, O my Lord and my God, can I see
thee in all thy glory ?   Shall my thoughts be fixed on thee as
surrounded by those worlds created by thee ?   Shall I think of
thee as dwelling in light inaccessible, worshipped by all thine

angels, who prostrate themselves before thee afar off? There is no place in the universe that is suited to thy greatness. All is so small compared with thee, so much at variance with thine infinity! But no : there is a place appropriate for the manifestation of all thy glory; that place is the accursed tree to which thou wast nailed. There I learn to know thee in all thy majesty far better than when surrounded by those millions who assemble around thy throne. All these conceptions of angels, of archangels, and of cherubim, who bow their heads before thee, are but mere types borrowed from man's ideas of greatness. But when bound to the cross for our sins thy glory is infinite. I can discover no trace of human grandeur there. There thou appearest in thy native splendour, in divine magnificence. Ah! no longer do I look with envy upon angels and archangels as they pay their homage before thee on thy heavenly throne! It is the part of man to worship thee on a more wonderful throne—to worship thee on thy cross. Angels forsook the skies when thou, O Lord! wast hanging there; for earth was the scene of a spectacle which heaven had never witnessed. At the foot of the cross I would stand to know thee, and to glory in it. "God forbid that I should glory save in the Cross of our Lord Jesus Christ!"

But if St. Paul gloried in the Cross of Christ because it revealed to him all the glory of God, he gloried in it quite as much because it taught him his own wretchedness. In what a state must he have been to have made it necessary that such an event should happen to effect his deliverance! It is true that there are voices enough, both internal and external, to teach us our nothingness; but how skilful are we in eluding their influence and in escaping from their appeals! With what false righteousness does man shield himself till he has seen the Cross of Jesus Christ; and how lofty the position he assumes till the Cross has humbled him! The Cross of Jesus Christ is the great bill of accusation which God holds up in the sight of the whole world. No one can behold it without being immediately convicted. It is folly for a man to suppose that he can have been innocent when the Son of God was made a sacrifice for his transgression. My brethren, the Cross of Christ will not speak ambiguously of your souls' disease. It will reveal the extent of your condemnation. It will show you the enormity of your sin. It will extinguish every spark of pride within you. Oh! thou who thinkest thyself of great value in the sight of God, come to the Cross of Christ and renounce that thought; come, and learn thy worth: it was necessary that the Son of God should shed his blood to ransom thee from death! Oh! thou who gloriest in the remembrance of thy virtues, come hither a moment, and examine them in the light of the Cross; they will fade away; they will be eclipsed; thou shalt see them sullied by egotism and pride, whereby they are rendered abominable in the eyes of God. Let the proudest of men draw near; let him stand at the foot of that cross erected for his salvation, and what will become of his pride? The Cross destroys that deceiving glass which magnifies us in our own eyes. It annihilates us. And on this account Paul glories in it; for he knows that in his present state the first object he can attain is to feel his own wretchedness. Nor ought we, my brethren, to have any other cause for glorying than that of Paul. We cannot be great in the eyes of God until we feel our worthlessness in his estimation. Oh! blessed be that Cross, which has brought us to our proper level, and which has shown us, in the consciousness of our insignificance, the source of all our glory!

But if St. Paul glories in the Cross of Jesus Christ because it reduced his false greatness, he glories in it especially because it raises him to the level of true greatness. The source of his glory is, that such a price should have been paid for the salvation of his soul; that the Son of God himself should have died for the sin which he committed; that the blood shed on the cross should have blotted out all his transgressions, and have acquired immortality for him. And in what, my dear hearer, does your glory consist, if not in the remission of your sins? What reason have you to lift up your head, if not because One died for you, and because it was that Being who made all things and who sustains all things by the word of his power? What! will you glory so earnestly in the smallest sacrifice that a mortal being makes for you, and in the least inconvenience that he bears; and will you not glory in the fact, that the Lord of all things, manifested in the flesh, was willing to shed his blood on the cross for your sake? It was not for his own transgressions that he was pierced, for even his judge declared, "I find no fault in him." It was not on account of the power of his adversaries; "could he not then have prayed to his Father; and he would presently have given him more than twelve legions of angels?" Why then did he die on the cross? It must have been for *your* sake, my dear brother; this is the only supposition we can entertain. Yes, the only cause for which the Son of God was nailed to the tree was the love which he bore for your soul, and the resolution he had made to save it. When he fulfilled his design, when he recoiled not before suffering, when he shrank not in the fearful hour, it was to save your soul. When he gave all his blood for you, when he was forsaken of his God, when his soul endured anguish of which we can have no conception, it was to save your soul. When he fought a great battle on the cross, when he overcame sin, the world, death, and hell, this too was to save your soul. He died— all is finished. He paid with his own blood the debt which you would have owed forever. You are reconciled. Your iniquity is blotted out. He is now "the author of eternal salvation" for all who obey him. Oh what a wonderful event is the death of the only Son of the Father,—an event which will be unequalled in the whole history of the universe,—an event, in view of the importance of which the angels will bow their heads unable to measure its grandeur! And will you, my dear brother, for whose sake this event took place, be the only one whom it shall not affect? Will you not glory in it? What event of celestial origin could happen on earth the occurrence of which could be more astonishing? At what price can you be ransomed if the very life of the being to whom you are indebted is not of sufficient value? At what price do you estimate yourself if the blood of the King of the earth is too inconsiderable? And what gift would you then receive if you so lightly esteem an eternity of glory? Ah! when you stand before the bar of God, and the eye of the Judge penetrates into the sinfulness of your soul, what will become of your hope,—what will become of your glory? What will strengthen your heart if you cannot say in the presence of your Judge, and of the multitude who stand before him, "Christ died for my sins"? Yes, my brethren, the unbeliever alone can gaze upon that Cross without discerning

in it the source of his glory; for there is indeed nothing there
for *him* to glory in.   But the believer discovers infinite glory
in it.   Lord! it is so; and the more humble thy Cross appears,
the more we will glory in it; for what greatness does such an
abasement announce to us! what glory is promised us in such
a humiliation!

But notice the motive which the apostle himself assigns.
"God forbid," he says, " that I should glory save in the Cross
of our Lord Jesus Christ ; by whom the world is crucified unto
me, and I unto the world."   This, my brethren, is indeed a
glorious advantage of the Cross of Jesus Christ.   It is the
great misfortune of man that he can not separate himself from
this present world and become a citizen of the world to come.
The Cross performs this miracle ; it crucifies him to the world,
and crucifies the world to him.   How forcible is this expression !   It will crucify you to the world, my brethren ; that is,
it will crucify sin within you, whereby you are made to live
for the world.   Since you acknowledge that it was on account
of sin that Christ died, will you not hate sin ?   Will you not
resist those impulses which affect your heart ?   Yes, my brethren ; the death of the Redeemer is the only thing that can
make you hate your own evil nature.   It is the true remedy
for your disease.   But the Cross of Christ will also crucify the
world to you ; that is, it will destroy in you all the attractions
of the vanities of this world.   You can not love both the Cross
and the world.   Of what value will all the pomp of this age
be to the man for whom the Cross shall have bought the riches
of the world to come ?   And how sincerely will he hate the
world, also, since it was sin that caused his Saviour's death,
and since the lusts and vices of the world were the instruments
of sin !   And, by crucifying man to this world, the Cross will
make him a citizen of the world to come.   By destroying within
him the old man, which is of earth, it will form within him
the new man, which is of heaven.   Where Christ is, there,
likewise, will be *his* treasure and *his* heart.   He will be risen
with Christ.   It is thus that the Cross effects the great change
which man needs, and makes the being whom it found in the
dust an inhabitant of heaven.   It is thus that it accomplishes
that to which both human law and human wisdom have ever

been found inadequate. Oh! God forbid that I should glory save in the Cross of our Lord Jesus Christ!

But the last motive which induced St. Paul to exclaim, as he was advancing into Asia, Greece, or Italy, or crossing the sea, that he desired no other glory, was his conception of the power of that Cross, and of the triumphs which await it. The great apostle knew that it was all-sufficient to give immortality to those who have fallen into the deepest misery. He knew that it had redeemed a great people, both in the cities of Galatia, to which he wrote, and in Greece, Rome, and Jerusalem. He knew its future destiny, that kings and nations would come and prostrate themselves before it, that "the people would bring their sons in their arms," and that it had received the ends of the earth for an inheritance. And as for ourselves, my brethren, we can see in part the things which the apostle predicted. That despised cross of Calvary has been raised up, and already it reigns over one half of the world. The prophecy of Him who hung upon it is constantly fulfilling: "I, if I be lifted up from the earth, will draw all men unto me." How many thousands of souls, in all ages, have gazed upon it as the Israelites of old gazed upon the brazen serpent in the wilderness, and were saved! How great a multitude, rescued by it from the kingdom of darkness, is now praising before the throne the salvation purchased by the Lamb! Old things have passed away; all things have become new. The breath of a new life has been perceptible in the universe for the last eighteen centuries. The Cross of Jesus Christ has already overcome many adversaries. Slavery, barbarity, effeminacy, have fled before it; so that, while saving individuals, it has become the true power of nations. As it advances, it effects the deliverance of the world. It puts to flight the powers of darkness, and we are left free. Struggling at once against superstition, which would put miserable human inventions in its place or by its side; and infidelity, which would fain destroy it, and persuade men that heaven is not open for the salvation of the earth; it is continually overthrowing its hideous enemies, on the right hand and on the left. Not satisfied with spreading its blessings over the scenes of its former conquests, it flies through the midst of the heavens to make new conquests. It is that stan-

dard which the Lord God sets up to the people. Its victories
increase. It gathers from all quarters those whom sin had
dispersed; and, trusting in its boundless strength, we can already foresee the time when it shall be said, "Now doth the
whole earth belong to our God and his Anointed!" Oh!
God forbid that I should glory save in the Cross of our Lord
Jesus Christ! Let the world trample upon thee; yet by thee
is the world saved! One drop of thy blood is more precious
to us than all the wealth of the universe.

THE OPINION OF THE WORLD.

Is this your language, my brethren? If such was St. Paul's
opinion, what is yours? There is perhaps no truth which
encounters so much opposition from the world as this. How
many are there who say, on the contrary, I will glory in any
thing rather than the Cross of our Lord Jesus Christ! Are
you not among this class, my brethren? Let your consciences
testify whether, even on this occasion, on this day of triumph
of the Cross, and since you entered this sacred edifice, and
have been listening to my words, there have not been some sentiments in your minds and hearts which are directly opposed
to those of St. Paul.

And why is it thus? Perhaps you ask, ' Is it necessary to
think so much of the Cross, when there are so many other subjects in religion of more importance than this.' Of more importance than the Cross! We might here remind you of what we have
just said, but we prefer to refute you by your own words. You
wish to set aside the Cross, as a thing of little importance ;
and yet you exclaim, ' We cannot conceive of such a thing as
that Cross, that expiatory death of God's only Son ; it is too
much for our reason.' How can such decisions be made to
agree? How can the Cross be at once so contemptible and so
astonishing? If it so greatly surpasses your comprehension,
why do you esteem it so lightly? You must explain this. The
Cross of the Son of God cannot exist if it be unworthy of
your attention. It is either true or false. If it be true, it is
the noblest affair on earth ; and you must come and acknowledge it, and prostrate yourselves before it in spirit. If it be
false, you ought to pronounce it an absolute imposture, as well

as all the holy volumes which proclaim it, and Christianity itself, which is a mere summary of it. You should, like those first
apostates of the Church, trample upon it, and swear by the
gods of this world. The Cross ought to be, in your opinion,
either the wisdom of God, or a falsehood of hell. It must be
the cause either of your salvation or of your destruction. There
is no medium between these paths. You can not be indifferent
to this subject.

'But,' you will say, 'it is this that perplexes us. If the
Cross be true, then it is certain that the foundation of all our
pretensions must give way, and that we must glory in it alone.
But is it true ? Is it true that the Son of God shed his blood
on the cross to purchase eternal life for us ?' Yes, my
brethren, it is true ; and the witness who will convince you of
this is God himself, *the only true God*, who has declared through
his messengers that " Christ reconciled both unto God in one
body by the Cross." But, without seeking a witness in heaven,
is not earth itself sufficient ? Think of the most striking events
of antiquity ; not a vestige of them remains ; and it is only
through the ancient chronicles which have been handed down
to us that we are acquainted with their existence. But it is
not so with the expiatory death of Christ ; this fact is *living* in
the world. The present state of the world bears testimony
concerning it. It is from the blood which flowed from that
cross that all those nations have sprung which have unfurled
the sacred banner over the globe which they rule. Among
them every thing speaks of it. Yes, the Cross of Jesus Christ
is above your reach ; you can not disturb it. This truth, on
which eighteen centuries rest, can not be laid aside as readily
as any vain imagination fabricated by the man who advances
it. Attacked at all times by the combined strength of men, it
has remained firm through every age. It has sustained itself
against the united efforts of infidelity and superstition. And
this fact of a sacrifice once offered up for the sins of all is forever extant in the world, proclaimed among the nations as the
most important fact acknowledged by humanity.

But is it possible that such a thing has happened ? Into
what a state of astonishment does this doctrine throw us ! And
how can we view it otherwise than as a piece of *folly ?* My

brethren, let us not enquire into the possibility of an event of which we have ascertained the reality. To ask whether that which *has been* is possible is a ridiculous quibble of sophistry; and the voice of sophistry must be silent when the Cross of the Son of God is concerned. You are astonished, you say; and tell me, according to what principles are our minds to measure the depths of Divinity? If God, when he gives life to a plant, performs a deed which confounds you, do you suppose that when he reconciles the world to himself, it need not astonish you? Man wonders at this, because he never conceived of any thing like it. But learn that God has sympathized with you in this feeling, and that he offers his Cross in the very same manner in which you receive it. He calls it *foolishness.* But may not this be for the purpose of teaching us that if we presume to dispute with him we shall find that what we call *wisdom* is *foolishness*, and what we call *foolishness* is *wisdom*? A little of the foolishness of the Cross is enough to confound all our philosophy. That Cross, which alone manifests all the attributes of God, and which alone satisfies all the wants of man, is the true *code of wisdom* of this universe. All the systems of human pride will be successively confounded by it. It has already overcome several; it will overcome many more. The man who does not know this deceives himself. The time is coming when all will wonder that they could have passed by it without attending to it; and when Christ, "having spoiled the principalities and powers" of human wisdom which are reigning in this world, "and having made a show of them openly, will triumph over them in his Cross."

But if the Cross of Christ is not your wisdom and your glory, what are you, then? To what religion do you belong? Are you Christians? Christians without the Cross? What novel form of Christianity is that, and in what school is it taught? You might learn from the very infidel that of which you seem to be ignorant. Go to the son of Jacob; go to the follower of the false prophet; ask either of them what is this Christianity which you profess. Though he does not believe in it, and is therefore not prejudiced in its favour, he will tell you that the Christians are a people who profess to acknowledge Jesus of Nazareth, born in Bethlehem, as the only Son

of God, and who believe that the death which that Jesus suffered under Pontius Pilate is the sacrifice which reconciles sinful
and rebellious humanity to God. What! do you not know
your own religion as well as those who are strangers to it?
They insult the Cross of our Jesus, but they do not profess to
believe in it; but *you* profess to believe in it, and yet, like
them, you are ashamed of it! Not to glory in the Cross is to
be an alien from the Christian church. If we look at those
who in every age have followed in the footsteps of St. Paul,
and whose names are written in the Book of Life, we see that
it is in this they glory. Those heroes of the Reformation
whom we honour as our fathers in the faith gloried in the
Cross. God forbid that, rejecting their example, you should
glory save in the Cross of our Lord Jesus Christ!

Ah! my brethren, shall we tell you why you do not glory
in the Cross alone? Because you do not believe in it. Shall
we tell you why you do not believe in it? Because you do
not know it. Shall we tell you why you do not know it?
Because you will not. Shall we tell you why you will not know
it? Because you do not feel the need of it. This is the point to
which the whole case refers. We seize with eagerness the aid
which we think to be necessary, but we despise it if we think
it superfluous. The Cross of Jesus Christ is designed to purchase eternal happiness for you; but you would fain purchase
it for yourselves. The Cross of Jesus Christ is designed to
procure sanctification; but you would fain procure it yourselves. Then what have you to do with it? In my opinion, it
is natural that you should reject it. The question is, Which
of the two is in the right: the Cross of Jesus Christ, which
makes salvation depend on itself, or you, who claim it as your
own work? This is the question; a question which, if not
answered before must be decided in that day when all things
will be judged and made manifest.

But perhaps you say—as some may say with truth—'I do
not deny the Cross of Christ.' That is true; you believe it,
but partially. You do not deny the fact, but you evade it.
You dare not believe, fully and openly, that the Son of God
was nailed to the cross for your sake; and therefore, so far as
its influence on your heart is concerned, it is a fact of no im-

portance. Ah! reject this pusillanimous faith. Forsake this ruinous *semi-Christianity.* Any form of Christianity of which *Christ crucified* is not the centre to which every thing tends and from which every thing proceeds is a false Christianity. Why should you not believe what St. Paul believed? The Cross of Jesus Christ is just as near to you as it was to him. We offer you *Christ crucified for you,* as St. Peter offered him to those who had nailed him to the cross. You behold his blood as they beheld it ; and it can wash away your stains just as it washed theirs away. Ah! what occasion can be more appropriate than this solemn hour when the Son of God was pierced on Golgotha for your sakes?

Yes, Lord! I will arise in this hour, and stand before thy cross! Thou didst bring an offering here for me ; I bring thee my offering. Thou didst make a sacrifice here ; I bring thee my sacrifice. I come, Lord! to forsake all things, and to declare that there is nothing in the world wherein I glory save in that cross to which I see thee nailed. I throw away all my greatness before thee ; thy cross eclipses and destroys it. I sacrifice the pollution of which I used to boast. I trample upon my own righteousness, Lord! I know that what I called righteousness was only iniquity. I trample upon my holiness ; I know that what I called holiness was only uncleanness. I trample upom my meritorious works ; I know that none of them are pure, and that the things which I thought worthy of life deserve nothing but condemnation. There is nothing left, Lord! Here am I as thou wouldst have me : in the dust. Here am I before thee, wretched, poor, blind, and naked. Give me thy gold, "tried in the fire, that I may become rich!" Give me "the white raiment" of thy righteousness, "that I may be clothed, and that the shame of my nakedness do not appear!" Ah! thy cross gives me back all I had lost, and gives it back in a far greater measure. It was for me, Lord! it was for me that thou wast thus bound! The blood which thou didst shed affords me peace. I will wash away all my stains in it. It blots out all my sins in the eyes of my Judge. It brings me near, and reconciles me to him. It utters for me " better things than the blood of Abel speaks." Thy cross becomes my wisdom ; thy cross becomes my righteousness ; thy cross becomes my sanctification ; thy cross becomes my redemption. Now am I rich, Lord ! I have acquired that title to glory which will admit to heaven, and will give me an eternal throne. " God forbid that I should glory save in the cross of our Lord Jesus Christ !"

Ah ! let that host of infidels who have in all ages made the cross of our Lord Jesus Christ the object of their blasphemy stand before us now ! We fear them not ; we will say to them : It is that *crucified God* whom we worship ; it is in that cross of Jesus Christ that we glory. Fickle and vain-glorious world ! We know that the contempt of the wisdom and greatness of this generation will fall on us at the foot of the cross of Jesus Christ ; but, covered with that contempt, we will brave your boasts, we will laugh at your magnificence, and we will despise your greatness. We " esteem the reproach of Christ greater riches than the treasures of Egypt. We glory in every scornful epithet ; and, trampling upon every thing of which we might become proud, we again repeat with the apostle, " God forbid that we should glory save in the cross of our Lord Jesus Christ !"

I will add but a word : Stand by that cross. You have answered my call, my beloved brethren ; you have approached that cross of our Lord ; thanks be to him who brought you there ! But that is not enough ; you must never leave it. Henceforth let nothing draw you away from it.

Stand by that cross. Weep over your days of ignorance there. Lament each moment that you lost when you knew not its power and its glory ; and, since you have lived so many years a stranger to it, and without God in the world, adopt, while you acknowledge your present happiness, the words of one of its venerable servants : " I have known thee too late ! I have loved thee too late !"

Stand by that cross. Since you have found that it is the true source of greatness, sacrifice all false glory. Sacrifice joyfully that pride, produced, in one of you, by the superiority of mind or of knowledge for which you are eminent ; in another, by your elevated place in society, or your extensive reputation ; in a third, by the wealth which you possess, or by the mode of life for which you are distinguished ; in a fourth, by the admiration of which you are the object, by the splendour which surrounds you, or by the flattery you receive. But how shall I enumerate all the sources of that puerile pride which you should sacrifice to the Cross!

Stand by that cross. Stand by it in your trials. Be comforted; the Cross has saved you; your redemption is accomplished; eternal life awaits you; not all the tempests of the world can disturb the peace acquired for you. Think but little of the burden you bear, in view of the punishment which the Holy One and the Just endured; and rejoice that you are led through the path of suffering by which Jesus went to glory.

Stand by that cross. And when sin is aroused in your members, when the world calls you, when the Evil One spreads his net, when your soul begins to stagger like a drunken man, then look to Jesus. Let the sight of what he suffered for your sins fill your soul with a sacred horror, and revive in your heart the dying flame of love.

Stand by that cross. And even if all things unite against it, if it be again surrounded by those who revile it and wag their heads, still let it be your glory to confess it boldly before all men; for "whosoever shall confess me before men," saith the Lord, "him will I confess also before my Father which is in heaven; but whosoever shall deny me before men, him will I also deny before my Father which is in heaven."

The day is drawing nigh when the vail which conceals that cross will be drawn back, and it will diffuse its light and glory on those who shall not have been ashamed of it. May God give you strength to be confessors of the cross of Christ during life. May God give you strength to be confessors of the cross of Christ in death. "I will not blot out his name out of the Book of Life," saith the Lord. Amen.

DISCOURSE III.

THE PUBLICATION OF THE GOSPEL.

"The poor have the Gospel preached to them."—MATTHEW, xi, 1.

MY brethren,—In the reign of the emperor Tiberius and his immediate successors a wonderful revolution took place in Asia Minor and Greece. The inhabitants of those countries were living in the midst of darkness, strangers to God and indifferent to the salvation of their souls. Some were meditating on absurd theories, shutting out the few beams of light which they had received from ancient philosophers; others were ruined by the indulgence of sensual appetites; many crossed the seas in eager pursuit of the objects of their speculations; and all, actuated by curiosity and by vague forebodings for which they could give no account, were anxiously listening to the tidings of events which rumour brought them. The apostolic historian particularly informs us, " that all the Athenians and strangers which were there spent their time in nothing else but either to tell or to hear some new thing." but suddenly tidings of a most extraordinary nature spread throughout those regions. First, Asia Minor hears the story, and soon it is repeated in Greece: the ships which go from Troas carry it to Neapolis; from Neapolis it spreads to Philippi; from Philippi it reaches Thessalonica, Corinth, and Athens. *The Gospel is preached.* A star has arisen in the East, and spreads its light around. A message has been brought from the great God, who made the heavens and the earth. A Hebrew, named Paul, has appeared, and has spoken at Iconium, at Derbe, and at Lystra. He proclaims to men the counsel of God's mercy; he announces that a heavenly kingdom is founded on earth; he declares to all, in every place, that to become citizens of this kingdom, they must be converted and baptized in the name of Jesus of Nazareth. Strange news! Must we believe it? Or must we reject it?

They examine the matter; they listen to Paul himself. Many find that he speaks the truth; they feel that this message is addressed to them; they forsake their superstitions, their customs, and every thing that practice had endeared to them; they believe; they receive eternal life. "They turn to God from idols," says the apostle, who was himself the instrument and the witness of this change, "to serve the living and true God, and to wait for his Son from heaven, even Jesus, which delivered us from the wrath to come."

We would now ask you, my brethren, whether you ever heard these tidings which were so remarkably propagated in all the countries of the East? Have they reached you? Have you listened to them? The aspect of the world at present seems to resemble but too strikingly the scene which was witnessed in Asia and Greece before this proclamation. Men are busy with the absurd theories of human wisdom; they are seeking joys which often prove fatal; they are absorbed in material interests; they are occupied as the Athenians were, in telling and hearing some new thing. But have they heard *the great news?* I know not; but I fear that there are many who are not yet aware that *the Gospel is preached,* and that it is preached *to the poor.* The object of this meditation shall be the instruction of those who are ignorant of this. We will first endeavour to settle the fact of the publication of the Gospel; secondly, we will describe the state in which we can best be profited by its publication.

THE GOSPEL IS PREACHED—IT IS PREACHED TO THE POOR.

These are the truths which we desire to develope. And do thou, O Lord! whose hand was with the apostles, when for the first time this news was published in the world, be with us now! May thy word be powerful, and subject many hearts unto thyself, bringing every thought into captivity and obedience unto thee! Amen.

THE GOSPEL IS PREACHED.

The Gospel is preached. What tidings does it bring? Oh, if men understood them, how soon should we see them arising out of their state of lukewarmness!—how soon would their excitement cease, and they stop to listen to them ! This news. which they esteem so lightly, is the most surprising and delightful message that can be proclaimed here below. It brings tidings of pardon granted, of reconciliation effected. It brings tidings of peace. It certifies to us that God, who dwells in heaven, has graciously approached the guilty human race; that he remembers our iniquities no more, and makes an everlasting covenant with every one who accepts the pardon he proclaims. At the same time, marvellous facts, calculated to dispel all fear in our hearts, are announced to us. The Son of God, the promised Saviour, expected from the beginning of the world, foretold to Israel by so many types, the object of enquiry in so many absurd superstitions of the Gentiles, has appeared in the flesh. He has given his life for those who were to be saved. The blood which he has shed obliterates their sins. And now the heralds of that Gospel address all men in these admirable words : " In time past ye were strangers from the covenants of promise, having no hope, and without God in the world; but now ye, who sometimes were far off, are made nigh by the blood of Christ. He came and preached peace to you which were far off, and to them that were nigh. He reconciled both unto God in one body by the cross. Now therefore ye are no more strangers and foreigners, but fellow-citizens with the saints, and of the household of faith." There is no want on earth which this heavenly message will not satisfy. God has sent it to put an end to all our sufferings. Now the disease of man is healed. With the forgiveness of his sins God has given him all things. Does he feel that he is a stranger to God, and does he mourn over that estrangement ? This message announces that he is adopted as a child through the beloved Son. Is he without hope and without any thing to console him in the midst of the misery of the present life ? This message announces that he is made " an heir of eternal life, heir of God, and joint-heir with Christ." Does he despair of subduing sin, which is powerful in his flesh ? This message announces that " he can do all things through Christ which strengtheneth him." Does he dread the attacks and snares of the world, and of all the enemies of his salvation ? This message announces that the Master whom he serves has received " all power in

heaven and on earth, and is at the right hand of God making
intercession for him." This message provides for every circumstance. Christ has brought us all we need. A new state
of things begins for the human race. Those who were weak
have become strong. " The grace of God that bringeth salvation hath appeared to all men."

What are the things which men call great, and which are
the subjects of their thoughts and conversations ? The Gospel is equal, nay, superior to them all. The most pompous
expressions of human language, those which recall the objects
of man's veneration, we can scarcely presume to apply to the
Gospel of Christ. The Gospel is a *Covenant;* but not a covenant between men; it is one in which *God* establishes peace
with *man;* the terms on the one hand are forgiveness of sins
and the gift of life everlasting; and on the part of man, repentance and belief on the name of the Lord Jesus Christ. The
Gospel is a *decree of amnesty;* but a decree emanating from
that being who is " God from everlasting to everlasting," and
publishing the revocation of the exile of the children of Adam,
and the restoration of their primitive glory. The Gospel is a
charter of freedom; but the great, the real charter of freedom,
given to the posterity of Adam—a charter which puts an end
to the only *real* slavery, and which is granted in pure mercy,
men having no title to it. The Gospel is the act of the mercy
of God, who stoops to relieve man lying in sin, and take him
to his arms.

If such be the contents of the Gospel, how important is it
that the tidings of it be spread every where ! The salvation
of man depends on its publication. " Whosoever will call upon the name of the Lord shall be saved. How then shall they
call on him in whom they have not believed ? And how shall
they believe in him of whom they have not heard ?"

My brethren, we have no reason to complain; the Gospel is
preached. God has taken proper measures. He has etablished
in the world institutions whose sole object is to proclaim his
forgiveness, and which will remain as long as the sinful race of
Adam exists.

In how many ways we can learn that God offers peace to
men, and that they ought now to be *friends !* God proclaims

this news in his word. It is a letter sent by him, addressed to all men, carried to every part of the world, on every page of which he says to every creature that "He so loved the world that he gave his only-begotten Son for it." God proclaims this news through his ministers. "Rise, and stand upon thy feet," he says; "I make thee a minister and a witness, and I send thee to the Gentiles to open their eyes." And they go and preach. Faithful to their charge, they preach "the Gospel of Christ, which is the power of God unto salvation." There is no person who cannot learn from these ambassadors the message which they bear. God publishes this news by his sacraments; the Holy Supper will "show the Lord's death till he come." This sacred mystery ever remains in the midst of the Christian people. And if the word of God were taken from it, if the voice of the ministers of God were hushed, this feast, commemorative of the death of the Lord, this bread, which is the communion in his body, this wine, which is the communion in his blood, would speak with a power increased by the fact that they would speak alone, and would announce to every humble soul eager to attain salvation, that "the Lamb was slain," that "the blood of the New Testament was shed for many for the remission of sins."

Yes, my brethren, the great tidings are announced in the world, and these voices which were to publish them have never been silent. Sooner would the sun cease to illuminate the earth than the publication of the Gospel cease to console the heart. If we look behind, we see a cloud of witnesses who have proclaimed it; if we look at the present time, we see a cloud of witnesses who are still proclaiming it. This news, that "giveth life unto the world," will be carried by the church unto all generations till the end of time. Our latest descendants will hear it as we have heard it, and will rejoice in it as we do now. And even if men kept silence, the very stones would cry out. Day unto day uttereth speech concerning it, and night unto night showeth knowledge.

The Gospel is preached. It is preached every where. The Lord has published the tidings of forgiveness in every language, to every tribe, to every nation, of the earth. "I saw an angel fly in the midst of heaven," says St. John, "having the ever-

lasting Gospel to preach unto them that dwell on the earth."
In the countries where the Church of Christ is already triumphant, the message is proclaimed, and all can hear it. Say not
that in so many places superstition or unbelief is still opposing
it. There is not an infidel who does not know that message;
and the very declaration that he will not believe it *proves* that he
knows it. In vain would superstition cover the pure gospel of
God with a human attire; the splendour of the truth pierces
the useless vail. There is not a being who does not know why
the Church exists, and what the object of the gospel of Christ
is on earth. And in those distant countries which the Prince
of darkness has shrouded, a voice of rejoicing is also heard:
"The feet of them that bring good tidings, that publish peace,"
are seen on every "mountain." "Their line is gone out through
all the earth, and their words to the end of the world." "The
day-spring from on high hath visited" all the inhabitants of
the world, "to guide their feet into the way of peace."

Thus, my brethren, the Gospel is really preached on earth.
No monarch ever took more pains to have his ordinances proclaimed than the Lord has taken to publish his ordinance of
peace, his decree of forgiveness. It is inscribed every where,
it is proclaimed every where. No one who sees and hears can
avoid seeing and hearing it. "Peace! peace to him that is afar
off, and to him that is near, saith the Lord; and I will heal
him. Declare ye, tell this, utter it even to the end of the
earth; say ye, The Lord hath redeemed his servant Jacob."

Athenians, who spend your time in nothing else but either
to tell or hear some new thing, shall I tell you something new?
Listen, then, to the news. It is this: God has made peace with
man; "the acceptable year of the Lord" is published over the
whole earth. This is the news. There may be other tidings
for nations, families, or individuals; but this is *the general news,*
the news for all nations, families, and individuals. And every
man ought for once, at least, to listen to it. He ought, some
time or other, to awake and exclaim, "This is a real and wonderful fact, which I never knew before. The Gospel is preached
to me. The Son of God was manifest in the flesh, and he gives
me peace. Oh, this is new to me; henceforth it shall be my
only treasure!"

How many, my brethren, are in need of hearing this message! How many fainting souls there are who "do hunger and thirst after righteousness!" There is a secret voice within the heart of every man that calls for the Gospel and for reconciliation with God. Mankind are in mourning till they hear it; for they have lost an inheritance. They know and feel this, and the Gospel alone can give you that inheritance back.

What joy there ought now to be on earth! The Gospel, "the good tidings of great joy," is preached. Rejoice, ye who "have wandered in a solitary way; the Lord leads you forth by the right way, that ye may go to a city of habitation." Rejoice, ye who were "sitting in darkness, and in the shadow of death; the Lord hath saved you out of your distresses, and hath cut the bars of iron in sunder." Rejoice, ye who were "afflicted because of your transgression, and because of your iniquities; for the Lord hath sent his word and healed you, and delivered you."

Lord! thy throne is in the heavens! O thou "who livest, and wast dead, and art alive for evermore," thou reignest! "All things have been put under thy feet," and now thou presidest over the preaching of that news which cost thee thine own blood! Then we will be of good cheer. Thou, Lord! wilt preserve it unto the end. Thou wilt overcome all thine enemies. Thou wilt not rest till thou shalt have "put down all rule and all authority and power" which opposes that Gospel of peace, and shalt have caused "all the ends of the earth to see thy salvation!"

IT IS PREACHED TO THE POOR.

But why, my brethren, do not all men, throughout the world, rejoice in the preaching of the Gospel? And if we ourselves have not yet received it, why is it so?

It will not be difficult to find a reason. Our very text gives us one. *The Gospel is preached;* but one qualification is necessary for those who hear it. It is preached to *the poor.*

But do not mistake, my brethren, the nature of the poverty required by the Gospel. It is not temporal poverty. The poverty or the riches of the earth are objects of indifference in the kingdom of God; they neither confer nor take away any privi-

lege. But this poverty is the poverty of the heart. "Blessed
are the poor in spirit," says Jesus elsewhere, in explanation of
the poverty of which he speaks. It consists in acknowledging
oneself destitute, not of temporal goods, or as receiving support
from others; but destitute of *eternal* goods, of pardon and merit,
and obliged to resort to another to obtain these.

Yes, my brethren, it is to the poor that the Son of God causes
his gospel to be preached. "He hath filled the hungry with
good things, and the rich he hath sent empty away," said Mary,
when she magnified the Lord. And in the parable of the Great
Supper, which was emblematic of the publication of the Gospel,
it was not those who had bought oxen and fields who sat down
at the table; but it was the poor, the maimed, the blind, and
those who were in the highways and hedges.

And how can God enrich those who think themselves rich
without his aid? How can he consent that the robes of his
righteousness should be merely an addition to the unclean covering of man's righteousness? What glory would he derive
from his mercy, if the mouth which sounded forth his praises
should unite a mortal name with his; and if his redeemed said
not with one accord, "It is thou that givest us all we have.
By thy grace alone we live. Thou art our Alpha and Omega;
we are of thee, and through thee, and belong unto thee.

But can *we* receive the news which is announced to us if we
are not poor in spirit? Of what use to us is a message that
speaks of reconciliation so long as we do not feel that we are
rebels? If so, we do not need *reconciliation.* How can a message which proclaims forgiveness of sins concern us so long as
we have not acknowledged that our sins have made us *guilty*
before God? We do not need *forgiveness.* How can we be in
need of those tidings which would deliver us from all iniquity,
if we have not discovered that "the power of sin binds us,"
and that we carry its bonds every where with us? We need
no *deliverance.* However frequently it may be announced, we
do not understand it, and can scarcely be said to hear it. Who
thinks of healing, when he has not felt the sore?

'But no,' you may reply ; there is another reason which
prevents me from paying attention to the news which the Gospel
publishes. Faith is no easy thing ; it is not given to every

one. If I do not believe, it is really because I have not the strength to believe!' Not at all, my dear brother ; if you do not believe, it is because you are not poor. Before we believe in the reality of the aid, we must believe in the reality of our want of it ; when we do that, the truth of the former becomes self-evident. If you acknowledge the true state of your soul, all your weakness and hesitation will cease. As the man who, on opening his eyes, sees that he is in imminent peril, and seizes with unwonted strength the help which is offered him ; so you would unhesitatingly seize the aid which this message tenders to you ; and the peace which it would immediately impart would show you, more clearly than any thing else can, that this really is God's appointed remedy ; and, still oppressed by some doubts, you would cast yourselves at the foot of the cross of the Redeemer who saves you, " saying with tears : Lord, I believe ; help thou mine unbelief!' "

'But no ; that is not the reason either : if I do not receive this news with eagerness, it is because I see nothing worthy of God in it ; there is, in the Gospel, ' no form nor comeliness when we see it.' In my eyes it is " despised, and not esteemed." And why do you not see that beauty in the glorious Gospel of our Lord which so many discern in it ? Ah ! learn your nakedness, and then you will learn "the unsearchable riches of Christ !" So long as you are rich, the Gospel will appear poor to you ; but become poor, and then you will find it rich. Our poverty restores its value to it. Oh, how glorious is the Gospel, when we know that it alone can save ! Thus the prodigal son, who in times of plenty despised his father's table, esteemed highly what he once despised, when forced to feed swine, and said, with bitterness, " How many hired servants of my father have bread enough and to spare, and I perish with hunger !"

'Well,' you perhaps continue, ' I can understand that this external humility of the Gospel may conceal Divine grandeur ; but it is not this that keeps me from approaching it. The distractions and occupations of the world prevent my doing so.' You are right, my dear brother ; we will not deny it ; the attractions of the world are a source of ruin to many ; our Lord teaches us this. But if a feeling of poverty came over you in the midst of the enjoyments of the world, do you suppose that they could drive it away ? With what scorn would you turn away from those empty phantoms, if your soul hungered after " the true bread, which cometh down from heaven !" Your poverty would drive you to the Cross of Jesus Christ, to seek for life there. How many " brands" have already been thus " plucked out of the burning !"

Yes, my brethren, the ignorance in which man is living, with reference to his own wretchedness, is the greatest obstacle to the reception of the Gospel ; it is the reason why this generation possesses neither peace nor salvation. It is this which impedes the progress of the kingdom of heaven. It is this that prevents the waters from flowing over the parched earth. This is the link by which Satan still holds the sons of Adam in chains, although deliverance has been proclaimed from the cross.

Become poor, then, my brethren, that ye may become rich. And is this poverty so concealed to you that you can not discover it ? How often have you had a feeling of emptiness in your soul ! When have you ever possessed that which an immortal being should have ? And is not that sense of emptiness *poverty* ? But if something is wanting in your heart, do you not also discover in it propensities rebellious to the law of Him who made you ? And have not these propensities been working upon your heart ? Ah ! far from being able to enumerate the rebellions into which they have led you, do you not find that your whole life has been one continued revolt against God ? And how will you cloak these faults from the eyes of your Judge ? Will you resort to any of your own works ? Which of them will you adduce that does not, in itself, deserve to be hidden from him ? Yet those crimes can not thus remain uncovered. Devoid of holiness, overcome by sin, self-accused at the bar of God, and without any thing to exculpate you—see, O see your misery ! Is it not evident to you ?

" Prepare ye, prepare ye the way of the Lord ! Let every mountain be brought low, and all flesh shall see the salvation of God." A message of pardon comes from heaven, and the earth must prepare to hear it. Forsake to-day, my brethren, all your proud thoughts, and behold your nakedness. You have acknowledged that you are of little value in the sight of God ; take now a more difficult step : acknowledge that you

are of none. So long as you hesitate to do this you can not
be truly poor. Cast off every covering, throw down your rich
habiliments, and humble yourselves in the presence of the
Lord. Conceal those robes now in this house, and seek only
the white robe of Christ's righteousness. It will be given you
then ; for " the poor have the Gospel preached to them."

And what season, my brethren, can be more appropriate, on
which t. preach that gospel to you, than this solemn day,
when you are about to receive the bread and the wine, those
sacred symbols of the body and the blood which were offered
up for our sins ? Generations pass away, and are called to
appear before the bar of God ; but as they pass they have the
Gospel preached unto them, to save them from the wrath to
come. I will then preach that Gospel to you too ; on this day,
and at this hour, I will proclaim in your midst that message
which the voice of the apostle once published at Iconium and
at Corinth ; I will bring it to this part of the Lord's heritage,
one of the smallest, it is true, but not less precious in his eyes
on that account, and a large flock of which will, I trust, stand
one day before the throne. " The Spirit of the Lord hath
anointed me to preach good tidings unto the meek ; He hath
sent me to bind up the broken-hearted, to proclaim liberty to
the captives, and the opening of the prison to them that are
bound ; to proclaim the acceptable year of the Lord." I come,
then, my brethren, in the footsteps of so many ambassadors
of Christ, who, in all ages, have preached the Gospel, to deliver
unto you, feebly, it is true, yet boldly and joyfully, this testimony which has been committed unto me : " God so loved the
world that he gave his only-begotten Son, that whosoever believeth in him should not perish, but have everlasting life."
" The Word was made flesh." " Christ gave himself for our
sins." " Peace, peace to him that is far off, and to him that
is near, saith the Lord ; and I will heal him." " Now then
we are ambassadors for Christ, and we pray you, in Christ's
stead, be ye reconciled to God."

Such are the tidings which are published, and which we
bring you to-day. That gospel which is preached over the
whole earth has come to you now. The tidings of great joy
are now published within these walls. Have you never heard

them before, my brethren ? Oh ! how many there are among
you to whom it is suited ! How many to whom God has caused
it to be proclaimed ! Oh ! ye who are poor in spirit, who weep
often over your sins, to you is the Gospel preached ! You are
told that the Lord forgets all your iniquities, and that in Christ
he communicates his eternal righteousness to you.   Oh ! ye who
are thirsty, who seek peace and happiness, and can not find them
either in yourselves or in any other creature, to you the Gospel
is preached ; the living fountain of happiness is open to you ;
" God hath given to you eternal life ; and this life is in his
Son."   Oh ! ye who have even become lukewarm, who have
been overcome by the allurements of the world, who have obeyed
the lusts of the flesh, and have wandered in the dark paths of
sin, to you the Gospel is preached.   For your souls Christ has
died ; his blood can wash away your sins too, and to you also he
can impart the pardon which he proclaims.   Then leave the
bondage of this death.   " Look upon him whom you have
pierced ;" be reconciled unto him, and receive from him a new
heart.

The Gospel is preached unto you now, my brethren ; this is
a certain truth, of which you are witnesses.   The Lord, who
designs to give peace to your souls, offers you reconciliation.
I display all his mercies before you.   This fact, I repeat, you
can see and hear, and you can bear witness to its truth.   *The
Gospel is preached unto you.*   Ah !   I doubt not that the angels
of God are rejoicing that such a favour is granted unto you ;
and what joy would there be in heaven if one soul awoke at the
sound of this proclamation, and formed an eternal covenant
with God, sealed with the blood of Jesus Christ !   The Gospel
is preached unto you ; give ear to this publication.   Henceforth
you can not stand before the throne in any other character than
as having had his gospel of peace announced to you at his command.   Oh ! may he never have to say to you, in allusion to this
hour, " I would have gathered you together, and ye would not !"

The Lord fulfils his work toward you.   The Lord causes his
pardon to be proclaimed unto you.   Receive it then with joy !
The Gospel is preached unto you.   God grant that, throughout
eternity, you may bless the hour when you heard it !   May it
be the instrument of saving your souls !   Amen.

DISCOURSE IV.

THE SERVICE OF JESUS CHRIST.

A HOMILY.

" Then came the first, saying, Lord, thy pound hath gained ten pounds. And he said unto him, Well, thou good servant: because thou hast been faithful in a very little, have thou authority over ten cities.—LUKE, xix, 16, 17.

IT is the destiny of man to serve. Having lost his innocence, he has lost his liberty. He serves even when he imagines that he enjoys the most perfect independence. He serves his own passions and prejudices, or the passions and prejudices of others, or else some other master. Within ourselves, or around us, we may be certain to find masters. It frequently happens that what we call freedom is but another species of slavery. A man who is at liberty to do what he pleases, a son, for instance, who has left his father's house, is perhaps at that very time living in a peculiarly painful slavery; for, instead of having one master without, he has several within.

Man must serve. Do you not agree with us, my brethren, in thinking that his welfare must depend on the nature of the master whom he serves? For you know that " Like master, like servant," is a popular axiom. Man will do right so long as he has a good master; but when his master is wicked, nothing but evil can be expected of him. Of all masters, there is one whom all will readily acknowledge to be the best. That Master is God. What an influence must he exert upon his subjects! And what blessings must he impart! To serve God is to serve sovereign truth and righteousness, and, consequently, to escape all the deluding tyrants who make us miserable. Oh, blessed slavery! which will release us from all other slavery. Oh, glorious slavery! which, in restoring man's innocence, gives him back his liberty also, true, eternal liberty.

Oh, blessed Master! who, in his mercy sets free those who were born in slavery, and receives them into his house as sons: "Ye are no more servants, but sons." Such are the words which the Gospel addresses to all. This is the Being to whose kingdom all other power should yield. This is the only Master who can benefit man. And this every one must, sooner or later, perceive.

But is God a master whom we may endeavour to serve? Yes, my brethren, God has chosen to give men the power to become his servants; and for this purpose he was manifested in the flesh, in the person of his beloved Son. God is now one of those masters among whom we may choose. We will consider with you to-day the practical part of this service of Jesus Christ. In this light only will we examine it. You will then acknowledge that, while every other service deludes and ruins man, this renders him useful on earth and happy in heaven. In our text we have the history of a certain master and his servant. We shall simply consider THE WORDS OF THE SERVANT, and THE WORDS OF THE MASTER.

The words of the servant will draw our attention to this world, and will teach us what we have to do here; the words of the master will transport us to heaven, and will teach us what we have to hope for or to fear, as we may have entered upon or forsaken the service referred to.

Do thou, O Father of our Lord Jesus Christ! give us the spirit of wisdom and understanding! Amen.

I. In considering the history of this servant, the question will naturally arise, Where did he find the means to serve his master? To whom did the money which he had so greatly increased belong? Was it his own? Had he acquired it by his own efforts, or had he inherited it from his ancestors? Not at all, my brethren; "Thy pound!" he says to his master; 'it is thine, Lord! I was a poor servant; I owned not a farthing; but when thou wentest away, thou gavest me a pound, and it was that pound which I have thus increased!' Behold then, my hearer, the source from which you must draw all power and strength; it is Jesus Christ; and it is only by means of what he has given you that you can gain something more. 'What!' you exclaim, 'have I not sufficient ability in myself? Do I not possess much penetration of mind, much activity, and many other qualities besides?' Perhaps you do, my dear brother; but these are not the things with which you must labour for that Master; or, rather, you must have the pound which the grace of Jesus Christ can give you, before you can use those talents to advantage in this service. The servant also had strength; yet if one pound had not been given him he could not have gained the other ten. So long as a man has not received love to God and man from Jesus Christ, the only object of all his labours is to benefit himself; he himself is the idol whom he worships and serves; and even while he seems to be seeking the interests of his brethren with the greatest earnestness, he is only working for himself. Having nothing of his own, he can give nothing away. Having no funds of his own, he can gain nothing. He must seek the necessary advance. He will find it in *the knowledge of Jesus Christ.* He must know that the Son of God gave himself for him, that he might redeem him from all iniquity." He must acknowledge that it is but reasonable that, having been "bought with a price," he should henceforth "glorify God." He must ask Christ to give him what he came to give the world; "a new heart and a new spirit," that he may serve him aright." This is the *pound.*" With it you will receive ability to do right. From that time your words and deeds will be blessings, for they will be prompted by charity. "He that abideth in me, and I in him," says Christ, "the same bringeth forth much fruit; for without me ye can do nothing." Begin to seek it then, if you have not received anything yet. Ask for your pound. Do not fear lest Jesus should refuse to give it. His work as a master is to distribute. "A certain nobleman," he says in this parable, "went into a far country. And he called his ten servants, and delivered them ten pounds, and said unto them, Occupy till I come." If he even gave a pound to the *wicked* servant, do you suppose that he will send you away empty?

But how much did the servant receive? Was it a great treasure? Was it a large territory? "Lord," he says, "behold, here is thy pound!" It was *a pound,* my brethren, that this *nobleman,* who was going to acquire *a kingdom* for himself, left his servant! How small a thing! Did not the servant despise this paltry sum? Was he not tempted, like the other servant, to wrap it up in a napkin, to bury it in the ground? By no means. On the contrary, he immediately began to use his pound in trade, just as though he had received a great treasure!

But perhaps, my dear brother, unlike him, you complain; perhaps you are anxious about your own destiny, when you look at the small value of the pound which you have received; perhaps you say, There are many to whom much is given; let them act, let them trade, let them serve God! These things do not concern me! Ah! my dear hearer, act well your part to-day, and to-morrow you will receive a greater sum. "Unto every one that hath," says Jesus Christ, "shall be given, and he shall have abundance." And Solomon says, "The path of the just is as the shining light, that shineth more and more unto the perfect day." But you can not contribute, you say, either to the welfare of your brethren or to the glory of God. You are seriously mistaken, my dear brother. Each has his duty in life, and can fulfil it: do not neglect yours. It is true that the Scriptures tell us, that sometimes the master gives a servant *ten talents*, which is a large sum. But this servant had received only one pound, yet he was active. O you who have received but little from the Lord (and certainly the majority here belong to this class), cease your distrust! Let your efforts be unceasing, and be of good cheer! If you are restricted to an unknown sphere, this is another reason why you should labour; for if *you* do not, who will? Let your weakness be a matter of encouragement, not of timidity; for the weaker we are, and the more we feel it, the more God will assist us; and a little of God's strength is worth all man's. "When I am weak," says Paul, "then am I strong." He who made the universe out of nothing, can certainly do a great deal with the little he has given you! The principles of his government are the reverse of those of the governments of the world. He has chosen small things to accomplish great objects. A few obscure and illiterate men, devoid of riches or of power, came forward to found his kingdom; and immediately the idols of the nation fell, the kingdom of darkness was overthrown, and the salvation of the world was established. Oh, how much more good would be done, if each did what little is in his power! It is not by great efforts that the foundations of real prosperity are to be laid, but by the insignificant labours of each in the sphere in which he is placed. The strongest wind can not shake the rock, but the drops of rain will loosen it from its place; it is not of importance whether we have much or little, but whether we are *faithful*. And if you were the most miserable of beings, you might be faithful in your misery, and do a great deal with the little that your faithfulness gains.

But what, then, have we to do? What did this servant work for? To accomplish his master's business, of course; the nobleman went away on a journey, and it was natural that he should leave it in the hands of his servants. Very well, my brethren; in what other bank, then, ought you to place your pound, that it may gain other pounds, than, to use your own expression, in the *business* of Jesus Christ? Jesus Christ has gone away; but he has left you here to manage his affairs. His ministry should be your ministry. If the Eternal Light dwells no longer in our midst, each of its servants should reflect its splendour. Behold, my brethren, this beautiful plan of life! And what are the affairs of Jesus Christ? Obedience and mercy. All that can contribute to the happiness of man or to the glory of God, then, should now become the great object of your life. Oh, there is a great work for the man who wishes to spend his life in "going about to do good!" Much assistance ought to be given to all who partake of the weakness of our nature. And how great is that weakness! We must "deal our bread to the poor; bring the poor that are cast out to our houses; and when we see the naked, we must cover them." "The true Light, which lighteth every man," must be manifested to all men, and all must find in Christ "wisdom, and righteousness, and sanctification, and redemption." How much ignorance still remains to be dissipated! how many diseases to be cured! how many unknown blessings to be given! And who but the servants of Christ will perform this work, which is the work of all men, and in all ages, and was the work of Jesus himself?— Yes, this is all very true, you say; it is the work of Christ's servants, the ministers of his word, but it is not ours! Not yours? We certainly acknowledge with joy, yet with fear, that this work is emphatically intrusted to the ministers of Christ; but how can any disciple of Christ be entirely exempt from it? It is true that the Scriptures teach us that Christ "gave some, apostles; and some, prophets; and some, evangelists; and some, pastors and teachers;" but, besides this ministry, to which you do not belong, he has established another, to which you do belong. It is that active ministry which he instituted, when he said unto all his disciples: "Let your light so shine before men, that they may see your good works, and glorify your Father which is in heaven." And, indeed, admirable as is the ministry with which we are clothed, yours is in no wise inferior to it.

Yes, my dear brother, acknowledge that which has been committed to you. You are the servant and minister of Jesus Christ. Were you not consecrated to the service of the living and true God in baptism? When you received your pound you were placed in the field of action. It was not to his apostles only, but to all his disciples, to all nations, and for all times, that Jesus Christ said, "Ye are the salt of the earth; ye are the light of the world." They ought, therefore, to be ever shining in the midst of darkness, and to purify that which is corrupt. How great is the ministry and how great are the transactions and speculations in which you are engaged! And in this there is nothing that you cannot accomplish. Jesus Christ fulfilled his ministry in the streets and highways. And it is in the same way that the duties of the priesthood to which you belong are to be performed; not in a lonely sanctuary, but in the midst of the world. Be compassionate toward all men, and you will be continually fulfilling the ministry of Jesus Christ. The churches in which he calls you to officiate are your own dwellings, and the places where you perform your duties. Mothers and the heads of families ought to perform this work in their houses. And the more you mingle with the world, the more opportunities you will have for serving the Lord.

But by what rules did the servant do his master's work? We have reason to suppose that he endeavoured to act in all cases just as his master had done. So faithful a servant must have loved his Lord's example. Ah! my brethren, shall we not, as the servants of so kind a master, take for our pattern the example that Christ set before us? How delightful it ought to be to us to do as Jesus did! Jesus did not "seek his own glory, but his glory that sent him." And in like manner let all efforts be made for Jesus Christ, who sends us. Let every thing we do be done for his sake, and because we owe him an immense debt. Jesus prayed to his Father when he was about to perform an action, and afterward he gave thanks to him." Let us not suppose, then, that we can do any good thing without having first prayed to our Master; and when it shall have been done let us return thanks to him who alone is the author it. Jesus took every opportunity to do good. When he happened to be at Cana, he performed his first miracle there; when he met a blind man he restored his sight. Let us likewise make it a rule not so much to seek extraordinary opportunities as to keep a vigilant watch for all those which daily life may afford us; then good works will not be wanting. Let us always do as Jesus did. Servants! let your Master's life be your example in all things.

And what was the final result of this servant's labours? "Thy pound hath gained ten other pounds," said he to the master. A single pound gained ten! The business in which the servant was engaged produced a thousand for a hundred! How great was this profit, my brethren! There are certainly not many speculations in this world which have been as successful as this! Such will be the result with you if you engage in the work of which we speak. God gives his blessing abundantly in this matter. Do not fear that he will be sparing in this; the glory of his name and the happiness of his creatures are concerned. In all your other labours success is doubtful; but in this it cannot be so. "Ye are labourers together with God;" it is his work to give you success. Ten for one is the rate of interest in the business of his kingdom. And even if you may not hold the ten pounds in your hand, do not suppose that your labours were of no avail. The deeds of God's servants are the seeds of life, which will sooner or later take root, and bear much fruit. "As the rain cometh down, and the snow from heaven, and returneth not thither, but watereth the earth, and maketh it bring forth and bud, that it may give seed to the sower, and bread to the eater: so shall my word be."

Perhaps it is the will of God to exercise your faith and your patience; and perhaps he will not let you see the fruit. Then sow as the husbandman does, trusting in that invisible power which will one day bring forth that which you have committed to Him. But your labour if it were lost upon others will not be lost for you. This we learn from the *words of the master.* Let us listen to them.

II. The servant had done his duty, and therefore the master rejoiced greatly in his conduct; he resolved to show his satisfaction by giving him a share in the government of his kingdom; he said to him, "Well, thou good servant; because thou hast been faithful in a very little, have thou authority over ten cities."

How great must have been the astonishment of the servant on hearing these words! This will probably be our first thought. 'What!' he must have exclaimed, 'the government of ten cities is given to me, because I put one pound to profit in thine absence! But, Lord! thou owest me nothing for that! Am I not thine? And is it not my duty to perform thy business?' Should you not say so too, my dear brother, on receiving the recompense which your Master will assign you? Will you not feel then that you have in no wise deserved it? What must you think of yourself, if you suppose that God owes you any thing? Are you not his servant? Do you not doubly belong to him, both as his creature and as ransomed by him? What then can you do beyond your duty? And which of your works do you suppose *deserves* eternal happiness? Select the purest of them; which of them is not so vile, when you consider it in the light of the word of God, of nature, or of the motives that prompted it, that you have reason to fear to present it to God, even as the fulfilment of your debt, much less as a merit which deserves immortality! No, my brethren, God no more owes you the recompense than he did the pound; he gave you one, of his own mercy, and it is his mercy that he will give you the other. "Have thou authority over ten cities." Oh, how deeply this unexpected gift will make the believer feel his unworthiness, and the incomprehensible riches of Christ!

Nevertheless, though this is a wonderful fact, it is also a certain one. The Lord gives *ten cities* to him who gained *ten pounds.* And indeed it is only to him who has gained the ten

pounds that he gives the ten cities; he who has gained nothing
cannot receive any thing. "*Because* thou hast been faithful,"
says the Master. The word "because" teaches us that it is
the Master's will that the work and the recompense should go
together, although their connection is not apparent. And this
also, my brethren, is the royal will of our King. This is a
fundamental law of his kingdom, and we preach it to you beforehand. "The faithful servant," and he alone, will be crowned. You will be judged *according to your deeds*, and he who has
been unprofitable shall be driven away in disgrace. And how
could it be otherwise? How can Jesus Christ, when he has
taken possession of his kingdom, receive as acceptable servants
those who have not applied themselves to good works? We
know what Jesus was during his pilgrimage on earth; we know
that he went about doing good; how then can those who have
remained idle please this Master who took no rest? We know
that the object of Christ's coming was to create man unto good
works, by restoring him to the glorious condition of a child of
God; now how can he who has attained the object which the
first coming of the Lord had in view obtain the glory which
his second coming will bring? We know by what mark Jesus
Christ recognizes *his friends:* it is that they do whatsoever he
commands them; how then can he call that man his friend who
has forgotten through life *the great commandment* of charity?
No, my brethren, we shall receive in heaven in proportion to
what we shall have done on earth. Christianity is emphatically
a law of activity. The great object here is to *labour*. The object of the Son of God in coming into the world was not to let
us go to sleep, but to gather a people from all parts of the
earth that shall be adorned with good works.

"Have thou authority," said the master to the righteous
servant, "over ten cities." This is written to instruct us respecting the greatness of the reward. For to assign authority
over ten cities to a servant to whom one pound had been entrusted, was certainly giving a great deal to one who had been
faithful in a very little. And this is what Jesus will give on
the last day; with this distinction, that all will be on a far
greater scale. There will be as little proportion between the
glory given above and the talent entrusted here below as there

was between ten cities and the servant's pound. Do not be anxious about the reward. The omnipotent Being who created the universe will be for ever occupied in giving it to you. "Eye hath not seen, nor ear heard, neither have entered into the heart of man, the things which God hath prepared for them that love him." Christ will share all things with us. His inheritance will be our inheritance; his kingdom will be our kingdom; his power will be our power; and his glory our glory. "Know ye not that ye shall judge angels?" says St. Paul; and Jesus writes to Laodicea, "To him that overcometh will I grant to sit with me in my throne." Do not suppose that such expressions are altogether figurative; it is certain that a kingdom will be given unto him who shall have glorified God amid the sin and misery of this age. But that kingdom will not give him any peculiar grandeur, nor will it fill him with pride. It will ever be his boast that he is a servant of Jesus Christ. Christ himself will always be the most precious crown of the believer.

But if the words of the master must have filled the righteous servant with joy, what an impression must they have produced upon those who were present and heard them! What must the unprofitable servant have thought? What must those who were not in this master's service have thought? What must others who were yet in the midst of their labours?

Ah! as to the wicked servant who, instead of improving his pound, wrapped it up in a napkin, and who, according to the parable, was coming up to render an account of it, how must he have been struck on hearing these words addressed to his companion: "*Because* thou hast been faithful in a very little, have thou authority over ten cities!" *Because*, says the master; what then will become of him whose pound hath gained nothing? He trembles; he is confounded already; already he hears those fearful words, "Out of thine own mouth will I judge thee, thou wicked servant! Take from him the pound and give it to him that hath ten pounds; and cast ye the unprofitable servant into outer darkness." To you, therefore, we speak, unprofitable servants! May you likewise listen to these words before it be too late. Oh, ye who have wrapped up your talent in a napkin, or have hidden it in the earth, think of the account that without fail will be required of you! Wicked servants! do you suppose that you will always be at your ease as you are now? Do you imagine that the dream in which you delight will last for ever, and that the dreadful truth that there is a Master who will one day require an account for the last farthing, will never be realized? Oh, ye who are sloth-ful in well-doing, do not suppose that any thing can screen you from the shame that awaits you! Whatever the cause of your sleep may be, unexpected ruin will fall upon you; whether the riches, pleasures, and luxuries of life detain you in a state of uselessness; or, trusting in what you call your virtues, your merits, or your righteousness, you fall asleep in the thought that you are acceptable in the eyes of the Lord, instead of en-deavouring to become so by serving Jesus Christ, and by your good works; or whether, glorying in your high privileges, and boasting of peculiar favours, you deny by your life the faith which you profess with your mouth; and, calling Christ your Lord, you do not the will of his Father. " Out of thine own mouth will I judge thee, thou wicked servant! Take from him the pound, and give it to him that hath ten pounds: for unto every one which hath shall be given; and from him that hath not, even that he hath shall be taken away from him."

But if "among them that stood by," of whom the parable speaks, who surrounded the king and heard his words, there were any who were not yet in his service, what must have been their feelings! " Because thou hast been faithful in a very little, have thou authority over ten cities!" Oh, how ardently they must have wished to enter the service of a master who acted so nobly and rewarded so generously! And you, my dear hearers, who are perhaps not yet in the service of the im-mortal King, you who are still subject to the world, or to sin, or to your own wills, forsake those masters; you receive no-thing but suffering in their service; but if you serve Jesus Christ, " ye will have your fruit unto holiness, and the end everlasting life." Yes, my brethren, we come to propose a new object for your ambition; we come to offer you authority in the kingdom of heaven—authority over ten cities! Why are you so anxious to possess the riches and kingdoms of the world? You can acquire a far nobler distinction, which will better supply the wants of a soul that will never die. By enlisting in the service of Jesus of Nazareth, you can obtain eternal treasures and kingdoms, without as much pains as you apply to obtain your worthless treasures and to win your paltry glory. Come and engage in this service. "Lay hold on eternal life, whereunto ye are also called;" enter into "the good fight of faith;" "count all things but loss for the excellency of the knowledge of Christ Jesus."

But perhaps there was some servant present to whom his master had also intrusted a pound, but who was still in the midst of his labours, and who had many difficulties to overcome. When he heard these words, with what new ardour he must have returned to his work! Let the sight of the same recompense give the same strength and the same joy to you, O servants who are still in the midst of your service! Perhaps you meet with many difficulties in the management of the pound which you have received; perhaps your service is painful, and you gain the ten pounds by the sweat of your brow; but look at the reward that awaits you! It is worth all and more than all your trouble. "Wherefore lift up the hands that hang down and the feeble knees." Perhaps you have to undergo trials that are foreign to your work; you must also drink of the bitter cup that is proffered to every member of the human family. Lift up your eyes, then! look at that "crown of righteousness which the Lord, the righteous judge, shall give you at that day;" enter by faith into those mansions which the Master is now preparing for you; "rejoice in hope; be patient in tribulation, continuing instant in prayer."

Would that these reflections might arouse us all! Would that we might receive new courage and strength to serve our God! Would that we might be made "steadfast, unmovable, always abounding in the work of the Lord, forasmuch as we know that our labour is not in vain in the Lord." Yes, my brethren, none but the servant who goes to the banks and public places to gain ten pounds by his pound will be accepted by his master. Dear hearer, where is your pound? What did you do with it when you received it? Unhappy man! you buried it in the ground! Go, dig it up, exchange it for current money, trade with it, barter, and let it not remain covered with rust. You must labour; you must gain your living; you must gain it here, penny by penny, and pound by pound.

Yes, Lord! we know and confess before all men that nothing but thy grace can save us; we know and confess before all men that nothing but the blood which flowed from the cross of Jesus Christ can blot out our sins! But we know, too, that, were we to glory in thy grace, and to rest upon thy bosom already, without having done our work, thou wouldest indignantly reject us, and say to us before all men, "I never knew you. Depart from me, ye workers of iniquity." Lord! let not this shameful lot be ours! Create us unto good works! Take us into thy service! Grant that we may be faithful; and in the day when thou comest to summon all mankind before thee, may we hear from thee the words, "Well done, good and faithful servant; thou hast been faithful over a few things, I will make thee ruler over many things; enter thou into the joy of thy Lord!" Amen.

DISCOURSE V.

THE DUTIES OF MASTERS TO THEIR HOUSEHOLDS.

" If any provide not for his own, and especially for those of his own house, he hath denied the faith, and is worse than an infidel."—1 Tim., v, 8.

MY brethren,—In our days, more than ever before, men seem to perceive the evils to which the lower classes of society are subject. Associations are forming in various countries which have for their object the prevention or the cure of those evils. It is true that among these classes there are individuals, and even families, who, having persevered in the faith, " live soberly, righteously, and godly." Honoured in their obscurity, they form part of the salt of the earth. But, generally speaking, who does not see that luxury, love of pleasure, intemperance, and liability to corruption have rapidly increased ? All this is but too easily explained. The evil which began above has come down. Indifference and infidelity at first attacked the higher classes; while the lower, guarded, as it were, by an invisible rampart, remained protected from the shock. But now, while the former are partly returning from their error, and partly acknowledging the impotency of the rules of human wisdom, and the necessity of principles of piety, while those who were dead are often seen restored to life, the poison has reached the lower classes, and is continuing its ravages among them. They now reap what others so zealously sowed many years ago. We find a great many self-styled philosophers among the common people ; some even attain the bewildering heights of materialism, and deny the immortality of the soul! The waters of infidelity, which first reached the highest peaks, are now gathering in the lowest parts of the earth. The paralysis which attacked the head has descended to the inferior members of the body ; and it were in vain to free the head ; the body can not move while

those parts are affected.   Thus, my brethren, it is not without
reason that attention is now turned to those classes.   We desire to-day to direct your solicitude to individuals who belong
to them, and who are within your reach : — to " those of your
own house," in the words of our text.   We will not remind you
that you ought to supply their wants, and give them wages
proportionate to their work ; nor will we speak of other similar
obligations, which we trust you have not failed to fulfil.   But
we would speak to you of a higher duty ; a duty which, perhaps,
you have not yet fulfilled ; a duty which relates to the moral
welfare, to the *salvation* of your servants.   It is not so much by
general measures that the evil which we have pointed out can
be remedied ; the cure must begin in every house.   The duty
which I have to insist upon is peculiarly applicable to those
whom I am now addressing.   In a language very different from
that of St. Paul addressing the Corinthians, I might say,
" There are not many poor among you, not many weak."   Listen, then, with attention, my brethren, and let your thoughts
be consecrated here during this meditation ; but, at the same
time, remember your own homes and those who dwell there, and
do not forget that your relations toward them are now concerned.
We will first point out a few motives for this duty ; we will then
present some directions respecting the manner in which you
should perform it.   And do thou, who art the Lord of masters
and of servants, enlighten us by thy Spirit !   Amen.

MOTIVES.

There are two things which ought to exert a great influence
upon man: the first is the thought of duty; and the second the
thought of usefulness.   The influence of these motives has always been irresistible to noble minds; either of them ought of
itself to be enough.   If we think it our duty to undertake any
enterprise, we ought to do so, even though we may not see all
the good that will result from it; and, likewise, if we perceive
its beneficial consequences, we ought immediately to turn our
whole attention to it, even though, in our peculiar position,
we may not suppose that it is a duty binding on us.   If these
two great principles were united, how powerful would they be!

Now, my brethren, on both of these we would rest our arguments. They afford us plenty of weapons ; we shall select but a few of the first that come to our hands.

And in the first place, since duty is concerned, consider yourselves in the character of Christians, and see what your duty is *toward Christ*. "If any provide not for his own," says our text, "and especially for those of his own house, he hath denied the faith, and is worse than an infidel." Yes, my brethren, if you have faith in Jesus Christ, you should take advantage of the opportunities you have to teach the truth and impart consolation in your own households. If you deprive others of the benefit of that faith, you become guilty with regard to it; you betray Jesus Christ.

What! when you know that the path in which men are walking leads to death, that "they have all gone out of the way, that there is none that seeketh after God, and that they have not known the way of peace;" that, if you had remained in that path, you would have drawn down upon yourself God's just condemnation—for this is your belief—when, I say, you know all this, can you live without doing something for those who dwell under your roof? Will you not endeavour to free them from the bondage of death, from the darkness of iniquity, of which you yourself have seen the fearful consequences? Ah! if you act thus, you will "deny the faith, and be worse than an infidel."

What! when you know that Christ is "the Way, the Truth, and the Life," that he is "the Door," and that "no man cometh unto the Father but by him," that "by him if any man enter in he shall be saved, and shall go in and out, and shall find pasture ;" when, I say, you know this—for this is your belief—can you live without directing those of your household who are wandering like sheep without a shepherd," to that Way and that Door? Ah! if you can act thus, you have indeed forsaken that way yourself ; you have renounced Jesus Christ ; you have "denied the faith, and are worse than an infidel."

What! when you know that "there is no distinction of persons," that God has called all men to obtain salvation through Jesus Christ," both bond and free," as St. Paul says ; that "Christ hath reconciled both unto God in one body ;" when you know this, I say—for this is your belief—can you still live without instructing your servants respecting those privileges which the Christian belief has offered them ? Can you withhold from them their portion of eternal life ? Ah ! if so, you have renounced Jesus Christ ; you have " denied the faith, and are worse than an infidel."

But if your duty toward Christ obliges you to take care of those who belong to your household, your duty toward your brethren in general lays you under obligations no less sacred. Do you not owe them an active manifestation of your love ? Oh ! it is sad to view the neglect which prevails in this respect ; a fatal but natural consequence of the absence of faith.

Perhaps you say, ' We are not idle ; we have often given alms to the poor.' But how is it then, we reply, that in your charity you forget those who are nearest to you ; and to whom do you owe more peculiar proofs of your fraternal love than to those whom God has placed under the same roof as yourselves ? Perhaps, desiring to justify yourselves in another way, you say, ' It is true that we are neglectful of the performance of good works, but really it is because we have no opportunities.' Ah ! we reply, in the words of an enlightened divine,[1] " Were you unable to do any thing beyond your domestic sphere, you might still, beneath your own roof, have your hands full of good works. Tell me, O man ! who are the hungry, the thirsty, the naked, the prisoners, the strangers, or the sick, but those of thine own family ? God, when he gave thee thy house, made it an *hospital*, and appointed thee a *steward* over it."

Perhaps you say, ' We have not forgotten our servants ; and when we have had any thing to give away, we have preferred giving it to them rather than others.' What gifts do you allude to ? An article of clothing, or a piece of gold ? Have you nothing better to give them ? Are not their souls naked, and do they not need the robe of righteousness ? Could you not give them some of that *pure gold* which you derive from the Gospel ? Of what use is it, my brethren, that Christian faith exists in your dwelling, if Christian works are not performed there ? Where there are no works, faith is but a dream and a delusion.

[1] Luther.

8 *e*

And if such be your duty toward the Saviour and toward your brethren, what is your duty toward God your heavenly Father in Jesus Christ? Our great duty toward God is to become like him, " to be perfect, even as our Father in heaven is perfect." In vain do we seek to please him by any other means, if we do not please him in this respect. To be like-minded with him, and to do what he does, is our rule. Now, how does God, who is our Master, act towards us, his servants? What care he takes of us! How his Providence extends to the most minute details! How continually does he act! Then do for your servants what God does for you. Especially let your desire to imitate God prevent you from forgetting the one thing needful. Does your Master, who is Lord of heaven and earth, and in whose house you are living, give you nothing but meat and drink? If nature works great miracles for the nourishment of your body, has not grace performed still greater miracles for your spiritual nourishment, and does it not still perform them? Hath not God given you Christ for your wisdom and your righteousness? Ought you not to spread blessings around you, as he spreads them over the whole world? and ought you not to act in your limited sphere as he acts in his universe? " Masters! know that ye also have a Master in heaven;" him must you imitate.

Thus, my brethren, the remembrance of our duty suggests important considerations. But this is not enough; we would also draw them from another source, and would lay before you some reflections in reference to usefulness.

And first observe how much good will result from the care given to those who belong to your household, for yourselves, for your own sanctification and happiness. It is in our own household that the Evil One lays the most dangerous snares. Perhaps it is not very difficult to appear to be a servant of Jesus Christ in public, and to seem very zealous for his cause and the advancement of his kingdom. But to be truly a servant of Jesus Christ in the retirement of the family, at all hours of the day, and among those in whose company life is to be spent—this indeed is difficult. And yet this must be done if your piety is sincere. If you neglect those who belong to your household, you will neglect yourself; but if, on the contrary, you devote all your efforts to them, it will be a powerful aid to your own perfection. And how can you lead a truly Christian life if there is no harmony on matters of faith in your home? How can that family be truly Christian where the servants are dissipated and slanderous, or even where their religious belief is at variance with that of their masters? There are a thousand things to disturb devotion and piety. Christian life requires harmony. If you and your servants are animated with the same spirit, they assist you in your progress in the path of sanctification instead of impeding you; a spirit of life pervades your whole family, unites its various members, and the way of salvation becomes easy. " Let the servants too be taught the word of God," says a father of the Church; " we shall find the practice of virtue easier if we have brought them up in it; as the pilot steers his vessel with greater facility if his sailors assist him."[1] And how often have the prayers of the faithful servant risen, a sweet savour, to the throne of God! How many servants, like Elisha's, have been instruments in assisting some widow of Shunem! How many masters have received from those who wait upon them not merely the food which perisheth, but also the Bread of Eternal Life?

But do you not perceive what good would result from your efforts to your servants themselves? The knowledge of God is assuredly an invaluable treasure to all men. But does it not possess peculiar advantages for those who are called to wait upon others? They are under the command of a human master; and oh, how delightful would it be for them to find *the great Master* who will never make them feel that his dominion is a wearisome one, who is "lowly in heart," whose "yoke is easy, and whose burden is light," and who can make up for all the exactions and caprices of others! They are not free; another commands them; and how precious would they find that *true freedom*, which can be acquired through faith in Jesus Christ, even by those who are in a state of servitude, the freedom which delivers from sin; for "they shall be free indeed whom the Son makes free." They are called at all times to sacrifice their will to the will of others; how desirable, then, that they should possess that knowledge of God which destroys self-

---

[1] Chrysostom.

will, which leads to the renunciation of self-interest, and which induces one to exclaim with joy and resignation, whatever may happen, "Lord, thy will be done!" You see then what precious advantages the truth offers to your servants; it would almost seem as though Christianity were made for them alone. And would you refuse them that which God has designed for them?

Perhaps you fear lest the attention given to your servants might prevent your taking the necessary care of your children. But, on the contrary, it is not possible for you to bring up your children properly unless you also rightly train your servants; and your family will derive the greatest benefit from your exertions in their behalf. How can your children be brought to the knowledge of the truth, and be led into the right path, unless moral order and discipline exist in your family; and unless the influences of Christianity surround them? If your servants themselves do not obey the precepts of the Gospel, they will ever be destroying the work of your hands. Their language, their actions, and their habits will be more forcibly impressed upon the minds of your children than all your instructions, and even than your example. The natural corruption of the heart of man leads him readily to receive bad impressions, and the enemy of our souls has particular designs upon the souls of children. O, how many have been ruined by the suggestions and examples of servants!

But if, on the contrary, your servants fear the Lord, how useful will they be to the younger members of your family! Be assured that they will be the best of teachers; they may, perhaps, have even more influence than yourselves. Thus, in the name of the interests most dear to your heart, we call upon you to fulfil the great duty which God's word lays upon you.

But what is this duty? We will tell you.

DIRECTIONS.

We must now, my brethren, give you rules for your conduct in future. This is a difficult task; but we shall at least endeavour to suggest a few directions, which we will place under three heads, and will say to you, If you wish to perform your duty to those who belong to your household, be their *equals*, their *masters*, and their *servants*.

O, masters! be the equals of your servants! This is the first thing required of you. Of this be well assured: you and your servants are equal in the sight of God; and in his book the same leaf upon which your name is inscribed contains theirs also. Let them be members of your family; let them be the companions of your life; let not the servants be a distinct class in each household, but let masters and servants be closely united. Paul, when he sent Onesimus back to his master Philemon, said to him, "Receive him not now as a servant, but above a servant, a brother beloved, especially to me, but how much more unto thee, both in the flesh and in the Lord?" In the eye of God there are no masters or servants. Christianity has done away with all those superstitious ideas according to which men believed that one class of human beings was of greater value than another. Christianity is the great law of perfect and universal equality. "In Christ there is neither bond nor free." Christianity teaches us that there is but one real inferiority, but one real state of bondage, namely, a state of sin. "I call the servant a master, even though he wear chains, if I see in him the evidence of a noble mind ; and, in my opinion, the man who is invested with the highest authority is but an insignificant being, if he has a servile soul. How many masters are lying drunken upon their beds, while those who wait upon them are erect and sober! Is there any other slave than the servant of sin?"[1] Christianity has abolished slavery, my brethren. Thanks to the law of liberty, one source of shame for man has been closed. But of what avail is it that slavery should have been abolished in name, if it still exists in fact? Do you suppose that the humiliating state of dependence, the marked distinction, the spirit of servility in which inferiors are held in so many families styled Christian, do not constitute real slavery? Ah! how many slaves, in by-gone days, were more generously treated than many servants are in our day! And by what right does one portion of the human race so lightly esteem another portion? The class of

---

[1] Chrysostom.

servants is in reality one of the most honourable of classes.
What other has such frequent opportunities of displaying that
noblest of qualities, forgetfulness of self! Christianity has
infinitely improved the condition of servants by telling them
that they do not serve men merely, but *the Lord;* and, by being
frequently reminded of this servitude, they are perhaps brought
nearer than any others to the glory of the saints and angels,
which consists in serving God. If you make your servants
feel the inferiority of their condition, it will be out of your
power to do them any good; but if, impressed with the great
law of equality, you treat them with that affection which the
Gospel requires, as brethren, as children, and as friends, their
hearts will be already gained over to the influence of the law
that annuls the sentence of servitude which the world has passed. The low habits and servile ideas which they may still retain will gradually become less common. Noble ideas will find
access to their minds. Their duties will still be the same, but
they will be fulfilled with higher and weightier motives; and,
when they appreciate their own worth, they will be more anxious for themselves and their eternal welfare. Their souls will
be better prepared to receive true Christianity, that supreme
law of deliverance. They will no longer regard religion, as
some do, as a yoke to which others wish to subject them, but
as a friend that would save them. They will be made a part
of Christian society. Do not say that the condition of your
servants is so far below such a state that you cannot think of
making any efforts of the kind; for what occasions their present condition but the course which you have hitherto pursued?
And if you alter it, what proof have you that the amelioration
of which we speak will not take place?

But it is not sufficient that you should become the equals of
your servants; you must also be their real *masters.* God forbid that we should even suggest the idea of that equality of
condition which is the prolific source of disorder. While we
remind you that you are their equals before the throne of Him
who casts down and levels all greatness, you must also act as
those who have been alloted to them as masters and superiors
in the present dispensation. But whereby are they to discern
the superiority you possess? Shall it be only by your com-

mands ? Shall it not rather be by the tender solicitude that you will show for their real prosperity, and by the kindness that they will receive from you ? The peculiar mark of a superior is that he gives away, not that others give to him. Why should a man be placed above others, if not that he may do them the more good ? Does not a large tree give much shade? When God appoints a king over a people, is it that he may deprive his subjects of the fruit of their labour and enjoy it himself ? Is it merely that he may command them and dispose of their possessions? Is it not rather that he may consecrate them to the good of those who are under his care ? And do you suppose that God has placed you above your servants for any other cause than this ? Do not say that the case is different, and that your servants are under greater obligations to you than subjects are to their monarchs; for if so, it would follow that you yourselves are under still greater obligations to them. Be then their *superiors*, their *heads*, their *masters;* that is, exert your authority for the good of those who obey you. In the eye of God, you renounce that character as soon as you cease to make a proper use of it. Do not let difficulties discourage you, even if they proceed from those who are the objects of your efforts. Exert the power entrusted to you.

But you wish to know more particularly what you have to do as *masters;* we shall therefore give you a few directions on this point. First, then, practise a wise superintendence over your household. " The eyes of the Lord are upon the ways of man, and he seeth all his goings;" and let your eyes also be every where; not with that restless look which pries into every thing, but with that look of love which would fain assist, direct, and reprove; with the look of a mother following the motions of her child, that she may hasten to it should it fall; so that not the slightest disturbance may escape your observation and correction. If your servants suppose that you do not care for them, then sin will have greater power over them, for the master's look is a second conscience for the servant. But if you watch over them, you will find that the eye of the righteous man bringeth righteousness.

And permit me, my brethren, to direct your attention as masters to a point of importance in this city: I allude to *sim-*

plicity in dress. The apostle commands that women should " adorn themselves in modest apparel, not with costly array." And how can a Christian woman allow even her servants to neglect the apostle's command ? Is it not too often the case that, far from preventing such conduct, the vanity of masters is gratified by the excessive love of finery of their servants ? Christian hearers, adopt some principle or other on this subject. The example you set will be imitated by others. How many young people might I mention who in their childhood received pious impressions, who learned to respect the word of God, and in whose hearts that word had borne some fruits of sanctification and righteousness, but who having come to one of our large cities, by degrees lost that portion of true riches which, had it been properly used, might have been increased. The love of dress is the destructive temptation by means of which the Evil One attacks them. One has not always the necessary means of satisfying it—and hence so much wickedness ! An establishment is now being founded in this city, by means of which, if instruction in the word of God and assiduous labour are made the instruments of correction, many wanderers may be led back from the path of perdition. May God bless this work ! And I cannot take leave of this subject without observing that the interest which is taken in establishments of this kind, the object of which is to alleviate the misery of mankind, is a work most acceptable to God. Would that I could see that spirit of usefulness developed among you which animates Christians in other lands, and which must necessarily exist wherever the Gospel of our Lord Jesus Christ is preached ! But, my brethren, while we admire such institutions, designed to repair the evil, do you not think it quite as important to endeavour to prevent its occurrence ? And you will succeed in doing this by striving to eradicate the love of dress from the hearts of your servants, and by preserving simplicity among them. Thus you will prevent their falling into that snare of Satan of which the Scriptures speak.

But let your watchfulness as masters extend still farther : see that your servants perform their religious duties faithfully. You are very sensitive when they forget the duties which they owe to you; and can you be less sensitive when they forget those which they owe to God ? Is it not your highest duty, as masters, to induce your servants to worship the greatest of Masters ? And how often have you hindered them from so doing ! How often have they been prevented on the Lord's day from going to the house where his holy word is expounded ! Persuade them rather to attend divine worship with regularity, and on proper occasions to receive the sacrament of the Lord's Supper. Let them not forget God in your houses. One of the most effectual and powerful causes of vice is found in the moments of idleness, when servants have nothing to do but to converse about their masters, or on other subjects, or to read books injurious to the cause of religion and morality. Could you not take away those books, and substitute others for them which breathe the pure spirit of the religion of Jesus Christ ? Especially, could you not give them the word of God ? Your servants might, by assembling together in the evening to read it, grow in temperance, righteousness, and piety. This is an easier thing than many suppose, and it has often been done.

Finally, my brethren, you should not only be equals and masters, but you ought also to be *servants.* If you are true servants of Jesus Christ, you should also be servants of all men, even of your own servants, for the sake of Jesus Christ. They serve your bodies, and you ought to serve their souls. " Whosoever will be great among you, let him be your minister," says Jesus. Like those pious heralds of the Gospel who became slaves themselves among slaves, that they might make them free indeed, so ought you spiritually to do, becoming the servants of your servants, that you may bring them captive to your Master. Since the Son of God became a servant to save us, shall not we become such ourselves that we may save our brethren ? No man can accomplish the salvation of men by any other means than by making himself of no reputation, as He did. And do not suppose that you must degrade yourselves for this purpose; you can be servants, and yet remain in the same position which you now occupy. Christ, although the servant of us all, has ever remained our superior. Become therefore the servants of your servants, for the sake of their salvation. Do this through charity. This sacred service is in reality nothing but *charity.* The man within whose heart this

4   D

Christian virtue exists is made the servant of all men by it. Love is the true strength of the Christian; by it he conquers the most rebellious souls. Thus, let there be no threatening, no bitterness, no capriciousness; let your conduct toward those of your household be full of patience, gentleness, and faithfulness; they will ask themselves what causes this; and they will find an answer in the Gospel of Jesus Christ. They will submit to that law of love which they will learn to know by your example.

Become servants in *your example.* Let them see that you have resolved to live for Him who once died for you. How many slaves, in the primitive times of Christianity, became converted when they saw that offerings were no longer placed upon the altars of false gods in their masters' houses, but that Christ the Lord was worshipped! Likewise let your servants see that in your houses those false gods of the world which are named wealth, pleasure, vain-glory, and pride, are no longer worshipped, but that, with things in heaven and things in earth, you bow the knee at the name of Jesus, who is Lord, to the glory of God the Father. Then, "turning to God from idols, they will serve the living and true God, and wait for his Son from heaven, whom he raised from the dead, even Jesus."

Such are the duties, perhaps unknown before to some, which we call upon you to fulfil. Masters, henceforth remember the work which God has given you to do! Do not look around you to see whether others guide their vessels rightly, but seize your own helms. If such efforts were made more and more by all masters, we might soon look for an amelioration in the condition of the lower classes of society. But you say, 'Servants constitute but a very small portion of society. How then can we hope for such extensive consequences from efforts like these?' Ah! my brethren, who can tell what good to all classes would result, if those who serve in our houses were brought up in the fear of God! In how many relations do they stand to others! A handmaid who becomes a wife and a mother will be accompanied in her own house by that piety in which she shall have been educated in the houses of her masters. The service of the rich will then be a school of virtue, not of vice; and from their dwellings, as from a precious nursery, will come forth sound and robust trees, which will soon give delightful shade in some other place. And to you, Christian women, to you to whom the government of the household particularly belongs; to you, Marthas, who are not called to serve the Lord in person but in the persons of your servants, to you more especially we speak in closing this discourse. Every man here below has a peculiar vocation. One is a magistrate, another a minister of the word, a third is engaged in his own affairs. And have you no calling? Assuredly you have. Do not neglect it; do not think yourselves forgotten in the universal distribution of labour. The peculiar vocation which you have received from God is the care of your homes and of those who dwell there. This is your ministry. How great is the influence of a Christian woman over servants who love and respect her! It is greater than that of any preacher. Oh, may they then revive that salutary influence which was exerted in brighter days of the Church! Let them live for their households, and no longer for the world!

My brethren, whatever may be your rank or your wealth, remember that all other things are of very little consequence compared with the opportunities which they may give you of doing good to the souls of your servants. May God assist you to profit by those opportunities! Amen.

DISCOURSE VI.

THE WORK OF SALVATION.

A HOMILY.

" Being confident of this very thing, that He which hath begun a good work
in you will perform it until the day of Jesus Christ."—Phil., i, 6.

IT was to the church at Philippi, a city in Macedonia celebrated for the battles which were fought there by the Romans during their civil wars, that the Epistle from which our
text is taken was addressed. We learn from the sixteenth
chapter of the Acts of the Apostles how this church was founded by St. Paul. The apostle was in Asia. Europe had not
yet received the light of the Gospel. A man of Macedonia,
the representative of many nations and ages, appeared in a
vision to the apostle of the Gentiles, according to the account
given by his fellow-traveller St. Luke, and prayed him, saying,
"Come over into Macedonia and help us! *Come over and help
us!* These are remarkable words, which Europe then addressed
to Asia, and which Asia now addresses to us in return. The
apostle concluding that the Lord called him did not hesitate:
he left Troas and soon arrived at Philippi; and was the first
herald of the Gospel of peace that set his foot upon our continent. But he was not idle; he left the city, went to the river-
side where prayer was wont to be made, and proclaimed the
news of which he was the bearer. His labours were not in
vain. St. Luke mentions several remarkable cases of conversion, particularly that of a certain woman named Lydia, a sel-
ler of purple, who heard the apostles, and "whose heart the
Lord opened, that she attended unto the things which were
spoken of Paul;" and the still more remarkable conversion of
the keeper of the prison into which Paul and Silas had been
thrown. At midnight an earthquake shook the foundations of
the prison; and that man who at first would have killed himself, supposing that the prisoners had been fled, being held

back by the voice of Paul, threw himself at the feet of the apostle and of Silas, exclaiming, "Sirs, what must I do to be saved?" "Believe on the Lord Jesus Christ," was the answer of the men of God, "and thou shalt be saved and thy house." Then they announced to him the word of the Lord; and soon, with his whole house, he rejoiced believing in God.

But before long St. Paul left Philippi; ten years of his life of labour and suffering passed away; he was now a prisoner at Rome. The Christian community at Philippi, which still regarded the apostle with tender affection, and deeply sympathized with him in his trials, and having learned what his situation was, had sent him assistance. Desirous of knowing his condition they had sent one of their brethren, named Epaphroditus, to Rome, where he fell dangerously ill; nevertheless God had mercy on him, and the apostle resolved, on his restoration to health, to send him back to his beloved flock with the letter from which our text is taken. Paul remained in bondage, and deprived of the company of his friend. Nevertheless he rejoiced at the remembrance of the believers at Philippi; and the first words of the letter which Epaphroditus carried to them inform us of the cause of this joy. "Paul and Timotheus," he writes, "the servants of Jesus Christ, to all the saints in Christ Jesus which are at Philippi, with the bishops and deacons: Grace be to you and peace from God our Father and from the Lord Jesus Christ. I thank my God upon every remembrance of you, always in every prayer of mine for you all making request with joy, for your fellowship in the Gospel from the first day until now; *being confident of this very thing, that he which hath begun a good work in you will perform it until the day of Jesus Christ.*"

Let us examine more closely, my brethren, this work which gave the apostle so much pleasure; it must be well worthy of our attention. We do not wish to present considerations more or less general at this time, but simply to explain to you each word which St. Paul here uses. By going thus to the fountain head, we shall have more reason to expect that your minds will submit to the truth. There are seven words in our text which need to be explained, and which shall successively engage our attention.

I. The work referred to: *a work*, says the apostle.

II. The scene of its fulfilment: *in you.*

III. The quality attributed to it: a *good* work.

IV. The author assigned: *He which hath begun.*

V. The apostle's opinion respecting this work: *He will perform it.*

VI. The certainty of this achievement: *being confident.*

And VII. The period in which this achievement will take place: *until the day of Jesus Christ.*

When we shall have explained these seven portions of our text, we shall have faithfully performed the duties of the servant of the word of God. May God our Father, for the sake of Jesus Christ our Lord, grant his Holy Spirit unto me, that I may explain his oracles according to the analogy of faith; and unto you, that you may understand them! Amen.

I. And first, my brethren, this subject relates to a work which was performed among the Philippians. This work is variously designated in the Scriptures. Sometimes it is called *repentance;* at others, *conversion;* at others, *regeneration;* at others again, *new birth;* and sometimes even *sanctification.* But whatever name it may bear, it is a work of the highest importance to every man. For this work men ought most sincerely to bless the mercy of the Father of every good gift, when they know and acknowledge that it has been accomplished. It is the thing most to be desired; even when the want of it is known and acknowledged. It is the great work which God requires of man. It is this that John the Baptist, the forerunner of the new covenant, required when he began his ministry, by crying in the wilderness of Judea, "Repent ye, for the kingdom of heaven is at hand." It is this that Jesus Christ, the Head of the Church, required when he likewise began his ministry, and said, as he walked by the shore of the sea of Galilee, "The time is fulfilled and the kingdom of God is at hand: repent ye, and believe the Gospel." It is this that the apostles, Christ's ambassadors, required when they too began their ministry, replying to the multitude at Jerusalem who exclaimed, "What shall we do?" "*Repent* and be baptised, every one of you, in the name of Jesus Christ." It is this that the successors of the first preachers of the Gospel have always required in all ages. Christianity would be destroyed on earth were the lips of the servants of God to become silent on this point. To proclaim this requirement is the duty of the Church. And consequently it is still the great appeal which ministers of the word ought to address, and do continually address with perfect freedom, to all men of every nation and language.

But what is this work? What is its history? What are the successive deeds which constitute it? The paths which lead to it are various, but the work is always the same. It was performed in the heart of Lydia, in that of the jailor, and in the hearts of all their brethren and sisters in Jesus Christ. Let us see wherein it consisted when performed in them; we may thus learn wherein it consisted when wrought in us.

In the first place, the Philippians to whom St. Paul preached the Gospel, were convinced of the wickedness of their own hearts and the evil course of their lives. They saw that there was not a single law written upon their consciences which they had not broken in some way or other, and that consequently they deserved condemnation. These sentiments we see strongly developed in the mind of the jailor; his slumbering conscience is awakened at the sight of the miracle performed in favour of the apostles: oppressed by the remembrance of his sins, he feels that he is lost; he casts himself at the feet of Paul and Silas, exclaiming, "What must I do to be saved?" Such should be the commencement of the work of which I am speaking within us.

But, secondly, this work consisted, among the Philippians, in their being brought to a knowledge of the salvation of which Jesus Christ is the author. St. Paul preached to them "the word of the Lord;" he had told them how the Son of God had become man, how he had lived thirty-three years on earth, in the land of Judea, that he might reconcile men unto God; how he had undergone great sufferings; how he had been nailed to the cross, and had died on it, and that for all men, that their sins might not be imputed unto them by their Judge, and that they might obtain eternal life. "Believe on the Lord Jesus Christ," said Paul. All these disciples had believed that these things had really happened, and that they had happened *for their salvation*, as the apostle told them. They had appropriated to their own souls the forgiveness of sins of which the cross

made all men worthy, and considered it as a gift to them.
This too, my brethren, is the faith which the Gospel requires
us to have. As we so often receive gifts from men, we ought
to receive this *gift of God*, which is *eternal life*, which no man
deserves, and which no man can obtain by his own efforts, but
which eternal love has designed, in mercy, to give freely to
every humble soul that comes and asks for it with faith and in
the name of Jesus Christ.

In the third place, this faith in Jesus Christ changed the
hearts and the lives of the inhabitants of Philippi; it made them
new men. From that time they began to walk in the footsteps
of their Saviour. This change was peculiarly evident in the
jailor. That man who but a few moments before had made
fast the feet of the apostles in the stocks, now filled with love,
washed their stripes. That man who but a few moments before was in deep despair, and would fain have killed himself,
was now the happiest of men; *he rejoiced*, we are told. Such
too should be the third and last effect of this work within us.
A total change of heart and life is the sealing act. Such is
the work of which the apostle speaks.

II. But where ought it to be performed? *In you*, replies
St. Paul. This is the second portion of our text, which we
must explain. The prophet Ezekiel had already foreseen that
the work which Christianity was to accomplish would be performed in the heart of man, and of this he informed his contemporaries in these words: "A new heart also will I give you
(saith the Lord), and a new spirit will I put within you; and I
will take away the stony heart out of your flesh, and I will give
you a heart of flesh." Our Lord told this to Nicodemus, saying to him, "Verily, verily, I say unto thee, Except a man be
born again he cannot see the kingdom of God." And the
apostles declared unto all men that "in Christ Jesus neither
circumcision availeth anything, nor uncircumcision, but a new
creature." Thus we have the unanimous testimony of our
Lord, of those who preceded him, and of those who followed
him, on this point.

There are many works peformed in the universe: many are
performed in heaven and on earth, in the east and the west, in
our houses and out of doors; but it is not in any of these places

that the work of which the apostle speaks must be performed; a very different place is assigned for it; it must be performed, he says, *in you*.

Yes, my brethren, it is *in you*, within your soul and spirit, that Christianity must perform its work; it is satisfied with nothing else. The sects of philosophers sought only to reach the understanding; false religions merely regulated external habits. But Christianity goes farther. It must take possession of your inmost heart; to make *all things new in you*, says the apostle.

This good work must be performed *in you*. The Scriptures speak particularly of *two* works. One was performed *without us;* the other must be performed *within us*. The first is the work of our *redemption*, which was performed by Jesus Christ, when he reconciled us to God his Father on the cross. This is the work which all the patriarchs and prophets foresaw, and rejoiced to see. By means of this work the good tidings of pardon can be and are proclaimed to every creature. This is the work which reconciled heaven and earth, and which, laying the foundation of a new order of things, will for ever fill the universe with joy. But we cannot profit by it so long as *the work within us* has not taken place. It was not for us that Jesus Christ came into the world and suffered on the cross, if repentance, faith, and sanctification have not performed their work upon our hearts. In that case, the death of the Son of God is to us a useless event in history. We are blind men who, in the brightest day, are neither enlightened nor gladdened by a single ray of light.

This good work must be performed *in you*. The apostle uses these words in order to take away all false confidence. Observe: it were vain for you to be Christians in outward appearance, to have been baptized in the Christian church, to have been taught the great truths of religion, to have partaken frequently of the holy supper of our Lord; it were vain for you to have avoided, like the Pharisee, being extortioners, unjust, or adulterers, unless the knowledge of Jesus Christ has exerted its omnipotent influence IN you; unless it has made you acknowledge your misery, forsake sin and the world, and become truly converted unto God. All these external things are unmeaning, and the essential work of Christianity is wanting: it

has not been performed *in you*. It were vain for you to be
perfectly conversant with the system of the Gospel, and to be
able to reason with facility respecting all the truths which it
contains; it were vain for you to say with your lips, *Lord!*
Lord! unless the work of regeneration through faith in Jesus
Christ has been performed within your hearts; unless you daily
present your bodies and your souls a living sacrifice, holy,
acceptable unto God; all the rest is nothing but show and
hypocrisy. "The kingdom of God is not in word, but in
power;" you must begin the whole work anew.

III. But what is the characteristic of this work? The
apostle calls it *a good work*. And who will not exclaim with
him, this is a good work!

It is good, for it has ended the darkness in which we were
lying. Oh, how many things we were ignorant of which we
know now! We were wanderers in the world, uncertain as to
whence we came, or whither we were going. But now all our
ways have been made manifest; and the knowledge we have
acquired fills us with joy. We did not know ourselves; but
now we have learned our present misery, as well as our former
greatness. We did not know God, and considered him as
possessing only a certain degree of power; but now we see
such holiness in his character as we never conceived of before,
such mercy as we could not imagine. Our ideas of a future
state were indefinite, and did not satisfy our desires; but now
the eyes of our understanding are enlightened, that we may
know "the greatness" of the hope of our calling. Yes, it is
a good work, by which we have been called out of darkness
into marvellous light!

This is a good work, for it puts an end to the estrangement
from God in which we were living. As we were living without any knowledge of God, we were also living without communion with him. We did not find it pleasant to raise our
thoughts to him, to read his word, or to do his will. But
now, thanks be unto him, the middle wall of partition hath
been broken down; he hath translated us into his kingdom; he
hath given us the spirit of adoption, whereby we cry Abba,
Father. We are his friends, his children. "I have rejoiced
in the way of thy testimonies as much as in all riches." Oh,

it is a *good* work that calls us back from the exile in which we were living.

This is a good work, for it puts an end to the dominion of sin. There were certain inclinations and favourite vices which we could not resist. When we rose above them, it was but to fall again. Oh, how many groans! how many struggles! Miserable beings that we were, what we would that did we not; but what we hated that did we. But we thank God, through Jesus Christ our Lord, that we have been delivered from the body of this death. God himself undertook what we could not do. "Being made free from sin, we became the servants of righteousness." Does not this work, which drew us out of such misery, deserve to be called *good?*

But its *goodness* is peculiarly apparent in the fact that it has made us participators in the remission of sins. The burden of our transgressions has been cast under our feet. All our sins have been thrown into the depths of the sea. We know this, and we repeat these words in which we shall ever rejoice: "There is now no condemnation to them which are in Christ Jesus." God will no longer hold us guilty. We need not fear punishment from the hand of the judge now, but we await the boundless riches of the Father. Oh, admirable work! the more we know thee, the more we love thee!

IV. But who is the AUTHOR of it? Who hath begun this good work in us? The apostle gives us an answer, and that answer is the fourth part of our text, which we shall consider. *He,* says St. Paul, *which hath begun a good work in you.*

It is GOD who begins this good work of man's conversion. St. Paul declares this, and our Lord himself says, "No man can come to me, except the Father which hath sent me draw him." "Every man, therefore, that hath heard and hath learned of the Father cometh unto me." In every event the first step is taken by God. He is in all things the first and the last, the beginning and the end, the Alpha and the Omega; and he is also the beginning, the very Alpha of our salvation. It is by the power of the Holy Spirit that we are to be made perfect, and that the smallest beginning, and even the least desire of regeneration, is to be effected within us. "It is God," says the apostle to these Christians of Philippi,

"which worketh in you both to will and to do of his good
pleasure."

The work of salvation is begun by GOD, not by *us*.   Let us
not venture to attempt it then.   Of ourselves we could never
begin it.   Let us go to God ; let us importune the throne of
his mercy, that he may say to our souls, Let there be light, as
he once said for the whole universe.   Let us stand by his word
as by a well of water springing up into everlasting life; asking
him to pour water upon him that is thirsty, and floods upon
the dry ground.

The work of salvation is begun by GOD, not by *us*.   Let us
therefore be attentive to what God does, and to what God says.
How often he may have called us already!   "Oh, Jerusalem!
Jerusalem! how often would I have gathered thy children together, even as a hen gathereth her chickens under her wings,
and ye would not!"   Alas for him who is called and will not
answer!   Do not attempt to justify yourselves for remaining
asleep, by saying, We can wait until God begins.   But say
rather, Let us fear lest he may often already have been willing,
and *we* would not.

The work of salvation is begun by GOD, not by *us*.   What an
antidote to pride this is ! Who will not humble himself when
he must say, If God had not called me I had not come.
"For," says St. Paul to all who hear him, " we ourselves also
were sometimes foolish, disobedient, deceived, hateful, and hat-
ing one another.   But after that the kindness and love of God
our Saviour toward men appeared, according to his mercy he
saved us."   What saint can glory in himself if he remembers
that, whatever height he may have attained, the foundation of
his greatness must ever rest upon the pure mercy of God.

The work of salvation is begun by GOD, not by *us*.   To him
then the believer will give the glory throughout eternity.   He will
cast his crown before the throne like the four-and-twenty elders,
saying, " Thou art worthy, O Lord, to receive glory and honour
and power; for thou hast created all things, and for thy pleasure they are and were created."   And he will fall down with
them, and worship him that liveth for ever and ever !

V. But what will " He who hath begun" do ? My brethren,
he who hath begun *will finish ;* he who hath begun *will perfect.*

Such is the promise given to us, and such is the fifth expression of our text which we have to explain.

The apostle Peter says in his first espistle, " Your adversary the Devil, as a roaring lion, walketh about seeking whom he may devour : whom resist, steadfast in the faith." He thereby declares that the Christian will meet with many difficulties in the work of salvation. And indeed we find many obstacles which might deter " the man who has put his hand to the plough," and has begun to turn his steps toward that " mark for the prize of the high calling of God in Christ Jesus."

One of the first obstacles you will meet with is *the influence of the world*. You have fixed your eyes, not on wealth which the moth and rust can destroy, but on the incorruptible riches of heaven. You seek not the glory which the world gives, but the unchangeable glory of Christ. You have seen that all the realities of the world are mere shadows, that the hopes of the Christian are alone realities. Nevertheless, do not suppose that you have been sheltered for ever from the influence of the world. It will soon find an opportunity to prove its power over you. It will come with its former attractions, covered with a hypocritical mask; and when you see its pleasures and its riches, you will say, " But these are real things; I do not see and feel those invisible things which I hope for; and who will warrant their reality?" It is thus that seduction will attack your souls. But fear not. " Resist, steadfast in the faith." He who hath begun the work in you will not suffer the world to regain the power over you which it has been forced to yield ; he will not let you become its prey again.

But a second trial is *unbelief.* It is by faith that you will work out your salvation, and therefore the enemy of your soul will endeavour to disturb it. ' There are few who believe in Jesus Christ,' your unbelieving heart will say; ' if Jesus Christ and salvation through his blood were realities, would not many more acknowledge him?' This and other similar artifices are familiar to the enemy of our souls, and he never fails to make use of them; but he is " a liar and the father of lies," says Christ. Believe him not; fear him not; resist him. Were you the only one who believed in Jesus Christ, he would still be the *Truth;* and even if no one believed on him, he would nevertheless be the *Truth ;* and all his sayings and promises would be *yea* and *amen.* The truth of Jesus Christ does not depend upon the dreams of our imagination. Our ridicule, our pride, our blasphemy can not for a moment disturb it : " He that sitteth in the heavens shall laugh; the Lord shall have them in derision." But a moment of the reign of Christ will have passed away when those who now deny his manifestation in the flesh will moulder in the dust. Yes, Lord ! "the heavens shall wax old as doth a garment, and as a vesture shalt thou fold them up, and they shall be changed : but thou art the same, and thy years shall not fail!"

A third trial, which may occasion the shipwreck of your soul before you reach the haven, is a deceitful tranquillity, a wandering away from God. You neglect the reading of the word ; you forget what you owe to Jesus Christ ; your prayers become colder and less earnest and less frequent; you often yield the victory to the world; you seem to be returning to your former state of death. Oh, fearful state ! a state which, if it last, must indeed destroy the work of salvation in your heart ! But God, who has begun the good work in you will not leave it to perish. He will say to you, " Stir up the gift of God which is in thee." " Awake thou that sleepest." He will go after you as a shepherd goes after the sheep that is lost, and will bring you back into his fold in his great mercy.

Yes, he who hath begun this work *will perform it.* He will daily revive his image in your souls. He will render your faith more and more simple and childlike. He will cause the growth of *sanctification* in your hearts. He will give you an increasing hope of riches to come. He will render your love more and more fervent. *He will perform the work.*

VI. But there may be many seasons when you will nevertheless be assailed by strong fears. As the man of business is sometimes seized with sudden alarm respecting an enterprise, so will it be with you who are engaged in a better enterprise. Your soul will be alarmed. ' Ah!' you will exclaim, ' my soul is downcast at times; it seems to me that God hides his face from me. Will he not forsake me? Will he perform what he has begun?' It was doubtless to dispel such anxiety that the apostle added the sixth portion of our text : *being confident.*

Being confident! This expression proves that St. Paul entertained *no doubt.* How then can you entertain any? Shall not your hearts be strengthened by this in that filial confidence in our Saviour which is the privilege of the believer?

You fear; your soul is terrified. But tell me, my brother, was not the grace of God toward you, in beginning this work, greater still than that by which he will continue it? Shall you not then expect *the lesser* from him who has already conferred upon you *the greater?* Will you not be assured that he who loved you *then* so greatly as to call you into his kingdom, will *henceforth* love you enough to keep you from forsaking it?

But your soul is in great danger; sin and the world threaten to destroy it. And what of that? Why is it cast down, and why is it disquieted within thee? Why does it not hope in God, who is the health of thy countenance and thy God? Is this the first time that you have been delivered when in danger? Look back upon your own life! See what your God has done for you. Is not the deliverance which you have already witnessed a presage of that which is to come? At one time the loud voice of your corrupt nature was heard; at another your faith was greatly disturbed by human unbelief, or by the suggestions of the Evil One, and you were already returning to the verge of infidelity; then you cast yourself at the feet of your God and exclaimed, with a deep feeling of your weakness, ' Do thou perform that which I cannot do!' Then he delivered you. Will not he who once answered your cry reply to it again? Is his arm shortened? Does he not hear his children while they are yet speaking? Ah! if we kept a daily record of all the mercies of our God, how would we blush at the very thought of doubting of his faithfulness!

And if the remembrance of past events in your life be not enough, look at the word of God, and learn on whom it is that you should rely. See how he strives to make known his love to you; he is continually reiterating his efforts; there is not a page of the holy volume that does not speak of it. What! in spite of his frequent assurances, can you still doubt that he loves you? And if it be true that he loves you, how can you believe that he will suffer you to be lost?

But what is this work which must be performed in you? It is that for which he gave his beloved Son! Do you suppose that he would have sent his only Son into the world to save you, if there were a possibility that after all you will not be saved? And what will he do for this work now, since he once did so much? I can suppose it true that any other work might fail, but I must always except this. Such is the argument of the apostle: "He that spared not his own Son, but delivered him up for us all, how shall he not with him also freely give us all things?"

You think it very likely that this work may not be performed. Ah! had it been begun by you, or by any mortal being, you would have good reason to fear; it is by no means certain that man will accomplish what he undertakes. But remember the Author of this work! Will not all that he begins be performed? While every skilful workman endeavours to render his work perfect, will *God*, the great workman, leave the work of his hands imperfect? Is the will wanting? Is the power wanting? Will he grow weary? Will he become exhausted? Will he be disgusted? Do you suppose that Sovereign Wisdom begins a work inconsiderately, and without knowing how it will end? What absurdities are these, my brethren!

But you may say, 'We are such insignificant creatures! Were we great saints, we might perhaps entertain such a hope; but we are so weak, so little!' And this, my brethren, is the very thing which ought to give you most reason for hope; for the more a man needs God, the more certain he is of finding him. It is upon the *feeble* that he delights to display his power, and upon the *small* that he is pleased to show forth all his greatness. "God hath chosen the weak things of the world," says the apostle, "to confound the things which are mighty; and base things of the world hath God chosen, yea, and things that are not, to bring to nought things that are."

And if such reflections have not entirely dispelled your fears, listen to the voice of your God, who speaks to you by his prophet Jeremiah: " I will not turn away from them; but I will put my fear in their hearts, that they shall not depart from me." And by his beloved Son: " It is not the will of your Father which is in heaven that one of these little ones should perish."

Again : " This is the Father's will which hath sent me, that of all which he hath given me I should lose nothing." And again : " I give unto my sheep eternal life, and they shall never perish, neither shall any man pluck them out of my hand." And the apostle in our text, certain of this grace, sings a hymn of triumph, in which all who walk in his footsteps must join : "I am persuaded that neither death nor life, nor angels nor principalities nor powers, nor things present nor things to come, nor height nor depth, nor any other creature, shall be able to separate us from the love of God which is in Christ Jesus our Lord."

VII. *Until the day of Jesus Christ.* This is the seventh and last division of our text; it does not need much explanation.

This day of Jesus Christ is the day of the resurrection, the day in which Jesus Christ will come to judge the living and the dead, and whereunto we are sealed by the Holy Spirit. It is the day which will end the present economy, and will open the economy of eternity.

In that day will be fulfilled all that remains incomplete. At the first coming of Jesus, every thing which had been foretold with regard to him was accomplished. At his second coming, every thing that has been foretold with regard to us, respecting the glory and immortality which he has acquired for us, will be accomplished.

In that day he will break with his own hand that seal with which he has sealed us here below, and which no power shall have been able to break.

He will come, bearing immortality in his right hand. The sound of the last trumpet will announce the end of the struggle, and will call together all the scattered soldiers around their Head. There will be no more sin, no more fiery darts of the Adversary, no more perfidious seductions of the world, no more death. These shall be swallowed up for ever. This corruptible must put on incorruption. This mortal must put on immortality. And all saints will exclaim with the apostle, " O death, where is thy sting ? O grave, where is thy victory ? The sting of death is sin ; and the strength of sin is the law. BUT THANKS BE TO GOD, WHICH GIVETH US THE VICTORY THROUGH OUR LORD JESUS CHRIST."

Such, my brethren, is the work of which we were to give you the history. Such is the work which was performed at Philippi when the apostle went to preach the Gospel there; and which should be performed in all ages throughout the world. In explaining the words of St. Paul, we have spoken as though that work were begun in you; it was necessary to do so, in order to give them the meaning which the apostle intended. Nevertheless, it is clear that when we treat of any work whatsoever, we must make a distinction between two different classes of persons ; those in whom it is begun, and those in whom it is still wanting. To know, with regard to the work we are now speaking of, who belongs to one or the other of these classes, or at least to know in whom it has not been begun, is not in the power of man, but in that of God alone. Scarcely do we know our own hearts; how then can we know those of our brethren? In how many souls may this work have been performed without any outward appearance of it! And is it the part of man to try the hearts and the reins? Nevertheless, these two classes exist, and we not only can but must believe in their existence.

Thus, remembering first those in whom the work of salvation has not yet been performed, we exclaim, O may they feel that this work is the only one whose issue is certain, the only one which gives happiness, and consequently the one to which it is wisest to devote oneself! May their hearts, like Lydia's, be opened by the Lord, that they may attend to the things which are written in the word of God! May they see that this is the work to which they are called as immortal creatures; the work which will restore them to the throne from which sin had driven them. "Ho! ye that have spent money for that which is not bread, and your labour for that which satisfieth not, incline your ear. and come unto me; hear, and your soul shall live, saith the Lord."

And to you in whom God has begun his good work, to you who, having laboured and been heavy laden, have found rest unto your souls in Christ, to you, O my beloved brethren, I address my closing words, and I say, Take courage: however small the beginning may have been, take courage. Be assured that he who has lighted your lamp, though its light may be very dim, will not extinguish it, but will always pour oil into it, that it may give more light. Take courage. Use with activity the strength which has been given you. Resist sin; grow in faith; apply your efforts to the performance of good works. This is your calling. Let your powerful weapons, before which every bulwark must fall, be these: *the word of God*, and *prayer in the name of Jesus Christ*. Do not stop to say, 'I cannot do it.' Those words do not exist in the language of the believer. What you cannot do *God can do*. He is now your only strength. Your duty is to advance without fear; it is for him to lead you to the goal. His strength will be made perfect in your weakness. "Fear not, thou worm Jacob, and ye men of Israel; I will help thee, saith the Lord, and thy Redeemer, the Holy One of Israel. I the Lord have called thee in righteousness, and will hold thine hand, and will keep thee."

"Now unto Him that is able to do exceeding abundantly above all that we ask or think, according to the power that worketh in us, unto him be glory in the Church by Christ Jesus throughout all ages, world without end." Amen.

DISCOURSE VII.

THE CHARACTER ESSENTIAL TO THE THEOLOGIAN. AND TO CHRISTIANS IN GENERAL IN THE PRESENT DAY.[1]

2 Timothy, iii

THE Church is entering upon a new era. The period embraced in the last twenty or thirty years will be designated as the Era of Revival in the Nineteenth Century; it has been characterized by an active, even an aggressive spirit. It has been a period of conquest; the great object seemed to be to advance into countries laid waste by the infidelity of the eighteenth century, or enslaved by Romish despotism, and plant the standard of the Cross there. All those to whom the name of Jesus was precious went forward with one mind, like one man. At present the aspect of things is changed. The world before us is still unconquered; and if we had that ambition in our Master's cause which Alexander had in his own, we would not falter.

But is it so? Do we not see the armies of the Lord, in many places, apparently satisfied with the ground they have gained, ready to halt, separate, and dispute concerning their uniform and discipline! Some are opposed to having leaders; others want leaders possessed of unlimited power. These disputes impede the general progress; and even those who wish to advance seem constrained to resist this tendency to anarchy. To conquer is not the sole concern now, as it was in the preceding era, but to defend; not to attack merely, but to maintain.

In this new era a new sentiment is necessary. In times of revival the most important quality was perhaps enthusiasm; in our day, the essential thing is a theological and Christian character; and it is of this peculiar want of our times that I desire to treat.

"In the last days, perilous times shall come," says the

---

[1] Delivered at Geneva, on the 3rd of October, 1844.

apostle in the chapter which has been read in your hearing. Alas! the fall of a stone is not more natural than the tendency of man and of the Church to turn away from the living God.

Now, what precept does the apostle give for resisting the evil which was to be developed in the last days? " Continue thou in the things which thou hast learned." *Continue :* this is the term by which St. Paul defines the theological and Christian character. To be without a character, to be wanting in character, is always deserving of blame; but it is peculiarly so with reference to the vocation to which you are to consecrate yourselves. To have a character, to display character, is on the contrary praiseworthy; and it is peculiarly so when the sacred ministry is concerned. No theologian has ever had much influence over the age, no mere minister of the word has ever been blest in his pastoral labours, unless he has had at least to a certain extent this mental quality.

Indeed, it is necessary for a man to have received an impression upon his own mind before he can communicate it to others. Go to a printing establishment, and ask a printer how he can stamp such distinct letters upon thousands of sheets which were perfectly white before. He will tell you, that when he placed those types in his forms they were clear and distinct. Had he used worn and mis-shapen types, the impression on the paper issuing from the press would have been illegible. So it is with the impression which the minister of the word is to produce. His own character must have been formed under the influence of the word of God by the work of the Holy Spirit, by persevering studies, and, if need be, by intercourse with men and with the world, before that character can be made fit to influence men and the world.

But what is this character? I will first refer you to the words of St. Paul: "Be ye of the same mind," or the same character, "which was in Christ Jesus." Yes, we ought to bear the image, the impress of the heavenly One. The sons who are begotten by the new Adam he begets according to his own image, as the old Adam did. It is by impressing us with his character that he designs to impress all our fellow-beings with that same character. "If any man have not the spirit of Christ," the character of Christ, "he is not one of his." Come then, my brethren; let your hearts be moved, and your eyes be fixed on Christ!

Is there not in our days a want of character, even among those whose hearts God has impressed with the great doctrines of salvation? How many Christians, how many ministers there are who, though at first they walked well, have since wandered away, have been drawn into dangerous paths, and have led others along with them, for want of character!

I do not mean that Christians who are still young in spiritual life can have a perfect character. That were indeed somewhat dangerous; for, as they do not possess the elements necessary for attaining this state, they might fall into error. We do not require in the child the strength of the strong man; but we do require a growth by which he may one day acquire that strength.

But among those who ought to be strong men in Jesus Christ, how great a want of character there is!

Does a man possess a character in the things of God when he has no fixed opinion with regard to them, no precise tendency, and who, like the wave of the sea, is tossed to and fro by the wind? He may be very talented; but what is talent in the church of God, without decided conviction? "It is," says a certain theologian, "a cloud upon which perhaps a thousand beams are shining, and which attracts the eyes of all by its splendour; but which, as it contains no water, passes over the earth without a blessing." A man may have much learning; but what is learning without the life-giving principle of a powerful conviction? It is like the chaff which is scattered by the wind without producing any benefit. To convince, one must be convinced: one must have character.

Or even in this case, should we have experienced certain convictions, they are produced arbitrarily, without any rule, without system, without foundation, without connection; unless the kingdom of God has become a unity in our minds: unless we have acquired in the doctrines of divine truth an unalterable consistency, a consistency which rules our whole lives: and if we are seen hurrying by turns in opposite directions, tasting of every thing, investing things with every variety of colour, passing from one extreme to the other, desiring to be every thing,

to do every thing: then, though I admit we may have many
other qualities, there is one at least which we lack: and that
is, a *character*.

How many Christians are wanting in character in other respects! The best way of exposing these wants is to hold up
to view the principal traits of the Christian character with reference to the present era. It is more easy to say who have
not a Christian character than to say who have. Nevertheless I will make a feeble attempt, by endeavouring to point
out excesses and guard against mistakes.

I.—PRINCIPAL TRAIT OF THE CHRISTIAN AND THEOLO-
GICAL CHARACTER.

ATTACHMENT TO JESUS CHRIST.

The Christian, and especially the theologian, should beware
of restricting himself to one single idea, or one single system,
even if that system be the truth. It is not a system that the
eternal Father has given us; it is his own Son. Whosoever
binds himself to one system only may forsake it for another;
but he who really attaches himself to Jesus Christ will never
leave him. The true secret of the wisdom of the theologian
and the stability of the believer is, an intimate communion with
the Saviour, for in him are hidden all the treasures of wisdom
and knowledge. Do not suppose then, as many Christian
students often do, that you must resort to books to be enlightened, and to Jesus Christ to be sanctified. From him alone
proceed both of these graces. It has been remarked that the
German nations have the greatest tendency to internal life and
to mysticism; and that the nations of the Latin race have most
inclination for systems and scholasticism. I acknowledge the
merits of the theologians now living in England, Scotland, and
America; and yet, when I attempt to account for the profound
knowledge and the attraction which I find among some theologians of Germany, I ask myself: Is it not because these men
belong to a people who have always been more closely attached
than we to our Lord Jesus Christ? Brethren, let us adopt
the principle of their wisdom and their life. But, at the same
time, let us reject that indolence which prompts men to forsake

those laborious studies by means of which Jesus Christ enlightens his disciples in our days. If a general is taught only
by continual battles, the character of a theologian is formed
only by constant labour. Luther once said that he needed
several days to translate one word of the Bible ; and you will
need many years of study to find one beam of light which will
afterward illuminate your path through life.

The attachment to Jesus Christ which has been referred to
is not only necessary to attain knowledge, it is also necessary
in practical life, and should be made the object of constant attention. " Thou therefore endure hardness, as a good soldier
of Jesus Christ." As soldiers in active service should daily
expect fatigue and peril, so the servant of Christ should be
ready to endure all things, thinking only of pleasing his Master.
At the first command of his Captain, he will go whithersoever
he is sent, even if it be to the mouth of the cannon at the risk
of certain death; for he knows that his Master can do for him
what no human general can do : He can give him his life if he
lose it, and even life everlasting. This devotion to our Lord
Jesus Christ is the basis of the true theological character. The
man who spends his strength in running after forms, human
inventions, novel systems, and doubtful questions, instead of
following Jesus, may perhaps be active as it regards his body,
but can never have a truly Christian character.

II. SECOND TRAIT OF THE CHRISTIAN AND THEOLO-GICAL CHARACTER.

INDEPENDENCE.

If we depend on Jesus Christ, we must not depend on any
man. This observation is the more important in our day, because so many various opinions are constantly promulgated.
It is by means of internal development and by real progress
that we must attain unto the truth. The doctrine we profess
must be the consequence of our own life, and not a foreign
garb, which we can lay off as easily as we put it on. Does this
mean that every one must learn only from himself ? God forbid !
The tree which grows in our fields derives from the atmosphere, from the earth, from all sides, the influences and the

strength which make it grow and yield its fruit in its season. Thus it is with our minds, and the most distinguished men of modern times are those who have best known how to profit by every thing. No one but a fool or a madman could wish to begin every thing anew. The truly wise man labours with others, and considers himself as a member of a vast community. He makes use of the tradition of ages; not by subjecting himself to it, as though it were the very word of God, but to gain light by it. He profits by another's path, to advance the farther himself. But all that he gathers he digests and appropriates ; he makes it really his own. It is thus that the tree of which I spoke, and which is exposed to every wind, turns all that it receives into sap and wood and bark ; and thus the food with which we nourish our bodies is transformed into our own flesh and our own blood. Let it be so with all that you learn. Do not look upon the instructions which are given you as a piece of bread which you must take and put in your pocket without breaking it. Foolish man ! make haste and break it, and eat it, and make it a part of yourself. You must not receive any thing merely because this or that master tells you to receive it, but because the Lord of lords commands it. Let each truth be infused into your whole being; let it have an effect upon you, upon your feelings, upon your imagination, upon your understanding, and upon your will. It is only when it has thus influenced every part of your being, and has left the traces of its passages every where within you, that this truth really belongs to you. Be not satisfied with the labour of your masters ; the essential labour must be performed by yourselves. " I speak as unto wise men; judge ye what I say."

III. THIRD TRAIT OF THE CHRISTIAN AND THEOLOGICAL CHARACTER.

SPIRITUALITY.

"The flesh profiteth nothing," said our Master; " the words that I speak unto you they are spirit and they are life." But man is always inclined to substitute something essentially earthly and material in the place of spirit and life. This was the sin of Rome. The Church, instead of being an assembly of brethren, became, in the middle ages, merely an external hier-

archy; its head was a man, and if Jesus Christ was present at
all,[1] it was in a grossly material sense.   We then, while we
defend the visibility of the Church, at the same time defend its
sacred spirituality; and in this respect let us always remember
the promise of its Head : " Lo ! I am with you always, even
unto the end of the world."   This is the grand doctrine of the
Real Presence, which is too much forgotten among us.   I do
not refer to the parody which the Church of Rome has substituted for it.   I mean a living, spiritual, and real presence of
Jesus Christ; a presence the token of which is the Holy Supper ; for if Christ invites us to his table, he certainly does not
intend to be absent from it himself.

Now if the theologian and Christian be an eminently spiritual man, let him fear to enter into the field of temporal things.
When our Saviour was asked to decide respecting worldly concerns he replied, " Man, who made me a judge over you?"
When, anxious to draw him into a discussion respecting political questions, they brought him a penny, he kept his eye on
that spiritual kingdom which he came to found here below.

So it must be with the servant of Christ.   I do not mean
that he ought not to take part as a citizen in national concerns.   His position in such matters must always be one of
moderation; but to forbid his taking any part in them would
be going beyond the commands of the Scriptures.   What I
mean is, that he must not confound politics with religion, nor
seek to find in temporal matters the strength of spiritual affairs.
I mean that he must not take up arms for the defence of the
faith; and that, rejecting all tendency to insurrection and disorder, he must ever, according to the command of the apostle,
" fear God and honour the king."   In the concerns of the
earthly kingdom he must be submissive to the powers that be;
but in the concerns of God's kingdom he must acknowledge no
Head but Jesus Christ.   What he should endeavour to establish is, not the reign of a law given by political bodies, or a
treaty made between cabinets, nor even any particular ecclesiastical form of government; but it is that eternal kingdom
which " is righteousness and peace and joy in the Holy Ghost."
The true theologian will dread that dependence on the State,

---

[1] That is, if they pretended that He was present.

that secularization of religious institutions which is a death-blow to the Church; and he will consider it his duty to labour with increasing energy for the re-establishment of the independence and spirituality of the Church. And here, my brethren, I must warn you against extremes. There are many faithful ministers who, in connection with the State, endure this union as an imperfection, and have no idea of glorying in it as an honour. May God give to all of us the piety and zeal which distinguish these brethren, and forbid our making the independence of the Church a question which absorbs all others, and even the doctrine of Christ. Still further : in claiming autonomy and independence for the Church, I require, it is true, that they should be entire. I am even convinced (for the examples of Scotland and America prove it) that the Church might always accomplish, with God's assistance, the duties which he imposes on it, might give the milk of the flock to him who leads it, and make those who have sown spiritual things in its bosom reap carnal things. I think even that the efforts which it may make to accomplish this apostolical precept will be very beneficial to it, and will awaken strength which is yet concealed within it; but at the same time I wish to see nations and the institutions of nations imbued with Christianity. (Alas! how far we are from this!) I do not wish to separate Church and State to such a degree that there will be no communication between these two bodies. I claim for the Church the right, if it judge proper, to have an understanding with the State for objects of public utility, such as the celebration of the Lord's day and of days of national fasts; general instruction; public worship, even in the armies, in hospitals, in prisons, and in other civil institutions. This understanding is, if you please, a union in reality; but it is a free and harmonious union. And the independence of the Church will be preserved; and its glory will consist in its dependence, not on the officers of the civil administration, but on our Lord and Saviour Jesus Christ. Yes, I believe in the Real Presence of Jesus Christ in the midst of his people. Papists and Socinians may seek another king of the Church; theirs is merely a dead Christ; but Christians cannot do so. O, how sad it is to see in our days so many who, though they had learned better things,

are attaching so much importance to union with the State, and
who appear to delight more, if possible, in their character as
officers of the public administration than in that of servants of
Jesus Christ! What a state of degradation for the Church,
when the principal boast of its adherents is that they have been
appointed by means of the election of a deliberative assembly!
The true theologian has no wish to have the minister of an
earthly king for his chief; his Master is in heaven. And when
he speaks, it is not according to the law of the year Ten,[1] but
according to the laws of eternity, which the angels contemplate
and adore.

IV. FOURTH TRAIT OF THE THEOLOGICAL AND CHRISTIAN CHARACTER.

ALL BY THE WORD.

The fourth characteristic which should distinguish the theologian and the Christian in the present time is this: ALL BY
THE WORD.

St. Paul, in the close of the chapter which we have read,
makes two assertions: first, that the word of God will do all
that is to be done in the Church: "It is profitable," he says,
"for doctrine, for reproof, for correction, for instruction in
righteousness;" second, that the man whose character is
formed under the influence of the word of God will be all that
the Christian need be: "That the man of God may be perfect,
thoroughly furnished unto all good works." Thus, the all-
sufficiency of the word of God is clearly established. Brethren,
if it be essential that soldiers should be perfectly familiar with
the weapons of their warfare, must not *we* be acquainted with
that "armour of righteousness on the right hand and on the
left," to wit, "the word of truth"? Resist every temptation
to resort to any other authority or weapon. With the word of
Christ you can do all that you ought to do. It is alone the
sword of the Spirit.

If then the traditions, either of primitive times or of the
Reformation, are offered to you as a rule, reject them. It has

---

[1] The tenth year (1802) of the French Revolution, in which the laws relating to religious worship were made by Bonaparte.— *Trans.*

been the glory of the Reform[1] that it has abolished all tradition as a religious authority (which does not mean that it has abolished history). And has it cast down idols to put itself in their place? If any one speaks to you of an unknown magical influence of the sacraments, by virtue of which, for instance, regeneration is effected in the infant the moment it receives the baptism of water, reject it. It is doubtless much easier to say, "I was converted in baptism;" this saves the trouble of being converted afterward. But these are vain inventions which are contradictory to the word. I have no fear lest He who said when on earth, "Suffer the little children to come unto me," should reject them in heaven. Do not their angels always behold the face of our Father which is in heaven? But we are regenerated and sanctified only by faith in the Word. The Scriptures declare it every where; and assuredly we can assert of children what St. Paul says respecting adults: "How shall they believe in Him of whom they have not heard?"[2] If you are presented with a visible ecclesiastical authority, and are required to submit to it, even though it be in opposition to the word of God, reject it. "He that abideth not in the doctrine of Christ," says the beloved disciple, "hath not God. If there come any unto you, and bring not this doctrine, receive him not into your house, neither bid him God speed."

This, brethren, is the great danger of the Church in our days. The traditions, the magical effect of the sacraments (*opus operatum*), the authority of the visible Church, are the shoals which begin to appear, and which have already been the cause of many sad shipwrecks. Let us dread them, even afar off. Let us remember that an invisible current, the current of our corrupt nature, draws us toward them, and will dash us against them, unless we firmly grasp the anchor of the word of God. The very strongest minds have been overcome by it.

---

[1] The word *Reform* is used here as elsewhere to designate the Church of Calvin.—*Trans.*

[2] Rom., x, 14. This Popish doctrine of Baptismal Regeneration, which the Lutheran Church had abandoned (De quibus nostris temporibus haud facile quisquam certet—MARHEINECKE, *Institutiones Symbolicæ*), is not only claimed now by an extreme party in the Lutheran Church, is not only the hobby of the Puseyite party in England, but has also gained adherents in the Reformed Church, at least in French Switzerland.

The pious *Sibthorp* was neither Puseyite nor Papist when he was travelling for the British and Foreign Bible Society, and freely explaining in the houses of Christians the holy word which he was endeavouring to spread. And yet what has he become? *Pusey* himself was neither Puseyite nor Papist when, on his return from Germany, where he had been intimate with the great Protestant divines, he published a remarkable work on Rationalism, which was received with praises even in Germany. But he fell, inch by inch, to the leeway. And now England waits the moment when, at the head of a hundred ministers, he will bow down before "the Man of Sin."[1]

Let us then, my brethren, abide by the word. I beg you to bear with me in my frequent appeals on this subject.[2] The

[1] I will perhaps be accused of entertaining unfounded fears, at least on the Continent, for those who are the nearest to that abyss may profess to be much opposed to the Pope, and may perhaps even write against him. But let us not be too easily reassured. The most Puseyistic of all the bishops of the Episcopal church who, by introducing the absurd ordinances of Popery, has caused much excitement in his diocese, and given occasion for those noble protests of laymen before which he was forced to furl his flag : the bishop of Exeter has just declared, in a public document, that "he in no wise sympathizes with any popish party in the church, and that he has given proof of this." At the same time he announces " that he desires to be, in this world and in the next, with the best and holiest theologians of England (who are called Puseyites, Tractarians, etc.), who preach *the whole Gospel, in all its parts,* in just proportions." Now what is this *whole Gospel?* Here it is: I translate it literally : [1]" The necessity of partaking of the sacrament for salvation, the new birth given to us by God in baptism, the actual communication of the body and blood of Christ (with the inestimable benefits of His passion) to the soul of whosoever faithfully receives the Lord's Supper, the privileges of the Church, which is the body of Christ, the sin there is in violating its unity, the Apostolical succession of its ministers, the want of all covenant promises and salvation to all who have never been united to the Church, or have renounced its communion." Such is the *whole Gospel* of a man who says he is not a *Papist!* But, as an Episcopal paper in England (the Record) very truly says, " There is not a single point specified in this profession to which a Papist would not subscribe. It is the pure popish doctrine ; in its essence, in its order, in its proportions, it is the good doctrine of the Pope." Thus one can have *Popery,* only leaving out Gregory XVI. May God preserve us from these *non-Papists,* and from every thing that might lead us toward them! Let us not only start back from the gulf; let us start back from the current leading to it.

[2] See the Discourses (Nos. X and XII,) entitled 'Lutheranism and Calvinism,' and ' Geneva and Oxford.'

[1] We are obliged to translate from the author's version of the original in this case as we have not the document referred to.—*Trans.*

word, and nothing but the word! Not indeed a dead letter, but the word in its light; the word with the abundance of light which dwells in it; the word, and the power unto salvation which God has deposited there. The word; not the Pope, nor the clergy, nor any human power imaginable; the word of Jesus Christ, I mean of Jesus Christ himself; this is the only power whose sovereign and perpetual authority we ought to acknowledge in the Church.

V. FIFTH TRAIT OF THE THEOLOGICAL AND CHRISTIAN CHARACTER.

ALL FROM GOD, ALL THROUGH GOD, ALL FOR GOD.

Yes, my brethren (and this brings us to the fifth characteristic), the Church, in the words of Peter Martyr, one of our greatest doctors, is like a notary to whose care a will is committed; this notary has no power over the last will of the testator; and if he were to make the slightest alteration, he would be a forger; in case the authenticity of that will were contested, his whole duty would be to prove it, for it alone has the power of deciding every thing. But such being the notary's duty, is it the part of a pious son merely to respect externally the will of his father? No; he will examine it, he will carry out its provisions even in the most minute particular. Now, I believe that this is the peculiar character of our Reformed Church. It has not recoiled before any of the commands of the word of God; it has adopted alike those which are most humiliating to man's reason and those which best satisfy the wants of the heart. And this is what I demand of you.

I do not here allude to the various tendencies of the Reform, which it is important for us to know, if we wish to comprehend the position which we occupy; tendencies which I described a few months ago in a discourse[1] to which I refer you, and which I support in all its bearings. But I allude to that doctrine which is the characteristic doctrine of our church; the doctrine of a gracious *election*. This should be the fifth trait of the Christian character, not merely in the Reform, but wherever the light of the truth shines. "All from, through, and for

[1] See the discourse (No. X) entitled 'Lutheranism and Calvinism.'

God." The sovereignty of God is the Majesty before which our church of all others humbles herself and bows down. It acknowledges that sovereignty on earth, declaring that the whole work of salvation, performed in every heart, is from its very beginning effected solely by the Holy Spirit. It acknowledges that sovereignty in heaven, attributing the origin of all grace solely to the tender mercies and the eternal counsel of the everlasting Father, accomplished on the Cross. Reformed Christians! this doctrine is the precious deposit which the Lord has intrusted to us; let us not be unfaithful stewards. The Most High has commanded us to follow this course; if we follow any other we lose our trouble, and we carry confusion into the work of God. When the general of an army orders one of his regiments to take possession of a difficult position, all the soldiers must march in that direction to the assault.

Nevertheless, my brethren, far be it from us again to run into any unhappy excesses. Let us be ready to recognize truth when it is found in other communions. I am convinced that on this point, whatever may be the vulgar opinion, there is little or no difference between Lutheranism and the Reform. I may perhaps demonstrate this at some future time; for this subject is singularly obscure in Germany, even to the most eminent minds. But however this may be, far from us be the idea that we can find no brethren among those who deny the doctrine of absolute election. There are many who, though less advanced in the knowledge of the truth than we, excel us in zeal.

Nevertheless, this truth should by no means weaken us. As for us, it is for this great doctrine of *grace* that we are to conquer. *In hoc vince*, the Saviour has said to us. I pray you, therefore, preach the duty of conversion; I entreat you, tell every man to begin immediately to strive to enter in at the strait gate; this ought to be your perpetual theme. But let the whole strength of your exhortation lie always in that remark of St. Paul, "It is God which worketh in us both to will and to do of his good pleasure."

VI. SIXTH TRAIT OF THE THEOLOGICAL AND CHRISTIAN CHARACTER.

ATTACHMENT TO THE TRUE CHURCH.

But ought we then to attach any value to our being Reformed Christians? That is a question which many put to themselves. It leads us to our sixth characteristic. There are two churches: the church on earth, and the church in heaven. There are many communions[1] on earth, and while we are dwelling here below we must belong to some one of them. Now, to which do we belong? I first ask those who have such a dread of a historical church which has already passed through a part of its developments in by-gone days, and who would prefer to efface every thing and begin anew: Which church would you then prefer to that in which you were born and baptized? Will you be an Irvingist, a Plymouthian, or a partizan of some other of those whimsical doctrines which are promulgated in the present day? If you are unwilling to enter any one of these will you form a new sect of your own? I beseech you, let us not increase the number of sects, but let us concentrate them all around Jesus Christ. No, no, my brethren, let us not, with a presumptuous hand, break every tie which binds us to the past, and rush into adventurous and uncertain inventions. History, too, is the domain of God. We have a church, the Primitive Christian church, reformed in the sixteenth century by the word of God; let us stand by it. As for myself, if I am asked to what church I belong, I reply immediately that I belong to that. I want no Arianism, no Puseyism, no Plymouthism, nor any other heresy, old or new. I am simply a Reformed Christian. This is not so novel; it is not so entertaining perhaps, but it is more safe.

Nevertheless, let us understand this well. The Reformed church does not, in my opinion, exist wherever the walls and seats remain which were once used in the days of the Reform. The church, like its God, is not restricted to "houses made with hands." It would be a very singular doctrine to maintain that a man must necessarily be the same being as he whose place he occupies. The Turks dwell within the walls and the

---

[1] I prefer this term to the modern expression *denominations*.

sacred places of Jerusalem, yet they are not the people of God. The Reform exists solely where the doctrines and principles taught by the apostles and professed by the Reformers are to be found. Not that we ought to reject with pride those churches which were formerly reformed, and are now, alas! deformed; let us rather bear them on our hearts and pray that God may reform and vivify them anew. But let us never forget that it will be out of our power to do them any good unless we firmly uphold the standard of the word of God, and refuse to make even the least concession to the spirit of error which has destroyed them. The Christian church, reformed in the sixteenth century, rectified, vivified, perfected, if needful, is our church. I know that in the last century it received many fearful wounds; I know that in many places its members are prostrate, and others are still trembling; but I remember too, the exploits which God has performed by it and for it. I gaze with filial piety upon the stakes of our fathers; I venerate that bloody Exodus, in which, not like Israel, bearing the treasures of their enemies, not even carrying their own goods, our ancestors left all to come and worship Jesus Christ at the foot of our mountains, and were even ready to go to the ends of the earth. It is something to be able to claim descent from an assembly which, like that of the apostles, bore the bloody baptism of the martyrs. I do not repudiate that inheritance. I do not run after modern inventions, unwarranted, untried, without struggles, without glory, without past, and without future.

But this is only the church on earth, the particular apartment alloted to us in the great mansion of the Master of the house. The true church is "the General Assembly of the first-born, which are written in heaven." If we should be connected with the former by a thread, we should be united by brazen chains to the latter. It has been said, and we ought never to cease repeating it, We shall not be asked at the day of Christ whether we are Presbyterians or Episcopalians, Reformed or Lutherans, but whether we belong to Jesus Christ. Let us loathe that narrow bigotry which would fain shut us up in our particular compartment, and isolate us from the other members of our Lord's body. I have already shown in a former discourse, that the principle of union and catholicity is one of the

essential characteristics of the Scriptures and the Reform.[1]
Whatever others may say of it, let us stand by it.

Moreover, this unity of the Church in heaven must one day
be manifested on earth. "There shall be one flock, and one
Shepherd." Precious promise! Yes, all barriers shall fall;
every sectarian banner shall be torn down, and Christ alone
will be King over his people. But when will this glorious day
arrive? There are those who would fain have it appointed by
orders of political cabinets, duly sealed and registered in the
offices of the civil administration. Others would hasten it on
by introducing into the Reform the hierarchical abuses and the
magical operations which it has rejected. Others again show
their inclination to be in favour of it by latitudinarianism.
Let us reject all these human expedients, and expect that union
from God, and not from man.

Nevertheless, we have something to do. On the one hand,
while waiting for the Lord, we ought to be sincere in our belief;
for if the object were to create a man by the union of a soul
and a body, would not the first thing required be that the soul
should be a real soul, and the body a real body? Would we
suppose that, by deforming the soul and the body, we would
prepare them for the union? On the other hand, let us above
all defend the great doctrines which are common to us.

You are aware of the proposition made on this subject in the
late General Assembly of the Swiss pastors at St. Gall.[2] But
a few weeks have elapsed since then, and already I have received several letters from various places on that subject. I
will mention, in particular, the following interesting communication from Scotland: "Our Provincial Synod, which met on
the very day when this good news came, unanimously resolved
to address a petition to our General Assembly, requesting it to
encourage the proposition from St. Gall." Assuredly, we are
advancing toward greater unity. Let us then forget all dis-
sensions, insults, derisive names, false accusations, and injurious
personalities. Let us not yield to a passionate, blind, offensive,

---

[1] Lutheranism and the Reform (No. X).

[2] In the summer of 1844. From this proposition and the favour with
which it was received at St. Gall have grown those measures which have
been since adopted in Great Britain to bring all Evangelical Protestants
into a Christian Union or Alliance.—*Trans.*

and bitter spirit, which would revive among us the disputes of
the sixteenth century.   Let us rather exclaim, with one heart,
" Lord Jesus! come quickly! "

VII. SEVENTH TRAIT OF THE THEOLOGICAL AND CHRISTIAN CHARACTER.

DECISION, FIRMNESS.

It is not enough to give a vague adhesion to the principles
which I have set forth.   You must *be* something; you must
know what you want; and you must be and know this firmly
and decidedly.   Who would wish to be wavering, unable to
take a stand either on one side or on the other ?   Thus decision
has become one of the watchwords of our day.   But if there
are some men who have not enough of this, there are others
who carry it to an extreme which we cannot recommend.   Are
we not perhaps too easily persuaded that none can be decided
but those who are on our side, or at all events, who are diametrically opposed to it?   We do not require you to renounce
from this time forth all the important questions which theological science presents.   Nay, we believe that sometimes a
theologian, whose views are very decided, may, after a long
career, preserve a respectful silence on some particular question
which, in his opinion, the word of God has not settled: A
narrow, false, exaggerated decision of opinion impedes the free
action of the mind, and prevents a man from growing in knowledge.   By such means are closed all the openings through
which greater light might enter.   So did not Paul.   "I reach
forth," said he, "unto those things which are before."   None
but narrow minds shut themselves up in their contracted views.
Men of character will advance, adapt themselves to their times,
and adapt their times to themselves.   There is a constant exchange going on between them and the times in which they
live.   The greatest theological characters, from St. Paul to
Augustine, from Augustine to Luther, from Luther to Chalmers.
have always passed through successive phases, and have even
undergone remarkable changes, which were brought on by internal developments, and by the ways of God himself.   If a
new opinion be the consequence of one held previously, it is a
mark of development, and not of contradiction, as the vulgar
may suppose.   It is thus that Augustine, after having believed

that man could do every thing, came to the conclusion that man has only half of the work of his salvation to perform, and finally acknowledged, at a still later period of his life, that the work of conversion belongs to God alone. We ask you to be firm in all essential matters, and to be decided, whenever you shall have wisely, truly, and firmly recognized the truth of a doctrine; we ask you not to be always uncertain, wavering, driven from side to side by the various tendencies which are manifested in the Church, attracted sometimes by one and sometimes by another, like those idle children amusing themselves in the market-place, who, instead of going to their work, are induced to visit this place and that place by all the wild children in the town. These men, said our Lord, will tell you, "Lo, here is Christ! or, there! believe it not: for there shall arise false Christs and false prophets. Wherefore if they shall say unto you, Behold, he is in the desert! go not forth; Behold, he is in the secret chambers! believe it not." Nothing is so necessary to the Church in our days as firmness in Jesus Christ. Seek, therefore, by constant study of the word, by continual prayer, by holy meditations and useful conversations, to obtain a proper, an enlightened, a Christian, and an immovable conviction. Be like a tree; its extreme branches are thin and flexible; you can bend its smallest boughs as you please; but as for the trunk and the larger branches, were you to strive with all your might, were you to call a thousand men to your assistance, you could not break them. Iron itself, which, says Daniel, breaks all things, will not move that conviction. Thus it was with Jesus Christ. Nothing could turn him away from his object; and it was by means of that indomitable and divine firmness he accomplished the task which was given him to do.

VIII. EIGHTH TRAIT OF THE THEOLOGICAL AND CHRISTIAN CHARACTER.

BOLDNESS OF PROFESSION.

Hence necessarily follows the eighth trait of the Theological and Christian character: *boldness of profession*. A man should have great freedom in expressing, and great courage in maintaining a conviction properly acquired. Of course, you should beware of defending your opinion with repulsive harshness and passionate zeal. That is not the boldness which we want;

true firmness is calm, temperate, considerate. When a man knows that he possesses the truth, when he is certain of victory, he can be gentle, pacific, and patient, as God is patient, because he is eternal.

But, at the same time, what is your conviction worth if you are ashamed of it, and even if you are unable, whenever it is proper and useful, to present it bodily?

We must take the oath which Luther took when he was made a Doctor of Theology: "I swear manfully to defend the truth of the Gospel." When a man knows the truth, he must know how to defend it with decision, and go forward with courage. This Christian characteristic demands energy, strength of mind, firmness, and manliness. Perhaps storms may rise against you; winds may arouse the waves of the ocean, and they may overwhelm you; but when the tempest has passed, and calm has returned, you will be found in the same place, proclaiming with the same tranquillity the words of truth and life.

This courage you will show especially by unweariedly opposing every error which may arise in the Church. I know it would be much more pleasant to keep silence, but then what would we be? "If a dog barks," says Calvin, "when its master is attacked, shall not I cry out when the doctrine of my God is attacked?" If, through fear of men, through a desire to please them, through indifference, or through indolence, you keep silence in presence of error, you will be dumb dogs, but you will not be true theologians. Look at your Master, in that nocturnal council, that senate of blood, where he appeared in the midst of the priests, already condemned by them in their own minds, already delivered into the hands of the soldiers, covered with contempt, without any hope of safety for himself; when the high priest puts to him that decisive question, "Art thou the Christ?" He answers with a calmness, a dignity, a boldness which strikes the interrogator with such astoundment that, rending his clothes, as it were to give vent to the anguish of his conscience, he cries out, "He hath spoken blasphemy!" That blasphemy was the simple and sublime reply, "Thou hast said; nevertheless, I say unto you, hereafter shall ye see the Son of man sitting on the right hand of power, and coming in the clouds of heaven!"

Such, my brethren, is your example; in the midst of whatever danger, maintain the truth in all its strength, but with great humility, and with perfect mildness.

Brethren, I have done. Such is the Theological and Christian character which you ought to make your own.

I will add but a few words. If this character be necessary at all times, it is particularly necessary in these days, which are so exciting and critical, in which all things are fermenting, and during which the church of God is to arise out of an immense chaos. The enemy is at work, and is sowing many tares in the field where the Lord has sown his word. Every where, among the ministers as well as among the members of the church, there are souls who have had enough of Jesus Christ, enough of his grace, enough of his Cross, enough of his Spirit of life. They want something new, something which has a peculiar relish; old things have grown wearisome to them. Scarcely has some meteor appeared on the horizon, when, turning away from the Sun of Righteousness, they hasten into the marshes toward which that deceitful light leads them. As there are bodies which are susceptible of receiving all diseases, so also there are minds which imbibe all errors. One day you will see them rushing into the arms of the prophets and apostles of Irvingism; on the next, into the radical ideas of Plymouthism; on the next, into the pretensions of Ecclesiastical Hierarchism, of which Puseyism and Popery are the finest expressions, but which finds among us a great number of transformations, modified and corrected, but by that very modification and correction made still more dangerous. So, if there appears any palpable folly, or any error like those which are discussed in the taverns, you will find minds that will adopt, imbibe, and proclaim them. This has always held true.

Thus, my brethren, we will close with the words we heard at the outset: "Perilous times have come." There is need, then, of strong men, created and renewed by the hand of God, who will come up to the breach for the sake of his cause.

Lord! create unto thyself, in holy pomp, that army covered with the armour of thy word; and do thou soon possess dominion over thine enemies!

DISCOURSE VIII.

THE CHURCH CALLED TO CONFESS JESUS CHRIST.

" Whosoever, therefore, shall confess me before men, him will I confess also before my Father which is in heaven. But whosoever shall deny me before men, him will I also deny before my Father which is in heaven. Think not that I am come to send peace on earth ; I came not to send peace, but a sword. For I am come to set a man at variance against his father, and the daughter against her mother, and the daughter-in-law against her mother-in-law. And a man's foes shall be they of his own household. He that loveth father or mother more than me is not worthy of me : and he that loveth son or daughter more than me is not worthy of me. And he that taketh not his cross, and followeth after me, is not worthy of me. He that findeth his life shall lose it : and he that loseth his life for my sake, shall find it."—MATTHEW, x, 32--39.

THE words you have just heard were uttered by our Lord in anticipation of times of trial. The state of the Church was to be represented for three centuries by that woman whom St. John saw in his Revelation, "clothed with the Sun," which is Jesus Christ our Righteousness ; having " upon her head a crown of twelve stars," the crown of the apostles ; " crying, travailing in birth, and pained to be delivered." It was necessary, then, that Christ should strengthen her in the confession of the Faith, that she might remain firm throughout her long and terrible sufferings.

My brethren, we are living in days which, perhaps, have some analogy to those in reference to which these words were pronounced.

Various signs seem to indicate that the times are drawing nigh when the church, so long restrained by boundaries too narrow, will spread abroad among all the nations of the earth; when Israel, converted, will be restored to their ancient home, and when the False Prophet of the East and the High Priest of the West will see their empires broken to pieces. The statesmen who are least acquainted with the prophecies, the newspapers of the most infidel sentiments, are already speaking of some of these events. The Jews are turning their eyes toward the Holy Land; at Constantinople the Turk feels the ground tremble under his feet; and, as a missionary who had been to Jerusalem, and had there been intimate with some of the highest Mahometan families, lately informed us a rumour is spreading all over the East that Mahometanism is about to fall; that Jesus Christ will soon come down and stand on the summit of the great mosque at Damascus, and will unite Judaism, Christianity, and Mahometanism into one primitive religion. These are the presentiments of the people.

But before these things come to pass, there will be final struggles; the Bible predicts this, and the present times confirm it. In truth, do we not see the enemies of Christ strengthened, the systems of infidelity and pantheism audaciously confronted with the cross of Jesus, the powers of Rome revived over the whole extent of the earth, monasteries building in France, a celebrated society, the most devoted cohort of Popery, establishing itself every where, and even in the bosom of our Confederation? Do we not hear of wars and rumours of wars? Is not the Levant crimsoned and furrowed constantly by the flashes of lightning which foretell the thunder-storm? Are not the powers of the East and the West assembled now around the Land of Revelation, that Judea, which is again becoming the centre of the world, that Jerusalem, of which it is said, "In those days shall Judah be saved, and Jerusalem shall dwell safely."

We do not pretend, my brethren, to know the times or the seasons; but if, on the one hand, we ought to display great discretion and reserve in these matters, would it not, on the other hand, be closing one's eyes to the light, to suppose that, both in a political and religious point of view, the world is now in a tranquil and ordinary state, instead of being in a critical condition? I think, then, that it will be proper to meditate with you upon the words which our Lord addressed to his disciples for the purpose of strengthening them during three centuries of persecution, and which will strengthen his children to the end of the world.

In such times as those to which we have referred, the great
work to which Christ calls his followers is, to confess his name
with boldness. This is, First, the duty of every Christian;
and, Secondly, the duty of the Church. Let us consider these
two duties; and may the Lord grant us strength to fulfil both.

I. We often meet with men (and perhaps there may be some
such in this assembly) who would fain be Christians, converted
Christians, but without saying any thing about it to any one,
and provided it might remain a secret to all save themselves
and their God. These feeble Christians have an excessive
fear of every thing that can make them known as such. You
will hear them say, to justify themselves, that "the kingdom
of heaven is within us," and that Christianity is too holy a
thing to be displayed before the world. But (though they
may not perceive it) it is their fear of the world that governs
and restrains them.

A notorious and corrupt church has adopted this miserable
hypocrisy. The Church of Rome permits that a man should
be converted without his acknowledging it. There are secret
Roman Catholics in Protestant countries, and especially among
the heathen. The many pretended converts in China, of
which Rome boasts so loudly, conceal their faith in that empire, and call themselves idolaters; there, too, we find that
Christianity without any confession of faith, which some wish
to see established in the bosom of Christendom.

But the Evangelical Christian church rests on principles
directly opposite, although some have been desirous, in our
days, of falsifying its nature in that respect. It declares with
the apostles that it is not enough to "believe with the heart
unto righteousness;" one must also "with the mouth make
confession unto salvation;" and instead of the accommodations
and subterfuges of Rome, instead of the silence, indifference,
fear, and respect of men, which characterize some Protestants,
who forget the rock out of which they have been formed, the
Evangelical church proclaims and duly heeds the firm and
sovereign declaration of Christ: "Whosoever shall confess me
before men, him will I confess also before my Father which is
in heaven; but whosoever shall deny me before men, him will
I also deny before my Father which is in heaven."

Yes, feeble and timid Christians! It is not enough to believe that we belong to Christ in our inmost hearts. If we
have truly embraced Jesus Christ, we will make him known
unto all men. What! when we have been saved by him from
eternal death, shall we not exalt him with all our souls? Ah!
let all men read in our lives an epistle written by the hand of
Jesus, and proclaiming his ineffable love!

"That is all very true," you reply; "but if we are not
obliged to suffer any thing for Jesus Christ, that is no proof
that we are unfaithful. It is an exaggeration to pretend that
a man can not be a sincere Christian without enduring persecution. Does not Christianity tend to produce harmony,
good-will, and peace every where? How can men persecute
us with contempt or hatred because Christianity has made us
better? Such things may have occurred in primitive times,
among the heathen; but in our days, in the bosom of Protestant Christendom, in our own church, no one can be tempted
to deny Jesus Christ through fear of persecution.

" Think not," Jesus Christ himself replies, "that I am come
to send peace on earth. I am come to set a man at variance
against his father, and the daughter against her mother."
Yes, if your conversion be a real one, if you truly confess Jesus
Christ, "think not" to escape from this universal rule. It is
very true that the *object* of Christ was not to bring a sword;
yet such has invariably been the *effect* of his coming wherever
he has appeared. And how could it be otherwise? Look at
the facts which occur around you. The Gospel has affected
the heart of a certain person of your acquaintance (perhaps
your own heart). It has effected a radical change, which is
visible in the whole tenor of the life of this new Christian.
This change inevitably draws the attention of his friends; and,
in the view of this work of God, they are driven to this alternative—either to undergo it themselves or to condemn it in
him. Unwilling to adopt the former, they choose the latter;
they condemn the conversion of their friend as an unreason-
able, enthusiastic, fanatical, methodistical measure. And if
this new Christian (whether it be yourself or some one else) be
a near relative, their irritation, as we constantly see, is only
increased; for the contempt and hatred of the world which the

believer draws upon himself are reflected in some degree upon them; the more closely the Christian is connected with them, the louder is the condemnation which they must pronounce against their own hearts. And it is to them that others look for the purpose of bringing back to his senses, as they say, the man who in their opinion is deranged.

Be not deceived then, my brethren; there is no need of extraordinary circumstances to make the confession of Jesus Christ a difficult thing. If you are upright and sincere in your profession, you cannot avoid opposition; this is the ordinary course of events in the world: "A man's foes shall be they of his own household."

Allow me then to ask you a question which your words suggest. What will Christ say of you? Is not the manner in which the world has hitherto received you a sure indication that Christ will one day reject you? No! you reply. Some prudence of course is necessary to escape opprobrium; we have made some little sacrifices, some unimportant arrangements. But what of that? If we have not been guilty of great crimes against Christian morals: if our only error has been to fail to confess Christ before our friends and our family as frequently and as courageously as perhaps we might have done: is that a proof that we do not belong to Christ, and that the Lord, for so light an offence, will deny us eternally? It cannot be!

Here again you shall be answered in the divine words which I preach to you, and not in my own language: "He that loveth father or mother more than me is not worthy of me," saith the Lord. "He that loveth son or daughter more than me is not worthy of me." If through fear of father or mother, brother or sister: if through love for your children, a fear of endangering the prosperity of a son or the marriage of a daughter, you yielded on one occasion, you kept silence on another, are you literally, in the sense of this declaration of the Master, worthy of Jesus Christ! With your own conscience I leave the answer.

Still further: suppose you confess Jesus Christ in the midst of your family: suppose even that you bear the reproaches of your mother or your son, and you walk faithfully in this path till the last hour; but that then, by the prospect of great op-

probrium and contempt from the world, or still more, in view
of persecution and of the stake, you are bewildered, you hesi·
tate, you keep silence, and you turn your back on Jesus Christ
as Peter did, then, notwithstanding all you may have done,
Christ will have a bitter reproach for you : ' Why didst thou
shrink back ?' he will say to you. ' Did I ever recoil ?   Did I
not bear for thee that cross which thou hast rejected !   Did I
not consent to be led to Calvary for thee ?   Did I not for thy
sake suffer my hands and my feet to be pierced ?   But as for
thee, thou hast loved thine ease, thine interests, thy life, more
than my kingdom and my glory.   I know thee not !'   " He
that taketh not his cross and followeth after me is not worthy
of me."

And why should we wonder at this severity of the Lord
when we remember that the course we pursue with regard to
him is very different from that of the world ?   Which of us
would not submit to a painful operation, if he knew that that
operation would secure permanent good to him ?   And shall
we esteem eternal life unworthy of the endurance of a few short
hours of suffering ?   Ah ! you have not now before you the
cross, the sword, and the scaffold ; I know that death is not
presented to your view now.   Nevertheless, it is at the cost of
this that we are to receive Jesus Christ.   No man belongs
really to Christ unless he is ready to lay down his life for the
purpose of confessing him.   It is thus the soul is saved.

This *semi-faith*, if I may so call it, which is seen in the
Church, and which will undoubtedly fail in the day of martyr-
dom, is a deplorable thing.   All are not called to confess
Jesus Christ on the scaffold, but all should be ready to do so.
And these words which we preach to you are as true with re-
gard to times of tranquillity as in days of trouble and blood :
" He that findeth his life shall lose it : and he that loseth his
life for my sake shall find it."

II. And now we will go farther; we will look abroad upon
the whole Church, and say, What is true with regard to each
individual is true for the Church.   If Christ, in the first place,
calls every Christian to confess him, he also and particularly
calls the Church to do so.   And when I speak of the Church,
it is still to you and to your duty that I refer, with this differ-

ence, that it is to your duty, not as an isolated individual, but as a member of a universal society, the Church.

The Church is called by its Master to confess him before the world. And is not the duty of each individual the duty of all? Is not the obligation of the soldier to be faithful to his standard binding on the whole army? And is it not a consequence of God's command to each planet to move, that the whole system must harmoniously pursue its course?

Every false church opposes the confession of Jesus Christ. "If any man did confess that Jesus was Christ," we are told by John, "he was to be put out of the synagogue." Every true church confesses the Lord. It is the duty of a minister, not merely as an individual, but also as the servant and representative of the Church, to imitate Timothy, and like him to profess "a good profession before many witnesses." The Church ought in all things to follow its Head. "Christ," the Scriptures say, "left us an example, that we should follow his steps." Now Jesus Christ, as we are told by Paul, "before Pontius Pilate witnessed a good confession." And what is the eulogium which Jesus Christ pronounced, not of an individual, but of a church, the church of Pergamos, when the cruel Domitian had shut up the faithful Antipas in a brazen ox heated by the fire, as we are told in the account of the life of that martyr?[1] The glory of that church, as Jesus himself declares, consisted in confessing the name of Christ, and in proclaiming its faith in the Lord. "I know thy works, and where thou dwellest, even where Satan's seat is; and *thou holdest fast my name, and hast not denied my faith,* even in those days wherein Antipas was my faithful martyr, who was slain among you, where Satan dwelleth."

Such, my brethren, is the duty of the Church; the Bible asserts this; and the church which does not as a body confess the great mystery of godliness, *God manifest in the flesh,* is quite as unfaithful and guilty as the Christian is who neglects to do so in his individual character. These are the conclusions of common sense.

And this the universal church has acknowledged. Yes, my brethren; we have not arbitrarily imposed this duty on the

---

[1] Bollandi, acta.

Church: on the contrary, it tells us that in its brightest days it always performed it.

It felt the need of fulfilling this duty when, in the beginning of the fourth century, a fatal heresy, denying the eternal divinity of the Son of God, began to spread throughout the world, and the universal Church was assembled at Nice, in the year 325, from the farthest parts of the East and the West, as represented by its bishops; and, rejecting the errors of Arius, declared, in the presence of the first Christian emperor, and before the whole world, "We believe in one Lord Jesus Christ, true God of true God; begotten, not made, consubstantial with the Father, by whom all things were made, both in heaven and in earth, who for us men, and for our salvation, descended, was incarnate."[1]

The church in Germany felt the need of performing this duty, more than three centuries ago, when, in 1530, at Augsburg, during the great revival of Christianity, in view of the terrible wars and fearful persecutions which seemed about to pursue it, and when summoned by the emperor Charles V to cease preaching the word of God, it replied through the margrave of Brandenburg, "Rather will I sacrifice my head than cease to confess my God and his Gospel." And when the Evangelical Princes solemnly assembled in the imperial chapel, in the presence of that dreaded emperor who ruled two worlds, and of a number of princes, bishops, ambassadors, and the powerful men of the earth, amid all the splendour of the age, the elector of Saxony and his brother in the faith arose, the chancellors advanced, and for two hours the renewed church, through its representatives, proclaimed, in the midst of the deepest and most impressive silence, its priceless faith: "Justification by the merits of Christ, through grace, and by means of faith."[2]

The church in France felt the need of performing this duty less than three centuries ago, when, on the 26th of May, 1559, not with splendour and royal magnificence, as at Augsburg, but in silence and mourning, enduring the contempt, and even the sword of their adversaries, and under the bloody reign of

[1] Θεου αληθινον ομοουσιον τω πατρι (symbolum Nicænum.)
[2] Fourth Article of the Augsburg Confession.

Henry II and Catharine of Medici, the deputies from all the churches then existing in France assembled at Paris; "At Paris," says Theodore Beza,[1] "because it was the most convenient place for the secret assembling of a great number of ministers and elders;" when, having entered the capital through the troops of the archers of Henry II, those ministers and members of the Church resorted, during four successive days, to a house in the quarter of St. Germain,[2] one by one, stealthily, from different directions, and there remained assembled for the confession of their faith, "surrounded by stakes and gibbets," says another historian, "which were erected in every part of the city;"[3] in the presence of the spies of the clergy, the emissaries of the parliament, and the soldiers of the king, and obliged almost to hold their breath lest they should be betrayed; and the Church of our fathers in France, protected by its humility, proclaimed that noble Confession of its Faith, which its ministers and elders then carried to all the provinces, and published boldly in the presence of the satellites of Rome, and over the ashes of martyrs, saying, in the tones which still sound in our ears: "We believe that from that general corruption and condemnation into which all men are plunged, God withdraws those whom, by his eternal and unchangeable counsel, he has elected, out of his mercy alone, in our Lord Jesus Christ, without any consideration of their works. We protest that Jesus Christ, God and man in one person, is our entire and perfect purification, and that in his death we have a full satisfaction to aquit us of all our sins."[4]

Yes, my brethren, it is thus that at all times the Church has had the courage to confess its faith, to obey its Master, and to "profess a good profession before many witnesses."

And shall not the Church in our days do likewise? Shall it remain silent? Has not Christ been crucified for it? Or has it no faith to profess? More than a century has passed since the Confession of Faith in Christ, our God and Saviour,

[1] Eccles. Hist., p. 109.
[2] A p.   Paris on the south side of the city.— *Trans.*
[3] Hist. of the Edict of Nantes, vol. i, p. 18.
[4] Confession of Faith of the Reformed Churches of France, Art. 12th, 17th, etc

was subverted in this church of Geneva; but a few months ago, it was subverted in the church of the canton Vaud. Almost every where the confessions of our fathers have been either overthrown or neglected. The Church is now, as it were, in the midst of immense remains. Ruins—ruins—nothing but ruins.

Ah! while the adversaries are so cunning in the work of destroying, shall the friends of Jesus Christ be so remiss in that of rebuilding? If the mouths of our fathers have been stopped so that they cannot speak of their ancient faith: if they have, so to speak, put them to death again, shall our lips remain silent? What! because those hands which presented to the world the Confession of the Eternal Word made flesh, have for three centuries been lying cold and rigid in the tomb; because those eyes which gazed with mildness and boldness on the kings and executioners, have for three centuries been closed and sightless; because those feet which hastened to the stake, if necessary, rather than cease to confess Christ, are disjointed and scattered; because those lips which exclaimed in the midst of the multitude, and when surrounded by flames, "Emmanuel! God with us! have been closed and silenced for three centuries in the dust of death: shall *we*, in our day, do *nothing*, confess *nothing*, say NOTHING! O corpses that we are! Since we are dead, let us renounce the very name of life; let us go and lie down in the grave, if we cannot speak any more than its inhabitants. That church which is beneath the ground, and which awaits the archangel's trump and the voice of the Son of man, would shudder in its dust, if it could know the lukewarmness of the church in our days. The courageous dead would rise from their sepulchres, and say, "*We* had arms to move, and lips to speak: have *you* arms and lips to remain quiet? And do *you* not hear that august and fearful voice which makes us tremble even in our tombs: 'Whosoever shall deny me before men him will I also deny before my Father which is in heaven'?"

My brethren, the Church needs a confession of faith, that it may manifest its unity. The duty of unity is a command prescribed by our Master. We cannot avoid it. Now it is not by an earthly head, by a worldly hierarchy, by uniformity of

8   F

worship and liturgy; it is not by crosiers, mitres, or censers; it is not by any of these things that the unity of the Church is manifested; it leaves these beggarly elements for the world. The true Church of Christ has no other bond than the unity of its faith and confession, in the charity and holiness of life. All external things, of which men make so much parade, are merely secondary with it. All is free in it, save only Jesus Christ. Let Rome talk of her false and lifeless unity; the Church of Christ will display a *living* and *true* unity; *unity*, not *uniformity*. Yes! in view of that dead uniformity of Rome, which is like uniformity of parade in the armies of the kings of this world, let us answer by a loud und unanimous confession of "the Lord our Righteousness," like that of the angels who lie prostrate before the eternal throne. The former unity is that of the children of this world; the latter, that of the children of heaven. What an admirable unity was that of the Church at its great revival in the sixteenth century! It was no servile uniformity; there was freedom on every point in which men can be free; but there was also a sublime and imposing harmony in the confession of divine truth. Take the confessions of Germany, Switzerland, Belgium, France, England, and Scotland; there is every where the same faith, the same God, the same Christ, the same salvation. In the church of Rome, the principal things are men—priests, bishops, and pontiffs; its unity consists in their being united. In the Christian Evangelical church, the principal things are faith, the heavenly doctrine, the truth of God; that is to say, God himself; and its unity consists in the unanimous confession of this truth. Every church which ceases to seek unity in that confession of the same doctrine, and would make it consist in union with the chiefs or companies who direct it, may indeed bear the name of "Protestant;" but in this it has adopted the essential characteristic of Popery. It is not walls which must soon fall, or leaders, ephemeral beings who to-morrow will be lying in the tomb, that constitute the essential thing in the church. The worshipper of the virgin and saints, in Spain or in Italy, obeys the pontiff who is at the head of the oldest church of the West; and the Turk at Constantinople bows down in the ancient halls of Justinian and

Theodosius.[1]   Stones are nothing; men are nothing; Christ is every thing.   To suppress the unity of faith and the confession of Christ is to suppress the Church.   Then there may indeed be a few Christians yet, scattered here and there; there may be walls, priests, and ruins; but there will be no Church; for no assembly of God can exist where there are only foreign, perhaps, opposing elements, without any divine and eternal bond to unite them.

My brethren, we must have a confession of faith of the Church; for it is by means of that confession that the Church must conquer.   What are "its weapons, mighty to the pulling down of strong-holds," as St. Paul says?   Those weapons are *the confession of Jesus Christ.*   This is the only strength of the Church.   What would become of it were the confession of faith wanting in it?   It would become an accidental aggregation of certain semi-civil societies, each of which acts according to its own good pleasure, or according to the pleasure of its rulers; like a tree, the trunk of which has been severed, and whose separated and scattered branches can only wither and die; like a body, whose head has been cut off, and whose members have been scattered to the four winds.   How could it, in this state, be victorious over its enemies?   Alas! this is but too truly the state of the Evangelical church in our days; and it is this that gives us much alarm in view of the dangers that threaten it.   But let the Church revive and be built up in its most holy faith and in its admirable unity; let it put on that strength and life which belong to a great community; let it unite with all the ends of the earth in confessing, with one heart and with one voice, Jesus its God; and these are the trumpets before which will fall down the strong-holds of infidelity and the walls of Rome.   "The people shouted," we are told by the Scriptures in the account of the siege of Jericho; "the wall fell down flat, so that the people went over into the city."

And shall it be said, my brethren, as it is often repeated in the world, that though it be true that the Church needs a bond, without which it can not exist (a concession which it were well to note), yet this bond exists in the universally-admitted princi-

[1] The Mosque of St. Sophia.

ple that the holy Scriptures are the only source of our faith.
"We do not need," say they, "to confess any doctrine ; the
Bible, and nothing but the Bible, is our confession." What !
the Bible! and nothing in it ! Is the Bible, then, simply a
certain volume, bound after a certain fashion, and of a certain
form, with nothing but white leaves in it? "Freedom of examination," they add, "and progress, constitute our church ;
it needs no doctrines ; each minister may have his own, and
preach them." Thus, my brethren, the poor Christian flocks
are to be given up to all the imaginations which may enter the
minds of their ministers! Each church is to change its religion whenever it changes its pastor! Whenever a new minister comes to a village, a new religion is to come with him!
One will preach Protestantism, another Anabaptism, another
Socinianism, another Universalism, another Romanism, and
another, even (why not?), Judaism, and, still another, Mahometanism ; for Judaism has more foundation in the Bible than
most of these other doctrines ; and Mahometanism professes a
more explicit faith in Jesus Christ than Socinianism itself.
And all this must be very good for the poor parishioners who
are obliged to pass, together with their children, through all
these forms of doctrines of their masters, just as the footman
puts on successively the various liveries of the families where
he serves. Ah! these latter, at least, only change their clothes;
but in your deplorable system, it would be faith, which is to
save for eternity, that would have to be changed constantly in
the soul!

"But," they continue, "are not freedom of enquiry, examination, and progress, enough?" Certainly we want freedom of
enquiry and progress, but we want to have them real, and bearing
fruits of salvation and life. To you those are only expressions by
means of which you can seal your indifference. What, I pray,
is the meaning of your *enquiry*, which, though it discerns, retains nothing? What is your *research*, which searches always,
and never finds? What does your *progress* signify, which, like
a certain fabulous traveller, is always advancing, but never
reaches any point? For we must remember that, in this miserable system, though the church is commanded to seek its
doctrine, it is forbidden to find it ; since, as soon as it finds it,

and consequently proclaims it, the system is destroyed; for then it would possess a doctrine, and would return to God's truth.

No, my brethren, it is impossible that the Church should have meditated for centuries on the oracles of God, which "enlighten the simple," and yet should not know what is found in them. It is impossible that the Church should believe in the Scriptures, and yet not know what the Scriptures tell it. The Church has known from the beginning; it knew in the days of Paul and Peter, of Athanasius and Augustine, of Luther and Calvin, it knows now, in every place, and at all times, what it rejects, what it believes, what it wants: GOD MANIFEST IN THE FLESH. And if there are any teachers, if there are, alas! any churches, which have withdrawn from this glorious and consoling confession, men only have fallen; the confession is still standing. The grass may wither, the flower thereof may fall away; but the word of the Lord endureth forever.

Thus, my brethren (and with this we will conclude), a courageous confession of the Lord arises from the ruins which lie heaped upon the field of God; and a loud and faithful voice sounds from the very interior of the Revival which is taking place.

But, you may enquire, do you then pretend to say that the Church in our days ought to confess its faith in an authentic and universal manner, as it did in the 16th century?

And why should it not, my brethren? Do we then suppose, as some do, that a command of God is binding in one century, and not in another? I do not say that the form ought to be the same as that of the 16th century; it might be wholly different; perhaps it ought not to be a confession made once for all, but frequent and repeated confessions; perhaps not confessions made with pen and ink, but living confessions made by the mouth and the life. "Every age has its peculiar manner of confessing Jesus Christ, as every age has its peculiar manner of persecuting those who confess him."[1] Nor do I assert that this must be done at all times. Finally, I joyfully acknowledge that there are lips which have spoken, and which still speak. But I simply say that "the church, over the whole

[1] Quesnel.

world, if it really awaits the coming of its Head, ought to confess, with a unity and universality far greater than it does now,
that Christ is indeed the Lord, to the glory of God the Father."

Then, you may say again; that concerns the ministers; you
ought to preach to them, and not to us! What! is the Church
composed of none but ministers? That is true only in the language of Popery. You are the Church, and you, as well as
we, must confess Jesus Christ. When the Church professed
its faith at Augsburg, before Charles V, there were none but
laymen there to do it. The princes would not yield that honour
to the theologians. Will you concede it now?

Let us, then, my brethren, be confessors of Jesus Christ; let
us be such, first, as individuals, as souls called out of darkness
into Christ's marvellous light, and proclaiming the virtues of
Him who hath redeemed us, by our words, by our lives, and
by all our actions.

Let us, then, be confessors of Jesus Christ, my brethren; but
let our confession be sustained by faith and by internal life.
Confession can be free and real externally, only so far as sanctification advances internally. A confession with the mouth,
without renouncing self, and without the life of the heart, is
hypocrisy, that is to say, an abomination in the sight of God.

Let us be confessors of Jesus Christ, my brethren; but let
us confess him with wisdom and charity; without uselessly
affecting singularity; without giving too much importance to
secondary objects; without forgetting that we must carefully
watch the dispositions of our own hearts. Perhaps your father
or your mother requires of you an act of conformity to the world;
you refuse to perform it; you do well; but if, in doing so, you
are violent, or wanting in respect, you sin against the Lord.

Be confessors of Jesus Christ, my brethren; but confess him
willingly, boldly, joyfully; not with that timidity, that mournful or gloomy aspect with which Christians are sometimes reproached. There is joy in the harmony of an identical and
universal confession; but there is sadness in the discord of human opinions. You have nothing to fear. " Whosoever shall
confess that Jesus is the Son of God, God dwelleth in him,
and he in God; and " greater is He that is in us than he that
is in the world."

Let us be confessors of Jesus Christ, and let each of us fulfil this duty in the station in which God has placed him.   Let the magistrate confess Christ in the council; let the mechanic confess him in his work-shop; let the man of business confess him amid his occupations; let the labourer confess him in the fields; let the mother confess him in her family; let the soldier confess him when in arms; let each, wherever he may be placed, look upon his situation as a sanctuary in which he is called to confess the Lord!

And you, young men[1] who have come back again from various countries, and have again left your homes to apply your minds to important studies, be confessors of Jesus Christ! Renounce the world and the flesh: be not the disciples and the servants of human masters; do not become great in your own eyes; but may you belong to Jesus Christ alone and entirely; confess Christ by your lives in the midst of this people, and at some future day, as lights of the Church in the midst of the world.

But shall we, my brethren, be content with individual confessions?   In all the works of God we find union and harmony, and we see, too, what great things are effected by these.   On our mountains, a drop of water fallen from a glacier mingles with another drop of water; rivulets unite with rivulets, torrents unite with torrents; and from all these collected waters proceed those beautiful rivers, which hasten far away to carry life and fertility to the plains.   At the dawn of creation, when, " all the sons of God shouted for joy," one world, at the Lord's command, approached another world, and " the morning stars sang together," and the heavens began that harmonious march of the universe which fills the soul with wonder and adoration. When the beloved disciple was ravished in spirit, and beheld a " throne set in heaven, and One sitting on the throne," one voice joined another voice; many angels around the throne united their songs; and there were " ten thousand times ten thousand," and " every creature which is in heaven, and on the earth, and under the earth, and such as are in the sea, and all that are in them," replied; and these united voices were " as the voice of many waters, and as the voice of a great thun-

[1] The students of the Theological Seminary.

der." Let us also, O ransomed of the Lord ! do likewise; let the voices of all here below, strangers, elect, and scattered throughout the world, unite in holy enthusiasm and courage to ascribe glory to Jesus Christ. Let us leave behind us our petty individualities ; let us not be satisfied with our feeble voices dispersed here and there; let there be on earth, also, a great concert, a magnificent harmony, to celebrate the praises of Him who hath bought us with his blood. Let the world, which hitherto has passed by without attending to Jesus Christ, be constrained to listen; and let this voice of the Church become so loud that "all the kindreds of the earth shall worship before the Lord."

Ah ! if my voice could sound beyond this house ! if it could be heard in the vast churches of this city, in which the faithful voices of our fathers once echoed ; if, reaching still farther, it could speak to the church of Vaud, to the church of France, to the universal church of the Lord, and could say to that great assembly, Let us confess the Lord ; for "Worthy is the Lamb that was slain, to receive power, and riches, and wisdom, and strength, and honour, and glory, and blessing."

Lord ! I cannot do it, and my feeble voice must remain within this humble house of prayer; but thou canst ! Speak then, Lord! and let thy servants every where hear ! Dispel delusions; tear away every vail; break with thy mighty hand every fetter which binds the noble minds whom thou callest to freedom; suffer none of thy servants to " confer with flesh and blood;" grant that every where they may be deaf to the thousand voices of the world that might induce them to keep silence, and may they hearken to thy voice which calls them to confess thee. The days are hastening on; the times are ripening for the manifestation of thy salvation ; call to thy church ; let every soul hear thine imposing voice before the approaching solemn day arrives, when, appearing seated on the clouds, thou wilt say of many, "O Father ! they have been ashamed of me, and now I am ashamed of them." Oh ! may we not have to endure that opprobrium, and rather let us all be of those to whom thou wilt say in the day of thy glory, " I have seen thy trials, I have seen thy humiliation, I have seen thy faithfulness, thy courage, the confession which thou didst make of my name ! Now I reveal them before the assembled universe ! Faithful servant ! enter thou into the joy of thy Lord !" Amen.

DISCOURSE IX.[1]

THE CONFESSION OF THE NAME OF CHRIST IN THE SIXTEENTH AND NINETEENTH CENTURIES.

" Whosoever will confess me before men, him will I confess also before my Father which is in heaven."—MATTHEW, x, 32.

THREE centuries have passed away since the princes of Germany, assembled at the Imperial Diet in the town of Augsburg, publicly and solemnly confessed Jesus Christ and his word in the presence of the emperor, of the princes who still remained under the rule of Rome, and of the ambassadors of Rome itself; and not only before Germany, but as it were before the whole world. That day is yet, and will be to the end of time, one of the brightest epochs in the history of Christianity. And at this time all the evangelical churches of Germany, as well as those of other countries, responding to the appeal of their princes and their pastors, commemorate with thanksgivings and songs of joy the third jubilee of that glorious day. In the words of an august personage, convoking the people whom he governs, " May the festival commemorative of the proclamation of that testimony of the faith of Christians, which is still and will ever be as true as it was three centuries ago, and in the spirit of which I heartily concur, contribute to strengthen and revive the true faith in the evangelical church, to awaken in all its members a unity of spirit, real piety, and Christian charity and tolerance." [2]

Will you not also, Protestant Christians of France, remember that day of confession of the name of Jesus? Have you not shared in its blessings? Were you not born, and do you

---

[1] This discourse was delivered on June 27, 1830, at *St. Quentin* (France), that day being the Third Centennial celebration of the Confession of the Protestant States of Germany at Augsburg. It was afterward repeated by request at Brussels.

[2] Ordinance of his Majesty the King of Prussia, May 4, 1830.

not dwell and fight beneath that spotless banner of the Gospel of Christ, which those noble men on that memorable day held up in the view of their enemies? Was it not your faith that those illustrious princes and divines confessed then before the universe? And do you not march on with flying colours to that holy war in which they fought with the powerful weapons of the word of God? But, alas! it is not so; we do not march as they marched! "Our hands hang down and our knees are feeble," and that heroic courage which in those bright days was the glory of the church of Christ seems to have forsaken it now. And this is the very reason why we ought to commemorate this day; to the end that, seeing we are surrounded by a cloud of those illustrious witnesses for the truth, those magnanimous confessors of the Cross of Jesus, who "through faith subdued kingdoms and waxed valiant in fight," we also may "fight the good fight of faith." "Standing fast in one spirit," they strove in the great day "with one mind for the faith of the Gospel, in nothing terrified by adversaries." Disciples of Christ, you are called upon to do likewise. The days in which you live are no less remarkable than those in which they lived, and the same courage is needed. Must we remind you, my dear hearers, that these battles are not fought with carnal weapons, and to shed human blood? Need we say that they are not to be performed in a spirit of violence or hatred? We need not say this; the examples which we will lay before you to-day might, were it necessary, give you sufficient knowledge on this subject. As the events which the evangelical church celebrates on this day are not so extensively known as they ought to be, we design to recall them to your minds, and then to draw some consequences from them. It is not our habit to deliver historical discourses. But is not every thing which can edify appropriate for the Christian pulpit? and have we not on this point numerous illustrious precedents? Was not the discourse of Stephen the protomartyr purely historical? Were not most of St. Paul's discourses, as recorded in the book of Acts, purely historical? We will not then reject as improper that which the Holy Spirit has thought proper. "These things," we are told by the word of God, "were for our example."

Spirit of God! who didst in former times inspire the heroes of the faith, do thou kindle the same flame within our hearts! Amen.

The emperor Charles V, who unquestionably swayed the sceptre over a kingdom more extensive than that of any other prince, and who, as the sovereign of portions of Europe, America, and other quarters of the globe, could boast, as it has been said, that "the sun never set on his empire," having, in the year 1530 (just three centuries ago), overcome his enemies, resolved to turn his attention to the religious Reformation which was then going on in Germany, and to endeavour to suppress what was termed a heresy. He was solemnly crowned on his birth-day, February 24, by the Romish pontiff; and these two personages remained together for some time in the same palace. The emperor promised the pope that he would exterminate Protestantism. It would even appear that he pledged himself to use violence and persecution for the purpose of accomplishing his object. At all events, he was asked to do so. When this news arrived in Germany, many advised the evangelical princes to go to the Alps and meet Charles, sword in hand, and prevent him from entering Germany until he granted them entire religious liberty. But this was a worldly proposition, and the great Reformer Luther, whom some would fain represent as being a man of violent temper, silenced those rash counsellors. "The weapons of our warfare are not carnal, but mighty through God."

But the emperor decided that it was wiser to begin by using other means than compulsion; he therefore convoked an Imperial Diet at Augsburg, and invited all the princes and representatives of states in the empire to attend it. Many persons, remembering the violence of the enemies of the truth, which broke out against the Reformers in the Council of Constance, entreated the Elector of Saxony, who was the leader of Protestantism, not to appear in person at Augsburg. But the Elector decided to accept the emperor's invitation; he wished to confess Christ in his presence; for that purpose he requested Luther, Jonas, Pomeranus, and Melancthon, four of his most distinguished theologians, to draw up a confession of faith of the Evangelical church; and having commanded that fer-

vent prayers that the Lord might grant him success should
be offered up every where throughout his states, he set out on
April 3rd for Augsburg.

A great number of princes, nobles, counsellors, and theologians accompanied the elector. The same spirit animated them
in their solemn journey, during which Luther preached frequently, kindling faith in those noble champions of the Gospel
by his discourses. At Weimar they all partook of the Lord's
Supper; at Coburg the elector parted with the Reformer, whom
he commanded to abide there secretly, while the Diet was in
session. He remained in a castle on the mountain, the upper
apartments of which he occupied; twelve knights guarded his
room day and night; but the servant of Christ was under safer
guardianship—that of the God whom he praised in a beautiful
hymn which he composed at that time, and which begins with
these words :

" A mighty fortress is our God !"

The elector arrived at Augsburg before any of the other of
the princes, to the great surprise of those who had supposed
that fear would have kept him back. But soon a multitude of
electors, princes, deputies, bishops, and a great number of
soldiers of every grade, entered the city, and Augsburg was
filled with the pomp and the splendour of the world. " Why
do the heathen rage, and the people imagine a vain thing ?
The kings of the earth set themselves, and the rulers take
counsel together, against the Lord, and against his Anointed."

In the midst of the tumult that surrounded them, the zeal
of the ministers of the word who accompanied the Protestant
princes did not grow cold; they preached the Gospel, and boldly
proclaimed the whole counsel of God. Many were alarmed and
displeased; the preaching produced the effect which the word
of God always produces when it is first preached in a place.
" The word of God is making a noise," said Luther. " It is
a hard saying; who can hear it ?" Some complained of their
discourses, although they simply preached the truth, without
any controversy. These wrote to the emperor, who was stay-
ing at a short distance from Augsburg; he sent word that he
thought it best that the ministers should cease to preach until
a decision had been made with regard to matters of doctrine.

The elector asked Luther's advice on the subject, and the Reformer gave another instance of his moderation: he advised that the preaching should cease if the emperor persisted in requiring it; "for," he said, "the emperor ought to be master in his own city." But the elector could not receive Luther's counsel. "To forbid the preaching of the word," he wrote, in answer to the command of Charles, "is to act in opposition to the conscience; especially in the present time, when we need constantly to seek consolation and help from the word of God." "Unless thy law had been my delights, I should then have perished in mine affliction." Thus spake another prince, David, the prophet-king.

While Melancthon, the friend of Luther, assisted by other theologians, was constantly engaged at Augsburg in drawing up the Confession which was to be presented to the Diet by the Protestant princes, Luther was suffering great distress at Coburg, both in body and in mind; and he had already selected a spot for the burial of his body in his *desert*, as he called it. The elector sent him the assistance necessary for the restoration of his health, and wrote him a very affectionate letter. Luther answered it in a strain well fitted to console that Christian prince in the midst of the fearful struggle with the enemies of the Gospel in which he was engaged. "It is really without cause," said he, "that you have deigned to be concerned about me. These weeks have passed by so rapidly that they scarcely seem like three days. But your grace is now in a painful and dangerous situation. O may our good Father in heaven assist you, to the end that your heart may remain stedfast and patient, relying on his mercy, which has been so richly manifested unto you. It is only for the love of God that you are called to suffer so much danger and anxiety, since all these princes and these furious enemies can find no fault in you save that you love the pure and living word of God; and since they acknowledge that in other respects you are an amiable, blameless, pious, and faithful prince. And it is certainly a great proof of the love of God toward you, that he not only gives you his holy word abundantly, but also makes you worthy of enduring so much hatred and reproach for its sake. It is this that affords much joy and consolation to the conscience; for to

have God for one's Friend is a greater consolation than to enjoy the friendship of the whole universe besides."

Strengthened by these words, the elector John awaited the
arrival of the emperor, who was delaying his journey. At
length, the 15th of June having come, all was ready for his
solemn entrance. Great pomp was displayed, probably for the
purpose of giving the Protestant princes a high opinion of the
power and glory of the emperor. The electors, the princes,
and an immense crowd went out to meet him. When they had
come within fifty paces of the emperor, they all dismounted.
The pope's legate took this opportunity to pronounce the papal
blessing; the emperor and the multitude listened on their
knees: but the elector and all the evangelical princes remained
standing; thus giving evidence of their belief and their firmness. The procession then continued its march. When it had
reached the bishop's palace, where the emperor was to stay, all
were invited to enter, with the exception of the noble elector of
Saxony and his generous brothers in the faith. They joyfully
bore this contempt for the sake of the cause of Christ, and soon
gave another proof of their undaunted courage; for King
Ferdinand, the brother of Charles, having, in the presence and
name of the emperor, demanded of them to command the cessation of the preaching of the word of God, as well as to attend
the procession of the holy Sacrament, which was to take place
on the morrow, the margrave of Brandenburg, in the name of
the others, exclaimed, " Rather will I kneel before your majesty
and sacrifice my head than cease to confess my God and his
Gospel !" The emperor having, on the evening of the same day,
sent a deputation to repeat this request, the margrave went to
him, with the other princes, at six o'clock on the following
morning, and said to him, " We are unwilling to sanction by
our presence such impious human superstitions, which are opposed to the word of God and to the commands of Christ ! On
the contrary, we all unanimously declare that we wish to see
those human doctrines abolished from the Church, and the
members of Christ's body who are still undefiled protected from
that deadly poison. Let not your majesty be offended if I
resist his requests, for it is written that it is better to obey God
than man. Wherefore I am ready, in confessing the doctrine

which I know to be the voice of the Son of God, the unchangeable and eternal truth, to risk any danger, and even death itself, with which, as I learn, those who confess the truth are
threatened." Magnanimous courage! admirable renunciation
of self and of the world! may our hearts imitate this example.
"He that loveth his life shall lose it," saith Jesus; "and he
that hateth his life in this world shall keep it unto life eternal."

The procession took place, and none of the Evangelical
princes attended it.

The princes showed the same firmness with regard to the
preaching of the Gospel. "The word of God," said they, " is
not to be fettered; to bind and restrict it is a sin against the
Holy Ghost. Besides," added these magnanimous men, " as
we are mere sinful beings, we need the preaching of that Divine word to console our consciences. We can not do without
the daily nourishment of the body; much less can we endure
privation of the word of God; for 'man shall not live by bread
alone, but by every word that proceedeth out of the mouth of
God.' "

Upon this, Charles V sent a herald through the city to proclaim with a trumpet that no minister would be suffered to
preach any more without special permission from the emperor.
" Thus;" as the elector of Saxony wrote to Luther, " our Lord
God is commanded to be silent at the Imperial Diet of Augsburg!" Happy is the Church when all, from the greatest to
the least, know the value of the pure and faithful preaching of
the Gospel of Christ! " More to be desired is it than gold,
yea, than much fine gold; sweeter also than honey and the
honey-comb."

At length, on the 20th of June, the Diet was solemnly opened. The introductory speech displayed the hostile intentions
of Charles. The war was declared. It was necessary to "be
strong in the Lord, and in the power of his might, to be able
to withstand in the evil day, and having done all, to stand."
On leaving the assembly, the elector of Saxony invited all the
princes, his brothers in the faith, to meet at his lodgings, and
there he exhorted them to stand boldly in the cause, which was
the cause of God, and faith in Jesus Christ. On the following
day, early in the morning, he commanded all his counsellors

and servants to withdraw; and the pious prince spent the whole day in his chamber, seeking consolation and courage in reading the Psalms of David, and beseeching God to grant him his assistance and his grace, that the glory of his gospel might be made manifest. The Protestants obtained permission to read their Confession in public on the 24th of June; but on that day other business engaged the attention of the Diet. They were required to give their Confession in writing; but they insisted on reading it in the presence of the assembly. The emperor granted their request; and all impatiently awaited the morrow, which, it seemed, was to decide the fate of the invincible truth.

Meanwhile Luther, at Coburg, was putting on the whole armour of God; he was constantly singing the praises of the Lord and reading his word, full of courage, hope, and joy. Not a day passed by in which he did not spend at least three hours in prayer. He addressed God as his Father; so we are informed by his servant. One day he was heard praying in his closet in these words: "I know that thou art our merciful God and Father; wherefore I am certain that thou wilt destroy the persecutors of thy children. If thou dost not, the danger concerns thee as well as us. The whole matter is in thy hands; we have done our duty; wherefore, O holy Father, thou wilt protect us."

"Were I in the situation of our friends," he once said to his faithful servant,[1] "I would have answered our adversaries, 'If your emperor can not consent to have the empire divided, our Emperor, the Lord, can not consent to have the name of God blasphemed. So you may boast of your emperor, and we will boast of ours. We shall see who will gain the victory!'"

The wise, gentle, and timid Melancthon, at Augsburg, did not feel the same confidence that Luther felt; he was full of fear and anguish. His friend Camerarius frequently saw him shed bitter tears. Luther, full of assurance, endeavoured to inspire his friends at Augsburg with the same courage. He wrote to Jonas from his *desert* (for thus he dated his letters written from Coburg): "It is philosophy, and nothing else, that troubles Philip; for our cause is in the hands of One who

[1] Veit Dieterich.

can say with truth, 'No man shall pluck them out of my hand.' I do not wish that it were in our hands. I have had many affairs in my own hands, and none of them have been successful; but all those which I intrusted to him have succeeded perfectly; for it is true that the Lord is our Refuge and our Strength. Whom has he ever forsaken that trusted in him? as it is written, 'Thou, Lord, hast not forsaken them that seek thee.' Let us, then, bid defiance to our adversaries, and let us be bold in the Lord Jesus; for, 'because he liveth, we shall live also,' even in death; and he will preserve the wife and the children of the man who shall have confessed his name at the cost of his life. Since he reigns, 'we shall also reign with him;' even now already we reign with him! Oh! if my presence was required at Augsburg, how soon, by the grace of Christ, would I be there! God be with you!"

He afterward wrote to Melancthon: "Grace be unto you, and peace, in Christ. In *Christ*, I say, and not in the world. Amen! Why art thou constantly troubled? If our cause be not just, let us abandon it; but if it be just, why should we make God a liar when he tells us to be contented, and 'of good cheer!' 'Cast thy burden upon the Lord,' he says. And again: 'The Lord is nigh unto them that are of a broken heart.' You are concerned about the issue of this matter, because you can not conceive what it will be. But I tell you that if I could guess that issue, I would not meddle with it, and still less would I be willing to have undertaken the affair. God has put our cause in a place which you will not find by means of your rhetoric or your philosophy. That place is called FAITH; and there are all those things which we can neither see nor understand. The man who endeavours, as you are doing, to see and understand these things, is rewarded by tears and anguish of heart.

"If Christ be not with us, where in the universe shall we find him? If we are not the Church, where is the Church? Is it the Duke,[1] or Rome, or the Turk and his fellows? If we have not the word of God, who has it? And, 'if God be for us, who can be against us!' If we fall, Christ falls with us, and Christ is the Lord of the earth! Christ has said, 'Be

[1] Of Bavaria.

of good cheer, I have overcome the world;' and I know that
this is true.   And why then should we fear the world when it
is overcome as though it were the conqueror?   O precious
word! many would go on their knees to Rome or Jerusalem
to get it; and we, because we have it, and can at all times
make use of it, esteem it lightly!   This is wrong.   I know
that it proceeds from the weakness of our faith.   Let us then
pray with the apostles, 'Lord, increase our faith!'"   "Though
a host should encamp against me, my heart shall not fear."
"No weapon that is formed against thee shall prosper, saith
the Lord."

The 25th of June, 1530, that day of triumph for the Church,
came at last.   At three o'clock in the afternoon, three centuries ago, to-day, all the electors and representatives of states
in the empire assembled at the palace in which the emperor
was residing, and in the chapel of which the Confession was to
be read, to avoid the concourse of the people.   The emperor
commanded that the princes and electors alone should be admitted; but the court of the palace was soon filled by a great multitude.   The two chancellors of the elector of Saxony, strengthened by the arm of the Lord which was stretched above them,
advanced into the middle of the chapel, holding in their hands
the *Confession*, one copy of which was written in Latin and the
other in German.   The elector expressed a wish that, since
they were in Germany, the emperor would permit the confession
to be read in German.   To this he consented.   Then one of
the chancellors delivered a short discourse in the name of the
Protestant states; after which the other began to read the
Confession in a loud voice, so that the immense crowd assembled
in the court of the palace could hear every word.   This occupied two hours.   It was listened to with the deepest silence,
and produced a most powerful impression.   No one had expected to hear such things.   We will not repeat this Confession
to you, my hearers; but there are a few principal points which
are worthy of being called to mind in these days. in which
many have forgotten "the faith which was once delivered unto
the saints."

"We confess and teach," said the Evangelical princes of
Germany in the presence of that assembly of kings who listened

attentively, "that there is but one God, and that in that only Being there are three Persons, God the Father, God the Son, and God the Holy Ghost, a Divine and eternal Essence, of infinite power, wisdom, and goodness, the Creator and Preserver of all things visible and invisible.

" We confess and teach, that since Adam's fall all men are naturally born in sin; that is, from their mother's womb they are full of evil lusts and inclinations, and can by nature possess no true piety, no real love to God, no sincere faith in God. We teach, that this innate sin is real sin, which condemns unalterably and punishes with eternal death all those who are not regenerated by baptism and the Holy Ghost.

. " We confess and teach, that God the Son became man; that he intimately united the two natures, human and divine, in one person, namely, Christ, who is true man and true God, and who, being really born, crucified, dead and buried, was a sacrifice, not only for the inborn sins of man, but likewise for all other sins, and thus appeased the wrath of God.

" We confess and teach, that Christ, having descended into hell, arose from the dead on the third day, ascended into heaven, sat down on the right hand of God, and reigns and rules eternally over all creatures; that he sanctifies by his Holy Spirit all who believe on him; that he purifies, strengthens, and consoles them; that he gives them life and all kinds of mercies and blessings, and protects and defends them against sin and the Devil.

" We confess and teach, that, since men are born in sin, do not fulfil the law of God, and can not by nature love God, we can not deserve the forgiveness of our sins by our works or by any mode of satisfaction, and are not justified before God on account of our works, but by the love of Christ, through grace, by means of faith, in consequence of which our conscience is consoled by the promises of Christ, and believes that remission of sins is truly acquired for it; that God is favourable to us and gives us eternal life through Christ, who, by his death, has reconciled us unto God.

We confess and teach, that such faith must bear good fruits and produce good works; that we ought to perform all the good works which God has required for the love of God, but without trusting in them to be justified; for when we shall have done all those things which are commanded us, we shall still have to say, ' We are unprofitable servants.'

" This," added the chancellor of Saxony, before proceeding to enumerate the abuses of the church of Rome, "is the summary of the doctrine preached in our churches for the instruction and consolation of consciences, as well as for the sanctification of believers.[1]

Having concluded the reading of this memorable document, the electoral chancellor approached the imperial secretary to hand to him the two copies of the Confession. But the emperor, who had not lost sight of them, reached forth his hand and took them himself. Then the representatives of the Protestant states thanked Charles, Ferdinand, and all the other princes for their attention. Thus a solemn act was ended. The adversaries, and several bishops even, were struck with the admirable exposition of the Christian faith which they had just heard; and who knows but that the impression made by it upon Charles may have been revived in the convent of St. Just, and have afforded him ineffable consolation on his dying bed!

Copies of the Confession were soon sent to all the courts of Europe, and the knowledge of the Evangelical Faith was thus spread with the seed of the truth to the most distant countries. As for the heroes of the faith who so boldly had just confessed Christ and him crucified, they were animated by a new sentiment, which from that memorable hour filled their hearts. They had confessed Christ before men; and their hearts felt that he would confess them also before his Father which is in heaven. "The Spirit of glory and of God rested upon them!" They had overcome; they had put to flight all the armies of the enemy; there was "everlasting joy upon their heads." From that day the destiny of the Evangelical faith was insured, and the Lord again declared to it: "The gates of hell shall not prevail against thee."

Such was the confession of the name of Christ in the sixteenth century. Shall not that glorious name be confessed in

---

[1] See the same truths proclaimed in the Confession of Faith of the Reformed Churches of France, articles 1, 6, 9, 10, 11, 13—18, 22.

the nineteenth with the same courage and fidelity?   O, my brethren! shall the adversaries of the name of Jesus, who could not prevail against it in that day, conquer in our times, and shall the voices of Christians be silenced now?   That very voice of the Son of God, which was heard by the heroes of the Faith who have carried off the palms of victory by their faithfulness and courage during three centuries, still addresses his people in our days, saying, "Whosoever shall confess me before men, him will I confess also before my Father which is in heaven."

But cannot all men confess the name of Jesus Christ in our days?   Those who confess him must first know him; and all do not know him.   The day which we commemorate shows us two distinct classes of men; and Jesus, in the text of this discourse, declares that there are those who confess him, and others who deny him.   There is, then, a great distinction, a great separation among men; this is the first truth derived from the picture which we have laid before your eyes.   This separation, which existed in the times of the apostles, existed also in the days of the Reformation, when those were seen, on the one hand, who made that noble profession of the truth; and, on the other, those who desired to destroy it; and it exists now also.   We do not now allude to the distinction which various external communities establish, "for God is no respecter of persons;" but we speak of that distinction which is found in every nation, in every external denomination, between those who confess and those who reject that unchangeable truth which the apostles and reformers professed.   It is an axiom, the truth of which has always been acknowledged, and which every form of philosophy, even, has proclaimed, that as there is a distinction between good and evil, so there must also necessarily be, on earth, a distinction between the good and the evil, the just and the unjust, the saint and the sinner; or, as the word of God forcibly says, "the children of God and the children of the Devil."   Christianity only separates these two classes, and declares that this classification exists in the eyes of God, and that all men will receive their recompense in accordance with it.   "Whosoever shall confess me, him will I confess; whosoever shall deny me, him will I deny." And the Saviour of the world himself, who is *the Truth*, says, with regard to the relative extent of each of these classes, of whom both Scripture and the event which we commemorate to-day remind us: "Enter ye in at the strait gate; for wide is the gate, and broad is the way, that leadeth to destruction, and many there be which go in thereat : because strait is the gate, and narrow is the way, which leadeth unto life, and few there be that find it." These words were true three centuries ago in the town of Augsburg; and they are still true in every part of the world. Thus, if there be now, as there was in the days of the apostles and reformers, a doctrine which is rejected in the world, in society, among the lovers of riches, of glory, and of the pleasures of the age; a doctrine which men refuse to embrace, which they deem extraordinary, which is left to a small number of persons, it is probably a proof that that doctrine is the truth. Thus, if there is a mode of life which is thought severe, exaggerated, contrary to the customs and tastes of a great many people, which none of them will receive, and which is adopted by a small minority, it is probably a proof that that course of life is the true one. Thus, if there is a form of Christianity against which men defend themselves, which is rejected by all who are wise in their own conceit, and who seek the glory of men and not the glory of God, it is to be presumed that that form is in harmony with the Gospel. And if I am on the side of the multitude, if I do as the world does, if I think as the world thinks, if I walk as the world walks, I have reason to tremble; for it is a proof that I am in the broad way leading to destruction. "There are few that be saved," says an inspired writer. "One of a city, and two of a family," says another. O my soul! thou art either with God, or far from him! Thou art either converted, or thou art not! Thou dost either confess Christ, or deny him! Thou hast entered into one of those ways; which is it? Is it the narrow way of life? Is it the broad way of death? Dost thou confess Christ, or deny him? O my soul! this is worthy of thine attention! Examine, prove, search, and find out distinctly what thou art! "Examine yourselves, whether ye be in the faith."

My dear hearer, you whose conscience tells you now, "Thou

dost not confess Christ! thou dost not know him! thou art still in the broad way! why will you not now be saved? Why will you not *to-day* turn into that way of life in which are the "fellow-citizens with the saints," and the confessors of Jesus Christ? There is but one thing that deters you: it is your want of faith in the powerful and saving name of Jesus. So long as you do not believe in that name, your sins will keep you away from God, and it is impossible for you to confess a name of the glory of which you are ignorant. But believe in that word, that eternal word, in comparison with which all is darkness and error, and which says to you, "Christ, being the brightness of the glory (of God) and the express image of his person, and upholding all things by the word of his power, *when he had by himself purged our sins*, sat down on the right hand of the Majesty on high." Understand what the word of God here declares to you. Christ, not by an angel, or by any of the heavenly principalities which he had created, but *by himself, purged the sins* of all who believe on him; that is, he purified them, redeemed them, separated them, delivered them from all their sins, and made them as pure as though they had never committed any. At the very moment when Christ died on the cross, having taken upon himself the sins of all, all the sins of his people, of all ages and nations, were blotted out. Can you suppose that Christ would have taken the trouble *of himself to purge the sins* of his people if a part of that stain which defiles them and hinders them from seeing God was still to remain? If, to use a comparison which all will understand, when a mother has washed the body of her child in pure water, and has said to it, Go, thou art clean, the child obeys, but to make it certain, goes, as the Scripture says, "and beholds his natural face in a glass," he thereby insults his mother by supposing it possible for her to lie. And so Christ himself, the Saviour-God, says to the man who believes on him, "Go, thou art clean; I have by myself purged thy sins; I have taken them all away; 'he that believeth on the Son hath everlasting life.'" And shall not we believe that eternal word of truth? Shall we suppose that Christ can lie? My brother, do you truly believe that Jesus is the Saviour? do you "believe him in your heart, and confess him with your

mouth?" If you do, I declare unto you, in the name of the
Eternal Word, "You are clean." All your sins are forgiven.
You have found grace with the everlasting God. "There is
now no condemnation unto you." "You were in time past
not a people, but are now the people of God; which had not
obtained mercy, but now have obtained mercy." Hearken,
then, to the voice of the Lord: He calls on you to forsake the
standard of error, and follow the standard of truth. Leave
the camp of its enemies; enter into the camp of its friends and
its children. Unite with its prophets, with its apostles, with
those glorious princes and teachers who once confessed its
name so gloriously. There is not one of you but can do it,
and that immediately; the door is open now; it is open to all.
O, why prefer the stained and worthless banners of unrighteousness and infidelity to the pure and immortal standard of
Christ? Behold, "the fashion of this world passeth away;"
already its greatness trembles, and must soon be destroyed.
What will remain for you? "Come out from among them,
and be ye separate, saith the Lord, and touch not the unclean
thing; and I will receive you, and will be a Father unto you,
and ye shall be my sons and daughters, saith the Lord Almighty."

But if you have known Jesus Christ, my beloved brethren,
if your names have been enrolled in the army of the ever-living
God, what a lesson the events of this day give you! Soldiers
of Christ, who fight under the eternal banner, who have known
that he is the Saviour: children of God, "strangers," as an
apostle calls you, "scattered" throughout the world: hear what
was said by a man who was poor and despised, and who "had
not where to lay his head," but whom, by the majesty and authority of his language, you will recognize as "your Lord and
your God:" "Whosoever shall confess me before men, him will
I confess also before my Father which is in heaven."

The confession of the name of Christ is perhaps even more
necessary and more difficult in our days than it was in those of
the Reformers. Then there was only one adversary—fanaticism, or superstition; but God, whose will it is that all the
enemies of the Church should display themselves, so that its
victory may be the greater, has suffered a new adversary, no

less formidable, to rise out of the ages which followed those glorious days, namely, materialism, or infidelity. Its fatal atmosphere spreads every where, to every height, in the low places of the earth, in the institutions of learning, in the work-shop in the country, in the bosom of the family, and has mingled its poison even with the fountains from which the nations are accustomed to draw life. Satan displays in our days the whole of his imposing army. With fanaticism on his left, and infidelity on his right, he attempts to pass over all the high places of the earth, and establish an uncontested empire over the whole world. Who will face him if you do not, O scattered children of God, who have the promise of your Head: "The God of peace shall bruise Satan under your feet shortly!" Therefore we call you, at this celebration of a great victory, to one still more glorious. "Be of good courage," we say to you, as the captain of the armies of Israel once said, on the day of a great battle against the children of Ammon; "and let us play the men for our people, and for the cities of our God; and the Lord do that which seemeth him good!"

Are not the events which are taking place around you suitable to arouse your courage? If the enemy of God increases his forces, when did Christ, the Head of the church, the Captain of your salvation, ever raise his standard higher? The soldiers of the adversary were shouting tumultuously, " Crush them! crush them!" but they themselves were crushed by the masses which they had raised to destroy the Being against whom they fought, and " the Lion of the Tribe of Judah" has lain down triumphant on their ruins. Do you not see many countries where, a few years ago, there was not a single voice to confess the name of Jesus Christ, that are now filled with his glory? " There shall be a handful of corn in the earth upon the top of the mountains; the fruit thereof shall shake like Lebanon: and they of the city shall flourish like grass of the earth." The distant isles awake and stretch out their arms to you; a sound of life pervades the world, as though a man were gathering his followers together, and preparing them for the battle. " The people shall be willing in the day of his power, in the beauties of holiness from the womb of the morning: the Lord has the dew of the youth."

8

K

Let us fight, therefore, O children of God! and let us fight
by the confession of the name of Jesus. Beloved brethren!
having been saved by Jesus, it is our duty, as well as our great
joy and glory, to be faithful to him and to confess him openly
before men. It is true that you are not called to make as
solemn a confession as that on which we have been meditating
to-day; perhaps the trumpet does not call you to a pitched
battle; but each of you must confess the Lord in the peculiar
situation in which God has placed him. There is an essential
difference between the two epochs which we are contemplating.
At the epoch of the Reformation, a few great names appear,
which seem alone to fill the whole battle-field. In our days,
the armies of the living God have no head on earth; all names
are lost in a blessed obscurity. One Captain arises in our
midst: it is Jesus Christ. O my brethren, let us feel how great
is the responsibility under which this fact places us! You can
not now rely on a few illustrious chiefs; each must fight at his
post, as though the victory depended on him alone. It is not,
perhaps, by great battles, but by a thousand struggles of individuals, that the King of Zion will establish his kingdom.
To each of you is intrusted a part of its destiny. " God hath
chosen the foolish things of the world to confound the wise;
and God hath chosen the weak things of the world to confound the things which are mighty; and base things of the
world, and things which are despised, hath God chosen, yea,
and things which are not, to bring to nought things that
are: that no flesh should glory in his presence." If Christ has
placed you in cottages, confess him in cottages. If he has
placed you in the houses of the rich men of the earth, confess
him in the midst of abundance and prosperity. If he has
placed you in the sanctuary, speak boldly there. If he has
placed you in the seat of the powerful, confess him at the very
steps of the throne, as the princes of the earth once did in the
palace of the king. Do not neglect a single occasion to confess Jesus faithfully in the midst of your families, in your conversation, in your vocation: " Sanctify the Lord in your hearts:
and be ready always to give an answer to every man that
asketh you a reason of the hope that is in you, with meekness
and fear." This is all that Christ requires of you in fighting

for him. This is your armour in this glorious battle. His name alone, without any human aid, gains wonderful victories; his name alone overthrows the kingdom of darkness, and drives the powers of darkness away. "God hath given him a name which is above every name: that at the name of Jesus every knee should bow, of things in heaven, and things in earth, and things under the earth."

Disciples of Christ! the truths by means of which you ought to obtain the victory over the world, and bring many souls captive to God the Saviour, are the same as those which those apostles, and those Reformers and illustrious princes, confessed, who were once, as it were, the arm of the Lord. Men change, but "Jesus Christ is the same yesterday, to-day, and forever." That Christ whom Paul, Peter, and John confessed, whom Luther, Calvin, and Beza confessed, that Christ *you* must proclaim. You must say, as they said, "We are by nature sinners and condemned." You must say, as they said, "We are saved through grace alone, by Christ through faith. You must say, as they said, "We must become new creatures before we can see the kingdom of God." Give your testimony with simplicity and gentleness to all the truths contained in the word of God, which is the testimony of God himself; this is confessing Jesus Christ. It is no doctrine invented yesterday, but the eternal truth, that you are to confess. Human systems of doctrine have always been changing; and at present no two of them agree; but the truth of God is always the same. You may be certain that Christ will be to the world, as he was in the days of the Gospel and of the Reformation, "an unknown God." Some will say, "These are old and superannuated doctrines;" others will say, "These are strange novelties!" Yes, the truth which you proclaim is always old, for it existed in the counsel of God before the creation of the world. Yes, that truth is always novel, for every time it is manifested in the heart of the sinner, he begins to see things of which he had no conception. Be not disturbed by vain clamour. Ever old and ever new, that truth has already saved and renewed the world twice; it has given proof of its authenticity. Let us stand firm; it will yet a third time save it, and that, we trust, forever. "I know that my Redeemer liveth, and that he shall stand at the latter day upon the earth."

Go on, therefore, soldiers of the Lord of hosts, and fight manfully. In these days we need resolution, strength, devotion, and entire self-renunciation; for if the weapons which the world uses are more subtle than they were in the days of the apostles and the Reformers, they are the more to be feared. The coldness and contempt of those who surround us, sometimes of our dearest friends, are flames which scorch our hearts still more grievously than those of the stake of the adversary; and the respect of men, the fear or the love of the world, has made more persons unfaithful than the sword of the executioner has. Therefore be strong, be of good cheer, and fix your eyes on the certain triumph which awaits the cause of God. The Chief whose steps you follow has already overcome all his enemies. "Having spoiled principalities and powers he made a show of them openly, triumphing over them in the cross." The conversion and subjection of the whole world is promised unto him. "I have set my King upon my holy hill of Zion. I will declare the decree," saith the Lord: "The Lord hath said unto me, Thou art my Son; this day have I begotten thee. Ask of me, and I shall give thee the heathen for thine inheritance, and the uttermost parts of the earth for thy possession." Already is the King of the universe preparing all things for the accomplishment of this promise. Already "the Gentiles seek the root of Jesse which stands for an ensign of the people." Already " the Lord sets his hand again the second time to recover the remnant of his people." Already, in the midst of our degenerate churches, the Lord is gathering unto himself from all sides a "willing people;" and "the bright and Morning Star" is rising above the earth, weary of the long and tedious night. Soldiers of Jesus Christ! fight, then, with joy and courage, knowing that the cause in which you are engaged is the cause of God himself, and that He prepared its triumph even before the creation; let your hearts be filled with sacred courage; be energetic and vigorous, for " God hath not given us the spirit of fear, but of *power*;" and " he that overcometh," saith the Lord, " shall inherit all things; but the fearful shall have their part in the second death." Believe and hope, if need be, against hope; for " through faith," says Paul, men have " subdued kingdoms, obtained promises, stopped the mouths of lions."

Nevertheless, my dear brethren, remember that the battle to which you are called is one of eternal charity. It is not by bitter zeal that we shall hasten the kingdom of God. What is to be your object? Is it not to be instruments in the hand of God for the salvation of souls? And how will you save souls unless you love them? Remember how Christ, your Head, in whose steps you ought to walk, appeared on earth. He appeared in love, and it is by love that he overcame the world and saved his people. "When he saw the multitudes" around him, "he was moved with compassion on them, because they were scattered abroad as sheep having no shepherd." "He went about doing good." Oh! if there were more charity in our hearts, how much more glorious would be the victories we would obtain over the prince of this world, and how many more "souls saved from death" we would see! Let us then, my brethren, love souls as God has loved them, and let that love animate and fill our souls! Let us beware of crying peace! peace! when there is no peace. But let us also beware of narrow-mindedness, of bitterness, of disputes, of a spirit of dominion and condemnation. Let us beware of abounding in the sense in which some understand it; but let us abound and superabound in the sense in which the Lord, who is love, understands it; let *truth* be as it were the body of the soldier of Christ, and *love* the robe that covers him; "for God hath not given us the spirit of fear but of *love*."

And finally, let us remember that in the confession of the name of Christ the battle which we are fighting is one of sovereign wisdom. It is not by precipitation or by carnal zeal that we shall hasten the kingdom of the Lord. This is sometimes the idea of those "novices lifted up with pride," of whom the apostle speaks; and for that reason he is unwilling that they should be bishops in the church of the Lord. What an example did our illustrious predecessors give us three centuries ago! Let us be distrustful of ourselves. Whenever we go forward in our own strength, in our own zeal, in our own wisdom, we do injury to God's cause. Let us consult the Lord before we act. Let us often wait; the servant of God should know how to wait. Let us judge with wisdom; let us always choose the noblest end, and use the best and most prudent

means of attaining it. Let us not " fall into the condemnation of the Devil." Let us have " the wisdom that is from
above, which is not earthly, sensual, devilish, but is first pure,
then peaceable, gentle, and easy to be entreated, full of mercy
and good fruits, without partiality and without hypocrisy;"
" for," says the apostle of the Gentiles, " God hath not given
us the spirit of fear, but of *a sound mind.*"

Ministers of the word of God, who are doubly my brethren,
to you and to myself I would now address the word of exhortation : may we all be found faithful in that sacred battle of
eternal love to which we are called ! Brethren, let us pray !
let us pray much for ourselves ; let us pray much for others !
Let us gird ourselves with truth and with charity; let us " hold
fast the form of sound words which we have heard;" let us
courageously proclaim the counsel of God ; let us clearly
and truly announce his whole counsel; " for," as the Scripture says, " if the trumpet give an uncertain sound, who shall
prepare himself to the battle ?" " Watchmen of Zion ! let us
blow the trumpet" when we " see the sword come," lest " the
people be not warned, and the sword take any person from
among them." Shepherds of the flocks of the Lord ! let us
feed them on the fruit of that " plant of renown raised up for
them, that they be no more consumed with hunger in the land."
Let us be " instant in season, out of season, reprove, rebuke,
exhort, with all long-suffering and doctrine." In doing this,
" we shall both save ourselves and them that hear us."

Elders in our churches who are called to labour with us ;
and you, great men of the earth ! follow the example of those
illustrious and generous princes whose faithfulness and glory
you have been recalling to mind ! Learn of them that the
doctrine of the truth is not the exclusive property of the ministers of the sanctuary, but that it is yours as well as ours, and
that you are called as we are to defend it. " Be not ashamed
of the testimony of our Lord;" but, like that assembly of
princes, confess Christ before the world. And as they were
the firm support of the ministers of the word of God, grant us
also on every occasion your affection, your prayers, and your
assistance. Let us unite in defending the doctrine of the
truth which God has entrusted to our churches. Let us esteem

the gift of a faithful minister a great privilege. "We beseech you, brethren," says St. Paul, "to know them which labour among you, and are over you in the Lord, and admonish you: and to esteem them very highly in love for their work's sake. And be at peace among yourselves."

And you, disciples of Christ of every age, of every rank and sex, "walk worthy of the vocation wherewith ye are called!" Confess Christ by your words with all humility and modesty; but especially confess him by your lives. "Comfort the feeble-minded, support the weak, be patient toward all men. "If your enemy hunger, feed him; if he thirst, give him drink. Follow that which is good, both among yourselves and to all men. Rejoice evermore. Show forth the praises of Him who hath called you out of darkness into his marvellous light. Let your light so shine before men that they may see your good works, and glorify your Father which is in heaven."

And soon the promise of the Lord to you will be gloriously fulfilled. He will come; he will appear surrounded by his holy angels. He will say to you, "Come, my brother! come, my sister! fear not! thou didst confess me before men; I will confess thee before my Father which is in heaven. Father! he is mine; he is my ransomed one; he is my friend; he is my brother! He has made a covenant with me by sacrifice. He has confessed me in the midst of the reproach of the world; I will confess him in thy glory. 'Give him a white stone, and write upon him the name of my God.' 'Lift up your heads, O ye gates!' 'Enter thou into the joy of thy Lord!'

DISCOURSE X.[1]

THE STUDY OF THE HISTORY OF CHRISTIANITY, AND ITS USEFULNESS IN THE PRESENT DAY.

GENTLEMEN,—My design is to address you on the History of the Reformation in Germany in the 16th century. Literature, the Sciences, the Arts, Philosophy, the Civil History of Nations, have been successively in this city, and in the midst of you, subjects of instruction by men justly celebrated.

I invite you to a new field—the History of Christianity. I ought, then, to assign the reasons of my choice. I ought to disclose the advantages which I discover in the study of that history at this epoch.

You are, perhaps, at this very time, my justification. That we should believe it possible to fix the attention of men in our day on the history of the Christian religion; that we should command an audience desirous of hearing it: this, gentlemen, is a sign of the times. It proves that men of the world, absorbed until now in the exterior forms, the ornaments, the splendid dress of nations, and of their history, have at length begun to consider what is, what ought to be their heart and life.

And yet, who is it who dares to venture on this new career? Who dares to follow so many men, admirable for genius, profound in knowledge, and skilful in the art of speaking; whose privilege it is to gather every winter in this city, an audience of every age, and of both sexes? Powerful must indeed be the motive which brings forward one who has been called, it is true, to preach the everlasting Gospel, but who has never yet ventured to speak, save in the sanctuary, and with the aid of

[1] Delivered at Geneva, January 2, 1832. This discourse was introductory to a course of lectures on the history of the Reformation and the Reformers in the 16th century.

that holy office which exalts the humblest and animates the most feeble.

This motive is the excellence of that study to which I invite you.

There are, in the life of each man in particular, and of nations in general, three great elements, *politics, letters,* (comprehending, of course, the sciences, the arts, and philosophy,) and *religion.* And it might almost seem as though these three elements have appropriated to themselves the three great modifications of man. The political has engrossed his will and vigour of action. The literary, his intelligence and all the variety of his imaginations and thoughts. The religious, his heart and the energy of his affections. But religion, enthroned, as it were, in the centre, extends over the whole man her sceptre of power.

There are then, according to these elements, three species of the history of man—the *political,* the *literary,* the *religious.* The History of Religion, it cannot be denied, is the least cultivated in our day. How zealously, on the contrary, do not men study political history, believing that they shall discover there, as augurs in the entrails of victims, the prognostics and the key of futurity! How many systems of history, now picturesque, now philosophical, are passing in review before us! How many eminent men, within our own walls, has not their narrative of national events immortalized! With what ardour is not the history of *letters* studied! Who has not read, again and again, the Lyceum of La Harpe, the works of Ginguené, of Schlegel, of De Staël, of Sismondi, and of so many others? Still more is done. Each fashions this history for himself: he approaches these documents, these materials, so formidable in the other two departments; he reads them, again and again, with delight, because they are the master-works of genius. Every educated man examines, compiles, judges, creates an entire history of letters in his own mind.

But as to the History of Christianity, who is engaged in that? Who studies it? A handful of our contemporaries, if indeed so many. And yet I regard it as undoubtedly the most worthy of the attention of men; as that which, in our age, furnishes the most salutary lessons, and in whose prophetic entrails we shall learn correctly what is sought in vain elsewhere.

Perhaps this first sitting will be suitably employed in the endeavour, at the outset, to remove the prejudices entertained in our day against studying the History of Christianity; and I shall afterward establish the usefulness of this history in the present age of the world.

One of the distinctive features of the past age was a spirit of profaneness and mockery. The History of Christianity was affected by it. This imposing edifice, which appeared as the *work of ages*, was assailed with sarcasms, that confounded, in one sentence of condemnation, Catholicism and Christianity, the church of men and the church of God. The structure of men, which might, perhaps, have resisted all serious assaults, soon crumbled with a loud crash, before the light breath of ridicule. But in its fall, it drew along with itself the power which had overturned it. Man passes not in vain through such a crisis. He acquired beneath the ruins a new temper. Baptized in blood, our age could no longer exist in the frivolous atmosphere of its predecessor. The profane La Harpe, in some respects the successor of Voltaire, in the office of President of the anti-Christian League, came forth a Christian from the dungeons of the Revolution, into which he had been cast an unbeliever. The tempest of the Revolution has not, however, entirely swallowed up the impious spirit which roused it. Still does it subsist among us, although a stranger, perhaps, to the characteristic spirit of our age. The History of Christianity is still assailed by ridicule, in which you may perhaps discover, at times, some grains of the wit of Aristophanes and Voltaire. That ridicule must leave some impression on light minds, which may thus, for a season at least, become indifferent to grave and useful studies. It is not expected of me to answer sarcasms: one word suffices. Doubtless, ye scoffers of the age! ye may find on this or that passage in the history of religion, a brilliant quibble or heartless raillery; but there is in Christianity and its annals something beyond your reach. History exhibits it as an angel, bearing from Asia to Europe, from Europe through the whole earth, and among all nations, light and life; destroying evil every where in its course, and leaving

every where the incorruptible seeds of good. Whoever has
met with it has been healed by the salutary influence which it
sheds around. Before such achievements of benevolence, the
weapons of ridicule are impotent. The pointed shafts of the
scoffer never can destroy the work of God. Childish arrogance
only could attempt it; timid weakness only could fear it.

There are men of a graver cast, though not less incredulous,
who attack with other arms the history of religion. What,
they ask, can the History of Christianity reveal? Why do you
thus unadvisedly ransack its annals? What can you derive
from them? Christianity has been injurious to humanity. Man
has been kept by it in swaddling clothes. Its influence on the
civil and political state of nations has been unfavourable. Such
words afflict the soul by the deep ingratitude, the utter blindness
from which they flow. We shall not even mention the blessings
of Christianity in eternity, though these are its chief object,
but shall stand on the very ground to which our adversaries
challenge us. " Take," will we say to them, " a map: lay before us a statistical view of nations. Where is light, and
where darkness? Where is liberty, and where slavery? Do
you not observe the shadows which rest on all the unchristian-
ized states, and the light which covers Christian countries?
What is it that rends the black and polluted vail which hung
so long over the shores of Otaheite, of Eimeo, of Hawaii?
What but Christianity? Take now a pencil; mark by successive
shadows the regions where knowledge, morality, religion prevail the most. You will find but one progress, that of Christianity itself. Wherever the Gospel shines the brightest, there
will you behold most abundantly the chief blessings of humanity.
The United States of America, Great Britain, other Evangelical countries, where the light of the eternal word is shed in all
its purity, will be at the top of the scale; and the transient
shades which lead us from Christian to heathen regions distinguish those portions of the earth where, though Christianity
exists, it is stifled by the human elements commixed with it.
But why have recourse to this geographical *coup d'œil?* The
history of Christianity will itself give the answer to your objections. There will it be seen elevating gradually, from age
to age, the character of nations. Still more, it will there be

discovered that even the corruptions of Christianity, those
against which you contend the most strenuously, have been
useful to humanity, whenever they have retained the least element of the religion of Jesus Christ. There will you behold
those monasteries (the just objects of our reprobation,) becoming, as it were, unconsciously, depositories for the preservation
of so many ancient monuments of letters, amid the deluge of
northern barbarians, and, when the flood had passed, again
sending forth those treasures. But there you will especially
behold that illustrious Reformation, some of whose features I
shall sketch, which delivered the human mind from the chains
which had oppressed it, and which has become to the nations
the dawn of a new day of light, evangelization, and life. In
its history Christianity is every where exhibited as the friend
of human nature.

But you must confess, say other men of the age, that the
history of Christianity reveals to us many things, intrigues,
wars, and the like, which can not but expose it, and diminish
that respect which you demand for it. This we deny. Christianity is a divine work, and, of course, perfectly pure. Whatever has flowed from itself is good. But, in descending from
heaven to earth, from God to man, it has suffered alloy. Christianity in man, and even in the holiest of men, is not Christianity in God, that is to say, in Jesus Christ. Impute not to
God that of which man only is guilty. The water which falls
from heaven is pure, and even the purest of all, for it has been
distilled in the wonderful apparatus of God. And yet scarcely
has it touched the earth, when it is already defiled. How
often, alas! will the hardened heart of man not suffer the life-
giving waters of Christianity to penetrate his bosom? To those
heavenly influences how obstinately is it closed! Man drives
away religion from his heart, and is content to wear it without as a cloak to his sins; and then the vulgar dignify with
the name of Christianity what is thus displayed to their eyes!
History will rend this hypocritical mantle, and will reveal the passions which it hid, and which were the only moving cause in him
who had enveloped himself thus artfully. There will you see,
for example, that those irreligious wars, called religious, sprang
not from Christianity, but from the immediate influence of that

very power of evil which Christianity came to destroy. There you will discover that those maxims of the governors, of the chiefs of the Church, which you justly condemn as disgraceful, were directed *against* the religion itself of Jesus Christ; that this was the victim which they immolated, not the tongue which uttered them. History justifies Christianity, dissipates every cloud and every prejudice, and all the hatred wherewith man has been pleased to surround that sublime and heavenly image, which dwells in the midst of ages, and exhibits it to the admiration of men, in all its simplicity, innocence, beauty, and glory.

If Christianity be innocent of all that is usually laid to its charge, at least, it will be said, the history of the Church is the most barren, the most destitute of life and emotion, and, consequently, the least interesting which can be imagined. Councils and decrees of councils, popes and bulls, metaphysical doctrines, subtile distinctions, scholastic systems, are not these all that it offers? Doubtless it would be strange that the history of this kingdom of God, which its founder said should be a living seed, that would become a great tree, full of sap, and casting all around its beneficent shade; or as leaven which should leaven the whole lump, that is, should communicate life to the world, that such a history should abound in unfruitfulness and subtilty. Not so, for there are two histories. There is, if you please, what we shall call "the History of the Church," that is, of human institutions, forms, doctrines, and actions; and "the History of Christianity," which has brought into the world, and still preserves, a new and divine life; the history of the government of that King who has said, "The words which I speak unto you are spirit and life;" the history of that regenerative influence of Christianity, through which so many individuals and nations have experienced a thorough change in their moral and spiritual condition; the history of that new and second creation, which fashions a people for God upon earth; the history of that invisible church, which is the assembly of the first-born. Most historians, it is true, have hitherto presented only the barren history of the exterior Church, because they themselves were only the outward man, and had scarcely even imagined the life of the spiritual man.

But is this a proof that it does not exist! Grant that human
forms have destroyed this new dominion of truth, justice, and
love which proceeds from the Father. Because you see at first
only a dry and hard shell, will you reject the delicious fruit
which is concealed under this homely covering? In seasons of
barrenness and death, the Church could only have a lifeless
and sterile history. But life, while descending to the Church
of our day, has descended also into its history. Reserve your
objections for those who may continue to drag on in the barren
field of rationalism and human opinions. The old man sees
in the field of the Church only dry bones. The new man there
discerns that spirit which blows from the four winds, and
creates for the Eternal " an exceeding great army." There
is, then, a new history of Christianity—that which we have
undertaken to unfold and defend, and not the history of human
forms and barrenness.

" Do you, then, imagine that you shall find in Christianity
life, elevation, generosity?" says a gloomy philosophy, which
pretends that the individual good of each man ought to be the
noblest object of his life. " What an illusion! those remarkable actions, that self-sacrifice of which the history of Christianity seems to furnish examples, are but hidden passions,
ambition, avarice, sensuality, envy, covered with obvious vails
—an egotism, somewhat more refined than that of the multitude. The only difference between the grossest of men and the
heroes of the Christian history is, that these know how to disguise somewhat more ingeniously the passions which governed
them. And if all be not thus explained, a deplorable fanaticism
and enthusiasm will account for the rest." Such is the language that has been held, more especially of the history which
I am called to lay before you, and of the most illustrious characters which it presents to your view. Gloomy and hideous
system! which, only taking account of the corruption of man,
is ignorant of those pure and sublime inspirations which proceed from the Spirit of God: a system which overturns the
whole moral hierarchy, since the most dissolute and the most
criminal of men would be at least sincere, by appearing such
as they really are; while the flower of humanity, men of disin-
terestedness and self-sacrifice, would be a band of deceivers and

knaves, whose only aim would have been to conceal the disgraceful motives of their actions. Seriously to refute such a system would almost be high treason against Divinity and humanity. The history of Christianity shall itself be, moreover, the most triumphant vindication. It will open to you the gates of a world different from that inhabited by the natural man. It will display to you a power which a narrow minded philosophy can not comprehend. The majority of men comprehend nothing but materialism. Some more enlightened attain to rationalism. The history of Christianity will carry us still higher. It will disclose to us spiritualism, which is the true, the primitive life of man, of which he was deprived, and which Christianity comes to restore. It will constrain us to acknowledge that life to be more certain, more real than rationalism, and even materialism. It will set before us, and we shall almost touch with our hands, a strength of faith, which is given from above to man, and which overcomes the world and all the passions of the heart. It will teach us to discern two classes of men upon the earth, and will teach us to understand this profound thought, " The first man is of the earth, earthy; but the second man is the Lord from heaven. As is the earthy, such are they also that are earthy; and as is the heavenly, such are they also that are heavenly."

'At least, however,' it will be said, 'it is certain and irrefutable, that the history of the Church most frequently presents us with controversies, agitations, quarrels, wars. What interest would you have us take in such things? How, indeed, could we esteem such a history?' Controversies, agitations, say you? And are such the motives for your contempt of the History of Christianity? But let me ask you, What beneficent principle, what fortunate conception for humanity has ever been established without agitation, without a struggle, without a conflict? Philosophers! had not your Galileo a contest to maintain while he was teaching the movements of the heavens! and do not you honour him the more for it? Literati! had not your Corneille to endure discussion and criticism while he was creating the language and poetry of France? And you, ye Liberals of the age! who, perhaps, chiefly assail the history of the religion of Jesus Christ: was your Mirabeau without

combats in the tribune? And when he blew the trumpet of
new-born liberty, was the war of which he sounded the signal
a short one? or, rather, are we not now as between two armies
of nations, in battle array against each other, brandishing with
impatience the arms which must decide the victory? And
Christianity, which attacks man in his dearest passions, though
they are the very cause of his misfortunes, in his love of riches,
his ambition, his vain-glory, in a word, in this inferior self,
which man idolizes, and of which a sublimer self is the slave,
shall this Christianity be alone exempt from struggles and
contests? The burdened atmosphere is only purified by tempests, and the crisis of his disorder is deliverance to the sick.
And, in like manner, that truth may possess the earth, she
must combat hand to hand with error. But the end, the result of Christianity, is peace. *Peace on earth!* Such was the
cry from heaven when the earth received its Saviour. We are
marching onward to peace. Let us, then, march onward, if
necessary, through the fire of battle.

But I am deceived if the history of the religion of Jesus
Christ do not present to you far other objects than agitations
and troubles. It exhibits a phenomenon altogether unique,
and to be found nowhere else. It offers to you peace in the
midst of trouble; meekness of spirit amid the conflagration of
the passions. It will lead you to the sanctuary of the men of
God; and while around them agitations, conspiracies, and terrible cries prevail, you shall behold them calm, cheerful, and
full of a peace which passeth all understanding. Satisfied
with having borne witness to the truth, they have committed
their cause to the Eternal, and remain tranquil and at rest,
waiting on him. Of this, the history of the Reformation, and
of that of Luther in particular, will furnish you illustrious
examples. The history of Christianity makes known the only
real peace which has ever been upon earth.

"Are not such studies," say respectable men, but of un-
settled opinions, "at least fitted to confuse us on religious
subjects, to strip us of our faith, and to lead us into scepticisms
and incredulity?" There is nothing, after the word of God,
better suited to save us from incredulity and superstition, and
to attach us to true Christianity, than the history of the re-

ligion of Jesus Christ.   Undoubtedly, if you take one ecclesiastical historian who presents a religion and the Church in
popes and councils; or another, who arrays them in meagre,
natural theology, lightly shaded with Christianity, and in the
barren instructions of human reason; or another still, who
exhibits them through metaphysical dogmas or scholastic distinctions, such would undoubtedly disgust you with what each
would call religion.   But where is the great evil?   Take, on
the contrary, a historian, who presents to you the religion of
Jesus Christ such as it is in reality, "The light and the life
of the world."   Such a history, I feel assured, would make
you love that religion.   There is still more.   If other considerations have shaken your faith, this study will strengthen
it.   The enemies of religion, of Christianity, and of the Reformation in particular, will perhaps exclaim that craft, enthusiasm, credulity or incredulity, have accomplished these two
great revolutions in the world.   They will tell you that men
had not time to examine; that they were accomplished by
means of a commotion, from which mankind were astonished to
find that they had come forth Christian and protestant.   Let
us stretch forth the torch of history, and all these phantoms
of a hostile imagination instantly vanish.   Then do you see
how every thing has been examined, discussed, tried; how
every inch of ground has been defended by the adversary?
Abandoning the field of history, does he occupy that of reasoning?   Are you gravely assured that Christianity is contrary to human reason?   Are all those objections repeated, so
much boasted of in our day, as the fruits of the advancement
of the age, and aimed against religion itself, against the
divinity of the Saviour, salvation by grace, and the fall of
man?   History still has something to say.   She teaches you
that these are shafts, long since used and broken; the ideas of
Greek and pagan authors revived; for she will point you to
them in Celsus, and Porphyry, and Hierocles, Greek and
heathen writers.   On the one hand, history shows that all
these objections, so vaunted in our day, were employed from
the earliest ages, against truth and the Church, which is its
depository; and, on the other hand, she shows you that very
Church advancing unceasingly amid these assaults, growing,

and extending every where its benefits. Fear not, then; for
these assaults will no more injure the Church and arrest its
progress now than they have hitherto. During eighteen centuries, the little prejudices of the human mind have accustomed
it to these attacks; and, with little or no anxiety on these
subjects, the Church marches onward through eighteen centuries to the triumph which her Head is preparing for her.

But is there not reason to fear that the history of the Church,
and of the Reformation in particular, may revive polemics,
above all against the Roman Catholics, and may re-open the
wounds of the Western church, as yet but imperfectly healed?
I believe the reverse. History will doubtless show us, in a
general way, truth on one side, and error on the other. But
she will also show us good and evil mixed here and there; she
will show us, on the side of the Catholics, many a true Christian, although in some respects certainly but little enlightened;
and on the side of the Protestants, many a man unworthy of
that name. She will show us Catholicism adding, without
doubt, many things to the word of God, but preserving, nevertheless, most of the fundamental doctrines of Christianity, the
depravity of man, salvation through the atonement, the essential Divinity of the Redeemer, the indispensable work of the
Holy Spirit in the heart. And to pass thence to the history
of the Reformation. I shall be a protestant. I proclaim it
beforehand; yet not as a sectarian, but as a Christian. I
desire not to be unmindful of the respect which is due to men,
in whose ranks have shone the names of Laurence de Bibra,
Sadolet, Borromeo, Vincent de Paul, Pascal, Fenelon. It
shall not be my province to strike Catholicism with redoubled
blows; that was the affair of Luther's age; it was done then,
and is not the business of our age; but it shall be alone my
object, if I can accomplish it, to invest with a touching influence the living principle which produced, in the 16th century, a great religious regeneration, and which must produce
the same in our day. I shall notice the evil deeds of Protestants when I meet them. I shall notice the good actions of
Catholics, whenever I see them; and perhaps a favourite trait,
incidentally mentioned by a narrator (I cannot say by a historian) of the Reformation, will soothe the mind more readily

than apologies for Catholicism, in the mouth of one of its priests.

But then, it is lastly said, you must confess that the study of Christianity is advantageous to theologians only, but that we have nothing to do with it; that to us it is useless. I adopt the distinction: certainly it is not necessary to salvation; the knowledge of Jesus Christ is alone sufficient; and if we were addressing those who were indifferent to all history, we should perhaps be less favourably situated for a reply. But we address an audience who have not neglected the literary and political history of nations. We then say to you, Why should you reject that of Christianity? If this concerns only divines, assuredly political history is the province only of magistrates and princes. Whenever the members of councils of state and of some other bodies shall be the only students of civil history, I may understand that only ministers of the Gospel should devote themselves to religious history. If there be a history which you desire to study, ought not that of religion to stand first? Of the three great elements of history—politics, letters, religion—is not religion the most universal, and that which ought above all to interest each member of society? Had you not a soul and a God, before you had literary and political sympathies? Is not religion paramount in whatever is most dear and sacred to man? Let us grant that hitherto you have repelled religion as to yourselves, and that you desire to study that only which influences the destinies of man, is not Christianity the moving principle of political development, of intellectual labour? What but this has given and still gives the most powerful influence to the social life, to the literary genius of modern nations? The study of the history of Christianity *useless!* Is not this saying, it is useless in a steam-boat to study the machinery which communicates motion to the whole vessel; that it is sufficient to study the vessel itself, the planks and rigging, which that machinery impels? The religion of Jesus Christ is the machine which moves the world.

But this very usefulness of that religion, especially at this present time, remains to be laid before you.

Jesus Christ founded in the midst of men a kingdom of God; and thenceforward the history of the human race, composed till

then but of scattered, unconnected fragments, possessed a centre to which every thing might and ought to be referred. This
divine kingdom gave unity to the nations of the earth and to
their history, and, through it, isolated members became a body.

One of the noblest and most essential ideas of our age, as
yet perhaps but indistinctly traced on many minds, but which
must continually become more and more the fundamental
thought of those who reflect and believe, is that in the new
period now opening before us there will be no longer, so to
speak, a personal history of nations, but a great history of human nature. Our age is the centre where the numerous threads
from various points are united, and thence issue in one cord.
And what is this new period but the fulfilment of the destinies
of Christianity ? While some philosophers saw indistinctly
but yesterday something of this vast centralization of the races
of men, Christianity, opening the annals of a people who had
crucified their Divine and eternal Founder, exhibits there to
the world the annunciation of this mighty event in the history
of man, declared, two thousand years before its occurrence, to
Abraham the Chaldean—" in thee shall all families of the
earth be blessed ;" and proclaimed still more clearly, two hundred years after, by an old man to his children around his
death-bed, when, casting a prophetic look on the future, and
announcing this Messenger, who was to issue from the midst
of them, he adds, " unto Him shall the gathering of the people
be." Words of peace which that mysterious person, when he
appeared here below, repeats to his disciples in language still
more striking, if that be possible : " There shall be one fold
and one shepherd." The religions of antiquity rendered impossible this vast assembly of nations. Like the languages
of Babel, they were so many walls which separated nations
from one another. The tribes of the earth worshipped only
national gods—those gods only suited the nations who made
them. They had no points of contact, none of sympathy with
any other people. Falsehood has a thousand strange faces,
not resembling each other. Truth only is one, and this only
can unite all the races of men. The idea of a universal kingdom of truth and holiness was a stranger to the ancient world;
and, if some sages had a vague and obscure presentiment of it,

with them it was but a conception, without the possibility of their even imagining what might be its reality. Christ came and immediately accomplished what the religions and sages of the world had not even been able to foresee. He founds a spiritual kingdom, to which all nations are called. He overturns, according to the energetic language of his apostle, the barriers, the middle wall of partition which divided nations, and "hath made both one," "for to make in himself of twain one new man, so making peace." Christianity is not, like the ancient religions, a doctrine adapted to a certain degree of development in nations ; it is a truth from heaven, which is able at the same time to act on man under every grade of improvement and climate. It bestows on human nature, whatever may be its rudeness, or the diversities of changes which letters and philosophy may have produced, the principle of a new and truly divine life. And this life is to be at once the great means of development to all nations, and the centre of their unity. With its appearance commenced in the universe the only real cosmopolitism. Citizens of Judea, of Pontus, of Greece, of Egypt, of Rome, till then mutual enemies, embrace like brothers. Christianity is that tree, of which the Scriptures speak, whose leaves are for the healing of nations. It acts at the same time on the most opposite states of society. It regenerates and vivifies the world, corrupted by the Cæsars, and soon after softens and civilizes the barbarous hordes of the north; and at this very time it produces similar effects on the citizens of London, Paris, and Berlin, and on the savages of Greenland, Caffraria, and the Sandwich Islands. The net is cast over the whole earth, and the day cometh when a heavenly hand shall hold captive in it all the races of men. Ye have perceived, men of the age, that we are passing out of the period of nations, and entering on that of human nature; but fashion not for yourselves a paltry standard for the union of nations. A new hierarchy, with its common frame, can not be the bond of unity, nor political liberalism, which carries tempests and discord in its bosom. Christ is this ensign of which the prophet speaks, and around which " shall the gathering of the people be."

But while many in our day hail at this moment the dawn of

a new reorganization, others, on the contrary, behold in it only an epoch of dissolution. And these two opinions, apparently opposite, are perfectly hormonious; since dissolution must precede reorganization. The two great powers of man have been unable to resolve the problem of human nature. The hierarchy had undertaken it, but failed, and the iron arm of Rome was broken. Human philosophy rushed into its place, and said, I will accomplish it; but the disorder of the nations has increased in a frightful ratio. There remains the power of God, or Christianity, which already, while human power was making its trials, has laid every where the foundations of the new edifice: and it will succeed. Do you exclaim, that in our day men walk in uncertainty? that all the doctrines for the welfare of nations are doubtful? It is true, that all does seem in our day to be dissolving. But, O man! listen to thy master, a master of eighteen centuries old, who has assisted more than once at the decline and elevation of nations, at the decomposition and recomposition of the world, and who has been the great organic principle of nations. Listen to what it has been, to know what it will be; and to what it has done, to know what it will do. Christianity is totally different from the religions of men. In these, it is man who gives strength to religion; in that, religion gives strength to man. While the republic was counting its days of glory, the gods of Rome shone with the greatest lustre. But when corruption had seized on domestic life, when personal ambition and venality had assailed public life, religion, worm-eaten at the base, decays and disappears with them. Jupiter falls, and is buried under the ruins of his own Capitol. Christianity, on the contrary, independent of man, remains firm amid the fall of nations (their annals testify this), and renews the world by its power. When all the social forms of humanity are destroyed, as at the epoch of the invasion of the Barbarians, the religion of Jesus Christ remains upright on their ruins, and her hand scatters amid the chaos that seed whence humanity shall rise anew. Fear not the mournful state of the world at this time. History, and especially that which we shall lay before you, demonstrates, that when corruption has extended its ravages the farthest over the world, the divine power of Christianity, which has not its roots in the entrails of human nature, rises with the greatest power. The Spirit of God is moving on the chaos, and out of it he will bring forth a new earth.

But the history of Christianity will teach you, moreover, that this religion is the instrument which he has chosen to accomplish his work. It will exhibit her mode of action, not as a continued influence, but as a succession of struggles and combats. The essence of Christianity is conflict with the world; and thus the true Church of Christ hath appeared from the beginning, as, " militant" amid the nations. Already have two enemies successively assailed her and been vanquished, however easily they promised to crush her. At first, she had to combat without against the idolatry and vices of paganism. Paganism fell. But scarcely had this victory been gained, when the danger appeared in the bosom of the Church. While men slept, according to the parable of the Divine and Eternal Founder of Christianity, the enemy came and sowed tares among the wheat. The evil continued to increase. The Church had been founded that man might seek for heaven in it, and there he sought only the world. Then the true Church shook off the dust of death. Arrayed, as it were, in an instant in the spiritual armour which God had prepared for her, she began a war, the most terrible, because intestine. Rome, vigorously assailed, tottered, and the crown fell from her head. This war we propose to lay before you. It remains for Christianity to obtain a final victory. An enemy, who is neither within nor without, as were the first two, or rather, who is both at the same time, advances to the last assault. I refer to the unbelieving, anti-Christian spirit of the age. More powerful, more terrible still than the first two adversaries, he casts upon Christianity that look of disdain which the gods of the Capitol once cast on the citizen of Tarsus, in chains at their feet ; and which, fifteen centuries after, Leo and the magnificent court of the Medici cast, with a smile, into the obscure cell of an Augustinian monk. Still more may be said: the anti-Christian spirit of the world, now lifting his banner so high, does not suspect the enemy which is to vanquish him. And yet he will be conquered; and the formidable giant of the age, who defies the God of the armies of Israel, struck in the forehead, shall

fall with his face to the earth, under the sling of the enemy
whom he has despised.

Is the question asked, By what arms shall this victory be
gained? Here, again, the History of Christianity will give
the answer. It shows you that this religion has twice regenerated the world, at least partially, by doctrines entirely
its own. To pretend that the religious system, which is to
accomplish the grand solution desired by all, consists of those
general ideas of religion to be found in Rabbinical Judaism,
in Mahometanism, and even in Pagan Philosophy, is a strange
error; for these ideas never have produced the regeneration of
the people who have known them. The power of Christianity
lies in its peculiarity. It compels man to feel the astonishing
contrast between his whole life and the law of its holiness. It
produces in him the desire of deliverance from so miserable
a condition. It reveals to him the magnificent work, which
the mercy of a God has accomplished for his rescue, in the
death of the cross. It proclaims, by the command of the
King of the world, an entire amnesty through all the world.
Now, we maintain two things. *First*, that this news of a full
pardon, of a perfect amnesty, proclaimed upon earth, that rebellious province of the empire of the King of kings, is alone
capable of touching, of changing the heart of man, and of inclining him, through love, to obey the Sovereign who reclaims
him. Ye politicians of the age, what advice would you give
to a king for the establishment of peace and subordination in
the midst of a rebellious people? Classifications, conditions,
scaffolds, or a generous amnesty without reserve, calculated to
win all hearts? And we maintain, *secondly*, that the submission of the heart to God, the inward power of Christianity, is
the only power which can now heal the diseases of nations.
Every bond is broken. Selfishness and the spirit of censure
are universal. There are but two methods for the re-establishment of order and peace among the rising and agitated
masses: exterior and violent measures of compression; or the
interior persuasive power of Christianity. What do I say?
There is but one; for as to the first, all nations have shown
its inefficiency. Three days have sufficed. By destroying
selfishness, and planting in the hearts of all the love of God

and the love of man, Christianity alone will resolve the great problem, and establish liberty among the nations, with order and peace. These truths, taught by the nature of things, history will confirm. As to the *first*, she will disclose to us the unheard-of power of Christianity. She will prove to us that these doctrines can accomplish an actual second birth of human nature. And as to the *second*, contemporaneous history shall instruct us. Enquire of her in what nations order and liberty are the most closely united, and she will answer by pointing to the countries where the Gospel is the most openly proclaimed, the most universally believed. But, above all, history will show that a power not of man hath produced those partial regenerations, which are symbols and precursors of that universal regeneration announced by Christianity. Call this power God, or the Spirit of God, or even Providence —the name is of little consequence; the fact is certain—something hath descended from heaven. Such is the present state of the world, that whoever believes not in this power, as independent of the world, may well despair. But, for ourselves, nothing terrifies us. "Give me," said Archimedes, "a place to stand on, and I will move the earth." Christianity is that point beyond the world from which it shall be one day entirely displaced, and shall revolve on a new axis of righteousness and peace. Then shall be poured out on all nations a mighty influence of the Spirit of God. Such are the most ancient promises. The Trojan war had just closed, and Rome was not yet founded, when, in the midst of the people, to whom God had intrusted the germs of religion for all the nations of the earth, these prophetic words resounded: "Until the Spirit be poured upon us from on high," "and the work of righteousness shall be peace."

Do you desire to know the obstacles which this renovation of human nature has to encounter, so that you may wisely remove them? The History of Christianity will point them out. They have been the same at all times. A wisdom, shall I say, or a folly, altogether earthly and carnal, which ridicules Divine things, and would contract God and his kingdom to the narrow dimensions of its own scale: a priestly despotism, which claims alone the privilege of manag-

ing heavenly things, which turns a deaf ear to examination
and research into the Divine word, and materializes religion:
a fanaticism which opposes, with all its might, the knowledge
of the truth; which being hostile to liberty, would silence those
who utter it; which labours to arm public opinion against
Christianity and Christians—whatever may be the name which
this fanaticism bears, such as Jewish, Pagan, Dominican, or
falsely liberal and philosophic — such are the principal obstacles which the History of Christianity exhibits.

Do you ask with the age for movement, for progress?
History will show you that Christianity is the religion of progress, and that she calls man, by continual advancements, to
the liberty and the glory of the children of God.   Let us carefully remark that there are only two spheres in which advancements can be made, viz., in the religion destined to renew mankind, or in man himself called to be renewed.   The
man of our age ascribes this progress to religion; religion, to
man himself.   Christianity came forth perfect from God, and
is unchangeable as its author.   Thou, O man! art thus continually to advance; and in like manner, that immense Christian Society which the truth enlightens.   The sun is not itself
advancing to perfection, but is ever perfecting the shrub,
which, receiving life from it, becomes a majestic tree.   It is
the same with Christianity and man.   The Gospel places the
goal, toward which that Christian Society ought to tend, beyond
the vail which separates the two worlds.   Thus, the Gospel
summons society to a progress incomparably beyond all that
human systems demand, and assigns a task which can only
be accomplished in eternity.

Will you speak of *enlightenment?*   Will you say that we have
reached an age too full of light for the trumph of Christianity?
The history of Christianity will show you that she fears not
that light, though frequently a false one.   I shall not speak
of the present epoch, when she lifts her head with more energy
than ever.   This age, at least, ought to be out of the question.
I shall not speak of the Reformation, preceded for half a century by the great events which signalized the revival of letters:
we shall soon attend to it.   But consider what the history of
Christianity records on its first leaf.   The age of Augustus,
when Jesus was born, is among the most brilliant in the annals

of mankind.   Christianity chose the noon-day for its appearance.   A religious system which had lasted as long as the nation was crumbling under the assaults of the reason of the age; and at that moment Christianity presents itself to be, in like manner, examined and assailed.   The raillery of the man of wit, the assaults of eloquence, the protracted warfare of philosophy and learning, it challenges all; it sustains the shock, and nothing moves it.   On the contrary, it advances, it leads the thoughts captive, in obedience to the God whom it announces; and in celestial triumph on the theatre of human glory, it often numbers around its car those who had been the most formidable of enemies.   Christianity is the true light: it is the sun which rises above all the lights of this lower sphere. "I am the light of the world," said Jesus Christ.

Lastly, will the age speak of the *future?*   Will attention be vouchsafed to a doctrine only so far as it relates to the *future?* The future belongs to Christianity.   She claims not to-day or yesterday, like the ephemeral prophets of our day.   She said so four thousand years ago.   The 17th century was that of the past; the 18th is that of the present; the 19th is that of the future, and this belongs to Christianity.   Men, if enlightened and sincere, can no longer continue strangers to the ancient promises of the future, laid up in the book of the nations. Following out in history the accomplishment of the oracles of God, they will arrive at those which declare that "the earth shall be full of the knowledge of the Lord," that "his rest shall be glorious."   Ever since the men who were the heralds of God uttered these words all has been advancing, and all are now moving onward to their glorious fulfilment.   Christianity is on her march, and she will never retreat.   Her work is scarcely rough-hewn; but she will finish it.   She will bring about a great revolution on earth, which shall change its very being. The times are not perhaps very distant when its destinies will be accelerated.   A new history commences.   Christ opens to the world the gates of a new future.   "Great voices" shall be one day heard, as a prophet tells us, saying, "the kingdoms of this world are become the kingdoms of our Lord and of his Christ."

These are my reasons for maintaining that the history of Christianity is the most important of all historical studies; not only in general but particularly with a view to the present epoch. Christianity holds in her hand the future destinies of the world. She bears in herself the regenerative force that will renew the nation, the bond which must unite them. Here is that beneficent power which will spread over the earth and establish righteousness, liberty, and peace. O ye men of the age! there only may you learn the direction which you ought to give to all your efforts and labours. Study in the past the history of that which must accomplish such great results in the future. Dedicate to this study your spirit of research and your profound meditations. Set the example of abandoning the beaten track of the world, and of seeking light, life, the future, where only they are found. Young men who hear me, be the first to comprehend the calling of the new generation: receive first for yourselves the light which Christianity has kindled, and then go forth the beacon fires of the nations.

I am now to ask your attention to the history of the Reformation in Germany, or, at least, of the most important period of that history. Perhaps you will enquire what has led me to solicit that subject, and what circumstances have induced this narrative. I saw Germany, and loved her for the sake of this excellent work, which I propose as my theme. The Reformation, at the festival of its third centennial jubilee, welcomed me on the road, and in the Germanic cities, on my arrival in 1817. I recall (and not without some pain, when I reflect how far from them was the spirit of the Reformation) those bands of students, who flocked to the famous antique castle of Wartburg, where we shall one day in the course of my review, behold Luther a captive. I love to believe that those youths were rather indiscreet than guilty! I well remember how the gates of that ancient fortress (to which those young Germans were ascending in solemn procession) opened immediately before me at the name of Geneva; and the emotions revive which I experienced when I found myself in the prison-chamber of Luther. I remember those melodious strains which, some days after, announced the festival within the walls of Leipsic, descending, before the dawn of day, from the summit of the invisible towers of the churches, as though they had been music from heaven. Again, I met the Reformation in illustrious teachers at Berlin. I shall name only Neander, the father of the new history of

Christianity, Neander, whose tender affection is so dear to my heart, and who has raised up in Germany that Christian instruction to which other friends, his juniors, the Tholocks and the Hengstenbergs, now impart life with all the strength of their faith. Again, I found it on the borders of the Elbe, in the midst of the kindred and friends of the simple yet profound Claudius of Wandsbeck, and of the sublime poet of 'The Messiah.' Again, I found it in the ancient and Catholic Brabant itself, near the throne on which sat the descendant of the Nassaus, the heir of *the Silent*, that noble hero of the Reformation of the Low Countries. There the earth soon trembled beneath my feet.[1] The throne which it bore crumbled at the sound of the fall of another throne. A Queen of Cities became, during four days, the bloody field of horrible combats. There I was a witness, and nearly a victim of unspeakable calamities. I returned to our mountains, after an absence of fourteen years, desiring, if God should give me adequate strength, to speak amid my countrymen of those admirable things whose glory and influence met me every where. Perhaps those noble, correct, and liberal manners, whose charm I experienced in a foreign land, have not been found by me in all at home. Subject, however, myself to human frailties, I shall know how to excuse and not to condemn them in others. I promise, then, a cordial welcome to all who are disposed to hear my simple narrative. We shall survey together the plains of Mansfeld, the cells of Erfurt, the halls of Wittemburg, the palaces of Augsburg, of Leipsic, and of Worms. You will behold the Reformation. You will examine all things. You will not suffer the yoke of man to rest on your necks. I have seen Wittemburg, I have seen the land where the despotism of Rome perished; let us not bow down before the despotism of the age. A freeman myself, I seek after freemen; and I believe I have found them. May the divine blessing rest on my narrative! May words be vouchsafed to me suitable to spread true light and true liberty! and while I am relating to you the history of a great event in the kingdom of God, may the image of Christ, the King of the Church, grow unceasingly before your eyes and in your hearts!

---

[1] Allusion is here made to the revolution, in September, 1830, in Brussels, and the overthrow of the united kingdoms of Holland and Belgium.

DISCOURSE XI.[1]

GENEVA AND OXFORD.

"Two systems of doctrine are now, and probably for the last time, in conflict—the Catholic and Genevan."—*Dr. Pusey's Letter to the Archbishop of Canterbury.*

GENTLEMEN,—I am in the habit, at the opening of the course of lectures in our Seminary, of calling your attention to some subject peculiarly appropriate to the wants and circumstances of the times. Several such subjects now present themselves to our consideration.

And first of all, there is one which is appropriate to every year and to every day, one which concerns the very nature of this Seminary. It has none of those temporal sources of prosperity, of endowment, and of power which nourish other institutions; it can exist only as a plant of God; it can be nothing excepting just as the Spirit of God—like the sap—diffuses itself, without cessation, through the principal branches, and through even the least of its twigs; adorning the whole tree with leaves, with flowers, and with fruit. Gentlemen, Professors, and Students, we are those twigs and branches. Oh that we may not be barren and withered branches!

There is another subject which begins greatly to occupy the most distinguished minds; it is the question whether the Church ought to depend upon the civil government, or ought to have a government of its own, having no dependence, in the last resort, but upon Christ and his word. Without entering here into this important subject, I would indicate two opposite movements, which are at this moment simultaneously taking place under our eyes in the world; the one in theory, the other in practice. On the one hand, an admirable work, the pro-

---

[1] Delivered at the opening of the session of the Theological Seminary, in October, 1842.

duction of one of the most profound thinkers of our age, Mr. Vinet,[1] leads some reflecting minds to acknowledge the independence of the Church ; and, on the other, many people are uniting themselves with new zeal around the institutions of the government; so that there are all around us convictions and movements which seem to carry away the people of our day by contrary currents. It is thus that a student of Geneva has just written to us, that the refusal to grant to him the exemption from military duty, which the law stipulates in favour of students of theology, will oblige him to quit our school. We will always respect authority, but we cannot refrain from remarking that if, as all parties maintain, there has been a radical revolution in Geneva this year, that revolution has not, assuredly, tended to establish among us that equality and that religious liberty without which all other liberty is but a useless and dangerous plaything. However, it is in France above all that this movement is taking place. A French student writes to us, in a strain of affecting regret, that he has united again with the Established church. When young men, after having pursued, in our preparatory school, those primary studies which present so many difficulties, desire to secure to themselves, by certain measures, a prospect of greater ease, or even to abandon our Institution for the purpose of placing themselves in one sustained by government, from which Unitarian and Rationalist doctrines have been banished, we shall be happy to think that we have been able to prepare them in part, with the aid of God our Saviour, for the work of the ministry, and we shall follow them in their career with the same affection, and we hope with the same prayers. But we ourselves, gentlemen, will make no advances to the political governments ; we believe that our sole resource is with the Government of Heaven ; and knowing the faithfulness of Christ toward those who seek only his glory, assured that there is a place for whomsoever he calls to preach his Gospel, we will ask of him the confidence that we, teachers and pupils, ought to have in his love, and to make us all continue to walk *by faith*, and not by sight.

The circumstances even of the Church in our country might also occupy our attention. Alas ! we have played this year

[1] Essai sur la Manifestation des Convictions Religieuses. Paris, 1842.

the part of Cassandra. In vain have we presented, as well as
we could, the correct principles of ecclesiastical government;
in vain, especially, have we shown that the elders of the Church
ought to be chosen by the people of the parishes assembled in
their places of worship with their pastors, after having invoked
the name of God, and not by municipal councils, over which
magistrates preside; our words, for a moment heard, have in
the end been in vain. We have witnessed a very strange spectacle; we have seen ecclesiastics, men in other respects truly
enlightened, and possessing undoubted talent, apparently afraid
of their parishes, and employing their powerful influence to
cause the rulers of the Church to be elected, not by the Church,
but by the magistrates charged to watch over the maintenance
of the roads and public edifices. And now that this election
has been made, what do people say? Surprising thing! Ex-
clamations of astonishment and grief are heard, that the political bodies to which some have wished to entrust the ecclesiastical elections, cost what it might, have made those elections
political; the fall of the Church is predicted, men are now
occupied with those who *are destined infallibly to share the spoils*,[1]
and nothing can equal the zeal which has been employed to
bring about this change, unless it be the grief which has been
manifested when, as we predicted, its inevitable results have
been discovered. Behold, gentlemen, how far men may be led
by ignorance of the first principles of ecclesiastical government
on the part of those who administer the Church, whatever may
be in other respects their illumination, their morality, or their
patriotism.

If we look beyond this Seminary, beyond this city, into the
religious world in general, there are other subjects which present themselves to our view. It is thus that we see pious men,
seduced without doubt by many truths mixed up with strange
errors, receive a system coming from a city in England,[2] which
teaches that there is no more Church, although Jesus has
promised that "The gates of hell shall not prevail against it;"
and that there ought to be no more pastors and teachers,

---

[1] See the Courier of Geneva of the 24th Sept., 1842.
[2] Plymouth. Those who are called "Plymouth brethren" are here referred to.

although revelation declares to us that Christ himself has established " pastors and teachers for the perfecting of the saints. for the work of the ministry, for the edifying of the body of Christ."

But, gentlemen, there is another error: it is that which is found at the other extremity of the theological line, and which I intend now to indicate to you. In the bosom of a university in England, that of Oxford, has grown up an ecclesiastical system which interests and justly grieves all Christendom. It is now some time since some laymen, whom I love and respect, came to me to ask me to write against that dangerous error. I answered that I had neither the time, nor the capacity, nor the documents necessary for the task. But if I am incapable of composing a dissertation, I can at least show in a few words how I regard it. It is even my duty to do so, since excellent Christians ask it of me ; and it is that which has determined me to choose this subject for the present occasion.

Let us clearly comprehend the position which Evangelical Christian Theology occupies.

At the epoch of the Reformation, if I may so speak, three distinct eras had occurred in the history of the Church.

1. That of Evangelical Christianity, which, having its focus in the times of the apostles, extended its rays throughout the first and second centuries of the Church.

2. That of Ecclesiastical Catholicism, which, commencing its existence in the third century, reigned till the seventh.

3. That of the Papacy, which reigned from the seventeenth to the fifteenth century.

Such were then the three grand eras in the history of the Church ; let us see what characterized each one of them. In the first period, the supreme authority was attributed to the revealed word of God. In the second, it was, according to some, ascribed to the Church as represented by its bishops. In the third, to the pope. We acknowledge cheerfully that the second of these systems is much superior to the third ; but it is inferior to the first. In fact, in the first of these systems it is GOD who rules. In the second, it is MAN. In the third, it is, to speak after the apostles, " THAT WORKING OF SATAN, with all power and signs and lying wonders."

The Reformation, in abandoning the Papacy, might have returned to the second of these systems, that is, to Ecclesiastical Catholicism ; or to the first, that is, to Evangelical Christianity.

In returning to the second, it would have gone half way. Ecclesiastical Catholicism is in fact a middle system—*a via media*, as one of the Oxford doctors has termed it, in a sermon lately published. On the one hand it approaches much to Papacy, for it contains in the germ all the principles which are there found. On the other, however, it diverges from it, for it rejects the Papacy itself.

The Reformation was not a system of the *juste milieu*. It went the whole length ; and, rebounding with that force which God gives, it fell, as with a single leap, into the Evangelical Christianity of the apostles.

But there is now, gentlemen, a numerous and powerful party in England, supported even by some bishops (whose charges have filled us with astonishment and grief), which would, in the opinion of its adversaries, quit the ground of the Evangelical Christianity to plant itself upon that of Ecclesiastical Catholicism, with a marked tendency toward the Papacy ; or which, according to what *it* pretends, would faithfully maintain itself on that hierarchical and semi-Romish ground which is, according to it, the *true*, *native*, and *legitimate* foundation of the Church of England. It is this movement which is called, after one of its principal chiefs, *Puseyism*.

" The task of the true children of the catholic church," says the *British Critic* (one of the journals which are the organs of the Oxford party), " is to unprotestantize the Church." " It is necessary," says one of these doctors,[1] " to reject entirely and to anathematize the principle of Protestantism, as being that of a heresy with all its forms, its sects, and its denominations." " It is necessary," says another, in his posthumous writings,[2] " to hate more and more the Reformation and the Reformers."

In separating the Church from the Reformation, this party pretends to wish, not to bring the Church back to the Papacy, but to retain it in the *juste milieu* of Ecclesiastical Catholicism.

---

[1] Mr. Palmer.   [2] Mr. Froude.

However, the fact is not to be disguised that, if it were forced to choose between what it considers two evils, it would greatly prefer Rome to the Reformation.

Men highly respectable for their knowledge, their talents, and their moral character, are to be found among these theologians ; and we must acknowledge that the fundamental want which seems to have decided this movement is a legitimate one.

There has been felt in England, in the midst of all the waves which now heave and agitate the Church, a want of *antiquity;* and men have sought a rock, firm and immovable, on which to plant their feet. This want is founded in human nature ; it is also justified by the social and religious state of the present time. I myself thirst after antiquity. But do the Oxford divines satisfy, for themselves and for others, these wants of the age? I am convinced of the contrary. What a juvenile antiquity is that before which these eminent men prostrate themselves! It is the young and inexperienced Christianity of the first ages that they call ancient ; it is to the child that they ascribe the authority of the old man. If the question be one respecting the antiquity of humanity, certainly we are more ancient than the Fathers, for we are fifteen or eighteen centuries older than they ; it is we who have the light of experience and the maturity of gray hairs.

But no ; it is not respecting such an antiquity that there can be any dispute in divine things. The only antiquity to which we hold is that of the "Ancient of Days;" "of Him who, before the mountains were brought forth, or ever he had formed the earth and the world, even from everlasting to everlasting, is God." It is "He who is our refuge from age to age." The truly ancient document to which we appeal is that "word which is settled forever in heaven," and "which shall stand forever." This, gentlemen, is *our* antiquity.

Alas! that which most afflicts us respecting the learned divines of Oxford is, that, while the people who surround them hunger and thirst after antiquity, they themselves, instead of leading them to the ancient testimony of the "Ancient of Days," only conduct them to puerile novelties. What novelties, in truth, and what faded novelties! that *purgatory,* that *human forgiveness,* those *images,* those *relics,* that *invocation of the saints* which these divines would restore to the Church![1] What an immense and monstrous innovation is that Rome to which they would have us return!

Who are the innovators? I demand; those who say as we do, with the eternal word, " God hath begotten us of His own will, with the word of truth," or those who say, as do the ' Tracts for the Times,' " Rome is our mother; it is by her that we have been born to Christ"? those who say, as we do, with the eternal word, " Take heed, brethren, lest there be in any of you an evil heart of unbelief in departing from the living God," or those who say, as do these divines, " In losing visible union with the church of Rome, we have lost great privileges?"[2] Certainly, the divines of Oxford are the innovators.

The partisans of Rome, that grand innovation in Christendom, are not so easily deceived; they hail in these new divines advocates of Romish novelties. The famous Romish doctor Wiseman writes to lord Shrewsbury, " We can certainly rely on a prompt, zealous, and able co-operation in bringing the church of England to obedience to the See of Rome. When I read in their chronological order the writings of the theologians of Oxford, I see in the clearest manner that these divines are approximating, from day to day, to our holy church both in doctrine and in sympathy. Our saints, our popes, become more and more dear to them; our rites, our ceremonies, and even the festivals of our saints and our days of fasting, are precious in their eyes, more precious, alas! than in the eyes of many of our own people." And do not the Oxford divines, notwithstanding their protestations, concur in this view of the matter when they say, " The tendency to Romanism is, in reality, only a fruit of the profound desire which the Church, greatly aroused, experiences to become again, as the Saviour left her, One."[3]

Such, gentlemen, is the movement which is taking place in that church of England which so many pious men, so many Christian works have rendered illustrious. Dr. Pusey had good reason to say, in his letter to the archbishop of Canterbury, " Upon the issue of the present struggle depend the des-

---

[1] Tracts for the Times, No. 90, Art. 6.   [2] British Critic.
[3] Letter of Dr. Pusey to the Archbishop of Canterbury.

tinies of our church." And it is worth while for us to pause here a few moments to examine what party we ought to prefer, as members of the ancient church of the Continent, and what we have to do in this grave and solemn crisis.

Gentlemen, we ought to profess frankly that we will have neither the *Papacy*, nor the *via media* of Ecclesiastical Catholicism, but will remain firm upon the foundation of Evangelical Christianity. In what consists this Christianity, when it is opposed to the two other systems which we reject ? There are things essential and things unessential in it ; but it is only of that which constitutes its essence, of that which is its principle, that I would here speak. There are three principles which form its essence : the first is what we may call its *formal* principle, because it is the means by which this system is formed or constituted ; the second is what may be called the *material* principle, because it is the very doctrine which constitutes this religious system ; the third I call the *personal*, or *moral* principle, because it concerns the application of Christianity to the soul of each individual.

The *formal* principle of Christianity is expressed in few words:—THE WORD OF GOD ONLY. That is to say, the Christian receives the knowledge of the truth only by the word of God, and admits of no other source of religious knowledge. The *material* principle of Christianity is expressed with equal brevity: THE GRACE OF CHRIST ONLY. That is to say, the Christian receives salvation only by the grace of Christ, and recognizes no other meritorious cause of eternal life.

The *personal* principle of Christianity may be expressed in the most simple terms: THE WORK OF THE SPIRIT ONLY. That is to say, there must be in each soul that is saved a moral and individual work of regeneration wrought by the Spirit of God, and not by the simple concurrence of the Church,[1] and the magic influence of certain ceremonies.

Gentlemen, recall constantly to your minds these three simple truths: *The Word of God* ONLY ; *The Grace of Christ* ONLY ;

---

[1] The words which are used in the French are *adjonction de l'Eglise*, and are employed to express that additional or concurrent influence which the Church is believed by the Puseyites to exert in regeneration by her ministration.—*Trans.*

The work of the Spirit ONLY ; and they will truly be a " lamp to
your feet and a light to your paths." These are the three
great beacons which the Holy Spirit has erected in the Church.
Their effulgence should spread from one end of the world to
the other. So long as they shine, the Church walks in the
light; as soon as they shall become extinct, or even obscured,
darkness, like that of Egypt, will settle upon Christendom.

But, gentlemen, it is precisely these three fundamental principles of evangelical Christianity which are attacked and overthrown by the new system of Ecclesiastical Catholicism. It
is not to some minor point, to some doctrine of secondary importance, that attention is directed at Oxford; it is to that
which constitutes the very essence of Christianity and of the
Reformation, to those truths which are so important that, as
Luther said, " With them the Church stands, and without
them the Church falls." Let us consider them.

I. The *formal* principle of evangelical Christianity is this :
THE WORD OF GOD ONLY. He who would know and possess the
truth, in order to be saved, ought to study that revelation of
God which is contained in the sacred Scriptures, and to reject
everything which is a mere human addition, every thing which,
as the work of man, may be justly suspected of being impressed with a deplorable mixture of error. There is one only
source at which the Christian quenched his thirst; it is that
stream, clear, limpid, perfectly pure, which flows from the
throne of God. He turns away from every other fountain
which flows parallel with it, or which would fain mingle itself
with it; for he knows that on account of the source whence
these streams issue, they all contain troubled, unwholesome,
perhaps deadly waters.

The sole, the ancient, the eternal stream, is GOD; the new,
ephemeral, failing stream, is MAN; and we will quench our
thirst but in God alone. God is, in our view, so full of sovereign majesty, that we would regard as an outrage, and even
as impiety, the attempt to put any thing by the side of his
word,

But this is what the authors of the novelties of Oxford are
doing. " The Scriptures," say they, in the *Tracts for the
Times*, " are evidently not, according to the principles of the

Church of England, the Rule of Faith. The doctrine or message of the Gospel is but indirectly presented in the Scriptures, and in an obscure and concealed manner."[1] Catholic tradition," says one of the two principal chiefs of this school,[2] "is a divine information in religious things; it is the unwritten word. These two things (the Bible and the Catholic traditions) together form a united Rule of Faith. Catholic tradition is a divine source of knowledge in all things relating to faith. The Scriptures are only the document of ultimate appeal; Catholic tradition is the authoritative teacher." "Tradition is infallible," says another divine![3] " the unwritten word of God, of necessity, demands of us the same respect which his written word does, and precisely for the same reason, because it is His word." " We demand that the whole of the Catholic traditions should be taught," says a third.[4] " Such, gentlemen, is one of the most pestiferous errors which can be disseminated in the Church. Whence have Rome and Oxford derived it? Certainly the respect which we entertain for the incontestible learning of these divines shall not prevent our saying that this error can come from no other source than the natural aversion of the heart of fallen man for every thing that the Scriptures teach. It can be nothing else than a depraved will which leads man to put the sacred Scriptures aside. Men first abandon the fountain of living waters, and then hew for themselves, here and there, cisterns which will hold no water. This is a truth which the history of every Church teaches in its successive falls and errors, as well as that of every soul in particular. The theologians of Oxford only follow in the way of all flesh.

Behold, then, gentlemen, two established authorities by the side of each other: the Bible, and tradition. We do not hesitate as to what we have to do.

" To THE LAW AND TO THE TESTIMONY!" we cry with the prophet; " if they speak not according to His word, it is because there is no light in them: and behold trouble and darkness, dimness of anguish; and they shall be driven to darkness."

We reject tradition, as it is a species of rationalism which

1 Tract 85.　　2 Newman, Lecture on Romanism.　　3 Keeble's Sermons.
4 Palmer's Aids to Reflection.

introduces, for a rule in Christian doctrine, not the human reason of the present time, but the human reason of times past. We declare, with the churches of the Reformation in their symbolical writings (confessions of faith,) that "the Sacred Scriptures are the only judge, the only rule of faith; that it is to them, as to a touchstone, that all dogmas ought to be brought; that it is by them that the question should be decided, whether they are pious or impious, true or false!"[1]

Without doubt there was originally an oral tradition which was pure; it was the instructions given by the apostles themselves, before the sacred writings of the New Testament existed. However, even then the apostle and the evangelist, Peter and Barnabas, could not walk uprightly, and consequently stumbled in their words. The divinely inspired Scriptures alone are infallible: the word of the Lord endureth forever.

But, however pure oral instruction may have been at the time that the apostles quitted the earth, that tradition was necessarily exposed in this world of sin to be gradually defaced, polluted, and corrupted. It is for this cause that the Evangelical church honours and adores, with gratitude and humility, the gracious good pleasure of the Saviour, in virtue of which that pure, primitive type, that first, apostolic tradition, in all its purity, has been rendered permanent by being written, by the Spirit of God himself, in our sacred books, for all coming time. And now it finds in those writings, as we have just heard, the divine touchstone which it employs for the purpose of trying all the traditions of men.

Nor does it establish concurrently, as do the doctors of Oxford and the Council of Trent, the tradition which is *written* and the tradition which is *oral;* but it decidedly renders the latter subordinate to the former, because one can not be sure that this oral tradition is only and truly the Apostolical tradition, such as it was in its primitive purity.

The knowledge of true Christianity, says the Protestant church, flows only from one source, namely, from the Holy Scriptures, or, if you will, from the *apostolic tradition,* such as we find it contained in the writings of the New Testament.

The Apostles of Jesus Christ—Peter, Paul, John, Matthew,

[1] Formula of Agreement.

James—perform their functions in the Church to-day; no one has the need nor the power to take their place. They perform their functions at Jerusalem, at Geneva, at Corinth, at Berlin, at Paris; they bear testimony in Oxford and in Rome itself. They preach, even to the ends of the world, the remission of sins and conversion of the soul in the name of the Saviour; they announce the resurrection of the Crucified to every creature; they loose and they retain sins; they lay the foundation of the house of God, and they build it; they teach the missionaries and the ministers of the Gospel; they regulate the order of the Church, and preside in the synods which would be Christian. They do all this by the *written word* which they have left us; or, rather, Christ, Christ himself, does it by that word, since it is the word of Christ, rather than the word of Paul, of Peter, or of James. "Go ye, therefore, and teach all nations: lo! I am with you always, even unto the end of the world."

Without doubt, as to the number of their words, the apostles spoke more than they wrote; but as to the substance, they said nothing more than what they have left us in their divine books. And if they had, in substance, taught otherwise, or more explicitly than they did by their writings, no one could at this day be able to report to us, with assurance, even one syllable of these instructions. If God did not choose to preserve them in his Bible, no one could come to his aid, and do what God himself would not wish to do, and what he would not have done. If, in the writings, of more or less doubtful authenticity, of the companions of the apostles, or of those fathers who are called apostolical, one should find any doctrine of the apostles, it would be necessary, first of all, to put it to the test, in comparing it with the certain instructions of the apostles, that is, with the canon of the Scriptures.

So much for the tradition of the apostles. Let us pass on from the times when they lived to those which succeeded. Let us come to the tradition of the divines of the first centuries. That tradition is, without doubt, of great value to us; but by the very fact of its being Presbyterian, Episcopal, or Synodical, it is no longer apostolical. And let us suppose (what is not true) that it does not contradict itself; and let us suppose that one father does not overthrow what another father has established (as is often the case, and Abelard has proved it in his famous work entitled the *Sic et Non*, whose recent publication we owe to the care of a French philosopher;[1]) let us suppose, for a moment, that one might reduce this tradition of the Fathers of the Church to a harmony similar to that which the apostolical tradition presents, the canon which might be obtained thus could in no manner be placed on an equality with the canon of the apostles.[2]

Without doubt, we acknowledge that the declarations of Christian divines merit our attention, if it be the Holy Spirit which speaks in them, that Spirit which is ever living and ever acting in the Church. But we will not, we absolutely will not allow ourselves to be bound by that which in this tradition and in these divines is only the work of man. And how shall we distinguish that which is of God from that which is of men if not by the holy Scriptures? "It remains," says St. Augustine, "that I judge myself according to this only Master, from whose judgment I desire not to escape."[3] The declarations of the doctors of the Church are only the testimonies of the faith which these eminent men had in the doctrines of the Scriptures. They show how these divines received these doctrines; they may, without doubt, be instructive and edifying for us; but there is no authority in them which binds us. All the divines, Greek, Latin, French, Swiss, German, English, American, placed in the presence of the word of God, are only disciples who are receiving instruction. Men of primitive days and men of modern times, we are all alike scholars in that divine school; and in the chair of instruction around which we are humbly assembled nothing appears, nothing exalts itself but the infallible word of God. I perceive in that vast auditory Calvin, Luther, Cranmer, Augustine, Chrysostom, Athanasius, Cyprian, by the side of our contemporaries. We are not "disciples of Cyprian and Ignatius," as the doctors of Oxford[4] call themselves, but of Jesus Christ. "We do not despise the writings of the fathers," we say, with Calvin, "but

---

[1] *Ouvrages inedites d'Abelard*, published by M. Victor Cousin, Paris, 1836. The introduction to this work, upon the History of Scholastic Philosophy in France, is a master-piece.   [2] *Nitzsch*, Protestantische Theses.   [3] Retract. in Prol.   [4] Newman on Romanism.

in making use of them we remember always that 'all things are ours;' that they ought to serve, not govern us, and that 'we are Christ's,' whom in all things, and without exception, it behoves us to obey."[1]

This the divines of the first century are themselves the first to say. They claim for themselves no authority, and only wish that the word which has taught them may teach us also. "Now that I am old," says Augustine, in his *Retractions*, "I do not expect not to be mistaken in word, or to be perfect in word; how much less when, being young, I commenced writing?"[2] "Beware," says he again, "of submitting to my writings, as if they were canonical Scriptures."[3] "Do not esteem as canonical Scriptures the works of catholic and justly honoured men," says he elsewhere. "It is allowable for us, without impeaching the honour which is due to them, to reject those things in their writings, should we find such in them, which are contrary to the truth. I regard the writings of others as I would have others regard mine."[4] "All that has been said since the times of the apostles ought to be disregarded," says Jerome, "and can possess no authority. However holy, however learned a man may be, who comes after the apostles, let him have no authority."

"Neither antiquity nor custom," says the Confession of the Reformed Church of France, "ought to be arrayed in opposition to the holy Scriptures; on the contrary, all things ought to be examined, regulated, and reformed according to them."

And the Confession of the English church even says, the doctors of Oxford to the contrary notwithstanding: "The holy Scriptures contain all that is necessary to salvation, so that all that is not found in them, all that can not be proved by them, can not be required of any one as an article of faith or as necessary to salvation."

Thus the Evangelical divines of our times give the hand to the reformers, the reformers to the fathers, the fathers to the apostles; and thus, forming, as it were a golden chain, the whole Church, of all ages and of all people, sings as with one

---

[1] Calv. Inst. Relig. Christ.   [2] Retractions.   [3] In Prol. de Trinitate.
[4] Ad Fortunatianum.

voice to the *God of Truth*, that hymn of one of our greates
poets:[1]

> " Speak Thou unto my heart; and let no sage's word,
> No teacher thee beside, explain to me thy law ;
> Let every soul before thy holy presence, Lord !
> Bow down in silent awe,
> And let thy voice be heard !"

What, then, is tradition? It is the testimony of history.

There is a historical testimony for the facts of Christian
history, as well as for those of any other history. We admit
that testimony; only we would discuss it and examine it, as
we would all other testimony. The heresy of Rome and of
Oxford—and it is that which distinguishes them from us—consists in the fact that they attribute the same infallibility to this
testimony as to Scripture itself.

Although we receive the testimony of History as far as it is
true, as, for example, when it relates to the collection of the
writings of the apostles: it by no means results from this that
we should receive this testimony on subjects which are false,
as, for instance, on the adoration of Mary, or the celibacy of
the priests.

The Bible is the faith, holy, authoritative, and truly ancient,
of the child of God; human tradition springs from the love of
novelties, and is the faith of ignorance, of superstition, and of
a credulous puerility.

How deplorable, yet instructive, to see the doctors of a
church which is called to the glorious liberty of the children of
God, and which reposes only on God and his word, place themselves under the bondage of human ordinances? And how loudly
does that example cry to us, " Stand fast in the liberty wherewith Christ hath made us free, and be not entangled again with
the yoke of bondage."

All those errors which we are combating come from a mis-
understanding of truths. We, too, believe in the attributes of

---

[1] Corneille.
> Parle seul mon cœur, et qu'aucune prudence,
> Qu'aucun autre docteur ne m'explique tes lois ;
> Que toute créature en ta sainte présence
> S'impose le silence,
> Et laisse agir ta voix!

the Church of which they speak so much; but we believe in them according to the meaning which God attaches to it, and our opponents believe in them according to that which men attach to it.

Yes, there is *one holy* catholic church, but it is as the apostle says, " The general assembly and church of the first-born, whose names are written in heaven." *Unity* as well as *holiness* appertains to the invisible church. It behoves us without doubt, to pray that the visible church should advance daily in the possession of these heavenly attributes; but neither rigorous unity nor universal holiness is a perfection essential to its existence, or a *sine quâ non*. To say that the visible church must absolutely be composed of saints only is the error of the Donatists and fanatics of all ages. So also to say that the visible church must of necessity be externally one, is the corresponding error of Rome, of Oxford, and of formalists of all times. Let us guard against preferring the external hierarchy, which consists in certain human forms, to that internal hierarchy which is the kingdom of God itself. Let us not suffer the form which passes away, to determine the essence of the Church; but let us on the contrary make the essence of the Church, to wit, the Christian life—which emanates from the word and Spirit of God—change and renew the form. *The form has killed the substance*—here is the whole history of the Papacy and of false Catholicism. *The substance vivifies the form*—here is the whole history of Evangelical Christianity, and of the true Catholic church of Jesus Christ.

Yes, I admit it; the Church is the judge of controversies— *judex controversiarum*. But what is the Church? It is not the clergy; it is not the councils; still less is it the pope. It is the Christian people; it is the faithful. "Prove all things; hold fast that which is good," is said to the children of God, and not to some assembly, or to a certain bishop; and it is they who are constituted, on the part of God, *judges of controversies*. If animals have the instinct which leads them not to eat that which is injurious to them, we can not do less than allow to the Christian this instinct, or rather this intelligence, which emanates from the virtue of the Holy Spirit. Every Christian (the word of God declares it) is called upon to reject "every

spirit that confesses not that Jesus Christ is come in the flesh.''
And this is what is essentially meant when it is said that the
Church is the *judge of controversies!*

Yes, I believe and confess that there is an authority in the
Church, and that without that authority the Church can not
stand. But where is it to be found? Is it with him, whoever
he may be, who has the external consecration, whether he possess theological gifts or not, whether he has received grace and
justification or not? Rome herself does not yet pretend that
orders save and sanctify. Must then the children of God go,
in many cases, to ask a decision in things relating to faith of
the children of this world? What! a bishop, from the moment
he is seated in his chair, although he may be perhaps destitute
of science, destitute of the Spirit of God, and although he may
perhaps have the world and hell in his heart, as had Borgia
and so many other bishops, shall he have authority in the assembly of the saints, and do his lips possess always the wisdom
and the truth necessary for the Church? No, gentlemen; the
idea of a knowlege of God, true, but at the same time destitute
of holiness, is a gross supernaturalism. "Sanctify them through
the truth," says Jesus. There is an authority in the Church,
but that authority is wholly in the word of God. It is not a
man, nor a minister, nor a bishop, descended from Gregory,
from Chrysostom, from Augustine, or from Irenæus, who has
authority over the soul. It is not with a power so contemptible as that which comes from those men, that we, the ministers
of God, go forth into the world. It is elsewhere than in that
episcopal succession, that we seek that which gives authority
to our ministry, and validity to our sacraments.

Rejecting these deplorable innovations, we appeal from them
to the ancient, sovereign, and divine authority of the word of
the Lord. The question which we ask of the man who would
inform himself concerning eternal things, is that which we receive from Jesus himself: "What is written in the Law, and
how readest thou?" What we say to rebellious spirits is what
Abraham said from heaven to the rich man: "You have Moses
and the Prophets, hear them."

That which we ask of all is to imitate the Bereans, who
"searched the Scriptures daily, whether these things were so."

"We ought to obey God rather than men," even the most excellent of men.

Behold the true authority, the true hierarchy, the true polity. The churches which are made by men possess human authority —this is natural; but the Church of God possesses the authority of God, and she will not receive it from others.

II. Such is the *formal* principle of Christianity; let us come now to its *material* principle, that is to say, to the body, the very substance of religion. We have announced it in these terms: THE GRACE OF CHRIST ONLY.

"Ye are saved by grace, through faith," says the Scripture, "and that not of yourselves: it is the gift of God; not of works, lest any man should boast."

Evangelical Christianity not only seeks complete salvation in Christ, but seeks it *in Christ only*, thus excluding, as a cause of salvation all works of his own, all merit, all co-operation of man or of the Church. There is nothing, absolutely nothing upon which we can build the hope of our salvation but the *free and unmerited grace of God*, which is given to us *in Christ*, and communicated *by faith*.

Now, this second great foundation of Evangelical Christianity is likewise overthrown by the modern Ecclesiastical Catholicism.

The famous 9th Tract, which I hold in my hand at this moment, seeks to explain in a papistical sense the Confession of Faith of the Church of England.

The 11th Article of this Confession says: "That we are justified by Faith only is a most wholesome doctrine."

This is the commentary of the new school of Oxford: "In adhering to the doctrine that faith alone justifies, we do not at all exclude the doctrine that works also justify. If it were said that works justify in the same sense in which it is said that faith alone justifies, there would be a contradiction in terms. But faith alone, in one sense, justifies us, and in another, good works justify us: this is all that is here maintained! . . . . . Christ alone, in one sense, justifies; faith also justifies in its proper sense; and so works, whether moral or ceremonial, may justify us in their respective sense."

"There are," says the *British Critic*, "some catholic truths

which are imprinted on the surface of the Scripture rather
than developed in its profound meaning; such is the doctrine
of justification by works." "The preaching of justification
by faith," says another divine of this school, "ought to be
addressed to Pagans by the *propagators* of Christian knowledge; its *promoters* ought to preach to baptized persons justification by works." Works, yes; but justification by them,
never!

Justification is not, according to these divines, that judicial
act by which God, for the sake of the expiatory death of
Christ, declares that he treats us as righteous; it is confounded
by them, as well as by Rome, with the work of the Holy
Spirit.

"Justification," says, again, the chief of these doctors, "is
a progressive work; it must be the work of the Holy Spirit,
and not of Christ. The distinction between deliverance from
the guilt of sin, and deliverance from sin itself, is not scriptural."[1]

The *British Critic* calls the system of justification by grace
through faith "radically and fundamentally monstrous, immoral, heretical, and anti-Christian." "The custom which
has prevailed," say, again, these divines, "of advancing, on
all occasions, the doctrine of Justification explicitly and mainly,
is evidently and entirely opposed to the teaching of the Holy
Scriptures."[2] And they condemn those who make "Justification to consist in the act by which the soul rests upon the
merits of Christ only."[3]

I know that the doctors of Oxford pretend to have found
here a middle term between the Evangelical doctrine and the
Romish doctrine. "It is not," say they, "Sanctification
which justifies us, but the presence of God in us, from which
this sanctification flows. Our Justification is the possession of
this presence." But the doctrine of Oxford is at bottom the
same with that of Rome. The Bible speaks to us of two
great works of Christ: CHRIST FOR US, and CHRIST IN US.
Which of these two works is that which justifies us? The
Church of Christ answers, The former. Rome and Oxford
answer, The latter. When this is said all is said.

1 Newman on Justification.   2 Tract 80.   3 Newman on Justification.

And these doctors do not conceal it. They inform us that it is the system against which they stand up. They declare to us that it is against the idea that, when the sinner "has by faith laid hold of the saving merits of Christ, his sins are blotted out, covered, and cannot reappear; his guilt has been abolished, so that he has only to render thanks to Christ, who has delivered him from his transgressions." "My lord," says Dr. Pusey to the bishop of Oxford, " it is against this system that I have spoken." Stop! Do not tear to pieces this good news, which alone has been, and will be in all ages, the consolation of the sinner!

Gentlemen, if the effect of the first principle of this new school would be to deprive the Church of all light, that of this second principle would be to deprive it of all salvation. "If righteousness come by the law, then Christ is dead in vain. O foolish Galatians, who hath bewitched you that ye should not obey the truth: received ye the Spirit by the works of the law, or by the hearing of faith?"

Men, the most eminent for piety, have felt that it is the very source of the Christian life, the foundation of the Church, which is here attacked: "There is reason," says the excellent bishop of Winchester, who, as well as several other bishops, and particularly those of Chester and Calcutta, has denounced these errors, in a charge addressed to his clergy, "there is reason to fear that the distinctive principles of our Church would be endangered, if men should envelope in a cloud the great doctrine which sets forth the way in which we are accounted righteous before God; if men doubt that the Protestant doctrine of justification by faith is fundamental; if, instead of the sacrifice of Christ, the pure and only cause for which we are graciously received, men establish a certain inherent disposition of sanctification, and thus confound the work of the Spirit within with the work of Christ without."

The school of Oxford pretends, with Rome and the Council of Trent, "that justification is the indwelling in us of God the Father and of the incarnate Word, by the Holy Spirit, and that the two acts distinguished from each other by the Bible and our theologians form only one."[1] What then?

[1] Letter of Dr. Pusey to the bishop of Oxford.

8

1. God remits to the sinner the penalty of sin; He absolves him; He pardons him. 2. He delivers him from sin itself; He renews him; He sanctifies him.

Are not these two different things?

Would not the pardon of sin on the part of God be just nothing at all? Would it not be simply an image of sanctification? Or should we say that the pardon which is granted to faith, and which produces in the heart the sentiment of reconciliation, of adoption, and of peace, is something too external to be taken into account?

" The Lutheran system," says the *British Critic*, " is immoral, because it distinguishes between these two works." Without doubt, it does distinguish between them, but it does not separate them. " See wherefore we are justified," says Melancthon, in the Apology for the Confession of Augsburg; "it is in order that, being righteous, we should do good, and begin to obey the law of God; see here why it is that we are regenerated and receive the Holy Spirit: it is that the new life may have new works and new dispositions." How many times has the Reformation declared that justifying faith is not an historical, dead, vain knowledge, but a living action, an act of willing and receiving, a work of the Holy Spirit, the true worship of God, obedience toward God in the most important of all moments! Yes, it is a living, efficacious faith which justifies; and these words, *efficacious faith*, which are found in all our Confessions of Faith, are there for the purpose of declaring that faith *alone* serves as a cause in the work of justification, that it *alone* justifies, but that precisely because of this it does not rest *alone*, that is to say, without its appropriate operations and its fruits.

Such is the grand difference between us and the Oxford School. We believe in sanctification through justification, and the Oxford School believes in justification through sanctification. With us, justification is the cause and sanctification is the effect. With these doctors, on the contrary, sanctification is the cause and justification the effect. And these are not things indifferent, and vain distinctions; they are the *sic* and the *non*, the yes and the no. While our creed establishes in all their rights these two works, the creed of Oxford compromises and annihilates them both. Justification exists no more, if it depend on man's sanctification and not on the grace of God; for "the heavens," say the Scriptures, "are not clean in his sight," "and his eyes are too pure to behold iniquity;" but, on the other hand, sanctification itself can not be accomplished; for how could you expect the effect to be produced when you begin by taking away the cause? "Herein is love," says St. John, "not that we loved God, but that he loved us; we love him because he first loved us." If I might use a vulgar expression, I should say that Oxford *puts the cart before the horse*, in placing sanctification before justification. In this way neither the cart nor the horse will advance. In order that the work should go on, it is necessary that that which draws should be placed before that which is drawn. There is not a system more contrary to true sanctification than that; and, to employ the language of the *British Critic*, there is not, consequently, a system more monstrous and immoral. What! shall your justification depend, not upon the work which Christ accomplished on the cross, but upon that which is accomplished in your hearts! It is not to Christ, to his grace, that you ought to look in order to be justified, but to yourselves, to the righteousness which is in you, to your spiritual gifts! . . .

From this result two great evils.

Either you will deceive yourselves, in believing that there is a work in you sufficiently good to justify you before God; and then you will be inflated with pride, that pride which the Scriptures say "goeth before a fall:" or you will not deceive yourselves; you will see, as the Saviour says, that you are poor and wretched and blind and naked; and then you will fall into despair. The heights of pride and the depths of despair; such are the alternatives which the doctrine of Oxford and of Rome bequeaths to us.

The Christian doctrine, on the contrary, places man in perfect humility, for it is another who justifies him; and yet it gives him abundant peace, for his justification—a fruit of the " righteousness of God "—is complete, assured, eternal.

III.—Finally, we define the *personal* or *moral* principle of Christianity. We have announced it in these words :—THE WORK OF THE SPIRIT ONLY.

Christianity is an individual work ; the grace of God converts soul by soul. Each soul is a world, in which a creation peculiar to itself must be accomplished. The Church is but the assembly of all the souls in whom this work is wrought, and who are now united because they have but " one Spirit, one Lord, one Father."

And what is the nature of this work ? It is essentially moral. Christianity operates upon the will of man and changes it. Conversion comes from the action of the Spirit of God, and not from the magic action of certain ceremonies which, rendering faith on the part of man vain and useless, would regenerate him by their own inherent virtue. " In Christ Jesus neither circumcision availeth any thing, nor uncircumcision, but [to be] a new creature." " If through the Spirit ye do mortify the deeds of the body, ye shall live."

Now the Oxford divines, although there is a great difference among them on this point, as well as on some others (some going by no means as far as others), put immense obstacles in the way of this individual regeneration.

Nothing inspires them with greater repugnance than Christian individualism. They proceed by synthesis, not by analysis. They do not set out with the principle laid down by the Saviour: "Except a man be born again, he cannot see the kingdom of God ;" but they set out with this opposite principle: " All those who have participated in the ordinances of the Church are born again." And while the Saviour, in all his discourses, excites the efforts of each individual, saying, " Seek, ask, knock, strive to enter in at the strait gate ; it is only the violent who take it by force ;" the Oxford divines say, on the contrary, " The idea of obtaining religious truth ourselves, and by our private enquiry, whether by reading, or by thinking, or by studying the Scriptures or other books, . . . is nowhere authorized in the Scriptures. The great question which ought to be placed before every mind is this: ' What voice should be heard like that of the holy Catholic and Apostolic Church ?'[1]

And how shall this individual regeneration by the Holy Spirit be accomplished, since the first task of Puseyism is to

[1] British Critic.

say to all, that it is already accomplished; that all who have been baptized have thereby been rendered partakers of the Divine nature; and that to preach conversion again to them is contrary to the truth? "It is baptism and not faith," says one of these divines, "that is the primary instrument of justification;"[1] and we know that with them justification and conversion are one and the same work. To prevent the wretched from escaping from the miserable state in which they are, would not the best means be to persuade a poor man that he possesses a large fortune, or an ignorant man that he has great science, or a sick man that he is in perfect health? The Evil One could not invent a stratagem more fit to prevent conversion than this idea, that all men who have been baptized by water are regenerated.

Still more, these doctors extend to the Holy Supper this same magic virtue. "It is now almost universally believed," say they, in speaking of their church, "that God communicates grace only through faith, prayer, spiritual contemplation, communion with God; while it is the Church and her sacraments which are *the* ordained, direct, visible means for conveying to the soul that which is invisible and supernatural. It is said, for example, that to administer the Supper to infants, to dying persons apparently deprived of their senses, however pious they may have been, is a superstition; and yet these practices are sanctioned by antiquity. The essence of the sectarian doctrine is to consider *faith* and not the *sacraments* as the means of justification and other evangelical gifts."[2]

What then? shall a child who does not possess reason, and does not even know how to speak, shall a sick man whom the approach of death has deprived of perception and intelligence, receive grace purely by the external application of the sacraments? Have the will, the affections of the heart, no need to be touched in order that man may be sanctified? What a degradation of man and of the religion of Jesus Christ! Is there a great difference between such ceremonies and the mummeries and charms of the debased Hindoos, or of the African savages?

[1] Newman on Justification.
[2] Tracts for the Times. Advertisement in vol. ii.

If the first error of Oxford deprives the Church of light, if the second deprives her of salvation, the third deprives her of all real sanctification. Without doubt, we believe that the sacraments are means of grace; but they are only so when faith accompanies their use. To put faith and the sacraments in opposition, as the Oxford doctors do, is to annihilate the efficacy of the sacraments themselves.

The Church will rise up against such fatal errors. There is a work of renovation which must be wrought in man, a personal or individual work; and it is God who performs it. "A new heart," saith the Lord, "will I give you, and a new spirit will I put within you."

By what right would they thus put the Church in the place of God, and establish her clergy as the dispensers of divine life?

Then it would be of little consequence that a man had led a dissipated life, and that the heart remained attached to sin and the world; would not a participation in the sacraments of religion suffice to put him in possession of grace? We are assured that already sad consequences are manifested in the life of many of the adherents of Oxford.

The system of Puseyism tends to lull the conscience to sleep by the participation of external rites: the Evangelical system tends to awaken it unceasingly. The work of the Spirit, which is one of the grand principles of Evangelical Christianity, does not consist only in regeneration; it consists also in a sanctification, fundamental and universal. If, instead of permitting ourselves to be enfeebled by trusting to human ordinances, we have truly the *Spirit of Christ* within us, we shall not suffer the least contradiction to exist between the divine law on the one hand, and our dispositions and actions on the other. We shall not content ourselves with abstaining from the grosser manifestations of sin, but we shall desire that the very germ of evil be eradicated from our hearts. We shall not content ourselves with abstaining from the grosser manifestations of sin, but we shall desire that the very germ of evil be eradicated from our hearts. We shall love the truth, and we shall reject with horror that sad hypocrisy which sometimes defiles the sanctuary. We shall not have in the communication of our religious convictions that reserve which Puseyism prescribes; "That which shall have been told to us in the ear, we shall proclaim on the house-tops." We shall not remain in a church whose most sacred truths we trample under our feet, eating the bread which it gives us, and lifting up our arm to strike it. From the moment that we shall have discovered that a doctrine is opposed to the word of God, neither dangers nor sacrifices shall prevent us from casting it far from us. The work of the Spirit will carry light into the most secret recesses of our hearts. "The King's daughter is all glorious within." The King whom we follow has said to us: "I am the light of the world: he that followeth me shall not walk in darkness, but shall have the light of life."

I repeat again in closing, gentlemen: the three great principles of Christianity are these : *The Word of God* ONLY,—*The Grace of God* ONLY,—*The Work of the Spirit* ONLY. I come now to ask you henceforth to apply to yourselves more and more these principles, and let them reign supremely over your hearts and lives. And why, gentlemen? Because every thing that places our souls in immediate communication with God is salutary, and every thing that interposes between God and our souls is injurious and ruinous. If a thick cloud should pass between you and the sun, you would no longer feel its genial warmth, and might perhaps be seized with a chill. So if you place between yourselves and the word of God the tradition and authority of the Church, you will no longer have to do with the word of God, that is to say, with a divine, and, consequently, a powerful and perfect instrument, but with the word of man; that is to say, with a human, and, consequently, a weak and defective instrument; it will have lost that power which translates from darkness into light.

Or, if you place between the grace of God and yourselves the ordinances of the Church, the episcopal priesthood, the dispositions of the heart, works, *grace will then be no more grace*, as St. Paul says. The instrument of God will have been broken, and we shall no longer be able to say, that " Charity proceeds from faith unfeigned," that faith worketh by love," "that our souls are purified in obeying the truth," "that Christ dwells in our hearts by faith.

Man always seeks to return, in some way or other, to a human salvation; this is the source of the innovation of Rome and of Oxford. The substitution of the Church for Jesus Christ is that which essentially characterizes these opinions. It is no longer Christ who enlightens, Christ who saves, Christ who forgives, Christ who commands, Christ who judges; it is the Church, and always the Church, that is to say, an assembly of sinful men, as weak and prone to err as ourselves. " They have taken away the Lord, and we know not where they have laid him."

The errors which we have indicated are, therefore, practical errors, destructive of true piety in the soul, a deprivation of God's influence, and an exaltation of the flesh, although in a form that " has the show of wisdom in will-worship and humility." If they should ever obtain the ascendency in the Church, Christianity would cease to be a new, a holy, a spiritual, a heavenly life. It would become an external affair of ordinances, rites, and ceremonies. This has been clearly seen by the servant of God whom we have already quoted: " Finally," says Sumner, bishop of Winchester, " I can not but fear the consequences that a system of teaching, which confines itself to the external and ritual parts of divine worship, while it loses sight of their internal signification and the spiritual life, may have upon the character, the efficacy, and the truth of our Church: a system which robs the Church of its brightest glory, and, forgetting the continual presence of the Lord, seems to depose him from his just pre-eminence; a system which tends to put the observance of days, months, times, and seasons in the place of a true and spiritual worship; which substitutes a spirit of hesitation, fear, and doubt for the cordial obedience of filial love; a slavish spirit for the liberty of the Gospel; and which, indeed, calls upon us to work out our sanctification with fear and trembling, but without any fore-taste of the rest that remaineth for the people of God, without giving us joy in believing."[1]

The universal church of Christ rejoices to hear such words. She beholds, with gratitude toward her divine Head, the firm-

---

[1] Charge delivered by Chr. R. Sumner, D.D., Lord Bishop of Winchester, 1841.

ness with which some bishops, ministers, and laymen of England meet this growing evil. But is this enough? Is it enough to retain, on the edge of a precipice, a Church and a people, hitherto so dear to the friends of the Gospel?

Oxford conducts to Rome; Mr. Sibthorp and others have proved it. The march of Puseyism, regularly inclining, from tract to tract, toward the pure system of the Papacy, demonstrates clearly enough the end to which it tends. And even if it should not effect a total conversion to Popery, what signifies it, since it is nothing else than a Popish system (in its essential features) transferred to England? It is not necessary that the Thames should go to Rome to bear the tribute of its waters: the Tiber flows in Oxford.

England owes every thing to the Reformation. What was she before the renovation of the Church? Blindly submissive to the Tudors, her forms of government, both political and ecclesiastical, were superannuated, without life and spirit; so that in England, as in almost all Europe, we might say, with a Christian statesman, " Despotism seemed the only preservative against dissolution.[1] The Reformation developed, in an admirable manner, that Christian spirit, that love of liberty, that fear of God, that loyal affection for the sovereign, that patriotism, those generous sacrifices, that genius, that strength, that activity, which constitute the prosperity and glory of England. In the age of the Reformation, Catholic Spain, gorged with the blood of the children of God, fell, overthrown by the Almighty Arm, and reformed England ascended in her stead the throne of the seas, which has been justly termed the throne of the world. The winds which engulfed the ARMADA called up this new power from the depths.

The country of Philip II, wounded to the heart because she had attacked the people of God, dropped from her hand the sceptre of the ocean; and the country of Elizabeth, fortified by the word of God, found it floating on the seas, seized it, and wielded it to bring into subjection to the King of heaven the nations of the earth. It is the Gospel that has given to England our antipodes.[2] It is the God of the Gospel who has

[1] Archives of the House of Orange-Nassau, published at the Hague, by Mr. Groen Van Prinsterer, Counsellor of State. [2] New Zealand.

bestowed upon her all that she possesses.   If in those distinguished islands the Gospel were to fall under the united attacks
of Popery and Puseyism, we might write upon their hitherto
triumphant banner, "ICHABOD, *the glory of the Lord is departed.*"

God has given the dominion of the seas to nations who bear
every where with them the Gospel of Jesus Christ.   But if,
instead of the good news of salvation, England carries to the
heathen a mere human and priestly religion, God will deprive
her of her power.   The evil is already great.   In India the
Puseyite missionaries are satisfied with teaching the natives
rites and ceremonies, without troubling themselves about the
conversion of the heart; thus treading closely in the steps of
the Roman Catholic church.   They endeavour to counteract
the efforts of evangelical missionaries, and disturb the weak
minds of the natives, by telling them that all those who have
not received Episcopal ordination are not ministers.

If England prove unfaithful to the Gospel, God will humble
her in those powerful islands where she has established her
throne, and in those distant countries subjected to her sway.
Do we not already hear a faint rumour which justifies these
gloomy presentiments?   The mother country sees her difficulties increase; unheard-of disasters have spread fear and terror
on the banks of the Indus.   From the chariot of this people is
heard a cracking sound, because impious hands have changed
the pole-bolt.   Should England forsake the faith of the Bible,
the crown would fall from her head.   Ah! we also, Christians
of the Continent and of the world, would mourn over her fall!
We love her for Christ's sake; for his sake we pray for her.
But if the apostacy now begun should be accomplished, we shall
have nothing left for her but cries, groans, and tears.

What are the bishops doing?   What is the Church doing?
This is the general question.

If the church of England were well administered, she would
only admit to her pulpits teachers who submit to the word of God,
agreeably to the Thirty-nine Articles, and banish from them all
those who violate her laws, and poison the minds of the youth,
trouble souls, and seek to overthrow the Gospel of Jesus Christ.

A few Episcopal mandates will not accomplish this.   We
undoubtedly believe that no power can take from the Christian

the right to "examine the Scriptures, and to try the spirits whether they are of God." But we do not believe in the supreme power of the clergy: we do not believe that the servants of a church may announce to it doctrines which tend to overthrow it. Did it not please the apostles, the elders, and the whole Church to impose silence upon those of Antioch who wished to substitute, as they do now at Oxford, human ordinances for the grace of Christ? Since when does a well-constituted Church speak only through isolated voices? Shall the Annual Convocations of the Church of England remain always a vain ceremony and an empty form? If their nature can not be changed, shall not powerful remedies be applied to counteract great evils? Will not the Church be moved in England, as formerly in Jerusalem? Shall not the "elders and the whole Church" form a council which shall, as tradition tell us they did at Nice, place the word of God upon an elevated throne, in token of its supreme authority, and, condemning and cutting off all dangerous errors, render to Jesus Christ and his word that supreme authority which usurping hands are on the point of wresting from him?

But if the Church still holds her peace, if she allows her sacred foundations to be sapped in her universities, then (we say it with profound grief) a voice like that of the prophet. will be heard, exclaiming, "Wo to the Church! wo to the people! wo to England!"

Gentlemen, there are two ways of destroying Christianity: one is to deny it, the other to displace it. To put the Church above Christianity, the hierarchy above the word of God; to ask a man, not whether he has received the Holy Ghost but whether he has received baptism from the hands of those who are termed successors of the apostles and their delegates: all this may doubtless flatter the pride of the natural man, but is fundamentally opposed to the Bible, and aims a fatal blow at the religion of Jesus Christ. If God had intended that Christianity should, like the Mosaic system, be chiefly an ecclesiastical, sacerdotal, and hierarchical system, he would have ordered and established it in the New Testament, as he did in the Old. But there is nothing like this in the New Testament. All the declarations of our Lord and of his apostles tend to prove that the new religion given to the world is "life and spirit," and not a new system of priesthood and ordinances. "The kingdom of God," saith Jesus, "cometh not with observation: neither shall they say, Lo here! or lo there! for behold, the kingdom of God is within you." "The kingdom of God is not meat and drink; but righteousness, and peace, and joy in the Holy Ghost."

Let us then attribute a divine institution and a divine authority to the essence of the Church, but by no means to its *form*. God has undoubtedly established the ministry of the word and sacraments, that is to say, general forms, which are adapted to the universal Church; but it is a narrow and dangerous bigotry which would attribute more importance to the particular forms of each sect than to the spirit of Christianity. This evil has long prevailed in the Eastern church [Greek], and has rendered it barren. It is the essence of the church of Rome, and it is destroying it. It is endeavouring to insinuate itself into every Church; it appears in England in the Established church; in Germany in the Lutheran, and even in the Reformed and Presbyterian church. It is that mystery of iniquity which already began to work in the time of the apostles. Let us reject and oppose this deadly principle wherever it is found. We are men before we are Swiss, French, English, or German; let us also remember that we are Christians before we are Episcopalians, Lutherans, Reformed, or Dissenters. These different forms of the Church are like the different costumes, different features, and different characters of nations; that which constitutes the man is not found in these accessories. We must seek for it in the heart that beats under this exterior, in the conscience which is seated there, in the intelligence which shines there, in the will which acts there. If we assign more importance to the Church than to Christianity, to the form than to the life, we shall infallibly reap that which we have sown; we shall soon have a Church composed of skeletons, clothed, it may be, in brilliant garments, and ranged, I admit, in a most imposing order to the eye, but as cold, stiff, and immovable as a pale legion of the dead. If Puseyism (and unfortunately, some of the doctrines which it promulgates are not in England confined to that school), if Puseyism should make progress in the Established church, it will in a few years dry up all its springs of life. The feverish excitement which disease at first produces will soon give place to languor; the blood will be congealed, the muscles stiffened, and that church will be only a dead body, around which the eagles will gather together.

All forms, whether papal, patriarchal, episcopal, consistorial, or presbyterian, possess only a human value and authority. Let us not esteem the bark above the sap, the body above the soul, the form above the life, the visible church above the invisible, the priest above the Holy Spirit. Let us hate all sectarian, ecclesiastical, national, or dissenting spirit; but let us love Jesus Christ in all sects, whether ecclesiastical, national, or dissenting. The true catholicity which we have lost, and which we must seek to recover, is that of "holding the truth in love." A renovation of the Church is necessary; I know it, I feel it, I pray for it from the bottom of my soul; only let us seek for it in the right way. Forms, ecclesiastical constitutions, the organization of churches, are important, very important. "But let us seek first the kingdom of God and his righteousness and all these things shall be added unto us."

Let us then, gentlemen, be firm and decided in the truth; and while we love the erring, let us boldly attack the error. Let us stand upon the rock of ages—the word of God; and let the vain opinions and stale innovations which are constantly springing up and dying in the world, break powerless at our feet. "Two systems of doctrine," says Dr. Pusey, "are now, and probably for the last time, in conflict: the system of Geneva and the Catholic system." We accept this definition. One of the men who have most powerfully resisted these errors, the Rev. W. Goode, seems to think that by the Genevan system Dr. Pusey intends to designate the Unitarian, Pelagian, Latitudinarian system, which has laid waste the Church, not only in Geneva, but throughout Christendom. "According to Romish tactics," says Mr. Goode, "the adversaries of the Oxford school are classed together under the name that will render them most odious; they belong, it is said, to the *Genevan school*."[1]

[1] The Case as It Is.

Certainly, gentlemen, if the Unitarian school of England and Geneva were called upon to struggle with the semi-papal school of Oxford, we should much fear the issue. But these divines will meet with other opponents in England, Scotland, Ireland, on the Continent, and, if need be, even in our little and humble Geneva.

Yes, we acknowledge that it is the system of Geneva which is now struggling with the Catholic system; but it is the system of ancient Geneva; it is the system of Calvin and Beza, the system of the Gospel and the Reformation. The opprobrium they would cast upon us we receive as an honour. Three centuries ago, Geneva rose against Rome; let Geneva now rise against Oxford.

"I should like," says one of the Oxford divines,[1] "to see the patriarch of Constantinople and our archbishop of Canterbury go barefoot to Rome, throw their arms round the pope, kiss him, and not let him go till they had persuaded him to be more reasonable;" that is to say, doubtless, until he had extended his hand to them, and ceased to proclaim them heretics and schismatics.

Evangelical Christians of Geneva, England, and all other countries! It is not to Rome that you must drag yourselves, "To those seven mountains, on which the woman sitteth, having a golden cup in her hand, full of abominations;" the pilgrimage that you must make is to that excellent and perfect

---

[1] W. Palmer's Aids to Reflection, 1841. This work contains some curious, and, without doubt, authentic conversations, which Mr. Palmer had at Geneva in 1836, with different pastors and professors of the Academy and the Company. "*July* 26. The public professor of dogmatic theology told me, when I asked him what was the precise doctrine of the Company of Pastors at that time on the subject of the Trinity, 'Perhaps no two had exactly the same shade of opinion; that the great majority would deny the doctrine in the scholastic sense.'—*August* 4. A pastor of the Company told me, ' That of thirty-four members, he thinks there are only four who would admit the doctrine of the Trinity.'" The author was almost as much dissatisfied with the Evangelical as with the Unitarian ministers. He relates that one of the former said to him, on the 12th of August, " You are lost in the study of outward forms, mere worldly vanities; *you are a baby, a mere baby,* he said in English."

Translator's Note.—The reader will remember that the above quotation is not in the original words, but translated from the French version by the author.

tabernacle "not made with hands;" that "throne of grace, where we find grace to help in time of need."

It is not upon the neck of the "Man of Sin" that you must cast yourselves, covering him with your kisses and your tears; but upon the neck of Him with whom "Jacob wrestled until the breaking of the day;" of Him "who is seated at the right hand of God in the heavenly places, far above all principality and power, and every name that is named, not only in this world but also in that which is to come."

Yes, let the children of God in the east and in the west arise; let them, understanding the signs of the times, and seeing that the destinies of the Church depend upon the issue of the present conflicts, conflicts so numerous, so different, and so powerful, form a sacred brotherhood, and, with one heart and one soul, exclaim, as Moses did when the ark set forward, "Rise up, Lord, and let thine enemies be scattered, and let them that hate thee flee before thee."

DISCOURSE XII.[1]

FAITH AND KNOWLEDGE.

" Si sanctus es, comprehendisti et nosti."—*St. Bernard.*

Ἐν τῇ πίστει ὑμῶν . . . . τὴν γνῶσιν.

" Add to your faith . . . . knowledge."—2 PETER, i, 5.

FAITH and knowledge, in the opinion of the world, are opposed to and exclusive of one another. It is said that
faith in revealed truth is incompatible with those glorious subjects of human science by which the depths of the earth are
sounded, the expanse of heaven is measured, and the still more
mysterious realm of the mind of man is examined. The names
of Bacon, Newton, Pascal, Leibnitz, Euler, and many others
have often been quoted in refutation of this singular assertion,
and have proved its absurdity; yet you will still hear it repeated
in the world, for there is not an error of any kind which man
does not endeavour to uphold.

We do not intend to occupy this hour in refuting this doctrine. We wish, rather, to enquire more deeply into the essence of faith, and to enter farther upon the domains of knowledge. We wish to consider a different sort of faith and knowledge, namely, the faith of the heart, or Christian life; and
theology, or the knowledge of God.

In truth, if we cross the threshold of the sanctuary of sacred
knowledge, we meet with the same pretension as in the world,
but applied to different subjects. Here faith is that new principle of life and holiness which the word of God and the Holy
Ghost develope in the hearts of God's elect.

Knowledge, or theology, is the philosophy of faith, the result of enquiry, of reflection, of the labour of the human mind
applied to divine things, and endeavouring to comprehend them

[1] Delivered at the Theological Seminary of Geneva, on the 3rd of November, 1834.

and discover the light, the tendencies, the systematic union of which they are susceptible.

In this new field, men condemn as incompatible, not knowledge, or a certain historical faith which all theologians must possess, more or less, but the living faith of Christians. Worldly theologians have attacked the latter kind in the same manner and with the same weapons with which worldly philosophers have attacked the former. According to them, there can be no harmony between living faith and theology.

And we must acknowledge that there is some ground for their assertions. Faith and theology have often been, and still are, separated in the minds of many ministers of the Gospel. Some are mere theologians, acquainted with the various branches of theological knowledge, and able to lay down with correctness the principles of the Christian system; but in their hearts there is no living faith. Others, on the other hand, possess the faith of the heart, the Christian life, but are unacquainted with theology, and regard it as a barren science, by which one may not expect to be profited.

My brethren, you are exposed to both these errors.

We think, with many theologians, that the ministers of Christ ought not to separate these two points, and that greater usefulness in the service of God would result from their proper combination. We have founded this Seminary in the name of faith and knowledge, of Christian life and theology. We believe that, in the words of the apostle, the *pastor* ought to be a *teacher*.

We shall, then, describe, in a few words, the relations which exist between Christian life and theology; we shall show the necessity of faith, and the advantages of knowledge, and we shall point out the dangers to be avoided.

I. FAITH. In the first place, I address those who, since they do not possess the living faith of Christians in their hearts, would fain supply its place with theology.

It is impossible for the Christian, and, consequently for the minister, to live without the life of faith. Do you then suppose that the scientific development of Christian doctrine will produce in you that living faith without which you can not exist? No, my brethren; the work of man can not create the work of God.

Theology is not the mother of faith; but faith is the mother of theology.

The cultivation of theological science has never produced a revival of Christian life in the Church. Such revivals have emanated from the simple preaching of Christian truths, from that faith of the heart, that internal conviction and experience, in accordance with which a man exclaims, with sacred enthusiasm, " I believed, and therefore have I spoken." If there have been instances of theological instruction being the means of producing faith in the heart (and there have been many such,) it has been owing to the element of faith which existed in that instruction, and not to the theological element. It is because the teacher believes, and not because he studies, that he becomes an instrument of regeneration. Faith produces faith, but thought produces nothing but thought. Correctness, explanation, and systematic arrangement of doctrine never produced life.

It is not to the school nor to the theologian that the minister or the layman must look for faith. They must go to Jesus Christ, the Head of the church. You must seek life from Him in whom " dwelleth all the fulness of the Godhead bodily;" not from the maxims of science. Every believer, and, consequently, every minister, is required, in his quality of prophet, to ask directly of Jesus the measure of grace. The character of a mediator between God and man proceeds no more from the science of the theologian than from the hierarchy of the priest. It is not in some Theological Summary, or *Commonplace Book*,[1] that you are to seek your faith, but in the Bible, in the Bible directly, by means of the light of the Holy Spirit which is promised to all.

But farther: theology, far from producing Christian life, is itself produced by that life. It is faith that supplies science with the means of knowledge, with the subjects of reflection, with the elements for combination. For real, enlightening science is composed, not of abstract ideas and dead elements, but of living doctrines and principles inspired by the Spirit of God.

---

[1] *Summa Theologica, Loci Communes:* usual titles of systems of theology, both before and after the Reformation.

And it is also that living faith which gives to the mind the elasticity, the liberal and profound views, and the activity necessary to set the primary elements at work, and to bring forth the system in all its branches. An era which was dead in faith never did and never will produce theology. The creating epochs of science have always been preceded, as history can prove, by a revival of Christian life in the Church. It was from the cradle of faith that those theological works came which marked the times of Augustine, the scholastics of the thirteenth century, and the Reformers.

If you want to be theologians, you must bathe in the stream of living waters. It is faith that will give you that impulse, without which no great work can be produced; that definite truth, without which you would wander into absurd systems; that life, without which you would only be walking in a field of dry bones.

Try the other method. If Christian life is not the source of your theology, you will fall into one of two evils: either you will rush as many have done, into the speculative distinctions of useless dialectics; or, receiving a negative impulse, you will assume a hostile attitude; you will take up arms against the objects you ought to defend; you will exert a destructive influence in the sphere assigned to you, and, instead of raising a monument to the living God, you will take pleasure in destroying that which exists, and in amusing yourself at the sight of the ruins, as too many theologians, alas! have already done.

And on what foundation, my brethren, would you have theology to rest if not on the word of God, on faith in the divine testimony, produced in the heart by the Holy Spirit? If this be not the foundation of theology, it must either rest on the momentary impulse of the spirit of the times, or on the adventurous speculations of human reason. With such support, science would make singular mistakes and experience many a fall, and would wander into strange and gloomy paths. If the tree of knowledge is to prosper, it must, as David says, be " planted by the rivers of water" of the law of God; it must derive constantly and solely from that pure water its sap and the elements of its life. Then it will " bring forth its fruit in its season; its leaf shall not wither; and whatsoever it doeth shall prosper." But if any foreign element happen to be absorbed by its roots, that tree will soon wither, languish, and die.

Plant it rather on the hill of Golgotha, under the shadow of the cross, under the look of love of the Crucified, who is the Wisdom of God and Life itself.

That which gives life to the humblest faith of the poorest believer gives it likewise to the most sublime knowledge of the greatest divine.

Faith is not only the creating principle of theology; it is also its renovating strength. We have but too many proofs that knowledge can separate itself from the word of God. It then goes astray; a fever of infidelity has taken possession of it; a crisis has occurred. What will cure it? What will bring it back into the right way? Will ordinances, laws, or acts of power? Assuredly those who superintend public instruction ought to watch lest, instead of adding life to it, they should put it to death. But an external power, the decisions of the civil government, or any human power, will never cure such a disease. If you imprison it for a time, it will only make the greater ravages within.

What then will save science? I answer, The life of the Church; the simple faith of the believer. That faith and that life existed before theology and independently of science; they cannot perish; there is healing power in them. They will react powerfully on theology. The teachers, surrounded on all sides by the manifestations of Christian faith, would be brought back in spite of themselves, by a superior power, to the source of all light and life. They would be constrained, one by one, to forsake all the positions in which chance might place them. Truth would daily gain power over the enemy's camp. The opposition would always increase in strength. Science itself, obliged to acknowledge that it had been separated from that to which it ought to be united, would soon raise its voice in opposition to the errors of science. Perhaps, as is usually the case, it was infidelity in the Church that carried infidelity into theology. The faith of the Church will revive faith in theology. That which gave the wound will heal it; that which struck will bind up. The light and life of the Church constitute the sun of theology. When that sun is vailed, science is darkened and dies. When it shines again, science is illumined and revived.

Thus, my brethren, if science is to be cultivated with success in a university, an academy, or a school, there must be liberty; but first of all there must be piety. There must be ideas; but above all there must be faith. There must be science; but there must be submission to the word of God. A theological school, if it is to prosper in science, must be a sanctuary. Away with a spirit of profanity and mockery; away with levity, indecency, looseness of morals, and conformity with a world lying in wickedness! It would be a death-blow to it, both as the temple of science and as the nursery of the prophets.

The holiness of a theological school is the most certain warrant of its progress in knowledge.

" THE LEVITES SHALL BE MINE, saith the Lord."

II. KNOWLEDGE.—Faith then is essential to theology. But there is another danger which we must point out; one into which many stumble who regard theology as a barren knowledge, unadapted and useless to the Church.

First, let us clearly understand what we mean by knowledge.

This is no proud and puffed-up knowledge, but a humble knowledge, which is aware that it knows nothing of itself, and ought to learn every thing from the Bible. It is not a knowlege separated from God, but one which God himself grants in answer to fervent prayer, to conscientious enquiries, to serious and holy meditation, the labours of which are vivified, and its influence made effectual by his Spirit.

The present state of the world, and especially of the French people, shows but too clearly the usefulness and necessity of knowledge. Why is Christianity so little known, and why are its fundamental principles so much despised? We do not hesitate, my brethren, to say that it is because, while all other sciences have risen rapidly, theological science does not exist among us for the present generation, or at any rate can scarcely be said to exist.

Perhaps there are eras in the social and intellectual development of a people when it suffices that Christian life should revive the Church. But it cannot be so in the present state of society.

When the entire being of man is developed, religion ought
to embrace man in his entire being. It is extensive enough to
do it, and there is no quality in man that ought to escape from
its influence. The faculty of knowledge that is within us also
finds the nourishment which it needs, and a field in which to
develope its strength. The understanding comes from God,
as well as affection or the will. To pretend, as some have
done, that it is enough that Christianity should speak to the
heart, and that it may leave the understanding unsatisfied, is
to oppose the rising of the sun over a part of God's creation;
it is to revolt against the order instituted by the Divine Being.

Christianity must maintain its place. It must keep its position as superior to all human wisdom. Theology must ever
be, in the bosom of Christian societies, what lord Bacon, the re-
storer of modern science, termed it, " the transcendent science."

And do not imagine that the existence of this science is useless for the conversion of souls. If so, why do we find in the
countries where theological science exists, as in Germany, so
many real Christians among laymen of education and intelligence, while among us we so rarely meet any in that class?

Nothing but the existence of science will explain this phenomenon. It has turned the attention of those learned men to
the instruction of God. It has also led them to look at this
branch of the tree which they cultivate. Science has made the
word of God and Christianity honourable in the eyes of the
learned. They enquired into it at first, perhaps, merely through
curiosity; then Christianity took hold of their hearts, and the
word of God saved them.

Let us lament, then, that while all other sciences have been
so highly honoured, and found so many worshippers among the
French people, theological science has no monuments or trophies; we might almost say, it has no name or existence. Let
us lament that, while all the branches of the tree of knowledge
under the shadow of which this generation rejoice, are full of
strength, and are covered with beautiful fruit, this branch,
though the principal one of the tree, is feeble, withered, leaf-
less, and sapless. This incalculable deficiency is one of the
greatest causes of the humiliation of the faith.

And still, the very reverse of this is generally supposed to be true. You will hear not only men of the world and enemies of the faith, but truly pious men and ministers, pretend that the whole evil proceeds from theology.

" Theology," say they, " with its precise definitions, its subtile distinctions, its fixed systems, is hurtful to the simplicity of faith, to the fervency of Christian life, and brings religion into contempt in the opinion of all enlightened men. Theology has been the ruin of Christianity. O, happy days, when there was no theology! O, simplicity of the Christian doctrine in the first centuries of the Church! would that you might return again!"

This simplicity of the early centuries, we will say in passing, of which so many boast, does not perhaps deserve so much eulogy as it generally receives. It frequently proceeded from ignorance, rather than from strict attachment to the line of truth; it was the simplicity of children who know very little, rather than that of the man who, perceiving what is right and what is wrong, stands by the right. And this simplicity, so often longed for by the men who would fain have piety without knowledge, was far from being free from errors, sometimes from grave errors.

But let us proceed to the objection we have just named. It is valid only with regard to the mistakes of science, not in respect to science itself. It is true that there is a false tendency of science which is repugnant to the simplicity of faith. It is only by means of Christian life that strength and prosperity will be pledged to science. When it is developed independently of that life, it loses itself in vain forms and absurd distinctions. It becomes a play of dialectics which stifles the last breath of life in those who cultivate it, and which deprives theology and religion of the esteem which they deserve.

But that is not science. That is not the true branch of the tree. That is a parasitic plant, which, in spite of the efforts it makes to unite with the tree to which it clings, and to mingle its dry branches and its yellow leaves with it, will be recognized by the owner of the tree to be foreign and pernicious to it, and will be torn away from it.

This objection therefore turns in favour of true science, which, emanating from the word of God, and intimately connected with Christian life, avoids these unhappy errors. It does not present a fleshless skeleton to the world as the symbol of truth; but a body covered with flesh, and filled with the Spirit and with life from heaven. It does not isolate any one of the faculties of man. In addressing his understanding, it also addresses his heart. What you reproach it with not having, it possesses emphatically. Consequently, it will do the reverse of what your fears imagined. By attacking every man, it will gain over all.

It is true, some say, that science is profitable for the world, for those without, as the Scriptures say; but it is of no use for the Church. Gentlemen, this is a singular delusion. We have defined true science as performing the most remarkable services for the Church. It preserves the Christian doctrine pure from foreign elements; and when it has been contaminated by them, it will purify it.

Such elements readily penetrate, first, into the Christian life, then into the spirit of Christianity, and, lastly, into science itself. This took place in the first eras of the Church. Foreign elements at that time united so closely with the scriptural elements, and were so thoroughly incorporated in the faith of Christians, that the true could scarcely be distinguished from the false. Teachers and believers presented an inconceivable medley of truth and falsehood.

This discerning of various elements, this separation of the true from the false, is one of the most glorious duties of true science. It is one of the tasks to which God has designed it. His piercing and certain eye distinguishes, in that mingled assembly, what is of God and what is of man. As a faithful servant of the master of the family, theology draws up that net which has been lying in the sea for centuries, and in the course of time has gathered together all sorts of things. With the torch of revelation in its hand, it brings to light and separates that which is vile from that which is pure. It puts the good portion in its boat and throws away the worthless.

And it keeps pure that which it has purified. It watches, like a faithful sentinel, lest the pride of human reason or the errors of enthusiasm should blight the plant which it has saved. As those officers who have charge of the treasures of a prince, and who prevent common elements from being mingled with the pure gold of which the royal jewels are made, so sacred theology has the care of the Lord's heritage, to preserve the Christian doctrine, that jewel of God, pure from human dross, and in the holiness and royal splendour which belong to every thing that is of heavenly origin.

But we wish to come nearer to you, students of this sacred theology, and who are called to be in future the dispensers of its treasures. How great are the advantages of science for the minister of the word! Of how much service will it be to you in the present times particularly! How necessary it is at a period when there are so many objections, doubts, and controversies; not merely with regard to certain points of minor importance, but also to the fundamental doctrines of salvation!

It is true science, gentlemen, science formed under the influence of the Spirit and the word, and blessed by God, that will give you a clear insight into the Divine revelations; that will show you new and unexpected treasures there, which are hidden to an ordinary perusal, and which, while increasing your knowledge, will enrich your experience and render your ministry more effectual.

It is science that, by leading you to make a proper estimate of the sacred doctrines, as well of the lamentable errors of the times, by manifesting the faith and unvailing the weakness of the Church, will show you the things that are, and those that ought to be, by means of those that have been, and will make up for your youth by the riches of well-tried experience.

It is science that will teach you to measure with a penetrating eye the present state of the Church; it will show you the evils against which you are to be guarded; it will keep you from exaggerated views, from hesitation, from hasty decisions, to which your heart is exposed; and, in the midst of the whirl-wind of human opinions that surrounds you, it will add to your convictions, views, and judgment, that clearness, correctness, and firmness which you would seek in vain within yourselves.

It is science that will make you capable of discerning good from evil, the useful from the hurtful, with relation to the Christian church in general, as well as to the flock which the Head of the church may intrust to your special care; it will qualify you for keeping an account of times, places, and circumstances; it will show you clearly the object which you ought to have in your career, and the means of reaching it; and will thus render your ministry more really and durably useful.

It is science that will teach you to shun those stumbling-blocks by which, as we so frequently see, the purest zeal, when not enlightened by knowledge, will be overthrown and destroyed; and which, by giving to all your labours a character of wisdom, reflection, and judgment, will make your ministry honourable, even in the eyes of the world.

It is science that will give you those characteristics so necessary to the Christian minister, and so rarely met in the same person; liberality, without latitudinarianism; exclusive submission to the word of God, without narrowness; and which, making your convictions both profound and extensive, establishing your mind, and enlarging your heart, will permit you to stretch out the arms of charity and to embrace all your brethren, without wandering from the only source of truth, the only impregnable centre of faith.

The science that emanates from God will guard you from that sad mechanism which so frequently attacks the evangelical ministry, and which turns the service of Jesus Christ into a paltry trade. For true science will always recall the spirit, idea, and life to your mind, in all your meditations and in all your labours. It will not allow your understanding to become like that of a workman. It will ever remind you that the Spirit of God ought to combine with the things of human life, the breath from heaven with the elements of earth. It will remind you that you are "wise men." It will oppose your being absorbed with material things. As the voice of God, it will keep your understanding from becoming gross, and your mind from growing dull.

The science which emanates from God will save you from Rationalism. Why are so many young theologians rushing into it, and passing so eagerly from one degree to another in it? Because they hope to find food for their understanding, for their reason. Vain hope! In the mean time, their hearts wither, their reason is degraded, and their intelligence contracted. It is Christian science that treasures up what their vague and sometimes proud but often noble desires are seeking. Young Levites! betake yourselves to it. It can satisfy you. Do not expect to find with your understanding, that lasts but a day, all that God has offered you in the depths of His eternity. Science will satisfy all your wants. It will show you in Christ all the treasures of divine intelligence. It will put you in possession of a light which, compared with Rationalism, is what the sun is to the *ignis fatuus* in our marshes. Then, discovering at once the paltriness of the erroneous productions of the human intelligence, and the grandeur of the manifestations of God's wisdom, you will exclaim, with the greatest of theologians, when, after wandering in the labyrinth of systems, he had found the divine science: "I have known thee too late!"[1]

The science which emanates from God will preserve you from that false enthusiasm which, eagerly receiving certain sensations, or snatching certain ideas out of their places, sacrifices them to an unruly imagination, where they bubble and ferment till they burst forth into deplorable excesses; at one time, into theosophical speculations; at another, into the disorderly flight of a vaporous mind; at another, into proud pretensions to gifts and offices which no longer exist, or to a fantastic state of the Church. Theological science will greatly assist you in discovering all these errors. It will show them to you in former times, together with the unhappy fruit they bore; it will acquaint you with their intimate connection with the corruption of the human heart, and with fatal doctrines; it will enable you to separate whatever may be good in these things from the evil, and will thus shelter you from a dangerous contagion.

The science which emanates from God will empower you to refute the absurd sophistry of the times; to attack specious errors with success; to enter into collision, if necessary, with the skilful, using the weapons of the understanding; with the learned, using the weapons of science; which weapons, as we have already said, cannot change the heart, but can often clear it of unfortunate prejudices, and thus prepare, to the joy of heaven, for the conversion of a sinner.

But, gentlemen, I ask myself whether it is necessary to prove the necessity of science for the minister of Christ, where-

[1] Augustine.

as its necessity for every disciple, for every Christian, ought to be a truth universally acknowledged.

It was to all those who have obtained a faith of like value with that of the servants of Jesus Christ that the Apostle Peter addressed the exhortation: "Add to your faith knowledge." It is true that there are branches of knowledge with which it is not absolutely necessary that every Christian should be acquainted, though it were desirable that all possessed them. But there is a Christian science in which all ought to make constant progress, according to their peculiar faculties and circumstances. Is it only those who are to teach the natural sciences that study them? Why, then, should none but theologians study theology, which is the science of God, that God "who is above all and through all and in you all"? In an unhealthy climate, do not all, at the approach of a dreaded contagion, endeavour to acquire medical knowledge? And is not science which treats of the remedy by which man can escape eternal death, great enough, important enough in the eyes of all, to be studied by all? How much more by you, ministers of Christ!

We hope that what we have said will suffice to demonstrate, to those who have seriously attended to it, the necessity of not separating faith from science, theology from piety, the pastor from the teacher. And we have thus endeavoured to make known one of the ends for which this seminary was established, both to those who, rejecting faith, speak only of science, and to those who, rejecting science, speak only of faith.

Thus, gentlemen, let us go to the study and the closet: to the closet and the study! Let us obtain the gift of God's Spirit, above all, by prayer. Let us abase ourselves in humility, before we exalt ourselves by reflection and knowledge; for, "if any man think that he knoweth any thing, he knoweth nothing yet as he ought to know." Like those aerial vehicles which the ingenuity of man has invented, we must empty ourselves of ourselves before we can arise into the lofty abodes of knowledge and contemplation.

Let faith be the key with which we unlock the treasure, to the possession of which we are invited. For faith makes known what the human understanding could never discover,

The life which comes from God explains that which meditation can not. Faith is the eye which we must have to penetrate into that unknown land of divine things which is the domain of theology. Faith is the true organ of the knowledge of God, It shows us the invisible, and explains the incomprehensible. "The things of God knoweth no man, but the Spirit of God. Now we have received the spirit which is of God, that we might know the things that are given to us of God."

Further: let holiness, a truly Christian life and conversation, give us an intelligence which can be obtained by them alone. For what is it but sin that obscures the mind and hinders it from understanding? Take the vail away, and you will see. The more you die unto sin, the clearer your eye will be, the brighter your knowledge, and the wider your perceptions. Every Christian work, all self-denial, is not only a step in sanctification, but also in science, in theology. If the angels know more than we do, it is because they are purer than we. Sin is darkness, and holiness is light. Let us walk in the light, that we may know Him who is light. "We shall see Him as He is. And every man that hath this hope in him purifieth himself, even as He is pure."

Thus, disciples of the science of God, we say to you, Let us pray; let us believe; let us be holy and blameless. But we will add, Let us study.

Let us labour, gentlemen. Let us carefully examine those great documents of sacred theology, the Old and New Testaments; those two pillars, at the foot of which the simple-hearted take refuge, and which, to the wise and skilful, raise their mysterious heads to the heavens.

Let us gather with care and a sound judgment all those facts, those instructions, theories, truths, and errors which history relates to us, as well as the light that philosophy sheds on the domain of science; always grasping firmly the guiding thread of our holy faith. Let us use our understanding; let us explain, discern, enquire into all the elements that science furnishes us. Let us weigh every point of doctrine considered apart and in itself; let us weigh its deepest meaning. And, at the same time, let us collect all the parts, learn to know their connections, their affinities, admire their completeness, their unity, and magnificent harmony.

Let us rise by sanctified meditation to the survey of the immense field spread out before us. Let us view science in all its aspects. Let us also stand on a holy mountain, whence we may see the land which the Lord has given us to conquer and possess. Let us keep near to the river, and then, if necessary, let us pursue its whole extent. Let us glance up to its source, and follow its current afar off. Let us distinguish its primary from its secondary streams; its principal branch from the accessory branches. Let us examine the march in which its pure water is corrupted, because the impulse of the former stream is wanting. Let us contemplate it when its fructifying waters are flowing along shores enriched by its gifts, and when its foaming waves rush on with impetuosity. Let us consider the tributary streams that bring foreign waters to it, and the various soils over which it rolls, that we may be well acquainted with the elements it derives from them. It is by all these branches of knowledge that science is formed. We must weigh all the influences, discern all the combinations, that we may derive from the Christian system, and construct sacred theology, which is man's noblest science, since it is the science of God.

Gentlemen! behold the ardour with which those who study either the body of man, or legislation, or the sciences of nature, are labouring. As disciples of theology, know and understand that yours is a grander field. Let the zeal of your contemporaries in the labours of their vocations cause you to reflect, and animate you with new zeal. You have to study *God and man.* Think of this.

Raise up science, which is calling on you, from the degradation into which it has fallen. Restore it to its primitive greatness. Let a sacred jealousy for it inflame your minds. On whom may we rely, if not on you?

And when you have become, as the Scripture says, " men of understanding," become, also, " in malice, children." Let our knowledge lead us to the faith of the simple, but to a firmer faith, less exposed to change, and which, explored in every direction, and well known in all its phases, may be firmly defended and wisely distributed by us, as milk to the babes and as meat to the strong men.

DISCOURSE XIII.[1]

THE VOICE OF THE CHURCH, ONE, UNDER THE SUCCESSIVE FORMS OF CHRISTIANITY.

" The Church, scattered over the world, proclaims, teaches, and hands
down this faith, as though it had but one mouth. For though there be
many different modes of expression in the world, the strength of the
truth, variously transmitted, is *one and the same* eternally ; as the sun,
that creation of God, is one and the same throughout the universe."—
IRENÆUS, *Adv. hæreses,* lib. i, c. 3.

GENTLEMEN,—How vast is the activity and how various
are the labours and efforts of men on earth! Yet time
levels most of their works; and even if they attempt to raise a
tower to the skies, their lofty structure is overthrown, and
mingled, after a few generations, with the sands of the desert.

Nothing but Christianity is durable here below. Christianity
alone is unchangeable like its Author. It is the rock of ages,
against which the waves have ever dashed, and will ever dash,
without shaking it.

If any man, therefore, is desirous of giving a character of
stability and perpetuity to his labours on earth, he must connect
them with Christianity. They will receive from that eternal
religion the imprint of immortality.

These truths, gentlemen, are not universally acknowledged;
and we find two capital errors among men on this point. Some
pretend that there is no perpetuity in the spirit of Christianity
itself. " The Christian doctrine," they say, " is merely a peculiar form of religious opinions. This form has succeeded
another, and will itself be followed by still another. The religion of the Saviour," they add, " was a necessary consequence of the state in which humanity was in the days of the

---

[1] Delivered at the annual meeting of the Theological Seminary in Geneva, on the 1st of May, 1834.

Cæsars; just as the blossoms and flowers of a tree come forth naturally in the spring." To this singular error rationalism has been obliged to resort; but it has been strikingly refuted by history. No; Christianity is not merely a human apparition. History, that unquestionable witness, shows that, far from harmonizing with the various tendencies of the human mind at the time when it first appeared, it was in direct opposition to them. It was not the wisdom of the world that gave it birth; on the contrary, it strove to crush it. Christianity was not the child of its own times; it was at once their enemy and their renovator. It was not from the dust of the earth that this precious fruit came forth; and it can not return to dust. Heaven committed to the world that unchangeable treasure, which successive generations were to hand down, uninjured, from hand to hand; we have received it in our day, and will reverently and carefully transmit it, in our earthen vessels, to our descendants; and it will remain unchanged among men until heaven and earth flee away, and there shall be found no place for them.

But if, on the one hand, we meet with the opinions of the levellers of Christianity, we find on the other the pretensions of an inflexible dogmatism, which would assign a constantly uniform appearance to Christianity throughout the whole existence of the Church. There is something in Christianity that never changes: and that is its essence; and there is something in it that does change; that is its aspects. It is by neglecting to distinguish the appearance from the reality that many have mistaken the unvarying nature of the religion of Jesus Christ. The appearance of a man changes in the various stages of his life; yet he is always the same man.

Like every thing else that enters into the sphere of humanity, Christianity was to be invested with a human form from the moment that it came down from heaven. The external circumstances of every epoch have exerted a decided influence on the development of Christian truths. One form has followed another. These successive forms have not been matters of indifference. One may have been preferable to another; but the same essential truth has always existed in all its past forms, and will always exist in the future ones.

Gentlemen, the work in which we are engaged to-day, and which we shall communicate to you, is a very feeble and paltry one; but its glory is, that it relates to the eternal work. If we wished to argue in favour of matters connected with some aspect of the religion of Jesus Christ, we should have no pledge of durability for the cause which we would defend. The next revolution of human society would send it to its grave, with every thing that is merely accidental. But if we keep hold of the very essence of Christianity, then the sacred cause to which our efforts are devoted will participate in the perpetuity of the work of God. We may fail; and soon, going the way of all the living, we shall fail; our Seminary may fail; but the cause to which it is consecrated will never fail, either in this city or in the world. In the words of an ancient oracle, "To it shall the gathering of the people be."

Yes, gentlemen, this is the foundation of our hopes, amid many difficulties and trials. It is this that, by God's grace, encourages us. And perhaps it will be worth our while to consecrate a few moments to acquainting you with this characteristic phenomenon of the religion of Jesus Christ: The unchangeableness of the doctrines of Christianity, in the midst of the diversity of its forms; *the Voice of the Church, one and ever the same in all ages.*

If we enquire into the various human forms which the unchangeable truth of God has successively taken in different periods of history, we find that they have been very numerous. We must collect them, unite them, and form them into an extensive whole. We shall thus obtain, as a last synthesis, four principal periods or forms. The first is the primitive form, or form of life. The second is the form of dogma. The third is the form of the schools. The fourth is the form of the Reformation. The Church of Christ, according to a scriptural comparison, is like one man. It has had its youth, its manhood, and its old age; and then, yet without dying, it has had, so to speak, a powerful resurrection. These have been the four eras or ages of the church of Jesus Christ.

We shall rapidly survey these four forms, so different, I may say so opposed in appearance, to see whether we will find in each the same unchangeable truth. We shall listen to the

voices of the teachers. It is true that the assertions of a single
man will not suffice to acquaint us with the belief of the Church;
but if, by consulting the writings of men who have lived in
various countries at a distance from one another, we find, amid
great variety of views, certain doctrines in which all agree,
may we not with reason conclude that those doctrines were
the doctrines of the Church, scattered over the whole world?
To what points then shall our enquiries be directed?

The whole of Christianity, as well as the whole of religious
philosophy, necessarily reverts to three principal points. In
the first place it refers to GOD; in the second place, to MAN;
and in the third place, to the relation which exists between
God and man, or the means by which God unites man to himself: that is, REDEMPTION. Let us see then what the voice of
the Church, in the various periods of Christianity, teaches us
respecting these three points.

THE VITAL ERA.—We exclude from the primitive period the
days of the apostles, which must be considered separately. In
our opinion, that primitive form begins with the successors of
the apostles, and extends to the times of Arius. The principal
characteristic of this period was *life*. The Christian truths
were not yet proclaimed with that precision and systematic
order for which they were afterwards distinguished. Men lived
for the Saviour in the midst of an idolatrous world; they died
for the Saviour in the arena or at the stake; and this without
much discussion respecting his person or his work. Christianity was content to exist, and to know and profess that it existed, without enumerating and classifying all the essential
parts which constituted it; in the same way that man is long
satisfied with possessing existence and life, without examining
or carefully explaining in what this existence and this life consist. A few rationalist doctors (who have not been undeceived
by a certain degree of learning which is only too superficial)
have very strangely concluded, from this characteristic of the
primitive form, that the Christian truths did not exist at that
early period, and that there were no dogmas, because there
was no dogmatism. But to infer, from this want of precision
in dogmas, that the Christian truths did not exist, is a mode
of reasoning as singular and as false as that of an unskilful

controversialist would be, if he pretended that the periods of his being of which a man can not give a precise and accurate account, never had an existence !

The result of this characteristic of the primitive form was, that the controversies of that period seldom had respect to dogmas. Their tendencies, rather than their dogmas, were different. We meet with families presenting various aspects, rather than sects sustaining opposite doctrines. Let us trace the consequence of these various families, before we state the doctrines which the voice of the Church then proclaimed.

The simple Christianity of the apostolic fathers followed the divine inspiration of the apostles. It seems that in this case the usual order was inverted, and that the ingenuousness and simplicity of childhood succeeded the power and maturity of the full-grown man. The Church, under the guidance of Ignatius, Polycarp, and many other faithful disciples, lived under the influence of the great idea of the approaching return of Jesus Christ. " There are three constitutions or dispensations of the Lord," says one of those fathers, Barnabus, who inclined to another direction: " the *hope* of life (the Old Testament); the *commencement* of life (the New Testament); and the *consummation* of life (the kingdom of heaven)." But by degrees this heavenward tendency seemed to cease in the Church. There arose a generation which did not penetrate so deeply into the spirit of Jesus Christ. Curious traditions were collected respecting the appearance of Christ on earth. Carnal Jews, who expected a human Messiah, preserved their gross views under the name of Christians. It seems as though the Church, weary of its upward flight, fell back to the earth. Let us not wonder at this; we almost always find a period of stupor following a great revival.

Then there appeared on the borders, and almost beyond the borders of Christianity, a tendency diametrically opposite. Oriental philosophy was desirous of uniting with the religion of Jesus of Nazareth. It deprived it of its practical character, and changed it into systems which soared among the clouds. Gnosticism substituted for the wholesome doctrine a fantastical cosmogony, by means of which it endeavoured to explain that which is inexplicable, and an enthusiastic theosophy, which

would fain have brought down to man on earth the sublime
contemplations of heaven.

The West shrunk back from the adventurous rambles of the
East. Tertullian and Irenæus displayed, in opposition to them,
in proconsular Africa and in Gaul, a simple, positive, and historical Christianity, and presented to men that faith by which
great and small live. Considering philosophy as the source of
Gnosticism, they began to look with distrust upon the wisdom
and scientific cultivation of the Greeks.

But this exclusive simplicity had its dangers also. Refined
and learned pagans, finding nothing which corresponded with
the requirements of their intelligence in the Christianity offered
to them, remained attached to the worship of false gods, or
rushed into the adventurous systems of Gnosticism. Eminent
minds were thus lost to the Gospel. Alexandria, seated on
the banks of the Nile, between the East and the West, observed
this. Alexandria, that great market of the sciences, to which
according to tradition, the Evangelist Mark carried the simple
word of Christ, undertook to become a mediatrix between these
two tendencies of man and these two parts of the known world.
Pantenus, Clement, and Origen founded a Christian science,
thereby approaching the views of the East, but, at the same
time, founding it on the Scriptures, and thereby approaching
those of the West; γνῶσις ἀληθινη—" the true science." Alas!
it was not wholly so; and although those divines did not forsake the fundamental principles of Christianity, philosophy
deposited in their systems the treacherous seed of the two
greatest heresies of the subsequent period, as well as of all
other periods.

The school of Alexandria gradually destroyed and supplant-
ed Gnosticism. But then it was against it that the attacks of
the severe and practical school of the West were directed. A
remarkable struggle took place, in the third century, between
these two churches, or rather schools. These opposite tendencies served to counterbalance each other, and contributed
powerfully to the prosperity of Christianity. Alexandria infused a theological spirit into the Church. It began to enlighten
and systematize the dogmas. It prevented a gross anthropo-
morphism from invading the heavenly doctrine of Jesus Christ.

The West always brought men back to the simple and literal interpretation of the written word. It reminded men that Christianity ought to be felt, undergone in the heart, and demonstrated in the life. It prevented that positive and wholesome doctrine from changing into vain and fantastical speculations.

Such, gentlemen, are the successive phases of the primitive form. In the midst of all these phases, a spirit of life animated the Church. It was the age of its youth. The Christians of the primitive days, delivered from the sins of Paganism, felt in their hearts the transforming strength of the Gospel with the more energy, because they could have compared what it had made them with what they had been till then. Their struggle with the world reminded them still more strongly of their vocation as soldiers of Jesus Christ. Every body lived for the Church; every body was moving. The Church received impulses toward heaven, and often toward the scaffold. And although its golden age was reserved for the new heavens and the new earth, yet Christian society presented features of celestial beauty in those days of its youth and life.

And what are the truths which were professed by the teachers and citizens of this new commonwealth, created in the midst of the world by the breath of God?

They knew a *living God*. They worshipped, in God, not only the author of all things (*the Father*), but also the Redeemer (*the Son*), and the Sanctifier of fallen humanity (*the Spirit*). They believed that the same God who created man in righteousness redeemed him from sin, and sanctifies him continually, until he reaches eternal life. They knew nothing of those singular errors, by which some would fain deprive God of the work and glory of redemption, to attribute them to a creature.

The idea of a holy Trinity in God is found at the very beginning of the primitive era, and is continually appearing in a more distinct manner. How the voice of those early soldiers of Jesus confounds the imprudent pretensions of our times!

Clement, a disciple of Paul, ascribing glory to the sovereign God, said at Rome, "One God, one Christ, one Spirit of

Grace."[1] Polycarp, a disciple of John, dying at the stake, gave eternal glory to "the Father, with the Son, in the Holy Ghost."[2]

Justin Martyr, the first of divines, in whom are united the Christian faith and the philosophy of the Greeks, a converted sage, who, under Antoninus, shed his blood for his master, proclaimed the "Unity in the Trinity."[3] Theophilus, a bishop of Antioch, professed the doctrine of the Holy Trinity about the same time, and in a still more explicit manner.[4]

A lawyer in Africa, Tertullian, who became a simple pastor of the flock of Jesus Christ, exclaimed, shortly after, "There is only one Divine Being, in three persons intimately united."[5] He preached the "The Trinity of one only Divinity, the Father, Son, and Holy Ghost."[6] And elsewhere he said, "Let us preserve the sacrament of our dispensation, which establishes the Unity in Trinity, acknowledging three: the Father, the Son, and the Holy Spirit, of one substance, one state, one power, because there is one only God."[7]

And with what energy did Irenæus, who had been compelled to leave the sacred shores of Asia to carry light into Gaul, and was the venerable bishop of a neighbouring city (Lyons), which was then distracted by the fury of the people against Jesus Christ, and is now distracted by other attacks:[8] with what energy, I say, did Irenæus defend the great doctrine of "God manifest in the flesh?" "Christ," he says, "unites in himself both God and man. If the *man* had not overcome man's great enemy (the Devil), that enemy would not have been really overcome. But if, on the other hand, *God* had

---

[1] Ἕνα Θεὸν, καὶ ἕνα Χριστὸν, καὶ ἕνα Πνεῦμα τῆς χάριτος.—Clem. Rom. 1 Cor.

[2] Δι οὖ, σὺν αὐτῷ, ἐν Πνεύματι ἁγίῳ δόξα.—Eus., *H. E.*, iv, 15.

[3] Μονὰς ἐν τριάδι νοεῖται, τρ. ἐν μον. γνωρίζεται.—Justin, *Expositio fidei.*

[4] Theoph., Aut. Autol., ii, 23.

[5] Una substantia in tribus cohœrentibus.—*Tertul.*

[6] Trinitas unius Divinitatis, Pater, et Filius, et Spiritus Sanctus.—*De pud.*, ii.

[7] Unitatem in trinitatem, . . . Patrem, et Filium, et Spiritum Sanctum, . . . unius autem substantiæ, et unius statûs, et unius potestatis, quia unus Deus.—*Tert.*, Adv. Praxeam.

[8] The author here refers to the political tumults which took place in Lyons in the year 1834.—*Trans.*

not brought us to salvation, we would not certainly possess it."[1]

Though but a few years had elapsed since the death of the oldest apostle, we find so many illustrious teachers preaching this doctrine of the Father, Son, and Holy Spirit, of which Christ has established a perpetual monument in his universal church by the institution of baptism. The greatest doctors zealously defended the consoling doctrine of God becoming man. The farther we advance, the more numerous are the testimonies given to this mystery in the churches of the Lord. Every where we find the eternal divinity of the Son of God deeply stamped upon the inmost convictions and the worship of the Christian people. And even one of the wisest of the heathen wrote to the greatest of their emperors, "They sing hymns to Christ as God."[2]

But if we enquire what these Christians of the Era of Life believed respecting *man*, we will not find that they, like the ancient heathen, and like many modern teachers, imagined that sin proceeded from man's natural organization, and that it is not in opposition with the holiness of God. This was their doctrine: The first man, having, by his disobedience, separated his will from the divine will, human nature has been abandoned to itself. Being thus separated from God, it fell under the dominion of sin.

Let us approach the college of the apostles, and question those who surrounded and followed them. Barnabas, Paul's companion, tells us: "Before we believed in God, our hearts were the abodes of corruption and sin; our hearts were full of idolatry; they were the habitation of demons."[3] Justin, who

---

[1] "Ἥνωσεν τὸν ἄνθρωπον τῷ Θεῷ.—Iren., *Adv. Hæreses*, lib. iii, c. 20.

[2] Quod essent soliti statuto die ante lucem convenire, carmenque Christo, quasi Deo, dicere secum invicem.—Plin., *Epist. ad Traj.*, x, 96.

[3] Πρὸ οὗ ἡμᾶς πιστεῦσαι τῷ Θεῷ, ἦν ἡμῶν τὸ κατοικατήριον τῆς καρδίας φθαρτὸν καὶ ἀσθενὲς, etc.—*Barnabas*, c. 16. (Some doctors have expressed doubts respecting the authenticity of the letter of Barnabas. Their motives, it seems to me, are weak. Several Rationalists, even—Bretschneider particularly - think it authentic. I name Bretschneider, because he is of great authority among Rationalists and Unitarians. We do not, however, suppose that the testimony of this divine, distinguished in some respects, is of much weight in ecclesiastical history. For, instance, he places

had in vain sought a key to man's history in all systems of philosophy, found one at last in the fall of Adam, which was brought about by the temptations of the Devil, disguised under the form of a serpent.[1]

The first man, according to the simple and practical Irenæus, was like a "prisoner," whose race was perpetuated in prison. The profound Tertullian calls the corruption of human nature "original sin" (vitium originis). "The first man," he says, "infected the human race which proceeded from him, and made it participate in his condemnation."[2] Cyprian, bishop of Carthage, that great light of the Church, had the same idea respecting the origin of sin. "The new-born child," he says, is in no wise sinful, save because he is carnally born of Adam, and, by his birth, has received the contagion of death."[3]

And if we are invited to resort to the school of Alexandria, hoping that those philosophical theologians will pronounce words flattering to our pride, we will lead you there, and you shall hear Origen say: "Adam turned away from the straight path of Paradise to enter the evil road of mortal life. Consequently, all his descendants, having come into the world, have turned away, and have, like him, become useless.[4] Every man is corrupt in his parents. Jesus alone entered into the world pure.[5] It is impossible for man, at the beginning of his life, to look to God; for it is necessary that he should first undergo sin."[6]

Thus, Egypt as well as Gaul, proconsular Africa as well as Asia, acknowledged that man was a fallen and sinful being.

Tertullian after Origen, making him live at the end of the third and the beginning of the fourth century, which is one century more than is necessary. See Bretschneider's *Grundl. des Ev. Piet.*, p. 342.)

[1] Dial. cum Tryph., p. 306.

[2] Totum genus de suo semine infectum suæ etiam damnationis traducem fecit.—Tertul., de Testim. An.

[3] Infans recens natus nihil peccavit, nisi quod, secundum Adam, carnaliter natus, contagionem mortis antiquæ prima nativitate contraxit.—Cyprian, Epist. lxiv, ad Fid.

[4] Omnes . . . . declinaverunt, et simul cum ipso inutiles facti sunt.—Origen, Comm. in Epist. ad Rom., lib. iii.

[5] Omnis ergo homo in patre et in matre pollutus est, etc.—Origen, Hom. xii, in Levit.

[6] Κακίαν γὰρ ὑφίστασθαι ἀναγκαῖον πρῶτον ἐν ἀνθρώποις.—Origen contra Celsum, lib. iii, 62.

And how was this polluted being to be reconciled to a holy God? What was the belief of that primitive age respecting the means by which God saved man? Let us again enquire of of those who surrounded the apostles. They will teach us those sacred doctrines of grace which were afterward more fully developed. "The Son of God suffered," says the apostolic Barnabas, "that his sufferings might give life to us. He offered up the vase of His Spirit (*his body*) a sacrifice for our sins." "Having learned to hope in the name of the Lord, and having received the remission of sins, we have become new men, and have been created anew" (vii, 16). Hermas, who was, perhaps, the same of whom St. Paul speaks, says, "Before man has received the name of a son of God, he is destined to die; but when he has received that seal, he is delivered from death and passes into life."[1]

"The law of God," says Justin, "pronounced a curse on man, because he could not fulfil it in its whole extent. Christ has delivered us from that curse, by bearing it for us."[2] Do we speak differently in these days?

Irenæus saw in circumcision a type of the saving blood of Christ, and in the tree of life a type of the cross of Christ. Elsewhere he declares that men ought no longer to strive to purify themselves with sacrifices, but with the blood of Christ and by his death. The lamb of the Passover was with him an emblem of Christ, who saves believers by the sprinkling of his blood. The two goats, one of whom, according to the law of Moses, was to be driven into the desert, and the other sacrificed to God, are emblems of the first and second coming of Christ; the first of which was to die, and the second to be glorified.[3] He opposed the obedience of Christ to the disobedience of Adam. "Christ," he says, "reconciled us with the Father, by atoning, by his perfect obedience, for the disobedience of the first man." And, pursuing his metaphor of man cast into prison and in the bondage of Satan, he declares that "Christ, by his sufferings, paid the necessary ransom to deliver man from that captivity."

Origen, likewise, viewed, in the death of Christ, the power

---

[1] Liberatur a morte, et traditur vitæ.—Hermas pastor, lib. iii.
[2] Dial. cum Tryph., c. 30.   [3] Dial. cum Tryph., passim.

which delivers man from sin. The whole primitive Church
looked upon the sufferings of the Lamb of God as the means
which opened to humanity the road which leads it back to
the Father. It is faith that makes man participate in that
deliverance, and, at the same time, communicates divine life.
"Called by the will of God," says Clement of Rome, a disciple
of the apostles, whose name, we are told by Paul, is in the
Book of Life, " we are justified, not by ourselves, or by our
wisdom, or understanding, or piety, or by any works we may
have done in the holiness of our hearts, but 'by faith,' through
which the sovereign God has justified men at all times. Shall
we be idle on that account, and cease to do good? On the
contrary, we ought to do good joyfully, as God, who hath
called us to himself, acts without ceasing, and rejoices in his
activity."[1]

Such was this holy church of the primitive era. Thus it
speaks, in the midst of its anguish, and, as it were, from the
stake itself. It confesses its own vileness, and, throwing itself
at the feet of Jesus, calls him "its Lord and its God." How
can we mistake the loud and truthful voice of its sincere piety?
And how lamentable is the occupation of certain doctors in our
day, who endeavour to despoil it of its white robe, to dress it
in the filthy rags of their own infidelity! This profane enterprise is, it is true, a mark of homage which they pay to it. Indeed, the very first Unitarians resorted to the same expedient.
But these efforts will be useless; and the primitive church will
ever address those who listen to them in the unchanging tones
of truth.

THE DOCTRINAL ERA. Though we have been able to glean
only a few ears in the great harvest before us, yet we have been
more diffuse, with regard to the primitive period, than befits
the limits of this discourse. We have done so, because this is
the only ground upon which the enemies of Christian truth
venture and hope for some success from their skilfulness. They
despair of all other periods, or rather, they make the loud, common, and public professions of faith which they find there, and

---

[1] Οὐ δι' ἑαυτῶν δικαιούμεθα, οὐδὲ διὰ τῆς ἡμετέρας σοφίας, ἢ συνέσεως, ἢ
εὐσεβείας, ἢ ἔργων ὧν κατειργασάμεθα ἐν ὁσιότητι καρδίας. Ἀλλὰ διὰ τῆς
πίστεως, etc.—Clem. Rom., 1 Cor., c. 32.

which are so contrary to their views, the subject of bitter reproaches and accusations. We shall not make great efforts to be victorious in a battle-field in which our adversaries already confess that they are overcome, and forsake us.

Let us look at the opening of that period of great teachers, great truths, and great heresies; that era in which Christian theology, the elements of which had been prepared in the preceding period, is carried, by illustrious men of God, to a great height; that day of Athanasius, Hilary, Gregory, Basil, Ambrose, Jerome, Augustine, and Chrysostom. Those were the times of strong men; it was the manhood of the Church. The flames of the last stakes of the confessors of Christ are extinguished; the memorable Council of Nice meets. The era of *life* is ended; that of *dogma* begins. God forbid that we should assert that there was no longer any life in the Church; but *dogma* was the ruling characteristic. Man is fond of distinct ideas; he likes to account for what he believes. It was so at that time. The Church, having no longer to struggle with its persecutors externally, could attend more thoroughly to internal matters, to the faith which it professed. The various tendencies of the primitive form became more decided, and, by a remarkable transformation, were changed into negative doctrines; just as the vague inclinations of the youth become more and more decided, and, in manhood, are changed into distinct traits of character, into positive vices or virtues. Great heresies appeared, conducted by Arius or Pelagius. But these very heresies became the means which God used to establish the Christian dogmas with still greater clearness and force. The Christian truths, thus laid down by the Church of that day, were faithfully transmitted to the succeeding periods. They were perpetuated, in spite of the disturbances and the barbarity which existed in the following centuries. This dogmatic form became, through divine grace, the armour which surrounded those doctrines in the midst of great struggles and revolutions; it was the hammer that beat them into the dull and gross minds of the barbarians. Yet we must acknowledge, such importance was ascribed to dogmas, even in their smallest ramifications, that the very essence and life of Christianity were sometimes forgotten in the view of forms of doctrine.

The East and the West preserved their peculiar characteristics. The East remained the land of profound speculations;
the West, that of practical questions. The East discussed
about God; the West about man. In the East we see Arius
and Athanasius; in the West, Pelagius and Augustine. But
in the East and in the West, the truth, violently attacked,
carried off brilliant and complete victories. Having passed
through the time of its youth, the Christian doctrine was, like
the first man, to undergo trial; but it was not, like him, to
fall. It resisted temptation and remained firm.

The doctrine of GOD was first exposed, in that era, with
majestic glory, because it was the first that was threatened by
man's presuming hand. A great teacher, Athanasius of Alexandria, viewed in the profound mystery of redemption the necessity for the eternal divinity of the Redeemer. The world
can have no Saviour unless that Saviour be God. In conse-
crating his life to the defence of the identity of substance between the Father and the Son, and in submitting to so many
exiles, Athanasius did not attach great importance to a mere
dialective subtlety; it was for the very essence of Christianity
and the salvation of souls that he fought. The object of Christianity is to restore communication between God and man. To
do this it was necessary to have a mediator. "But if the Son
of God," says Athanasius, "is in his essence different from the
essence of God, he needs another mediation to unite him to
God. None but a being who needs no mediation to unite him
to God, but who himself partakes of the divine essence, can
establish a real communication between God and man. Such
a being is the Son of God. If he were a creature, even the
holiest of creatures, he would, by interposing between God and
man, have separated instead of uniting them."[1]

But let us listen to the entire Church in the symbols of its
faith. "The Catholic Faith," it says, "is this: That we worship one God in Trinity, and Trinity in Unity; neither con-
founding the Persons nor dividing the Substance. For there
is one Person of the Father, another of the Son, and another
of the Holy Ghost. But the Godhead of the Father, of the
Son, and of the Holy Ghost is all one: the Glory equal, the

[1] Athan. Oratio contra Arian.

Majesty co-eternal. Such as the Father is, such is the Son, and such is the Holy Ghost. The Father uncreate, the Son uncreate, and the Holy Ghost uncreate. The Father is God, the Son is God, and the Holy Ghost is God. And yet there are not three Gods, but one God." "For the right Faith is, that we believe and confess that our Lord Jesus Christ, the Son of God, is God and Man; God, of the Substance of the Father, begotten before the worlds; and Man, of the substance of his mother, born in the world; perfect God and perfect Man; equal to the Father, as touching his Godhead, and inferior to the Father, as touching his Manhood."[1]

A struggle of more than sixty years (from 320 to 381) was necessary, to decide, explain, and defend the doctrine of Christ's divinity. New struggles began for the purpose of deciding another dogma. Soon after Athanasius and the other theologians who followed in his footsteps, we see in the Church a teacher who seemed to have received from God the mission of explaining and defending the doctrine of the Scriptures respecting *man*; a teacher no less remarkable for his profound intellect than for his ardent piety. It was Augustine. Already had several doctors demonstrated by their profession the unchangeableness of the Christian doctrine. "In Adam's sin alone," says Hilary of Poictiers, "all mankind have sinned."[2]

"We have all sinned in the first man," says Ambrose of Milan; "in him human nature sinned."[3] But it was when the great doctor of the West, under whose influence all those were educated, for centuries, who have clear views of the truth: it was when Augustine appeared that the depths of human impotency were revealed.

He first forsook Manichéism, and then Platonism, finding in neither of them that internal peace which he needed in the storms of life. He firmly laid hold of the Gospel, which dissipated his doubts, consoled his heart, and spread new light on all his ways. In the midst of his struggles with sin and

---

[1] . . . . . ut unum Deum in trinitate et trinitatem in unitate veneremur: neque confundentes personas, neque substantiam separantes, etc.,—Creed called Athanasian. (This œcumenical creed was composed by a Latin writer posterior to Athanasius.)

[2] In unius Adami errore omne genus humanum aberravit.—Hilar., in Matth., c. 18.   [3] Apol. Davidis, c. 2.

philosophy, he learned to know the corruption of the human heart by that of his own; and *that* was the string that vibrated in all his instructions. Pursued, at the same time, by a sublime idea of holiness, and all the allurements of lust, he saw, in the concussion of these conflicting elements, the depths of his heart opening before him, as the tempests of ocean reveal the profound abyss. He found himself in the presence of a man who, without any definite plan or object, and in circumstances of no extraordinary nature, took but a superficial view of human nature, and indulged in fantastic notions of the moral ability of man. Augustine entered upon a conflict with Pelagius; and this conflict was not one between men merely, but between two principles, two great tendencies of the mind of man, which are met with in every age. Augustine saw that the first man had wandered away from God; from that estrangement proceeded sin; from that sin proceeded the moral disorder which has invaded human nature. To him, the human race appeared to be " a heap of ruin."[1] The consequence, as well as the punishment of the fall of the first man, was to his descendants " an obligation to sin."[2] Man has lost his liberty as well as the ability to do any really good thing.[3] He could no longer possess any thing which God had not given him. If some men attained the faith of the Gospel while others did not attain it, the reason is not to be found in man, since both are alike incapable of doing right. That reason can be found only in the particular action of God, in a secret counsel of the Divine Being, in an election by grace.[4] After a struggle of more than thirty years in Africa, Italy, and the south of Gaul, truth triumphed, and the doctrine of man's total impotency remained in the Church.

Then, gentlemen (and this leads us to the third point we are to examine,) the doctrine of *grace* was clearly exposed by these doctors. Already had the excellent Hilary said: " Redemption is given gratuitously, not on account of the merits of works, but by the free will of the Giver, according to the election of the Redeemer."[5] " In this," says Augustine, " consists the grace of God through Jesus Christ. He justifies us, not

---

[1] Massa perditionis.—Pecc. or., 21.   [2] Obligatio peccati.—C.D., xiv, 1.
[3] Prædest., S. S., 3.   [4] Quæst. ad Simpl.   [5] Hilary, in Psalm.

through our righteousness, but through his own."[1]   But he insists especially on the idea that grace excludes all merit, all natural disposition of man to receive salvation.   God is the *Alpha* of salvation, as well as the *Omega;* the beginning as well as the end.   " What God began by operating," says he, " he finished by co-operating.   In commencing the work, he operates to the end that we may be willing; and to conclude the work, he co-operates with those who now possess the will."[2] He that glorieth let him glory in the Lord.

Thus, in this period of dogma, Christian science made great progress.   The doctrines of God, of man, and of salvation, which the doctors of the first period had seen in the Scriptures, were sounded more thoroughly, and explained more perfectly by those of the second.   Theology advanced under the influence of the Spirit of God; for, gentlemen, there is a progressive march in theology.   What will those answer, who, in our days, would fain lead us to forsake those advanced degrees of sacred science, not merely to make us return to the primitive elements, but receive sad errors which the Church long since refuted and rejected ?   " Leaving the principles of the doctrine of Christ, let us go on unto perfection, not laying again the foundation."

THE SCHOLASTIC ERA.—A new era followed that which had taken the place of the primitive.   After.times of darkness, we see, in the middle of the eleventh century, a great intellectual movement taking place in the West.   It is from this movement that scholasticism arose.   The school (*scola*) endeavoured to separate from the Church, which, till then, had ruled alone. It wished to obtain authority and influence independent of the hierarchy.   Free men, who, in the beginning, at least, were usually neither monks nor ecclesiastics, sought to form free schools distinct from those which had existed till then.   Soon the University of Paris, that mother of scholasticism, issued from these schools.   The spirit of the schools (we might now say the spirit of the university or of science) became the general characteristic of scholasticism.   Its tendency was, to apply

---

[1] De Gratiâ Dei, 52.   Suâ, non nostrâ justiciâ, etc.

[2] Co-operando perficit quod operando incipit.   Ipse ut velimus operatur incipiens, qui volentibus co-operatur perficiens.—Aug., De Gratiâ et Lib. Arb., sec. 33.

philosophy to Christianity; to reduce the Christian doctrines to systems; to show their connection, their internal proofs; to gain for them not only the heart, but the understanding also. So that if the first period was that of *life,* and the second that of *dogma,* the third can be regarded as that of *system.* There is still life among many; there are still dogmas among all; but system is the principal feature. It was then that every doctor published his system, his *Summary of Theology.*[1] It was the old age of the Church, which naturally succeeded the first two eras of youth and manhood. In truth, old age loves to systematize the truths which it has already collected. It meditates. It has but little power of impulse, and more of reflection. And although there were many strong men in that era of middle age, yet the tendency to systematize was its ruling characteristic.

At that time, historical studies were insignificant. Exegetical studies were of but little more importance. And yet intelligence was strongly aroused amid the European nations which had so long been slumbering. A guide was necessary to lead it. That guide was dialectics. And as theology was the science of that age, it became the field into which the human mind ventured under the auspices of its reasoning guide. This tendency of scholasticism might have led to Rationalism and infidelity; but its first teachers sheltered sacred theology from these attacks. "The Christian," says Anselm, the father of scholasticism, "should attain knowledge by means of faith, not faith by means of knowledge. I do not seek to understand for the purpose of believing, but I believe for the purpose of understanding. And even I believe, because, if I did not believe, I would not understand."[2] Soon Abelard and his school took possession of the principle of scholasticism, and became the defenders of free enquiry. They wanted to understand first, and then to believe. Faith, said they, when strengthened by examination, is much more solid. The enemies of the Gospel must be attacked on their own ground. If we must not discuss, then we must believe every thing, false-

---

[1] Summa Theologiæ, by Alexander of Hales (Venice, 1576;) by Albert the Great (Basle, 1507;) by Thomas Aquinas (Paris, 1675,) etc.

[2] Neque enim quæro intelligere ut credam, sed credo ut intelligam, etc.,
—Anselmi Epist., xli. Prologion, c. *i*.

hood as well as truth.[1] Yet, notwithstanding this tendency, and the condemnation of the Church, these Rationalist theologians can not be reproached with abandoning any doctrine of the faith.

We will not wholly absolve scholasticism. It frequently disfigured Christian truth. Its tendency, and the state in which the Church was then, made this a necessary result. Human reason never presumes to touch any of those great truths which surpass all comprehension without stumbling. The school of the Middle Ages, like that at Alexandria, weakened the doctrines, in attempting to strengthen the Christian system. Nevertheless, scholasticism produced great minds. Though it may surprise some, I do not hesitate to say that there was some progress made under its influence, not in Christianity, but in science, in theology. The doctors who were the light of those ages communicated many salutary instructions to the crowds that filled their schools, and followed them, when it was necessary, by thousands into the deserts, where they erected a pulpit for instruction.

In the opinion of the greatest infidels among men of the world, orthodox Christianity was an invention of the *Middle Ages*. This trivial accusation of the *wise men* of the 18th century is certainly very honourable to the Middle Ages; more so, I think, than they deserve; and it might, at least, exempt us from the necessity of proving that the Christian doctrine existed then. Let us, however, question some of those doctors.

We will see what exposition of the doctrine of salvation is made of Anselm of Canterbury, that powerful man, who united the labours of philosophy with the purity of faith; who was perhaps the most influential of the philosophical theologians of those days, and the second Augustine of the Latin church. By him the Bible system of redemption was developed and brought forward in such a manner as to anticipate all objection, and satisfy at once the understanding and the heart. "All reasonable beings," says he, "ought to submit their wills to the divine will. This law was transgressed by the first man's sin. Thus the harmony of moral order was destroyed in the world. The

---

[1] Si enim cum persuadetur aliud, ut credatur, nec est ratione discutiendum, quid restat nisi ut æquè tam falsa quam vera prædicantibus acquiescamus ? Abel., Intro. ad Theo., c. 3.

law of eternal justice requires, either that the human race should
be punished, or that, by an atonement proceeding from humanity, order should be re-established.   Otherwise it would not
be in harmony with the moral order of the universe that vile
man should be restored to the communion of happy spirits.
Man could not accomplish that atonement *of himself.*   As by
one being human nature had been corrupted, so by *one being* the
atonement was to be effected.   But he who was to effect this
must have had something to give that is above all creation.
He must have been God himself.   And, at the same time, he
must have been man, to make his atonement applicable to man.
This being could, therefore, be none other than the God-Man.
This God-Man voluntarily gave himself up to death; for he
was not subjected to death.   He exercised the most perfect
obedience in the midst of the greatest sufferings.   God owed
Christ a reward.   But since Christ, as God, amply sufficed for
himself, he needed no reward.   Therefore Christ could transfer
his merits to the world, and ask as a reward the salvation of
believers."   Thus wrote Anselm in his work entitled, *Why did
God become Man?*[1]

But what is remarkable, considering their ordinary reputation, the scholastics insisted particularly on the sanctifying
influence of faith.   "The sufferings of Christ," says Peter
Lombard, that illustrious Master of Sentences, who ruled the
schools for centuries, "delivered us from sin; for that immense
sacrifice of divine charity kindles love to God within us, and
that love sanctifies us."[2]   "The just man who lives by faith,"
says Robert Pulleyn, " is already sanctified internally; and he
receives good works as a token of his faith and righteousness.
Faith produces first the righteousness of the heart, and that
produces works."[3]   "Man, in his original state," says Alexander of Hales, the irrefragable doctor, "did not oppose God.
Therefore he only needed a *forming grace.*   But now he has
something in him that is in opposition to God, and which
can be taken away by God's power only.   Now, therefore, man
needs a *transforming grace.*"[4]

It is true that there were differences and controversies be-

---

[1] Anselm, Cur Deus homo? lib. ii.   [2] Sententiarum, lib. iv.
[3] Sentent., lib. viii.   [4] Gratia reformans.   Summa, etc.

tween the scholastic doctors; but those very controversies prove that they were grounded on the common foundation of the great truths of salvation. For instance, Anselm, Thomas Aquinas (the angelic doctor), and others, believed that Christ's sacrifice effected man's redemption by virtue of an intrinsic quality (*ex insito valore*); whereas other scholastics, and Duns Scotus in particular (the subtile doctor), maintained that that redemption was only a consequence of the counsel, the design of God, who had attached the redemption of man to that price. In these things they differed; but all said, " Man, who was lost, is saved by the death of the God-Man."

THE ERA OF THE REFORMATION.—Such is the testimony given for centuries by the Church and the school, without speaking of numerous witnesses to the truth, such as *Wickliffe*, *Waldo*, and others, who were the forerunners of the great movement which was about to take place in the world. The church had gone through its youth, full of life; its manhood, full of strength and clearness; its systematic and reasoning old age; but after the days of scholasticism, even its reasoning passed away. The hierarchy wished to embrace all in its chains: life, dogma, and systems; and to place a tombstone over all the noble tendencies of the Church. It wished to reign alone. Vain wish! The Church in its strength burst these bonds of death asunder; the stone was rolled away; the sepulchre opened, and it came forth like a man brought back to life. And here, gentlemen, we salute the fourth era, the fourth form: the form of the Reformation.

If the three successive forms which we have reviewed have seemed to possess characteristics, such as *life*, *dogma*, and *system*, what is the characteristic of this?

Gentlemen, a reformation is a return to old forms. But this reformation was not effected at the expence of any one of the preceding forms. The Reformation re-established and reunited the three successive forms which had till then been isolated in the Church of God, and formed a wonderful combination.

Yes, gentlemen, this is the characteristic of the fourth era. The Reformation took the form of *system*, and added to it that of *dogma*, then it joined these two united forms to that of *life*.

Or, rather, it inverted this order: it began with *life*, proceeded to *dogma*, and crowned the whole with the form of *system*. The Reformation united the wisdom of the three preceding forms.

It began with *life*. Luther felt in his heart, through divine grace, the living influence of Christianity as perhaps no doctor of the Church had ever felt it before. The Reformation came forth living from the Reformer's heart, where God had placed it. The era which was under the exclusive influence of the Wittemberg doctor was, we may say, an era full of life. This is so true, that Melancthon, the theologian of the Reformation, in an admirable work which he published at that time (we allude to the first edition of his *Loci Communes*), omits the doctrines of *the nature of God* and of *the Trinity*, not because they seemed unimportant to him, for, on the contrary, they formed the basis of his system, but because, he says, it is better to adore than to sound these mysteries.

But, at the same time, beneath this life you will find the strongly-constituted members of the Christian *dogma;* and soon, in the second period of the Reformation (that which begins with the Augsburg Confession, composed by Melancthon himself,) these doctrines stand forth and appear in all their power; the Trinity, man's entire corruption, and especially the doctrine of grace, justification by faith—these are exposed with a clearness and profoundness which were scarcely equalled in the era of dogma. And already you discover the system in the harmonious distribution of these various members of the body of the Christian doctrine. But the system was formed, especially in the third era of the Reformation, under the influence of two great theologians, Melancthon in Germany and Calvin at Geneva. The Christian Institutions of our Reformer will ever remain one of the finest monuments of the Christian system.

How loud were the voices which in that era proclaimed the immovable truths of the Gospel! Listen to the doctor of Wittemberg, the great Luther, respecting the divinity of Jesus Christ. " If Christ remaineth not the true and essential God, begotten of the Father from all eternity, and the Creator of all creatures, then we are lost; for of what avail are the sufferings and death of Jesus Christ to us, if he was but a man like you and me ? Then, he can not have overcome the Devil, sin, and death. We need a Saviour who was really God, above all sin, above death, hell, and the Devil. What though the Arians exclaim, ' Christ was the noblest, the most sublime of all creatures.' They want by this means to disguise their shameful error, so that the people may not discern it. But if the faith is injured, even in the slightest degree, we are undone. If they take away Christ's divinity from him, we have no deliverance from the anger and condemnation of God."[1]

And what does the Reformation say with regard to *man ?* It dashes to pieces the various subtile distinctions of scholasticism, and exposes, with admirable clearness and simplicity, the real doctrine respecting man. Even before he published his famous theses on indulgences, Luther had published several on man ; and these are a few of those truths which that great doctor declared himself ready to defend in the Church at the very dawn of the glorious day of the Reformation.

" It is true that man, who has become a worthless tree, can not but do and desire what is evil."

" There is nothing on man's side to anticipate grace, save impotency, and even rebellion."

" There is no moral virtue that is without pride and misery, that is to say, without sin."

" He who is without God's grace sins constantly, even if he does not kill, steal, nor commit adultery."

Shall we speak, gentlemen, of the homage which the Reformation pays to the doctrine of grace ? It was by that doctrine that it overthrew all the bulwarks of Rome. The Reformation was not willing that man should put his confidence and rest his salvation in any thing performed by him or in him. Christ is the only foundation, and faith in his name is the only means of grace. Every other doctrine can only lead to pride or despair.

Listen to Luther, writing to his friend Spenlein : "Art thou weary at last of thine own unrighteousness ? Dost thou rejoice and trust in Christ's righteousness ? Learn, my dear brother, to know Christ and him crucified ; learn to despair of thyself,

---

[1] Luther, Interpretation of the First Chapter of the Gospel according to St. John, t. ix.

and to sing this hymn unto the Lord: ' Lord Jesus ! thou art my righteousness ; and I am thy sin.   Thou hast taken what was mine; thou hast given me what was thine.   Thou didst become what thou wert not, to make me what I was not.' "[1] "Works are not taken into consideration," he says again, "when justification is concerned. True faith will no more fail of producing them than the sun will fail of shining ; but it is not works that induce God to justify us."[2]

"Without doubt, says Melancthon, "the renewal of the heart must follow faith ; but, if justification be referred to, turn thine eyes away from that renewal, and gaze only upon the promises and upon Christ, knowing that we are justified only for the love of Christ, and not on account of our renewal. Faith justifies us, not, as thou hast written, because it is the root of the good tree in us, but because it lays hold of Jesus Christ, for the love of whom we are made acceptable."[3]

" We offer nothing to God," says Calvin ; " but we are anticipated by his pure grace, without any regard to our works."[4]

All the Reformers, however they may differ on some points, agree on this.   In Germany, Switzerland, France, Great Britain, Holland, Italy, and even Spain, they proclaimed justification by faith, and said, " If this article remains, the Church remains.   If this article falls, the Church falls."

But is it necessary to insist on this subject ?   Have we not in our hands the confessions of their faith ?   And do not the adversaries as well as the friends of that faith agree in acknowledging that this was the doctrine of the Reformation ?

Gentlemen, a fifth period, a fifth form is now beginning in the Church ; a form mysterious and unknown, the characteristics of which it is not yet given us to discern.   But there is one thing which the history of past forms teaches us.   The same fundamental truths will constitute the essence and the glory of the future form.   That salutary doctrine which we have found every where will not forsake the helm of the Church. It will not give up this precious ship to the perfidious but ephemeral wind of the heresies of a Theodotus, an Arius, a Pelagius, or a Socinius.   That which has been will be.

---

[1] Luther, Epist., t. i.   [2] Luth. ad Melancthon, opp.
[3] Melanc. ad Brentium, opp.   [4] Calvin, in Epist. ad Titum.

Besides, gentlemen, the history of past forms is to us a pledge that the future form will unite all that was good in those which no longer exist. God does not suffer any thing to be lost in his Church or for it. And this leads us to touch upon an error of some pious Christians, whose intentions are good, but who are constantly speaking of returning to the primitive form, caring but little for all that lies on their road thither. The Church can no more avoid the influence of the successive forms through which it has passed than a tree can rid itself of the layers with which every spring has clothed it, or than the full-grown man can cast off the growth of many years. As for ourselves, gentlemen, let us not turn away our eyes from the future; but let us not reject the past either; the past will be in the future. Life, dogma, system, all will be found united in the new form.

But still, will there not be something to characterize it, and thus to distinguish it from the form of the Reformation? Certainly there will; but that characteristic is yet to appear, and who shall say what it will be? Nevertheless, I will venture to speak. Will not that characteristic of the new form be a universal activity in carrying to every race of men and to every individual that which the preceding forms have produced ? Did not the period of the Reformation unite all the isolated blessings of the first three, so that the new era might take hold of those blessings and spread them throughout humanity? Should not life, dogma, and system, or, to speak more perfectly, Christian *science*, become the property of our race, as they have not been heretofore ! I will be silent on these subjects, which are still covered with a thick vail.

But there is one thing which we ought to know. Gentlemen, we are entering upon a new period and form both as to Christian science and the Church; and this generation will be God's instrument to give its first impulse to this era. In this there is a vast work to do, and there are but very few labourers. My voice will, at least, be heard now by you, whose ears it can reach. Prepare yourselves for this emergency, O scribes and teachers, who are destined, under God's hand, to open the new path of science and piety ! Learn that to overcome strong unbelief you need strong faith and knowledge. Enrich yourselves with the past to make ready for the future. Young men,

who are called to serve the churches of Him who has given his
life for his sheep, or who are already appointed over the Lord's
flock, you should fully understand what sound theology requires
of you. Profit by the lessons of history. Let them lead you
to go beyond the narrow sphere to which prejudices may perhaps have restricted you. Let them bring you out of the low
path in which none but servile spirits can creep. Live, not
merely in the passing moment, but in the by-gone ages. History calls them up; they surround you; they give you their
weighty testimony. Will you reject the faith of the whole
Church for that of one isolated doctor ? Will you, despising
the glory which comes from God, seek that of the world ? Continue that wonderful chain, of which the Lord is the first link,
and which comes down to you, formed of the great doctors of
Christendom in all its periods. Do not stand aside in the service of some obscure heresy. Were you alone among your
fellow-disciples or your colleagues, alone in your church, or
alone in the world, in confessing *God manifest in the flesh*, you
should console yourselves with the thought that you are with
all those illustrious witnesses of so many various forms and
eras, whose voices have echoed to-day. History shows us that
Christianity has not ceased, throughout all ages, to act powerfully upon the thoughts and the lives of men; but it also shows
us that it has always been by means of the same doctrines that
this regenerating influence has been exerted. The orthodox
doctrines of Christianity have alone the power to renovate individuals and nations. Other doctrines serve only to amuse
or to ruin souls. You will never find *life* where *truth* is not to
be found. Do you wish to follow the career of a rhetorician,
to divert people by sonorous sentences ? Or do you wish to
become a benefactor of man, to save him by the wisdom of God ?

Cling to that which is sound, immovable, and eternal. Go
forward like a sacred cohort ! Let many and powerful efforts
be made in Switzerland, in France, in Germany, in Holland,
in Great Britain, in America, to raise sound theology in the
world, and to establish the throne of truth.

And do thou, O most holy God ! by that light which alone
can make us see, enlighten us, and open to us the gates of that
knowledge all the vast treasures of which are hidden in Jesus
Christ !

DISCOURSE XIV.[1]

FAMILY WORSHIP.

"As for me and my house, we will serve the Lord."—Joshua, xxiv, 15.

"LET me die the death of the righteous, and let my last end be like his!" We have said, my brethren, on a former occasion, that if we would die his death, we must live his life. It is true that there are cases in which the Lord shows his mercy and his glory to men who are already lying on the death-bed, and says to them, as to the thief on the cross, "To-day shalt thou be with me in paradise." The Lord still gives the Church similar examples from time to time, for the purpose of displaying his sovereign power, by which, when he is pleased to do so, he can break the hardest hearts and convert the souls most estranged, to show that all depends on his grace, and that he hath mercy on whom he will have mercy. Yet these are but rare exceptions, on which you can not rely absolutely; and if you wish, my dear hearers, to die the Christian's death, you must live the Christian's life; your heart must be truly converted to the Lord, truly prepared for the kingdom, and, trusting only in the mercy of Christ, desirous of going to dwell with him. Now, my brethren, there are various means by which you can be made ready, in life, to obtain at a future day a blessed end. It is on one of the most efficacious of these means that we wish to dwell to-day. This mean is *Family Worship*; that is, the daily edification which the members of a Christian family may mutually enjoy. "As for me and my house," said Joshua to Israel, "we will serve the Lord." We wish, my brethren, to give you the *motives* which should induce us to make this resolution of Joshua, and the *directions* necessary to fulfil it.

[1] Published at Paris in 1827 ; it was preached, however, at Brussels.

MOTIVES.—Family worship is the most ancient as well as the holiest of institutions. It is not an innovation against which people are readily prejudiced ; it began with the world itself.

It is evident that the first worship which the first man and his children paid to God could be nothing else than Family Worship, since they constituted the only family which then existed on the earth. "Then," says the Scripture, "began men to call upon the name of the Lord." Family Worship must indeed have been for a long time the only form of worship addressed to God in common; for as the earth still remained to be peopled, the head of every family went to live separately; and, as a high-priest unto God in the place which was alloted to him, he offered unto the Lord of the whole earth the homage due to Him, with his wife, his sons and daughters, his man-servants and maid-servants. It was only by degrees that, when the number of men was greatly multiplied, various families happened to settle near each other; then came the idea of adoring God in common, and *Public Worship* began. But Family Worship had become too precious to the families of the children of God to give it up; and, if they began to worship God with the families of strangers, how much more was it their duty to worship him with their own families! Thus if, leaving the cradle of the human race, we go to the tents of the patriarchs, we again meet with this Family Worship. Let us go with the angels to the plains of Mamre, when Abraham is seated at the door of his tent in the heat of the day; let us go in with him, and we will find that the patriarch, with all his household, worshipped the Lord together. "I know him," said the Lord concerning the Father of the faithful, "that he will command his children and his household after him, and they shall keep the way of the Lord, to do justice and judgment." Public Worship was instituted by Moses; he gave numerous ordinances; a magnificent temple was to be erected. Will not Family Worship be abolished? No; by the side of that temple in all its magnificence, the lowliest house of a believer is to contain the word of God. "These words which I command thee this day," said the Lord by Moses, "shall be in thine heart: and thou shalt teach them diligently unto thy children, and shalt talk of them when thou sittest *in thine house,* and when thou walkest by the way, and when thou liest down, and when thou risest up." Joshua, in our text, declares to the people that they may worship idols if they choose, but that he will not join in their profane festivities; and that alone in his dwelling he and his house will serve the Lord. Job "rose up early in the morning, and offered burnt-offerings according to the number of his children; for he said, It may be that my sons have sinned!" David, whose whole life was one continual adoration of God, and to whom one day spent in the courts of the Lord was better than a thousand in the tents of wickedness, did not neglect the family altar; for he exclaimed, "That which our fathers have told us we will not hide from their children." If we pass on to the times in which our Saviour appeared, we find domestic instruction practised in the pious families of Israel. Thus St. Paul could say to Timothy, "From a child thou hast known the holy Scriptures, which are able to make thee wise unto salvation. I call to remembrance the unfeigned faith that is in thee, which dwelt first in thy grand-mother Lois, and thy mother Eunice; and I am persuaded that in thee also." Jesus during his ministry laid the foundations of Family Worship among Christians, when he said, "Where two or three are gathered together in my name, there am I in the midst of them." St. Paul recommended it, saying, "Rule well your own houses; speaking to yourselves in psalms and hymns and spiritual songs, singing and making melody in your heart to the Lord; giving thanks always for all things unto God and the Father in the name of our Lord Jesus Christ." Yes, my brethren, if we enter the humble dwellings of those primitive Christians, after having visited the tents of the patriarchs, we shall still find the same Family Worship offered up unto the Lord; we shall hear afar off those hymns, which may perhaps betray the presence of the disciples of the Crucified to their persecutors, and cause their destruction, but which joyfully arise to the throne of their Saviour, because it is better to fear him than to fear men; we shall see them assembled around the Sacred Book, which they afterward conceal with care, to preserve it from the hands of those who would fain destroy it.

Clement of Alexandria, an illustrious doctor of the Church, near the beginning of the third century, advised Christian husbands and wives to make it a daily practice to pray and read the Bible together in the morning, and he added, "The mother is the glory of the children, and the wife is the glory of the husband; all are the glory of the wife, and God is the glory of them all." Tertullian, shortly before gave this admirable description of the domestic life of a Christian couple; "What a union is that which exists between two believers, who have in common the same hope, the same desire, the same mode of living, the same service of the Lord; like brother and sister, united both in spirit and in flesh, they kneel down together; they pray and fast together; they teach, exhort, and support each other with gentleness; they go together to the house of God, to the table of the Lord; they share one another's troubles, persecutions, and pleasures; they conceal nothing from each other; they do not avoid one another; they visit the sick and succour the needy; the singing of psalms and hymns is heard among them; they rival each other in singing with the heart to their God. Christ is pleased to see and hear these things; he sends down his peace upon them. Where two or three are thus met he is with them; and where he is the Evil One can not come."

If we leave the humble dwellings of the primitive Christians, it is true that we shall find the practice of Family Worship becomes less and less frequent; but how gloriously it reappears at the epoch of the Reformation! How great an influence it exerted then upon the creed, the manners, and the intellectual development of all the nations which returned to primitive Christianity! It is not very long since it was still to be found in all evangelical families. If our fathers were deprived of its light, our forefathers were acquainted with it. It flourished especially in the evangelical provinces of this kingdom;[1] and many precious remains can still, we trust, be found here.

My brethren, such has been, in all times, the life of piety. And will we be Christians, or will we not? Shall we invent a new mode of piety which will harmonize with the world, or

---

[1] The Netherlands. This discourse was delivered previous to the separation of Belgium and Holland in 1830.

shall we hold fast to that which God has commanded us to possess? Shall we not say, in looking at that worship which passed from the tents of the patriarchs to the houses of the primitive Christians, and was finally established in the dwellings of our fathers, "As for me and my house, we will serve the Lord"?

But, my brethren, if the love of God be in your hearts, and if you feel that, being bought with a price, you ought to glorify God in your bodies and spirits, which are his, where do you love to glorify him rather than in your families and in your houses? You love to unite with your brethren in worshipping him publicly in the church; you love to pour out your souls before him in your closets. Is it only in the presence of that being with whom God has connected you for life and before your children, that you can not think of God? Is it, then, only, that you have no blessings to ascribe? Is it, then, only, that you have no mercies and protection to implore? You can speak of every thing when with them; your conversation is upon a thousand different matters; but your tongue and your heart can not find room for one word about God! You will not look up as a family to him who is the true Father of your family; you will not converse with your wife and your children about that Being who will one day, perhaps, be the only husband of your wife, the only Father of your children! It is the Gospel[1] that has formed domestic society; it did not exist before it; it does not exist without it; it would, therefore, seem to be the duty of that society, full of gratitude to the God of the Gospel, to be peculiarly consecrated to it; and yet, my brethren, how many couples, how many families there are, nominally Christian, and who even have some respect for religion, where God is never named! How many cases there are in which immortal souls that have been united have never asked one another who united them, and what their future destiny and objects are to be! How often it happens that, while they endeavour to assist each other in every thing else, they do not even think of assisting each other in searching for *the one thing needful*, in conversing, in reading, in praying, with reference

---

[1] It is obvious that the Author here uses the word Gospel as synonymous with Christianity, and in the sense of true religion.

to their eternal interests!   Christian spouses! is it in the flesh,
and for time alone, that you are to be united?   Is it not in the
spirit, and for eternity also?   Are you beings who have met
by accident, whom another accident, death, is soon to separate?
Do you not wish to be united by God, in God, and for God?
Religion would unite your souls by immortal ties!   But do not
reject them; draw them, on the contrary, tighter every day,
by worshipping together under the domestic roof.   Voyagers
on the same vessel converse of the place to which they are
going; and will not you, fellow-travellers to an eternal world,
speak together of that world, of the route which leads to it,
of your fears and your hopes?   "Many walk thus," says St.
Paul, "of whom I have told you often, and now tell you even
weeping, that they are the enemies of the Cross of Christ;"
but "our conversation is in heaven, from whence also we look
for the Saviour, the Lord Jesus Christ."

But if it be your duty to be engaged with reference to God
in your houses for your own sakes, ought you not to be so engaged for the sakes of those of your households whose souls
have been committed to your care, and especially for your
children? You are greatly concerned for their prosperity, for
their temporal happiness; but does not this concern make your
neglect of their eternal prosperity and happiness still more palpable? Your children are young trees intrusted to you; your
house is the nursery where they ought to grow, and you are
the gardeners. But oh! will you plant those tender and precious
saplings in a sterile and sandy soil? Yet this is what you are
doing, if there be nothing in your house to make them grow in
the knowledge and love of their God and Saviour. Are you
not preparing for them a favourable soil, from which they can
derive sap and life? What will become of your children in the
midst of all the temptations that will surround them and draw
them into sin? What will become of them in these troublous
times, in which it is so necessary to strengthen the soul of the
young man by the fear of God, and thus to give that fragile
bark the ballast needed for launching it upon the vast ocean?

Parents! if your children do not meet with a spirit of piety
in your houses, if, on the contrary, your pride consists in sur-
rounding them with external gifts, introducing them into

worldly society, indulging all their whims, letting them follow their own course, you will see them grow vain, proud, idle, disobedient, impudent, and extravagant! They will treat you with contempt; and the more your hearts are wrapped up in them, the less they will think of you. This is seen but too often to be the case; but ask yourselves if you are not responsible for their bad habits and practices; and your conscience will reply that you are; that you are now eating the bread of bitterness which you have prepared for yourself. May you learn thereby how great has been your sin against God in neglecting the means which were in your power for influencing their hearts ; and may others take warning from your misfortune, and bring up their children *in the Lord!* Nothing is more effectual in doing this than an example of domestic piety. Public worship is often too vague and general for children, and does not sufficiently interest them; as to the worship of the closet, they do not yet understand it. A lesson learned by rote, if unaccompanied by any thing else, may lead them to look upon religion as a study, like those of foreign languages or history. Here, as every where, and more than elsewhere, example is more effectual than precept. They are not merely to be taught out of some elementary book that they must love God, but you must show them God is loved. If they observe that no worship is paid to that God of whom they hear, the very best instruction will prove useless; but by means of Family Worship, these young plants will grow "like a tree planted by the rivers of water, that bringeth forth his fruit in his season: his leaf also shall not wither." Your children may leave the parental roof, but they will remember in foreign lands the prayers of the parental roof, and those prayers will protect them. "If any," says the Scripture, "have children or nephews, let them learn first to show piety at home. But if any provide not for his own, and especially for those of his own house, he hath denied the faith, and is worse than an infidel."

And what delight, what peace, what real happiness a Christian family will find in erecting a family altar in their midst, and in uniting to offer up sacrifice unto the Lord! Such is the occupation of angels in heaven ; and blessed are those who anticipate those pure and immortal joys? "Behold, how good

and pleasant it is for brethren to dwell together in unity! It
is like the precious ointment upon the head, that ran down
upon the beard, even Aaron's beard; that went down to the
skirts of his garments; as the dew of Hermon, and as the dew
that descended upon the mountains of Zion; for there the Lord
commanded the blessing, even life for evermore." O what
new grace and life piety gives to a family! In a house where
God is forgotten, there is rudeness, ill-humour, and vexation of
spirit. Without the knowledge and the love of God, a family
is but a collection of individuals who may have more or less
natural affection for one another; but the real bond, the love of
God our Father in Jesus Christ our Lord, is wanting. The
poets are full of beautiful descriptions of domestic life; but,
alas! how different the pictures often are from the reality!
Sometimes there is a want of confidence in the providence of
God; sometimes there is love of riches; at others, a difference of
character; at others, an opposition of principles. O how many
troubles, how many cares there are in the bosoms of families.

Domestic piety will prevent all these evils; it will give perfect confidence in that God who gives food to the birds of the
air; it will give true love toward those with whom we have to
live; not an exacting, sensitive love, but a merciful love, which
excuses and forgives, like that of God himself; not a proud
love, but a humble love, accompanied by a sense of one's own
faults and weakness; not a fickle love, but a love unchangeable as eternal charity. "The voice of rejoicing and salvation
is in the tabernacle of the righteous."

And when the hour of trial comes, that hour which must
come sooner or later, and which sometimes visits the homes of
men more than once, what consolation will domestic piety afford! Where do trials occur if not in the bosoms of families?
Where, then, ought the remedy for trials to be administered if
not in the bosoms of families? How much a family where there
is mourning is to be pitied if it has not that consolation! The
various members of whom it is composed increase one another's
sadness. But if, on the contrary, that family loves God, if it
is in the habit of meeting to invoke the holy name of God,
from whom comes every trial, as well as every good gift; then
how will the souls that are cast down be raised up! The mem-

bers of the family who still remain around the table on which
is laid *the Book of God*, that book where they find the words of
resurrection, life, and immortality, where they find sure pledges
of the happiness of the being who is no more among them, as
well as the warrant of their own hopes.   The Lord is pleased to
send down the *Comforter* to them; the Spirit of glory and of God
rests upon them; an ineffable balm is poured upon their wounds,
and gives them much consolation; peace is communicated from
one heart to another.   They enjoy moments of celestial bliss.
" Though I walk through the valley of the shadow of death
I will fear no evil; for thou art with me; thy rod and thy staff
they comfort me."   " O Lord, thou hast brought up my soul
from the grave! Thine anger endureth but a moment: in thy
favour is life ; weeping may endure for a night, but joy cometh
in the morning."

And who can tell, my brethren, what an influence domestic
piety might exert over society itself? What encouragements all
men would have in doing their duty, from the statesman down
to the poorest mechanic! How would all become accustomed to
act with respect not only to the opinions of men, but also to
the judgment of God! How would each learn to be satisfied
with the position in which he is placed! Good habits would be
adopted; the powerful voice of conscience would be strengthened;
prudence, propriety, talent, social virtues, would be developed
with renewed vigour.   This is what we might expect both for
ourselves and for society.   " Godliness hath promise of the life
that now is, and of that which is to come."

DIRECTIONS. If you wish to profit by all the blessings of
Family Worship, what are you to do? What measures are you
to follow? We have still, my brethren, to give you a few.

And first, so far as it is in your power, let not these exercises
of domestic piety be wanting in *spirituality, truth, and life ;* let
them not consist merely in reading certain passages, and repeating certain forms of prayer, in which the heart is not concerned.   It would, perhaps, be better to have no Family Worship than to have such as this.   These dead forms are still to
be found in some families.   But at the present day, when the
Church is every where struggling to rise out of its ruins, and
when the wind of which Ezekiel spoke is breathing every where

upon the dry bones to impart life unto them, we must return to Family Worship and revive it, not in a state of languor and death, but in a state of life and strength. How shall we attain this object? Let us perform the exercises of family piety, not merely as though it were a good work which we ought to accomplish, for then we might fall either into the error which we have just pointed out, or into pride; but let us perform them rather like miserable beings who want riches; as famished creatures, who want food to nourish that which is most noble in them. Do it as a duty, if you choose; but do it rather on account of your own wants. The little child knows how to ask for a piece of bread, or even for its mother's milk; and do not we know how to go to God and ask of him his pure and spiritual milk? " Blessed are they which do hunger and thirst after righteousness; for they shall be filled."

We will give you another rule, my brethren: do not adhere too exclusively, too servilely to any one particular form. First establish such a service in accordance with your own wants and those of your family; let there be entire liberty; let it be conducted one day in one manner, and the next in another, if you choose; let it be prolonged at one time and abridged at another. Perhaps it were better that this exercise should not, at first, embrace all the members of your household, but should have a smaller and more intimate sphere; this will make it more easy and edifying. Follow these various suggestions; the great matter is, that God be not forgotten under your roof. " Stand fast, therefore, in the liberty wherewith Christ hath made us free, and be not entangled again with the yoke of bondage."

But how are these moments consecrated unto God to be occupied.

In the first place, the *word of God* should, of course be read, and sometimes, perhaps, other Christian books. In how many families that admirable Book, that Book of the nations, has been in all ages, and is still the most precious of treasures! In how many dwellings has the Bible diffused righteousness, peace, and joy in the Holy Ghost, and submission to all authorities appointed by God! The various books which compose the Bible are almost all of a different nature from one another; it were diffi-

cult to have a greater variety in one volume, though the same
Spirit of God is in each. This circumstance makes it remarkably appropriate for the nourishment of families; and hence so
many poor and obscure families in Protestant countries, possessing that Book, do without any others, and by it are brought
to the acquisition, not only of eternal life, but of a remarkable
intellectual development. The child, the old man, the woman,
and the full-grown man alike find something to interest them
there, and to lead them to God. There is something for every
situation in life. What abundant consolation have all troubled
and afflicted but faithful souls derived always from the Psalms
of the Royal Prophet! It is well to read throughout some book
of the Scriptures, but it is not necessary to follow the order in
which the different books are placed in the Sacred Volume.
On the contrary, it is, perhaps, best to turn from the New
Testament to the Old, and from the Old to the New; from one
of the Prophets to one of the Epistles of the Apostles, and then
to one of the historical books of the Old Testament. It is
desirable that the person who reads should make some remarks
on the passage read. You know how to speak about any other
book that you read; is it only here that thoughts and words
are wanting? Do you find nothing there that is applicable to
the state of your heart, to the situation of your family, to the
character of some one of your children? Read that book always,
not as a history of past times, but as a book written for you,
addressed to you now; you will readily find circumstances
and occasions which render it suitable. Nevertheless, if nothing has been given to you, be content with asking the Holy
Spirit to impart to every heart the fruits which he has promised for his word. "As the rain cometh down, and the
snow, from heaven, and returneth not thither, but watereth the
earth, and maketh it bring forth and bud, that it may give
seed to the sower, and bread to the eater; so shall my word
be that goeth forth out of my mouth; it shall not return unto
me void; but it shall accomplish that which I please, and it
shall prosper in the thing whereunto I sent it."

Another act of worship is, *prayer in common*, or together.
It is true that there are good written prayers; but can you not
pray to God aloud yourself? You know very well how to speak

to a friend; why should you not know how to speak to God?
Is he not your greatest and most intimate friend? How easy
is it to approach him when it is in the name of Christ crucified
that we come! "Thou art near, O Lord," says David. "While
they are yet speaking," God has said, "I will hear." If you
can pray in secret, can you not pray aloud? Do not be so
anxious about what you shall say; "Prayer requires more of
the heart than the tongue, more faith than reasoning." How
can it be otherwise than salutary, when, for instance, a father or
a mother prays aloud for the children who are present, and enters into detail respecting their sins before God, asking him to
give his help and his grace. And how often a family is in a
situation in which it is called upon to offer up prayer unto God,
for deliverance, for assistance, for consolation! "Ye shall
seek me and find me, when ye shall search for me with all your
heart," saith the Lord.

A third act of worship which ought, if possible, to form part
of domestic devotion, is *singing*. In these days man has asso-
ciated singing with his occupations, and especially with his
pleasures; but to praise God was certainly its primitive object.
It is to this that the Royal Prophet consecrated it, and shall
not we do likewise? If so many profane things are sung in
some houses, why should we not sing to the honour of the God
who has created and redeemed us? Still more, if sacred hymns
are sometimes sung for the sake of the beauty of the sound,
shall they not be sung with humility and fervour to celebrate
the Lord? "Admonish one another in psalms and hymns
and spiritual songs, singing with grace in your hearts to the
Lord."

But some will perhaps say, At what time ought we thus to
think of God and approach him together? I answer, whenever
you choose, at the most convenient hour, when you will be
least disturbed in your other business. This is generally in the
evening; perhaps it were better, on account of the fatigue of
the day, that it should be in the morning; and best of all both
morning and evening. When you have eaten your morning
meal, or even while you are eating it, could you not spend that
time which is usually spent either in saying nothing or in talking of trifles, in reading a few words which would raise your

thoughts to God, or in hearing them read? I am about to begin the day by the first function of the animal being; but wilt not thou, O my spiritual and immortal soul, do any thing or receive any thing now? I am about to feed my body with that which God has created; but do thou, O my soul, awake and receive thy food from the Creator! O God! thou art my portion forever! O God! thou art my God; early will I seek thee! What a blessing, my brethren, will such a beginning bring down upon the whole day, and what a happy disposition of mind it will give you!

And to you, Christian parents, let the evening of the Lord's day, that season when the children of irreligious parents run to places of dissipation, be peculiarly precious and sacred. Instruct your household in the way of the Lord, and your instructions at that time will be particularly blessed, provided your children see that you are really in earnest in the work which you are performing.

To all this, my brethren, add the essential thing: a life in accordance with the sacredness of the worship which you offer unto God. Be not one man before the altar of God and another in the world, but be truly one man at all times. Let your behaviour throughout the day be a living commentary upon what you have read, heard, or said in the hour of devotion. "Be ye doers of the word, and not hearers only, deceiving your own-selves; for the sacrifice of the wicked is an abomination to the Lord; but He loveth him that followeth after righteousness."

Such is Family Worship. We would remind you, my dear hearers, of all the motives which ought to hasten its establishment in your families, and we entreat you, and particularly those of you who are husbands or wives, fathers or mothers, to put your hands to the plough.

But do you say, 'This is so strange a thing'? What, my brethren! Is it not more strange that a family professing to be Christian, professing to have a firm hope for eternity, should advance toward that eternity without giving any sign of that hope, without any preparation, without any conversation, perhaps, alas! without any thought concerning it? Ah! *this* is very strange!

Do you say, 'This is a thing of very little repute or glory, and to which a certain degree of shame is attached'? And who, then, is the greatest: that father who, in former and happier days, was *the high priest of God* in his own house, and who increased his paternal authority and gave it a divine unction by kneeling down with his children before his Father and the Father of them all; or that worldly man in our days, whose mind is engaged only in vain pursuits, who forgets his eternal destiny and that of his children, and in whose house God is not? O what a shame is this!

But perhaps you say, 'Different times have different customs; those things were well enough then, but all has changed now'? It is precisely because all has changed that we must make haste and raise up the family altar in the midst of families, lest the feeble tie that still holds back these families should be broken, and they drag both Church and State into ruin. It is not when the disease has spread with great violence that remedies become useless; and before a man's life is despaired of, the most powerful preservatives are given to him.

Thus, then, do you, who, by the grace of God, are well disposed, and have made good resolutions, make an attempt, and be not discouraged; make another still; resort to prayer; ask God to guide you himself, to sustain you, and give you success; ask Jesus Christ to be with you; for "where two or three are gathered together in his name there is he in the midst of them."

But, my brethren, if you wish to erect an altar unto God in your house, you must, first of all, erect one in your own heart. And is there one there? I ask you, my brethren, Is there one? Ah! could I draw back the vail, could I now penetrate into the hearts of those who listen to me, what would I see? Or, rather, O Lord! what must thou see in our hearts—thou, from whom nothing is vailed, and before whom all things are naked and visible!

In your heart, my dear hearer, I see an altar erected to pleasure and worldliness; there you offer up your morning sacrifice; there you sacrifice, especially in the evening; and the incense arising from it intoxicates and bewilders you even at night.

In your heart, my dear hearer, I see an altar erected to the good gifts of this world, to riches, to Mammon.

In yours, my dear hearer, I see an altar consecrated to yourself. You are the idol whom you worship, whom you exalt above every thing else, for whom you wish for all things, and at the foot of whom you would fain see all the world kneel.

My brethren, is there an altar in your hearts erected to the only living and true God? Are you the temple of God, and does God's Spirit dwell within you? So long as there is no altar erected to God in your souls, there can be none in your houses; "For what fellowship hath righteousness with unrighteousness? and what communion hath light with darkness? and what concord hath Christ with Belial? and what agreement hath *the temple of God with idols?*

Be converted, then, in your hearts! Die to the world, to sin, to yourselves even, and live to God in Jesus Christ our Lord. Immortal souls, Christ hath redeemed you at a great price! He gave his whole life on the cross for you. Learn, then, "that he died for all, that they which live should not henceforth live unto themselves, but unto him which died for them, and rose again." "Wherefore come out from among idols, and be ye separate, saith the Lord, and touch not the unclean thing; and I will receive you, and will be a father unto you, and ye shall be my sons and daughters, saith the Lord Almighty."

O happy is that family, my brethren, which has embraced that God who says, "I will dwell in them, and walk in them, and I will be their God, and they shall be my people"! Happy for time, and happy for eternity! How can you hope to meet with those whom you love near Christ in heaven, unless with them you seek Christ on earth? How shall you assemble as a family there, if you have not as a family attended to heavenly things here below? But as to the Christian family which shall have been united in Jesus, it will, without doubt, meet around the throne of the glory of Him whom it will have loved without having seen. It will only change its wretched and perishable dwelling for the vast and eternal mansions of God. Instead of being a humble family of the earth, united to the whole family of heaven by the same ties, it will have become an innumerable and glorious family. It will surround the throne of God with the hundred and forty-four thousand, and will say, as it said on earth, but with joy and glory, "Thou art worthy, O Lord, to receive glory and honour and power."

O, my brethren, if but one father or mother would now re-solve to meet together in the presence of the Lord, if one single person not yet bound by domestic ties were to resolve to raise an altar unto God in his house when he shall be so bound, and would, in some future day, so act that abundant blessings would descend upon him and his, I would give thanks unto God for having spoken!

Dear hearer! may the Lord so affect your heart that you may now exclaim, "As for me and my house we will serve the Lord!" Amen.

ESSAYS.

ESSAY I.[1]

LUTHERANISM AND CALVANISM.

THEIR DIVERSITY ESSENTIAL TO THEIR UNITY.

" Each of these religions deems itself the most perfect: CALVINISM believes
itself to be most conformed to what Jesus Christ has said; and LUTHER-
ANISM to what the Apostles have done."—*Montesquieu, Esprit des Lois,*
Book xxiv, Chap. 5.

THE times are pressing. It is becoming necessary to aim
at the useful; not to be involved in useless discussions, but
to seek, according to the apostolic precept, that which will
truly contribute to the edification of the Church. This thought
has determined me to lay before you the following question:

What in our Reformed French churches has characterized
the past year?

It is, if I mistake not, a new manifestation of principles
which have frequently been designated by the names of parties
opposed to us, but which, we desire to mention only in terms
of kindness; and for this reason we will call them (using a
name dear to us) the principles of Lutheranism.

Lutheranism and the Reform[2] possess distinct characters,
but they are not separated so much by errors as by diversities.

---

[1] This essay, originally in the form of a discourse, was read before the
Evangelical Society of Geneva, at its anniversay in 1844.

It is thought best to add, that much of what is said of Lutheranism in
this discourse is applicable only to that of Europe, and cannot be said of
that of this country.—*Trans.*

[2] The reader must remember that the author uses the term *Reformation*
to designate the grand work of the sixteenth century in general, while the
word *Reform* is employed when the work of Zwingle and Calvin is especially referred to.—*Trans.*

God has chosen that this diversity should exist, that in the end
the Reformation might be complete. Having in the beginning
proposed to make immense bodies move round the sun, his
powerful hand impressed them with two contrary forces; the
one tending to drive them from the centre, the other to attract
them toward it. It is from these apparent contradictions that
the motion of the universe and the admirable unity of the
heavenly system results. So it was in the days of the Reformation. Opposite tendencies were necessary for this work,
and these very tendencies enhance its admirable unity.

> " In the garden of my Master
> There are many kinds of flowers." [1]

So wrote a Christian author.[2] Shall we then look for one
blossom only? Ah! let us not, like unskilful gardeners, tear
up those indigenous plants, the culture of which is suited particularly to our soil and climate, and supply their place with
exotics, which require other soil, and which would perish in our
hands.

Yes, let us understand this well: there is not only friendship
and harmony between Lutheranism and the Reform; there is
more than this—there is *unity*.

First, they possess that thorough unity which results from
the same living faith animating both. They believe alike in
man's entire inability to do good; they believe in God manifest
in the flesh; in atonement by his blood, and regeneration by
his Spirit, in justification by faith in his name, in charity, and
in good works by virtue of their communion with him. But
it is not of this unity of *identity* that we wish to speak at present. We go much farther: we intend to show that Lutheranism and the Reform are one, in their very diversities; whence
we infer that, instead of being effaced, most of these diversities
—and especially those relating to the Reform which we have
to defend—should be carefully preserved. Such is our position.

And those who, hearing us to-day, enumerate the characters,
so different in themselves, that distinguish Lutheranism from

[1] " Dans le jardin de mon Maître
Il est toutes sortes de fleurs."
[2] Tersteegen.

the Reform, would fall into a grave error should they exclaim with painful surprise, "What, then! are not these so many friends the less, and so many enemies the more!" The body and the soul differ vastly in their respective attributes, yet they form but one being. Man and woman have very opposite capaities and duties, yet are but one flesh. In Christ, humanity and divinity were certainly distinct, yet they together constitute but one Saviour. So Lutheranism and the Reform, though very different, are yet in unity.

Shall we speak of their strifes? But is there never any strife between the body and the spirit? between the husband and the wife? Was there not strife in Christ himself, between his humanity and divinity? "My soul is exceeding sorrowful, even unto death. Father, if it be possible, let this cup pass from me," cried his humanity, shuddering at the approach of the cross. Strife, indeed, but strife when overcome, far from being opposed to unity, is essential to it, at least on earth.

I believe that the time is now near at hand when the struggle shall be over, and the union of Lutheranism and the Reform will be triumphant, if the rash friends of the former do not endeavour to force the latter to submit to its laws. Bear in mind that the Reform, which is essentially the friend of proselytism, does not strive to make proselytes within the pale of Lutheranism; it loves it; it venerates it; it leaves it to its own strength, or rather, to that of its God. But, strange to say, Lutheranism, (certainly not that of Germany nor of Geneva,) Lutheranism, generally passive in its character, advances heedlessly, seemingly desirous of taking from us our patrimony, and substituting itself for the three centuries' work of our Reformers. It is indeed necessary in order to effect unity, to destroy one of the two members? This may be one method, but it is not ours. Lutheranism has important duties to discharge toward the Reform, and too well do we know the noble principles of the excellent men who, in Germany, are its true supporters, not to be convinced that they will perform them well.

If one of two friendly and allied armies has been beaten and dispersed by the common enemy while the other has remained in its camp, marshalled under its leaders and its standards, shall this latter seize that opportunity to assert its supremacy, and impose upon the other its own colours? Will it not rather generously help them to recover the ancient standards of their fathers? It is this that we now ask of Lutheranism.

We need not assert that we have no prejudice against Martin Luther. If there exist in the history of the world a man whom we love above all others, it is he. We venerate Calvin; we love Luther. Lutheranism itself is dear to us, and for weighty reasons. There are principles in the Reform which we would fear, if there existed not the counterpoise of Lutheranism; as there are also in Lutheranism those which would alarm us, were it not for the counterpoise of the Reform. Luther and Lutheranism have not, even in Germany, not even at Wittemburg, more zealous friends and admirers than ourselves.

But if this question be proposed, Should the Reform in France, in Switzerland, or elsewhere, give way to Lutheranism? We reply, without hesitation, Certainly not!

Now we think this is the question which, during the past year, has been brought before our churches.

Have they at all times answered as they should have done? We think not. The Reform is misunderstood, even among the Reformed themselves. Two centuries of persecution and humiliation have caused it to lose its finest traditions. Principles opposed to it find eloquent and pious advocates. Even within its bosom there are distinguished minds, which hesitate, and are irresolute at the moment of revival, and which, mistaking one voice for another, are ready to undergo a most wonderful transformation. One would say, judging from what is passing at the present day, that the Reform may organize societies, may exercise a certain external activity, but with regard to *principles*, Lutheranism alone must establish them, so that it only remains for us to place ourselves under its guardianship. Our standard, which is three centuries old, is called radical and innovating; and colours rejected by ten generations begin to be raised up here and there, in this presbytery and in that church. Some communities, even, which are wholly Reformed, are ready to advocate it. There are countries covered with eloquent ruins, and strewed with the sepulchres of the saints, where such things are going on, and where, if they be not stopped, the very stones will cry out.

We firmly believe that the Swiss and French of the Reformed church have no need to ask directions of any foreign church, particularly of one with which, it is true, the same faith and the same charity ought to unite them, but which does not know them, and which, we must say, has, though with many remarkable exceptions, been frequently wanting in justice and impartiality toward them. If the Reform is to live, it must possess a life peculiar to itself. It has in its own traditions an abundance of most sublime inspirations, but, unfortunately, it does not know how to appreciate them; and instead of exploring the golden mine of its antiquity, doubtless with some trouble, and by the sweat of its brow, it prefers receiving with eagerness coin already stamped, but stamped with foreign arms.

In order that the Reformed church should preserve the principles God has intrusted to it, it must know them. What are they then? It is to this research that we appropriate this essay. We shall only lay before you truths acknowledged for three centuries past, but which seem, in our day, to be completely forgotten.

A great mind, the genius of *Montesquieu*, perceived a fundamental difference between Lutheranism and the Reform, when he said, in his 'Esprit des Lois:' "Each of these religions deems itself the most perfect: the Calvinistic deeming itself most conformed to what Jesus Christ has said, and the Lutheran to what the apostles have done." This language, undoubtedly, implies that the Reform has for its basis the word of God, while Lutheranism has the acts and usages of the Church. This distinction is profound, and, generally speaking, contains much truth.

But let us examine more minutely these differences, without, however, pretending to enumerate them all. Let us lay aside peculiarities of doctrine, and particularly that of the free and eternal grace of God, which is our most precious jewel. Let us not speak, at present, of the election of the Father, nor of the manner in which humanity and divinity are united in the person of the God-man, nor of the nature of the Lord's Supper,

nor of the doctrine of Baptism; these are well-known peculiarities from which all others flow. Let us confine ourselves
especially to questions relating to the Church; which is daily
becoming the greatest, and, so to speak, the all-engrossing
subject.

I. The Reformed church lays down as the ground-work of
Christianity the *Scriptural principle*, that the *word of God* is *the
positive rule, the absolute law, the sole source of faith, and of the
Christian life;* whereas Luther lays down as the basis of his
Reformation a principle not less to be venerated, but entirely
different, namely, *faith*, or *justification by faith*.

We think it was well that these two fundamental principles
should have been established at the same time. In this particular, the combined action of Lutheranism and the Reform
was admirable; that of Lutheranism especially fills us with the
deepest veneration. Not only did Luther and his friends set
forth the capital doctrine of justification in a manner still more
explicit than did the Reform, but, had they not done so, we
boldly assert that there would have been no Reformation.
Why was not the great Reformation accomplished by the sects
of the middle ages, which originated the principles of the
Reform? For several reasons, undoubtedly, but principally
because they were not fully impressed with the importance of
this great idea, of which Luther, after St. Paul, was the most
faithful promulgator.

The Reformation, and, prior to it, nascent Christianity, had
two fundamental principles: that of the Reform, which was
simple, and that of Lutheranism, which was material. The
Reform required faith also; Lutheranism, too, required the
Bible. But each of these principles was distinctively and spe-
cially intrusted to a faithful guardian. These were the two
forces which were to urge on the new world created in the sixteenth century; and herein we admire with gratitude the most
perfect unity in the diversity of the work of God.

However, we would not justify the consequences to which
Luther carried his principles. Applying them to the word of
God with a boldness which astonishes us, he declares, in the
preface of his translation of the New Testament, that the
Gospel of St. John, the Epistles of St. Paul, particularly that

to the Romans, and the first Epistle of St. Peter, are the true *marrow* of the Scriptures, because they treat especially of faith; he considers the Gospels inferior to the Epistles; lightly esteems the Revelation by St. John, and speaks of one of the Epistles (that of St. James) in terms so well known that I need not repeat them here. Rationalism, which shakes or revokes all the canonical writings, has appeared, and, as it seems to us, could only appear in the Church of Luther.

The Swiss and French Reform could not be reproached with this want of respect. On the contrary, in throwing off the authority of the Church, it had recourse to that sovereign authority, which the Church itself had always exalted, that of the holy Scriptures. "Forsaking," says one of its leaders,[1] "the decrees of the popes and the fathers of the Church, 1 went to the very fountain-head. My soul was there refreshed, and from that time I strongly maintained this principle: the Bible alone should be our guide, and all the additions of men rejected."

"The church of Christ," said the pastors of Berne, in the famous dispute which decided the Reform of that canton in 1528, "has made neither laws nor commandments in addition to the word of God. This is the reason why all human traditions called ecclesiastical are obligatory only so far as they are contained and commanded in this holy word." And in the 17th century, Chillingworth, an English Reformer of the Episcopal church, chancellor of the diocese of Salisbury, all of whose opinions we should not uphold, but who, having been a Papist, understood well in what should consist the spirit of the Reform, uttered these sublime words: "The Bible, the whole Bible, nothing but the Bible, is the religion of the Reformed church." Let us here remember, that the church of England is a *Reformed* church, and not Lutheran. It is such, not only by the name it bears, but by its admirable articles of faith, and especially by the testimony it therein renders to the word of God.

This principle of the Reform is of even earlier date than the views of Luther; for it was not only the principle of the pri-

---

[1] Wolfgang Joner.

mitive church, of Wickliffe, of the Waldenses, and of many other fervent Christians, but it was proclaimed in the very morning of the Reformation, in the year 1518, by Carlstadt, who says, in those theses which Dr. Eck so violently attacked. "We prefer the letter of the Bible, not only to one or many doctors of the Church, but even to the authority of the whole Church itself."

Every thing in the Reformed church reveals this grand principle of the exclusive authority of the word of God. While the Augsburg Confession is silent with regard to the sole authority of the Scriptures, all the Confessions of the Reformed church are unanimous on this subject.[1] While the Lutherans uphold the Apocryphal books, and frequently select from them texts for their sermons, the Reformed distinguish them from the canonical writings with scrupulous care, and, if necessary, contend earnestly for this distinction, as did the British and Foreign Bible Society not long since, excited by the example of Scotland, that eminently Reformed country; and they regard it as a matter of the highest importance to define exactly the extent of the word of God, and carefully to exclude all human additions. While the text of the Lutheran Bibles does not distinguish human from divine words, in all our translations of the Bible, on the contrary, the words not found in the original are printed in italics, in order that the reader may, as far as is possible in a translation, discern between the word of God and the word of man. And it may be remarked that the translation of the New Testament published a few years since in Lausanne, which is purely and simply a *fac simile* of the original, has been prompted by the spirit of the Reform. We do not think that such a translation would have appeared among Lutherans.

It is not true, however, as has been recently pretended, that the Reform presents the Bible to us as a book all-sufficient in itself, whatever doctrine may be deduced from it. "We are persuaded," says the Helvetic Confession, "that a solid knowledge of true religion depends on the internal enlightening of

[1] Gallican Confession, Art. V; Confessio Belgica, Art V; Confess. Helv., Art. I, II; Conf. Aug., Art. VI; Conf. Bohem., Art I; Conf. of Westminster (of Scotland), Chap. I.

the Holy Spirit. We only regard as real and orthodox those explanations which are drawn from Scripture itself in conformity with the analogy of faith and the law of charity." Nor is it true, as has been asserted, that the Reform possesses no kind of tradition. There is not a century, not a generation, to whose voice the Reform is not ready to listen, and from which it is unwilling to derive instruction. Only it places the great voice above all smaller voices, and instead of judging of the import of Scripture by tradition, it judges, according to the principles of the fathers, of the truth of traditions by the Scriptures. Such then is our first principle :

The Reform is pre-eminently the confession of *the Bible.*

Never shall such man-worship be found among us, even of the men of God in the Church, as has been justly called elsewhere Lutherolatry. Never will there be seen among us such writings as have been published in Germany with these titles: *Luther, a Prophet—The Second Moses—An Elias—A Star—A Sun.* We have no other prophet than Jesus Christ, and no other Sun than the Bible. And while, for a long space of time, all sorts of relics of Luther were preserved with a religious veneration, we hardly know where the great Calvin resided; there is not even a small stone in our cemetery to mark the place where his ashes repose ; and four venerable trees, which were to be seen five or six years ago shading the ground where it is said the mortal remains of this great servant of God were laid, have been hewn down to make room ! . . . This is undoubtedly going too far ; but its import is striking: it reminds us that Calvin forbade that a monument should be erected to his memory, because he desired that the word of God alone should be honoured in his Church.

Yes, the Rock of the word of God is the foundation of the Reform ; we know of none other. Let other churches boast of their ecclesiastical basis ; we will boast only of our *Bible* foundation. And in this we believe ourselves more truly ecclesiastical than those who mingle with the Divine Rock the quicksands of human tradition. We will not forsake this our foundation for any price, not for the Pope nor for Luther— what do I say, not even for our Reformers themselves. Far distant be the day when the Reformed church shall glory in

being called the church of Calvin or Zwingle. The Bible—
—the Bible—the whole Bible—nothing but the Bible!

We asserted at the outset that the principle entrusted to the
Lutheran church was, in the days of the Reformation, of at
least equal importance with that which God entrusted to the
Reformed church. Which of the two is of most importance in
our day?

I dare not decide. But I will say, however, that the principle of the Bible appears to me at present at least as important as that of faith. Which are the powerful adversaries called
upon to fight the battle of the nineteenth century? *Evangelism
and Ecclesiasticism.* And by what means shall Ecclesiasticism
be silenced, and those clouds of human traditions and human
works which envelope it be dispelled? By the Bible.

If we hesitate on the importance of the principle of the
Reform, shall we not be instructed by the cry which is now
sounding on all sides: *The Church! The Church!* and would
put the visible church above the word of the Lord? Shall we
not, by that proud pontiff who calls us *sectaries of the Bible,*[1]
and who with "*that audacious mouth which spake very great things,*"
as says Daniel the prophet, has just uttered a cry from the
depths of the magnificent chambers of his Vatican, and, stretch-
ing forth his arms in terror in the midst of his Apollos, his
Venuses, and all those trophies of Paganism with which he is
surrounded, has rung throughout all Christendom that watchword of alarm and dread—THE BIBLE! THE BIBLE! What
then? has He who reveals all secrets "made known to him,
in the silent watches of the night, what shall come to pass
hereafter"? Has he shown him the Bible at the gates of
Italy? Has he shown him already suspended in the air, over-
hanging Rome, "the stone that was cut out of the mountain
without hands," that is to break in pieces the ancient statue,
and lay it low in the dust, amid the ruin and devastation of
twenty centuries? Ah! if there is a time when the Reform
should remain faithful to its principles, it is the day in which
we now live. To conquer by the Bible, or to perish, is the
only alternative before us.

One thing among others which alarms us concerning the

[1] Circular of the Pope, dated the day after the nones of May, 1844.

state of England is, that recently (about a month since) in London, while the assemblies belonging to particular churches (Episcopal or dissenting) crowded the vast extent of Exeter Hall, for the first time the meeting of the Bible Society had comparatively but few present. It is not our intention to draw too serious consequences from this; we know it may have arisen from various causes, but we confess that the knowledge of this fact caused us to shudder, and with sadness we recalled to mind these words, " *Ichabod! Ichabod!*" Hath thy glory indeed departed?

II. But if the Reformed church places the word of God so decidedly above any word of man, and gives it pre-eminence even above faith, on the other hand it places faith above the church. One of the oldest doctors, (Irenæus of Lyons) has called attention to this great antithesis: *Where the Spirit is, there is the Church;* this is the principle of the Reform; and *Where the Church is, there is the Spirit*, is the principle of Rome and Oxford; and it is also, though in a milder form, that of Lutheranism. A distinguished theologian, Dr. Lange, who occupies in the university of one of our confederate cities the professorship which was intended for Strauss, has recently brought to mind that antithesis, wording it thus: *The Church comes of faith, or faith comes of the Church.* We do not hesitate to say that both these propositions are true in a certain sense, and provided the visible Church be not confounded with the invisible; for there is a marvellous alternative between faith and the Church. But observe: while Lutheranism places emphasis on the latter, and declares that, since the foundation of the Church, God converts men only by means of the Church, the Reform on the contrary lays stress on the former, and asserts that faith, that faith which God implants in the heart, alone begets the Church. Hence the Reform does not say, The Church (which is the *assembly* of the faithful) exists first, and then follows each individual believer; but it says, First each believer exists, and then comes the *Church*, which is the union of all. Lutheranism says, First the species, then the individual; the Reform says, First the individual, then the species. We are ready to allow that both are right, but we add, that it should be our especial care to uphold the principle of the Reform.

And why so ? Because if we assert in an absolute sense that *faith comes of the Church*, we establish at once the principle that leads to the Inquisition, and which gave rise to it in times past. Now at the period of the Reformation, when for centuries all those who did not humbly receive their faith from the visible Church had been stretched on the rack, it was necessary that the renewed Church should loudly proclaim opposite principles. The Reform is then in direct opposition here to Rome, and also to ultra-Lutheranism. By this name we call that extreme Lutheran orthodoxy which, in the days of Calow and Quenstedt, revived the scholastic system, and placed above all other doctrines that of the Church and the means of salvation.

The Reform, on the contrary, remembering that Christ saves his people soul by soul, gives, has given, and always will give the first place in Christian theology to what concerns the individual work, the regeneration, the justification, and the conversion of the believer.

Thus, what distinguishes Lutheranism is the importance attached to the Church, to the Church collectively, and particularly to its ministers. In truth it is not very far from that *sacerdotalism* which is the essence of Rome and of Oxford. The Lutherans do not hesitate to give their pastors the name of priests; and in a celebrated book on *Practical Theology*, written by a German whose memory is very dear to us, Claude Harms, prevost of Kiel, one of the sections is entitled the *Preacher*, another the *Pastor*, and a third the PRIEST.

This too was essential to our unity. The individual element of the Reform might have brought on dissolution and dispersion of the members of the Church, which would have proved fatal to the whole body, had it not been restrained by the ecclesiastical element of Lutheranism; as also the tendency of the latter would have been to languor and certain death, had it not been restrained by the spontaneous and vivifying influence of the Reform. It is the combination of these two forces, the one centripetal the other centrifugal, which has launched into the universe a new world, and which sustains it.

Shall we abandon then the principle of our strength, as we are called upon to do ? God preserve us from this invasion on the eternal decrees of his all-wise providence! Let us not

look on one side only; let us examine both, and contemplate
the magnificent *ensemble* of the work of the Lord. If a man is
a Lutheran, he is right, quite right; if a man embraces the
Lutheran faith, he is right still; but if he is Reformed, if he
converses with the Reformed, he should neither act nor speak
as though he were Lutheran, or as though he were addressing
Lutherans, to counteract, impede, and destroy the Reformed
principle in the bosom of the Reform itself.

We shall not enumerate here the numberless evils to which
too strict an application of the Lutheran principles has led.
From this arose *clerocracy*,[1] or the excessive authority of the
pastor, or more properly speaking, confessor (for among the
Lutherans each individual has a pastor to whom he gives that
name), so that, in the last century, these confessors having become infidels, and the unsuspecting Lutherans continuing to
submit to them, infidelity spread throughout their churches
with inconceivable facility. It has even been asserted, in Lutheranism, that each individual should cling to his spiritual
guide, appointed by the competent ecclesiastical authority, even
though that guide were a stranger or entirely opposed to the
true faith! The Reformed Christians will never acknowledge
this as their maxim. They will ever rank the Bible above the
pastor, and, if there is a decided disagreement between them,
rather than allow themselves and their children to be led by
them into infidelity, they will forsake their pastor, and take
refuge beneath the word of Christ. In so doing they carry
the Church with them, leaving to themselves both the sect and
the pastor.

It is from this *Ecclesiasticism* that originates the different importance which the Lutherans and the Reformed attach to the
confessions of faith of the churches. The Lutherans look upon
them as rules of faith—*normæ normatæ;* and they have even
gone so far as to assert that their authors had a kind of inspiration, such inspiration as the Roman Catholics call *deutero-
canonical*, when speaking of the Apocryphal books. In the
Reform, symbolical writings are, on the contrary, but the ex-

---

[1] This word, as well as another here used (*ecclesiasticism*), though coined
by the author, is none the less significant and appropriate for its novelty.—
Trans.

pression of the faith of the Church. "Our churches do not say to those who desire to occupy our pulpits, *Believe!* but they ask them, *Do you believe?*" Thus spoke, in the true spirit of the Reform, two men who are dear to us, Cellérier and Gaussen, when, twenty-five years ago, they republished the Helvetic *Confession of Faith* in Geneva. Although this privilege belongs, by right, to another here present, allow me to pay a passing tribute to the memory of this faithful servant of Jesus Christ,[1] who was taken from us a few weeks since, in a good old age, and whose glory it was to have been the first, after a century of infidelity, to raise again in our country the standard of the Gospel and the Reform.

Again I repeat: *The Church comes of faith, rather than faith of the Church.*

This is our watchword. And who will dare assert that the time is come when we should lower our colours, and meekly march under those which others offer us, and which Papacy itself has shown for so many centuries past? If any of our brethren deem it their duty so to do, we openly declare we will not; convinced that, in this day, to uphold and vindicate the principles of the Reform is to save the Reformation.

But, it may be said, if the maxim that faith comes of the Church leads to the *Inquisition*, the maxim that the Church comes of faith leads to *separation*.

We do not deny that this is the excess of the principle, nor that this excess is to be seen in our day. But we deny that the abuse of a principle can ever subvert it. No; the principle of the Reform is not essentially a principle of separation; nor does it necessarily flow from that principle, that Christendom should be divided into a thousand sects. Undoubtedly, it is a right and a duty of a Christian, as was done in the days of the Reformation, and has been repeatedly done since, to separate from a community which no longer confesses Jesus Christ, "God manifest in the flesh," the only righteousness of his people. But to make separation a constantly-recurring duty, is, according to the Reform, to trample under foot numerous passages of the word of God; it is to invite what the Apostle

---

[1] The author alludes to the recent death of the venerable Cellérier, an illustrious servant of God in Geneva.— *Trans.*

Paul declares should be rejected, " strifes, seditions, and heresies."

" I assert," says Calvin, " that we should not, for slight dissimilarity of opinion, separate from a church where the fundamental doctrine of salvation is preserved, and where the sacraments are lawfully administered according to the institution of our Lord."[1]

However, if choice must be made between uniformity and error on the one side, and diversity and truth on the other, the Reform does not hesitate; it always sides with the truth; truth being always its great aim.

III. But the Reform has always distinguished itself by a liberal spirit of Christian charity; and this third characteristic triumphantly answers the charge of separatism; it has ever held out a brotherly hand to all communions that preserve pure the doctrines of salvation. So that, while a sectarian spirit has animated other confessions in various degrees, the Reform has ever worn on her brow the seal of true catholicity.

We shall not here speak of the sectarian spirit of Rome or of Oxford; these are well-known topics; but history obliges us to acknowledge this spirit even in Lutheranism. The Lutherans, like the Romanists, have always aimed; not at fraternally uniting with the Reform, but at absorbing it.

Exclusiveness is a feature of Lutheranism. Here it will be asked, What becomes of your unity? This exclusiveness itself was necessary for it. It is one of the wheels which must form part of the admirable machinery which the hand of the Great Architect prepared three centuries ago. *Exclusiveness* is essential to the Church. Who was more exclusive than he who said, " *No man cometh unto the Father but by me ;*" and again. " *Without me ye can do nothing*"? The Church needs a holy jealousy for the eternal truth of God. Latitudinarianism is fatal to it. The history of all ages has proved this, and none can show it more clearly than that of our own age. It was this *exclusiveness* with which Martin Luther was charged; and although he was mistaken in carrying out his exclusiveness, not only with regard to the fundamental doctrines, but even respecting the different methods of understanding the same truth; although it

[1] Christian Institutes, book iv, chap. i.

was against our Reform that his darts were hurled, yet we love, we admire Luther, even in his errors; and we behold in him, not a *furious Orestes*, as he was called by Bucer and Capito themselves, but a *Prometheus*, who, anxious that man should lift his eyes toward heaven,

.   .   .   .   *erectos ad sidera tollere vultus,*

and having taken fire from on high to inspire him, was cast down in consequence of his very elevation, and his entrails devoured by ruthless vultures. "*Let him that thinketh he standeth take heed lest he fall!*" Luther believed that the real presence of Christ was a truth of God, and he went too far to defend it. May God teach us what Luther did not know, to distinguish truth from falsehood, what is essential from what is secondary! God grant unto us what Luther could not do, to instruct with mildness those who entertain opposite opinions! But God grant at the same time that, like Luther, we may be inflamed with devotion to truth and filled with zeal for the house of God!

Here again, however, we can not justify every thing. History is inflexible, and points out sad excesses to us. This is the most painful part of our task; for Luther is our father (we speak after the manner of men), a father whom we regard with profound veneration, and tender filial affection. The true Lutherans are our friends, our beloved brethren; they are among those whom we hope one day to join in the kingdom of our Lord. If, then, their opposition draws from us a sigh, let it never cause in our hearts the least bitterness of feeling toward them. Be it remembered that the violence of controversy, far from proving us to be declared enemies, is a proof of the closest bonds uniting us to Lutheranism; for at all times, and in all matters, the more united we are on essential points, the more we are carried away by differences on minor ones.

It was Luther, that great man of God, who in this, as in every thing else, advanced at the head of his Church. When, in 1527, the Reformed pleaded for brotherly love and Christian concord, he answered, "Be such charity and unity cursed, even to the bottomless depths of hell." He himself relates to one of his friends that, at the conference convoked at Marburg by the Landgrave of Hesse, to unite the Lutherans and the Reformed, Zwingle, moved to tears, approached him, saying,

" There are no men on earth with whom I so much desired to be united as with the Wittemburgers." And Luther repulsed the Zurich Reformer, answering, "Your spirit is not our spirit!" and refused to acknowledge Zwingle and the Swiss as *his brethren*.

Since that day a sectarian spirit has always pervaded Lutheranism. When, in 1553, the unhappy Reformed were driven from London by the unfeeling order of bloody Mary, they were cruelly repulsed, in the midst of winter, by the advice of the Lutheran theologians, from the walls of Copenhagen, of Rostock, of Lübeck, and of Hamburg, where they asked for shelter. " Better Papists than Calvinists," said they; " better Mahometans than Reformed." And on one house in Wittemburg was written, " the words and the writings of Luther are poison to the Pope and to Calvin." The name of Calvin was given to cats and dogs. Books were published with such titles as these: "Proofs that the Calvinists have six hundred and thirty-six errors in common with the Turks:" " Brief evidence that the present attempt at union (1721) with the self-styled Reformed is in direct opposition to the Ten Commandments, to all the articles of the Apostles' Creed, to all the petitions of the Lord's Prayer, to the doctrine of holy Baptism, the power of the Keys, the holy Communion, as well as the whole Catechism." In a Lutheran Catechism of the beginning of the 16th century this question is asked : " Dost thou believe that, instead of honouring and worshipping the true and living God, the Calvinists honour and worship the Devil? Answer: I do, from the bottom of my heart." A Lutheran doctor, who is still living, and is remarkable for his piety and zeal, applies the following passage from St. Paul to the Reformed: " Be ye not yoked with unbelievers." It is well known that the Lutheran missionary societies have recently dissolved their connection with that of the city of Basle, which, however, comes nearer Lutheranism than any of the Reformed churches.

What shall we say concerning these excesses? We will say, with St. Paul, " They have zeal without knowledge;" and we will add with a smile the well-known words of Jerome of Prague, when he saw a peasant approach with a load of wood to deposit on his stake, SANCTA SIMPLICITAS! and then we will repeat the Lutherans are our brethren, our well beloved brethren!

A spirit of conciliation, of union and fraternity, has pervaded
our Church in all ages, and is, perhaps, its most beautiful ornament.   Zwingle, Œcolampadius, Calvin, and Farel always extended a brotherly hand to Luther and his friends.   Calvin,
even, does not hesitate to assert that, in his sight, Luther is
far superior to Zwingle: "For if these two are compared, you
are aware how much Luther surpasses him."[1]   And he writes
thus to Bullinger on the 25th of November, 1544: "I hear that
Luther is lavishing the most cruel invectives upon you and all
of us.   I scarcely dare ask of you to be silent; but I earnestly
entreat you at least to remember how great a man Luther is;
what admirable qualities distinguish him; what courage, what
faithfulness, what skill, what power of doctrine he possesses
to bring down the reign of Antichrist, and to propagate the
knowledge of salvation.   I say, and have frequently repeated,
that even though he should call me *Satan*, I would not cease to
honour him and acknowledge him to be an illustrious servant
of God."   These are sublime words; let the Reform never forget them!   And observe, they come from Calvin, that man
who is represented to us as so irritable and so proud.

At different times, proposals for peace and projects of union
were offered by the Reform.   The Reformed of French-Swit-
zerland particularly showed on this score the most unshaken
perseverance.   At the period when the ultra-Lutherans, West-
phal, Timann, Von Eitzen, and many others had discharged
their heavy artillery upon the Reform, Calvin and his friends
appeared on the field of battle, with the olive branch in their
hands.   This same year (1557) when Theodore Beza and Farel
travelled throughout all the cities of Switzerland, to excite the
public sympathy in favour of the Waldenses, who had been
cruelly massacred in the valley of Angrogna, they also visited
Germany, where they presented a Confession of Faith of the
churches of Switzerland and Savoy, designing to unite all the
Reformation, by convincing the Lutheran churches that they
also were brethren and fellow-soldiers in the war against Antichrist.   In 1631, the General Synod of Charenton, near Paris,
took the lead, accomplished this union, and passed a resolution

---

[1] Nam si inter se comparantur, scis ipse quanto intervallo Lutherus ex-
cedat.

which declared that "the churches of the Confession of Augsburg agreeing with them in all the articles of true religion, the members of these churches may be allowed to present themselves at the holy table without any previous abjuration." In our days it is from the Reformed that propositions and efforts to re-establish true union in the Church have always proceeded.

And wherefore this difference between Lutheranism and the Reform? Undoubtedly it proceeds in great part, as far as Luther and the Lutherans are concerned, from the importance they attach to the real presence of Christ in the Lord's Supper, from that unshaken attachment to what they believe to be the truth, which we sincerely respect; but we must say that it also results from that difference which we have already designated. The *Biblical* tendency of the Reform must lead all the Reformed to attach slight importance to *Ecclesiastical differences*, and much to *Bible truth;* consequently, to endeavour to extend a brotherly hand to all churches, and all individuals who hold to the *Bible.* It is thus from sound principles that beneficial consequences always flow. Let us remain faithful to this spirit of true catholicity. Let us not forget these memorable words of the apostle, "One God, one Lord, one body, and one spirit." To uphold these is the special mission of the Reform.

IV. But if the Reform possesses great liberality, it is none the less distinguished for a genuine profoundness. It is not merely a reformation of faith, as is Lutheranism, but a reformation of life; and for this reason it is more universally Christian. Undoubtedly Antinomianism is foreign to Lutheranism; Luther himself opposed it. Still there is great difference in the manner in which Lutheranism and the Reform view the law. A singular and characteristic feature points out one of the principal differences. In the Lutheran Catechism, the Ten Commandments are placed before faith, before dogmas. Their use is to convince man of sin, and bring him to Christ. On the contrary, in the Reformed Catechism the law is placed after faith, and after the doctrine of salvation, as an expression of the gratitude of the child of God for his redemption through Christ. The law, according to Luther, is for the unconverted only. According to Calvin, it is also addressed to believers.

Luther did not accomplish a reformation of morals, nor did he even attempt it. This was not undoubtedly because he did not think it of the highest importance. "How," as he wrote to the brethren of Bohemia, who desired him to establish such discipline, "how can we, who live in the midst of Sodom, of Gomorrah, and of Babylon, bring about order, discipline, and exemplary life?" Luther thought that the Reformation of morals should proceed simply and naturally from the influence of sound doctrine.

Let us here observe again how necessary the diversity of Lutheranism and the Reform is for the unity, and even the existence of the Reformation. Who does not discern a profound Christian truth in the doctrine that faith leads to sound morals? Was it not necessary, after centuries in which the discipline of the Church had caused innumerable troubles, and still greater superstitions, that there should be a protestation against these fatal errors? Was it not necessary that besides the strength of the Reform, which has a sectarian tendency, there should be another force in the renewed Church that should tend to enlarge the views of the faithful? Was it not necessary that above all that men can do, above all their efforts to rebuke the disorderly and to watch over the Lord's inheritance, there should be a finger to point to heaven, and that a loud voice should pronounce this oracle: "The good shepherd goeth before his sheep, and his sheep follow him, for they know his voice"? But if one of these was necessary, the other was not less so. The work of Christian vigilance and pastoral guardianship was intrusted to the Reform; and we are reformed.

Zwingle started from this principle: "A universal renovation of life and morals is as requisite as a renovation of faith." Immediately after the Reformation in Zurich, Berne, and Basle, ordinances for the promotion of good morals were published, prostitution was abolished, pensions and enlistments in foreign service were suppressed; and when afterward the pope, according to his ancient custom, required troops from Zurich, the citizens offered him instead two thousand monks and priests whom they could spare! Would to God that in our day we sent not Swiss soldiers to Rome. The morals of ministers were particularly insisted on: "As the word of Truth is solemn, the life of its servant ought also to be grave," said the ordinance of 1532.

But it was especially in Geneva that this principle was fully carried out. Calvin with the zeal of a prophet, and the resignation of a martyr who submits himself unreservedly to the severe word of God, exacted of the Church under his care *absolute obedience*. He struggled hard with the party of the Libertines, and by the grace of God he overcame. Geneva, which was so corrupt before, was regenerated, and evinced a purity of morals and a Christian simplicity so remarkable, that it drew from Farel (after an absence of fifteen years) an expression of admiration in these memorable words: "I had rather be the last in Geneva than the first elsewhere."

And fifty years after the death of Calvin, a fervent Lutheran, John Valentine Andreæ, having passed some time within our walls, said on his return, "What I have seen there I shall never forget. The most beautiful ornament of that republic is its tribunal of morals, which every week enquires into the disorders of the citizens. Games of cards and chance, swearing and blasphemy, impurity, quarreling, hatred, deceitfulness, infidelity, drunkenness, and other vices, are repressed. Oh! how beautiful an ornament to Christianity is this purity. We Lutherans can not too deeply deplore its absence among us. If the difference of doctrine did not separate me from Geneva, the harmony of its morals could have induced me to remain there for ever."

This moral character was not confined to Switzerland and Geneva alone; it spread through France, Holland, Scotland, and wherever the Reform made its way. It has in a measure remained in some of those countries to the present day. A German author, Mr. Goëbel, having related that a traveller, also a German, was unable to find in the churches of Scotland which he visited a single instance of adultery and divorce, and very little impurity, exclaims, "Let the frightful immorality of Germany be contrasted with this; in the country as well as in the city let only the pastors be interrogated, and one will be filled with astonishment and terror." Alas! we can not pride ourselves on such a state of things at present. These morals are no more. We do not pretend to say that there was nothing in this discipline adapted to hasten its fall; on the contrary, we think that the part the State took in these matters must inevitably have destroyed it. We reject all Christian discipline exercised by constables and soldiers; but we think we can lay aside all public force, retaining the power of vigilance, of charity, and of the word of God.

This was not done, and what is the result? Senebier said, " The prosperity of Geneva was long the fruit of Calvin's wise laws. In the purity of our ancient morals consisted our glory. We can prove that one of the causes of our misfortunes is the diminution of their influence. Thus Rome was lost when its censors could not make themselves heard any more, and Sparta fell with the credit of those whose charge was to cause virtue to be respected." If Senebier spoke thus in 1786, what shall we now say?

Ah! who could fail to understand what Montesquieu said, that the Genevese ought to bless and celebrate the day of Calvin's birth, and that of his arrival in their midst? But what the most profound politician of the eighteenth century clearly saw the Genevese have not comprehended. Instead of celebrating the birth-day of the Reformer, they and their children celebrate that of a noted sophist, a man of an ardent soul, of unsurpassed talent, but who sent to the hospital the sad results of his libertinism! They have erected a magnificent statue to the memory of Rousseau, and they have erected none to Calvin! "We will do it at Edinburgh," said a Scotch divine to me last year. "Edinburgh," added he, "is now the metropolis of the Reform."

The revival of faith and sound morals among the Reformed is the statue which Calvin, that great but unassuming man, would have desired. Shall we not erect it? And if now, as in Saxony in the days of Luther, a too rigid law is inapplicable, shall we not at least remember that whoever asks for a reformation of morals possesses the spirit of the Reform, and that it is the most sacred duty, not only of ministers but of all reformed Christians, to cause all those who invoke the name of the Saviour to be " *blameless and harmless, the sons of God without rebuke in the midst of a perverse nation.*"

V. This leads us to a fifth consideration. The Reform has,

both in its principles and its progress, something more decided than Lutheranism. The principle of Lutheranism was *to preserve in the Church all that was not condemned by the word of God;* while that of the Reform was *to abolish in the Church all that is not prescribed by the word of God.* Lutheranism is a reformation of the Church; the Reform its renovation; or to express this distinction by the different pronunciations of the same word, Lutheranism is a *reformation*, the Reform a *re-formation*. Lutheranism took the Church, such as it was, contenting itself with effacing its stains. The Reform took the Church at its origin, and erected its edifice on the living Rock of the apostles. While Luther, hearing what Carlstadt was doing, writes, "We must remain in the middle path," and opposes those who cast down the images, Carlstadt, the first Reformed, from the year 1521 boldy reforms the church of Wittemberg, of which he was the prevost, abolishing the mass, images, and confessions, the fast days, and all the abuses of papacy. Zwingle, almost at the same time, proceeds in the same manner at Zurich; and as to what took place at Geneva, we shall merely transcribe here an inscription which, for nearly three centuries, remained on the walls of our City Hall, from 1536 to 1798, and which expresses better than we could do the uncompromising character of the Reform. At the time of the jubilee of 1835, it was to have been placed in the Church of St. Peter, but it has not yet been done.

" In the year 1535, the tyranny of Roman Antichrist having been overthrown and its superstitions abolished, the most holy religion of Jesus Christ was established here in its purity, and the Church better organized, by an extraordinary blessing of God. And at the same time, this city itself having repulsed its enemies and put them to flight, was again set free, but not without a remarkable miracle. The Council and the people of Geneva have here erected this monument to perpetuate its memory, so that the testimony of their gratitude toward God should descend to their posterity."

What has resulted from this difference between Lutheranism and the Reform ?

Two very distinct courses, each of which has its favourite aspect. The course of Lutheranism is defensive, successive;

that of the Reform is offensive, acquisitive. To Lutheranism belongs the principle of resistance and *passivity;* to the Reform that of activity and life.

Is it necessary to recall to your mind that these two tendencies are important to the prosperity of the Church ? Must we insist that in a well-organized community immobility of principle should be joined to mobility of life ?

There is not even a family where two opposite tendencies are not to be found. To counterbalance the decisive and imposing authority of the father, the conciliating and indulgent tenderness of the mother is requisite. Thus in a political State the conservative and the liberal elements should be constantly combined. An exclusive immobility leads to violence, hatred, and revolution. Had we not an example of this during the reign of Charles X ? An excess of mobility leads to levity, superficiality, agitation, and pride. Do not nations furnish us with a demonstration of this ? These two elements are so indispensably necessary to the life of the whole body, that if, by some means, you could annihilate one of the two, it would soon reappear. In France, in 1830, the ancient *conservators* being excluded, those who, for fifteen years, had played the part of *liberals* became themselves conservators.

And what is necessary in the State, and even in each family, would you exclude from the Church? Would you by some revolution drive away some of these two elements? Impotent conspirators ! Could you succeed in destroying the element of the Reform, you would be compelled to become Reformed yourselves.

But undoubtedly Lutheranism had much to suffer in the 16th century for having carried its principles too far. Halting between the Bible and the Church, between that which it should retain and that which it should reject, its progress was in consequence somewhat impeded, its Reformation could not attain the height to which it had before aspired, and Luther, naturally of a gay character and joyful temperament, ended his days in sadness and weariness. While the Reform, possessing a visible and unclouded aim in the Bible, and nothing but the Bible, advanced with power; Calvin, Farel, Knox, and even

Zwingle, died joyfully and triumphantly. What a death was Calvin's; how touching his dying words!

Lutheranism, paralyzed from the beginning, witnessed, after the death of Luther, its *conservativeness* turned into *stagnation*.

The Lutheran princes, unfaithful to the glorious memory of the Diet of Spire (1529), opposed every extension of Protestantism, and were but too well seconded by their theologians.

Even now a new society, which we hail with affection and respect, the Society of *Gustavus Adolphus*, faithful to this Lutheran principle, endeavours, it is true, to support the Protestant churches which are tottering, yet declares itself opposed to any activity beyond the sphere of acknowledged Protestantism, as well as to all proselytism.

It is not thus with the Reform. It advances, it gains every where. Our evangelical Societies of Paris and Geneva, with their essentially proselyting characteristics, all our missionary societies, are the fruits of the Reformed spirit.

But it is principally in the relation between these two churches and the Papacy that we see the characteristic which distinguishes them. Lutheranism, which took the *offensive* with regard to the Reform, rested on the *defensive* with regard to the pope; while the Reform, holding out the right hand of fellowship to Lutheranism, boldly and courageously took the *offensive* toward Rome. Melancthon, at Augsburg, in 1530, said to the cardinals, that but a trifle separated him from the pope; but an immense abyss separated him from Zwingle.[1] Lutheranism, to which the visible church is of so much moment, could capitulate with Rome. The Reform, which will have nothing but the Bible, must fight Rome boldly. Wherever are found superstitious fears of a struggle with Papacy; wherever extreme circumspection is observed; wherever it is supposed, for instance, that prudence should keep Protestants from offering a fraternal hand to priests who reject the Pope, and confess Jesus Christ, there you will perhaps find ultra-Lutheranism; but there most assuredly the spirit of the Reform is not.

Inspired with a holy love for souls, and a deep conviction

---

[1] Dogma nullum habemus diversum ab ecclesia Romana. Parati sumus obedire ecclesiæ Romanæ. (*Legato Pontificio Melancthon.*) Ambeunt (reformati) colloquium cum Philippo; sed hic hactenus recusavit.—*Brentius.*

that Rome leads them to perdition, the Reform seized the sword of the word three centuries ago, and commenced with the papal power a war, the issue of which is life or death. Notwithstanding the constant and violent opposition of the most powerful monarchs of Europe, notwithstanding the redoubled efforts of that hierarchy which fettered the whole world, the Reform, has advanced, like little David against that gigantic Goliath, having nothing in its sling but a few round pebbles of God's word; and it conquered in the name of the Lord of hosts.

We certainly acknowledge all that Christian princes have done, especially the immortal Gustavus Adolphus. But that was the work of a prince, and perhaps was done with political views. With us it is the business of the faithful, and the work of faith. It is the Reform which saved the Reformation in troublous times, and the Reform will save it yet in our days.

It is true that it saved it at the price of its blood. While the Lutheran church numbers scarcely any martyrs, ours are counted by thousands; and their faithfulness filled the best Lutherans with respect and admiration, such Lutherans as the sympathizing Spener and Zinzendorf. In Switzerland, Scotland, and England, and especially in Belgium and France, the Inquisition, the daggers and the scaffolds of Popery, have covered with corpses the soil of the Bible. The Reform witnessed it, but it bowed not its head. It saw its children joyfully shed their blood, trusting in Jesus Christ, and it continued its onward march.

A circular, written in the name of a priest, who calls himself Count of Lausanne, and Prince of the Holy Roman Empire (although since the beginning of this century there has existed no Holy Empire), has dared to say recently in that city, "Always, and every where, since the time of the apostles, the Church (of Rome), its pontiffs and its priests, have been persecuted. The holy pontiffs and priests of Jesus Christ, labouring from the origin of Christianity for the conversion and sanctification of souls, have never employed other means than those which the Gospel, conscience, and reason approve."[1]

This is really too much and a sigh escapes us. What! you dare hold such language in this city, in the midst of a people

---

[1] Circular of the Bishop of Lausanne and Geneva, of May 17th, 1844.

formed, so to speak, from the fragments that escaped from your wheels, your racks, and your knives! We are accustomed to the effrontery of Rome, but we never had such a sample of it.

Men of no memory! To whom belongs the bloody application of these words, *Constrain them to enter?* By whose commands were shed those torrents of blood of the Waldenses and the Albigenses which inundated the Middle Ages? Who, if not your pope, on the night of August 24th, 1572, amid nuptial festivals, caused the venerable Coligny, on his knees, and 60,000 Reformed, to be cruelly butchered? Who ordered all the bells in Rome to be rung in merry peals, and the cannon of the castle of St. Angelo to resound, and medals to be struck? Who, in 1685, razed to the ground more than 1600 churches in France, slaughtered thousands and thousands of Protestants, and forced others to flee? In our days, who forbids, in nearly all Romish countries, the preaching of the Gospel? Who compels the poor inhabitants of Zillerthal to leave their father-land? Who makes laws in Austria against conversion to Protestantism? Who condemned to prison that *Maurette* who struggled here last winter with the priests, charged with having merely read *your circular* from the pulpit? Who, two months since, in a village near our frontier, within three miles of this place, caused a poor peasant to be arrested, thrown into a dungeon, and condemned to the galleys, for having committed no other crime than that of reading his Bible? Who, not in the 14th or 15th century, but only a few weeks since, condemned to death Maria Joaquina for having refused to worship the Virgin, and to believe the doctrine of transubstantiation? And you speak of Rome as a *persecuted* church! And you assert that it has never employed other means than the voice of conscience and of persuasion! . . . Men of no memory! . . . Come, come! when you persecute, you are consistent with yourselves. Persecution ought to be, and is, in fact, a dogma of yours. No one will envy you that opprobrium, no one will rob you of that glory. . . . *Your church* is a church of murderers; ours is a church of martyrs.

VI. We shall select but one more characteristic among all those which yet remain. It is a consequence of that characteristic on which we have just remarked. It is the difference which exists between these two communions, both as to liberty of the Church, and liberty of the State.

Whatever his enemies may say to the contrary, Luther was a humble and submissive monk; and however great may have been the power which he acquired by his language, he ever remained within the bounds of the most perfect obedience to his emperor and his prince. And even in 1530, Luther, who in 1522 had written a book entitled, 'Against the State, falsely called *spiritual*, of the Pope and the Bishops,' appeared, as did Melancthon also, entirely ready to acknowledge all bishops, provided these bishops would acknowledge the authority of the Gospel. Luther's reformation was essentially monarchical in its relation to the State, and hierarchical in its relations to the Church. The people are never brought forward in it otherwise than as modestly receiving that which is given them by the higher authorities. It is true that Luther at last made quite a proper distinction between the two swords of the Church and the State; but after him, and even in his day, the Lutheran princes, invested with the territorial episcopacy, absorbed all liberties, and all ecclesiastical independence.

It is necessary to observe that Lutheranism possesses peculiar excellence in this respect? The vehicle which bore the human mind was, in the 16th century, at the top of a steep declivity. The Reform boldly seated itself on the coachman's box; with one hand it seized the reins, and with the other it used the whip; and away went the coach. What was necessary to prevent a terrible catastrophe at the foot of the mountain? To use a vulgar comparison, the *wheel-lock* must be used; that lock was Lutheranism. By this means the progress is rapid though safe; and if it be true that the dreaded danger has been realized, it is because both Lutheranism and the Reform have lost their essential characteristics, and their intrinsic excellence during the past century; it is that the *wheel-lock* has been taken off, and the driver thrown to the ground.

In this, therefore, consists a new difference between the Reform and Lutheranism; and it was not unaptly that Bossuet said, in the presence of the court of Louis XIV, *The Calvinists are bolder than the Lutherans.*

The Reform, in its very origin, was essentially democratic. Switzerland, where the Reform is developed, is an assembly of small nations in which the people are the sovereign. There the reformation comes from the people; and when the councils are opposed to it (as, for instance, at Basle), the people make it prevail. The political rights and liberties, which were trodden under foot by Papacy, and which Lutheranism gave up without reluctance, are zealously claimed by the Reform. They advance with it, and are established wherever it goes. The reformation of the Free Cities of Germany, now Lutheran,[1] was the most striking act of their unfettered will; but in making this supreme effort they lost their energy and their freedom, and from that time they fell under the influence of their formidable neighbours.

But the Reform, on the contrary, wherever it goes, makes sacred the ancient liberties and bears new ones with it. Why is it that the fate of Geneva, a free imperial city, is at present very different from that of Augsburg, Nuremberg, and many other towns, which were once as free and independent as it is? History will answer. In 1559, when Geneva, was in dread of a siege, Calvin himself helped on the work of raising another rampart. To the same spirit which animated Calvin, Geneva owed her capability of maintaining her independence against formidable enemies for three centuries. Every where is this distinction between Lutheranism and the Reform apparent. In our own days, for instance, when, on the fall of Charles X in 1830, the Christians of France and some other countries rejoiced, and the Christians of Germany were astounded and scandalized, perhaps the simple reason of this was that the former were Reformed and the latter Lutherans.

This has long furnished the Roman Catholics with a favourite subject for reproachful language toward the Reform. Well, be it so. Only let us remember the continual commotions of Popish countries, of Italy, Spain, Portugal, Poland, Belgium, Ireland, France, and (but three days since) the battle of Trient (Valais). Let us remember the anxiety, the uneasiness, and the sad groans of the Lutheran states of Germany. Let us

[1] Save Bremen; there the Reformed church and doctrine prevail.—
Trans.

remember the mighty and fruitful liberties which are peaceably enjoyed by the Reformed countries at this time; by Scotland, Holland, England, America, and by some Swiss cantons. And if, in America, the quiet city of William Penn, once the city of brotherly love, is now defiled by bloody riots, whence is it? We do not say that the Protestants have been in no wise wrong. On the contrary, we grant that in this case probably *the salt has lost its savour*. But it is perfectly evident that the disaster which has occurred in Philadelphia is an act by which Popery and Ireland signalize their invasion there.

As it regards political freedom, Popery is in a state of revolution, Lutheranism in a state of fermentation, and the Reform in a state of possession.

Let no one say, There are democratic sympathies in the Reform; it is therefore not suitable for monarchies. This would be a singular anachronism; it would be reasoning in the style of the age of Louis XIV. Do not the greatest minds of the day acknowledge that democracy, under one form or another, is a future state toward which all nations tend! Now, if the Reform, as M. De Tocqueville himself asserts, possesses the light and the strength necessary to lead and moderate democracy, is it not essential to the future interests of all states? To reject it now would be to send off the seaman, to chase away the pilot, to throw overboard the compass, and to break the rudder, at the very moment when the ship is about to sail and go forth into the open sea. "Let us reform the morals of democracy by religion," says De Tocqueville. The Reform is the golden bit, powerful, yet easy, which a Divine hand has prepared for the mouth of liberty. True *pacific democracy* is the Reform. You will find it nowhere else.

But, if the Reformed church gives freedom to the State, it is because it possesses freedom itself. In the Reform, the government of the Church does not proceed from certain individuals whose functions place them above all the rest, but from the Church as a body, from the vote of each believer, so that, if any are raised above the rest, it is only as instruments or delegates of the Church. All necessary precautions are taken to hinder domination from entering it. "Let the moderator have the presidency" (say the ordinances of Schaffhausen), "but nothing more, lest a *monarchy* should take the place of *democracy*."

The Reform does not establish a church of the clergy; it establishes, observe, a church of the people; not of a worldly people, but of the people of God; that is to say, a church essentially, though not exclusively, composed of those devout and holy men whose thoughts have been led captive to the obedience of Christ.

Finally, as to the independence of the Church—we do not say entire separation from the State, for we shall not enter upon that subject in this discourse—as to the independence of the Church, that is not less essential in the Reform. Zwingle, to be sure, who never met with any opposition from the State, and who, on the contrary, received all kind of help from it, regarded the Church as a society embraced in the State, protected, cared for, and even, in some measure, governed by the State. But had Zwingle been living in a day when the State attacks Christian truth, for the benefit of Popery or Socinianism, do you suppose that he would have given up the Church to its rule? No! he would have separated from it.

Even before Calvin asserted this, the Synod of Berne, in 1532, declared that the State ought not to interfere with religious matters except in respect to external order. "But as to the work of grace, it is not in the power of man, and is dependent on no magistrate. The State should not meddle with the conscience; Jesus Christ our Lord is our only master. If the magistrate meddle with the Gospel, he will only make hypocrites."

But it was especially Calvin, the head of the Reform, who reclaimed the autonomy, autocracy, and independence of the Church. He was not, like Zwingle, a citizen by birth of a republic, but a subject of a monarchy, and as such he felt less than the former, that he was an integral part of the State. The organization of a monarchy, moreover, gave place, much less than that of a republic, to that confusion of Church and State which Zwingle realized.

Luther was a German, Swingle was a Swiss; but nationality found but a secondary place in the great mind of Calvin; Christ and the Church were every thing to him. He was

neither French, nor Swiss, nor Genevese; he was of the City of
God. On leaving France he sacrificed all that was most precious to him; he did not build up new idols to replace his old
ones. Doubtless he loved Geneva; it was his adopted country;
but the remembrance of his great nationality was above that
of all lesser ones. Nothing was so insupportable to him as
national egotism. Turning away from those narrow places
in which others chose to remain, his eagle eye was continually
fixed on the Church as a whole. His colleagues in the cantons
endeavoured to form a Swiss national church; but this scheme
seemed too paltry for his lofty genius; and, passing over rivers
and mountains, he constantly aspired to the Universal church
He knew none other than the holy nation, none other than the
ransomed people.

His very principle, which bound him to biblical and apostolical antiquity, led him back to the church of the first three
centuries, and made him view the independence of the Church
as its normal state. And how could Calvin, at the sight of
the State united in France to the Romish hierarchy, and roaring like a wild beast at the humble followers of the man of
Galilee, resist the desire of sheltering the Church from its attacks? Nor was it merely the oppression of Francis I or of
Henry II which he rejected, but the protection of Reformed
magistrates also gave him much uneasiness. He viewed the
relation which existed between the Church and the State in
Zurich and Berne as something servile, which hindered the
free movements of the Church, and was encroaching on its
holy liberty. "I do not believe that we are so slavishly fettered," he writes, in 1557, to Bullinger,[1] who insisted on the
authority of the magistrate.

Calvin, therefore, entirely rejected the idea of having the
State govern the Church, even though the State might have
become evangelical. He wanted it to form a community *sui
generis*, of which each member would have a certain share in
the government. He made of each church a small democracy,
and of the union of these churches a Confederation.

Nowhere, perhaps, was the spirit of Calvin so strongly
manifested, with regard to the independence of the Church as

---

[1] Non puto tam serviliter nos constrictos teneri.

in the canton Vaud. The Church in that fine country stood between Geneva and Berne, as between two conflicting forces. The spirit of independence and liberty seemed wafted to it from the walls of Geneva by the mighty breath of Calvin ; while the military republic of Berne, desirous of preserving that power of the State, which for several centuries contributed to its greatness, endeavoured, with a strong arm, to draw tighter the bonds and forms by which the State was attempting to restrain the Church. Berne could not permit any part whatsoever of the public power to be withdrawn from the mighty hands of the State, not even in religious matters. And thus, when the Vaudois[1] church claimed the free exercise of ecclesiastical discipline, the State feared lest, if this power were granted, its independence might thereby be acknowledged in some degree. It was willing to allow discipline, but it wanted to exercise it by means of its own officers.[2]

Nevertheless, Viret, Theodore Beza, and a number of other ministers, maintained the principles of independence in the canton Vaud. The ties uniting it to Berne were daily slackening, and all turned their eyes to Geneva. These two great systems, placed in opposition to each other, rendered a crisis unavoidable. "A rupture was inevitable," says the learned Hundeshagan (who is now a professor at Berne), in his history of the struggles of that church. Thus, in the 16th century, two hundred and fifty years previous to its emancipation, the independence of the Church was probably on the point of giving political independence to the Vaudois people. But the bear[3] was the stronger. It rushed down roaring from its mountain heights; and Viret, and Beza, and Marlorat, and Merlin, with about forty of their brethren, all friends of the freedom of the Church, had to flee from the country where they had preached the Gospel of Christ with so much joy, and went to enrich Geneva and the Reformed churches of France with their piety and their learning. The Free Church of Scotland

---

[1] *Vaud* is a Swiss canton ; the term *Vaudois* must not be confounded here with the French name of the *Waldenses*, which is spelt in the same way.—*Trans.*

[2] Ordonnance de réformation des seigneurs de Berne. Voir Ruchat, 1837, tome iv, p. 522.—*Pieces Justificatives.*

[3] The bear is the emblem of the Bernese Republic.

was allowed to remain in the very scene of the struggle; but
the *Free Church* of Vaud, having its strongest limbs broken,
and its hands chained together by a powerful Republic, was
obliged to leave its smiling villages, its valleys, and its mountains . . . . . and the *fettered church* alone remained. The
whole classis of pastors was imprisoned for two days in the
castle of Lausanne; and not one was allowed to leave that prison until he had promised to appear at the first summons. At
the same time the State withdrew from the Church the power
of convoking other classes or colloquies [1] in future. Thus Vaud
was the scene of the complete triumph of the State over the
Church. *" Order reigned in Warsaw."* That *order*, which followed one of the most memorable struggles of Christianity, has
endured for three centuries, and the influence of the Bernese
principles has so pervaded that beautiful country, in the course
of time, that if the eloquent voices of Viret and Beza are heard
here and there amid the ruins, claiming the rights of the
church of Jesus Christ, those sounds which have lasted for
three centuries are, strangely enough, taken for modern words
and theories of the day.

Without doubt, there were relations between Church and
State in Calvin's system; but they were so little essential that,
two years since, at the time of our revolution, it was enough
that a few voices recalled these principles of the Reform, to
place these relations in imminent danger of being broken. Let
us then mark this, that, although there is now a recrudescence
of nationality in some minds, though there are some honourable Christians who preach a blind submission, and who are
opposed to allowing citizens and believers to request respect-
fully in petitions that the liberty which has been promised them
by oath, and has been secured to them by the Constitution itself of their country, should be given them; still, let us mark
this, that such a mode of acting is an invasion of Lutheranism, of a false Lutheranism, as well as a great deviation from
the principles of the Reform.

Freedom in matters of the Church and in those of the State
is our antiquity; this is our custom; this is our tradition;

---

[1] The *Classis* is equivalent to our *Presbytery*; the *Colloquy* to our *Conference.— Trans.*

and we are its preservers. It would be a revolutionary deed to take from the Reform that noble love of freedom.

It is come to close.

"The Catholic church," says Lange, "is the church of priests; the Lutheran church is that of Theologians; the Reformed church is that of the faithful." We accept this definition, observing, nevertheless, that Lange's idea is, that the very catholicism of the Reformed church makes it attribute, both to doctors and pastors, the place belonging to them.

Were it necessary to give a motto to the Reform, what ought to be inscribed on its banner? I would choose this:

Above,   GRACE.

Below,   CATHOLICISM AND LIBERTY.

GRACE, for its doctrine. *Grace* in its fulness and its eternity, from the first movement of the regenerated heart to the entire accomplishment of its salvation.

CATHOLICISM and LIBERTY for the Church.

Catholicism. Assuredly the Reformed church possesses it, for it has never ceased to make the great Christian union one of its most fervent desires, one of its dearest objects. It possesses it in a far higher degree than the self-styled Catholic church, which has ever unhesitatingly cut off from its communion every man who has had any degree of truth and life. It did so to Jansenius, and almost to Fenelon.

But if *Grace* is the sun of the Reform, and if *Catholicism* is one of its poles, *Liberty* is the other pole. Catholicism for that church as a body, and liberty for its individual members. Individuality and catholicism are both equally essential to it; and to rise against either of them is to cease to be Reformed.

Thus, in the day when the Lord will bring his army together in holy solemnity, in the day when the body of Christ will unite its scattered members, the Reformed church will advance, bringing, as a gift to the new church, these three things, which will abide: *Grace, Catholicism, Liberty.* What other church can bring so sublime an offering?

We say then, in conclusion, let us be intelligent, faithful, and unchangeable sons of the Reform; let us be such, not only here, in Geneva, but in Lausanne, in Neuchâtel, in all Switzerland, in France, in Holland, in Scotland, in England, in

Germany, in America. The fate of the Church depends on this.

Shall we forget our fathers, their principles, their struggles, their faithfulness, their blood? While they took such care to preserve the Reform pure, not only in relation to Popery, but also in all its secondary aspects, shall *we* lightly forsake the precious principles of their faith? Shall we walk over their tombs, treading under foot their bones, and scattering their ashes to the winds?

Doubtless, Lutheranism has its work as well as we. Doubtless, Lutheranism and the Reform ought to walk hand in hand beneath the banner of Christ, to the conquest of the world; and that we should do our ally the service which he has a right to expect of us, *we must be ourselves.* And are we that?

Ah! He who wrote those revival letters to the seven churches of Asia speaks to us also. Seeing how many there are whose "hands fall down, and whose knees are feeble," He exclaims to the Reform, "Hold that fast which thou hast, that no man take thy crown. That good thing which was committed to thee keep by the Holy Ghost which dwelleth in thee."

The Reform is the church of the present day; the *Confession of the present*, as a German writer calls it.[1] Its special work. assigned to it by the Lord, is the bringing together of the nations. Let it then advance with freedom and courage in the world, and let it there accomplish the sacred functions which it has received from the Most High; and, as the sixteenth century was the century of a great separation, may the nineteenth become, through the prayers and labours of the Reform, the century of a great union.

"I will make thee a pillar in the temple of my God."

[1] "Die Confession der Gegenwart."—*Lange.*

ESSAY II.

THE VOICE OF THE ANCIENTS TO THE MEN OF THE NINETEENTH CENTURY; OR, READ THE BOOK.

"But the word of the Lord endureth for ever."—1 Peter, i, 25.

PROLOGUE

BETWEEN THREE YOUNG MEN OF THE NINETEENTH CENTURY.

First Young Man.

SOCIETY is dissolving. What bond is there that can hold it closely together? What sentiment shall pervade it? It is true that there is one: it is egotism. And, as a sequel to egotism, despair often follows. And then often, in the train of despair, comes suicide. What can cure this disease that rages among us?

Myself. Faith.

First Young Man. Ay, faith; that is, doubtless, a noble sentiment; but what kind of faith? Do you mean that which the sergeant had who blew his brains out, exclaiming, " I believe in Victor Hugo"? or that of—

Myself. Faith in God.

First Young Man. Does not every body in France believe in God in one way or another? and yet we are not healed.

Myself. Faith in God does not consist merely in believing that God exists, but also in believing what God says. When we have faith in any one, we believe his word; now in France men do not believe what God has said.

First Young Man. I know what Cousin, Hugo, Lamartine, and Chauteaubriand have said, for their works are within my reach. But where, I pray, am I to find what God has said?

Myself. In the BIBLE; that is, the *Book;* the Book of the nations, the Book of God.

First Young Man. The Bible; yes, I have heard of it, but I own that I have never read it, nor even seen it. It cannot be as widely spread as Lamartine's Meditations or Beranger's Songs. It is scarcely spoken of at all in France. And is it ever mentioned out of France?

Myself. The Bible has been translated into one hundred and fifty languages; it is disseminated among all nations and tribes. There are dialects in which it is the only written book. The savages of the islands assemble in crowds to lie down and sleep before the humble dwelling of the missionary, where it is printed in their own language, each eager to be the first to possess it, sheet by sheet; and the two or three hundred millions of inhabitants of China are now receiving it.

First Young Man. It must be very old to have travelled so far.

Myself. When the earliest of its authors was composing his works, the Greeks had not yet learned the art of writing.

First Young Man. What has it been doing since it has been in the world? Has it produced any effects to be compared with those of the writings of our day?

Myself. When the world was crumbling into dust in the times of the emperors of Rome, this Book triumphed over the corruption of the South, and created a new world. And when the barbarians threatened to crush reviving Europe, this Book triumphed over the barbarity of the North, and created modern society. It can save us a third time, and it has already converted the ends of the earth to the true God.

First Young Man. I am sure that, if these things were known and understood, men would pay more attention to that Book.

Myself. It ought to be read; it ought to be in every school, in every cottage; every Frenchman ought to possess it.

Third Young Man. My dear city friends, here you have been talking about religion for half an hour, and you have not mentioned either the Church, or the bishop, or the curate. We in the country are not so far gone as that, and we have great respect for what you, gentlemen, do not even think of. Learn that, in France, people still go to confession, and still believe in the priest, who 'alone has a right to direct us. Now, sir, the Church forbids that the Book which you are advocating should be read by the people.

Myself. How can men of God forbid that God's Book should be read?

First Young Man. What are you saying? Why I saw a notice of that book in a paper, and it said that it was published under the patronage of the archbishop of Paris.

Myself. What! the priests forbid that the people should read the holy Scriptures! This is just as if the king's ministers were to forbid Frenchmen reading the charter which it is their duty to execute.

First Young Man. Some rogue will soon say that the priests have good reasons for not letting others see what there is in that Book.

Third Young Man. Never mind. The Church is always the same; it still commands that which the holy fathers commanded in former days, in spite of the pretensions or mockery of this generation. We must submit to what has, from all antiquity, been acknowledged as true.

Myself. And who has told you that the Church wants to keep to itself the treasure which it has received to deal out bountifully to others?

Third Young Man. If the ancient doctors of the Church have desired that it should be read, why is it not shown to us?

First Young Man. If the book is what you say it is, why is no appeal made to this generation that it should read it?

Myself. (To the first). You ask for an appeal to men of our age. (To the Third). You want to hear the voice of the ancients. Well, then; if such an appeal and such voices are to be heard, you must promise one thing.

First Young Man. What is that?

Myself. To listen seriously.

Both. We promise to do so.

THE VOICE OF THE ANCIENTS TO THE MEN OF THE NINE-TEENTH CENTURY.

I. O ye nations! listen to the voice of the Lord!

God hath spoken. He who in the beginning made heaven and earth hath spoken to men. His voice is mighty as the strong wind which splits the mountains and breaks the rocks to pieces. His voice is mild and comforting; it penetrates the heart and cheers the soul like a soft and gentle sound coming down from heaven.

O man! Thy Creator, thy Father, thy Friend, thy Saviour, thy God hath spoken here below, and thou hast not listened yet!

Thou hast heard the voices of thy companions in pleasure; their tales, their jokes, their boisterous laughter hast thou heard; but the words of thy God hast thou not yet heard!

Thou hast listened to the voices of tempters, whose words are flattering, whose lips seem to drop with honey, while their words are bitter as gall; who say, "Come with us" but whose steps lead down to death, and whose paths end in the grave: but to the words of thy God hast thou not yet listened!

Thou hast listened to the voices in the market-place, or in the stores of those who are buying or selling; to the voices of business-men, and the servants of Mammon; to the voice of thine own heart, saying, "Heap up! heap up!" but to the words of thy God thou hast not yet listened!

Thou hast listened to the voice of the courier who has said, when passing by, "Such an event has just happened," and to the voices of thy friends, asking, "What is the news?" and to the voices of those who read the debates of statesmen or the combats of soldiers: but to the words of thy God thou hast not yet listened!

O man! Thy Creator has spoken on earth. Thou hast listened to all other voices; but to the voice of thy God alone thou hast not listened!

II. O ye nations! listen to the voice of the Lord!

Can He who hath given thee life forget thee? Can not He who hath formed thee out of nothing show thee the way to happiness? Doth not thy Maker know thee very well, and doth he not know what is good and profitable for thee?

O man! Where wilt thou find a more powerful friend? Where a more tender friend than thy Creator and thy God? To whom wilt thou listen if not to him?

It was on an evening early in spring; all was quiet. The moon in its mild radiance beamed through the windows into the houses. The people had played, they had laughed and danced till a late hour. The young men and the maidens had separated. The calm of night followed the noise of festivity; and they reflected. The hearts of some were aroused, and they said: "Yet this is not happiness; we want something else. The time of our life is as nothing before God. There is other happiness; eternal happiness. What shall give it to us? What shall point out the way?" And methought I heard a voice from heaven answering, 'THE WORDS OF YOUR GOD.'

O sons and daughters of men! The words of your God will show you that path. Read those words.

It was summer. All was active in the city and in the country. The citizen was busy in his counting-house, the workman in his shop, the mother in her family, the soldier on the parade-ground, the labourer in the field. There was a sound like the buzzing of insects at noon; but it was loud, for it was the buzzing of men. And many said, with a hollow look and a sad tone, "Ah! there is no true happiness in this bustle and business. What shall show us where to find it?" And methought I heard a voice from heaven answering, "THE WORDS OF YOUR GOD. O ye children of men, the words of your God will teach you the road to happiness. Read them."

It was an autumn day. The wind had bared the trees, their dry leaves covered the ground, and the old men and women were sitting before their houses and exposing their weakened limbs to the sunshine, while their children were at work. And every one was thinking to himself, "Soon my last sun will shine; soon the wind of death will loosen me, like these leaves, from the tree of life, and will lay me on the ground like them. What shall give me an assurance of immortality? what shall bring me eternal life?" And methought I heard a voice from heaven answering, "O ye aged! THE WORDS OF YOUR GOD will give you this. Read them."

It was winter. All was dry; all was frozen; all was dead. It was the time when men, meeting together, incite one another to sin; but it was also the time when God speaks with power to souls. The conscience, that invisible witness which each of us carries about in his heart, seemed to be awakened in some. Men and women, the young and the aged, in the town and in the country, were weeping over their sins. One

8   U

of these voices said, in a tone of terror, "I have sinned.   Ah!
death, which reigns over nature now, has entered also into my
soul.   I do nothing but evil.   Who can sustain the day of the
Lord's coming?   Who will stand when he shall appear!   My sin!
my sin! who shall deliver me from it?   Who shall save me?"
And methought I heard a voice from heaven answering, "JESUS
CHRIST! Jesus Christ will deliver thee!   He has come to seek
and to save that which was lost.   READ THE WORD OF THY
GOD, and thou wilt know the Saviour, thou wilt possess
salvation!"

III. Listen to this word, which is the complaint I make
concerning you, O house of Israel!

It seems as though there was a charm upon men.   Notwithstanding such entreaties, they will not take that Book,
which is so pleasant to the heart, and wherein the word is
written.

This Book was offered to a woman with white hair, with
fleshless fingers, and trembling limbs.   She replied, "Ah! leave
me alone with your word of God!"   And she rejected the Book
and him who offered it, and closed the door.   O God! the
children of this generation seek worthless books; but they
have despised thy word!

This Book was offered to a stout man, with a proud look
and a powerful frame.   He laughed loudly at this offer, as the
demons of hell laugh.   He uttered a horrible oath, and the
Book fell back into the hands of him who offered it.   O God!
the children of this generation seek vile books; but they have
despised thy word!

A man came forward.   At first sight he seemed venerable.
His palate seemed sweeter than honey, but his words were as
sharp as a two-edged sword.   Beneath a sheep's clothing
gleamed the cruel eyes of a devouring wolf.   He exclaimed,
"You must not read the words of your God!"   Then he
blasphemed against them, and snatching the Book from the
hands of an old man who found in it the hope of eternal life
and his highest comfort, he threw it into the fire with his sacrilegious hands, and the flames arose and consumed it.   I
looked, and instead of the oracles of Israel I saw nothing but
ashes.   O God! the children of this generation seek fables

cunningly devised, and doctrines of lies; but they have despised thy word!

You must not read the words of God, say they. And yet the voice of the ancients has spoken. The exhortations of the Lord's saints have been heard.

All the teachers of Christ's people, in the past times of its glory, have entreated men to read the sacred writings of the Lord, and to listen to the oracles of the mighty God.

But alas! Christianity is degenerate; it no longer listens to the voices of its first benefactors.

O rash tongue, which hast said "You must not read the words of God," didst thou not fear lest the breath of the mouth of the Lord should be sent forth, and should paralyze and silence thee forever? And you, sacrilegious hands, which took the word of God from that old man and burned it before him, did you not fear lest death should stretch its bony fingers over you, and make you as dry and lifeless as itself?

O ye nations! listen to the voice of the saints of the Lord, of the teachers of truth, of the fathers of the Church of Christ, of those who are now in the kingdom of heaven with Abraham, Isaac, and Jacob.

Christian people! they speak to you from those stakes and crosses where they were put to death here below for the sake of Christ's name. They speak to you from the heavens, where they now reign with Christ in his glory. Listen to their voices; they are friendly voices. They fought while on earth for that Gospel to which you owe every thing, both the consecration of your little children and the peaceful rest of your old men, and the light of your full-grown years, and the joys of the domestic fireside, and the arts of peace, and, above all, ETERNAL LIFE.

Child of man, whoever thou art, whether man or woman, young or old, layman or priest, wise or ignorant, rich or poor, listen: this cloud of witnesses calls to thee from heaven to take the words of thy God into thy hands, to read them, to treasure them in thy heart, and to practise them in thy life.

Come, then; travel through the primitive ages; but first put off thy shoes from thy feet, for the place to which thou drawest

nigh is holy.   He whose name is I AM, the Head and Finisher
of our faith, is about to speak.

IV. In the beginning was the Word, and the Word was
with God, and the Word was God.   The same was in the beginning with God.   All things were made by him; and without him was not any thing made that was made.   And the
Word was made flesh, and dwelt among us (and we beheld his
glory, the glory as of the only-begotten of the Father), full of
grace and truth.   His name was JESUS CHRIST.

Eighteen centuries ago God became man.   I say unto you,
there was great joy on earth then.   All who heard him and
believed on him had eternal life.   Darkness fled before his
light.   Ah! we can hear him no more!   We can see him no
more!   He has returned to heaven.   Sons of men! you can
hear him.   His word is in your midst.   Why do you not read
it?   He who was in the beginning and became man eighteen
centuries ago, to save man, fixed his penetrating eye upon the
ages to come.   He saw that future generations would also cry
out for eternal life.   He wished to leave on earth the means
by which they might be saved.   He opened his mouth and
gave them a commandment.   O ye nations! listen to the commandment of Jesus Christ!

"SEARCH THE SCRIPTURES; FOR IN THEM YE THINK YE HAVE
ETERNAL LIFE: AND THEY ARE THEY WHICH TESTIFY OF ME."

Thus spake Jesus Christ.   This is the first and great voice.

Lord! make us to understand these words.

V. Sons of men, read the Book.

A man had encouraged the murderers of the first martyr,
and kept their garments while they were stoning him.   And
this man, lying prostrate on the earth in the highway, heard a
voice speaking unto him.   And he said, "Who art thou?"
And the voice answered, "I am Jesus whom thou persecutest."
Then the voice continued, saying, "Arise, and stand upon thy
feet: for I send thee to the Gentiles, to open their eyes, and to
turn them from darkness to light."   And this man became
the great labourer whom God employed to replant the tree of
life in the dreary dwelling of man.   His name was ST. PAUL.
Asia, Macedonia, Greece, and Rome heard his voice.   A celestial fire inspired those dead bodies.

Men of this century, there is instruction still for you; there are still words addressed to you.

There are some who, in the error of their minds, say, "All Scripture is not good. It is not sufficient to instruct, to save, to fit for good works."

O ye nations! listen to the words of St. Paul: "All Scripture is given by inspiration of God, and is profitable for doctrine, for reproof, for correction, for instruction in righteousness: that the man of God may be perfect, thoroughly furnished unto good works."

This is the second voice.

Lord! make us to understand these words.

VI. Sons of men, read the Book.

The Son had scattered the seed; the Holy Spirit made it fruitful; the minds of the Jews and the heathen, a field long barren, showed symptoms of life, and sacred churches were seen to arise every where, like trees covered with blossoms and fruit.

Among the Jewish believers there were some who deserved the name of *noble* and the praises of the Holy Ghost. These were the BELIEVERS OF BEREA. And why? Because they read the Book daily. And because they would not believe what their preachers told them unless they found it in the Book. Yet these preachers were great apostles; they were Paul and Silas.

Children of our age, imitate the Christians of Berea; do not believe your preachers unless what they teach you is in the Book; wherefore read it.

St. Luke says: "Those of Berea were more noble than those in Thessalonica, in that they received the word with all readiness of mind, and searched the Scriptures daily, whether those things were so."

This is the third voice.

Lord! make us to understand these words.

II. Sons of men, read the Book.

Sixteen centuries ago, where the waters of the Rhone and the Saône unite, there was a great light. A son of the east, a disciple of Polycarp, who was a disciple of the apostle whom Jesus loved, had come across the seas, had ascended the Rhone, had stopped at the city of Lyons, and had become its bishop. And all the people who inhabited the banks of the Rhone and the Saône, as well as those still farther off, were ravished by his doctrine. They forsook their idols, and worshipped Jesus Christ. Christ blessed them with his pierced hands, and they began to live. This man's name was St. Irenæus, a.d. 177.

O ye nations! listen to the instructions which St. Irenæus gave, sixteen hundred years ago, on the banks of the Rhone and the Saône. You assert that the Scriptures are obscure and ambiguous. Irenæus says, "These things are laid before our eyes, *openly* and *without ambiguity*,[1] in the various parts of the Scriptures. All the Scriptures, the Prophets, the Gospels, can be heard *equally by all*,[2] openly and without ambiguity. Those who close their eyes to so clear a revelation[3] seem very stupid,[4] and are not willing to see the light of instruction."

This is the fourth voice.

Lord! make us to understand these words.

VIII. Sons of men, read the Book.

A man eager in pursuit of knowledge, who was still a slave to the worship of false gods, travelled over Greece, Iona, and Italy, and attended, in all these countries the schools of worldly philosophers, for the purpose of finding truth there. And he drew nigh the banks of the Nile, to the city of learning; and he heard Jesus Christ preached there. He believed. He received the remission of his sins from the Redeemer, and broke his idols to pieces. Soon he himself spread the light of Christ in Egypt, at Jerusalem, and at Antioch. Thousands of ministers of God were educated under his care. His name was St. Clement of Alexandria, a.d. 190.

Men of our days, you say that "The spirit of the age and evil doctrines have caused many to err; for such the Scriptures were not made. They can not understand them." Hear what the doctor from the Nile replies; "Let those whose eyes are dimmed by a bad education and by evil doctrines hasten to approach the light, the truth, the sacred Scriptures, which

---

[1] Aperte et sine ambiguo.   [2] Similiter ab omnibus audiri possint.
[3] Tam lucidam.   [4] Valde habetes. (Irenæus, bishop of Lyons; five books against all the heresies. Book ii, chap. xlvi.) As it would take too much time and space to give the Latin and Greek quotations in full, we will quote but a few passages, and refer the reader to the original.

will reveal to them things that can not be written. The sacred Scriptures light the spark of the soul; they open its eye that it may see; and, like the husbandman who grafts a tree, they communicate something new to the soul."[1]

This is the fifth voice.

Lord! make us to understand these words.

IX. Sons of men, read the Book.

Persecution was raging among the churches of Egypt. The people arose in tumult against the Christians, and Severus crushed them with his sceptre. A young man, sixteen years of age, stood by when soldiers seized his father. In vain he cried out; Leonides was cast into a dungeon. The young man wanted to run to the courts of the pagans; he, too, wanted to confess Jesus Christ; he wanted to sacrifice his head to the murderers of his brethren, while his father was sacrificing his. But his afflicted mother enfolded him in her arms, and, seeing that he was about to escape from her, took his toga and his tunic, and hid the garments of her son to save his life. Then the young man, unable to share his father's lot, exclaimed to him, "Beware, at least, that you do not renounce the name of Jesus Christ for our sakes."

Leonides died the death of a martyr, and left his wife a widow, his son without a guide, and six small children orphans. And the young man became a doctor, and sat down in the seat of Clement. And if Clement taught a thousand, the son of Leonides taught ten thousand.

His name was ORIGEN, A.D. 220.

Men of our age, listen to the voice which ravished the East; listen to it in your cottages, in your palaces, and within the walls of your cities.

You say, "Who shall teach us this Scripture? Shall men reveal its mysteries and explain their meaning? Shall a human tribunal?"

This doctor of the Church answers: "My son! first of all read the holy Scriptures attentively; but I say *attentively*, for it is with much attention that those divine writings ought to be read, lest they should be too hastily spoken or judged of.

---

[1] Πρὸς τὸ οἰκεῖον φῶς βαδιζέτω, ἐπὶ τὴν ἀληθινὴν, τὴν ἐγγράφως τὰ ἄγραφα, etc.—*Works of St. Clement of Alexandria. Stromatum,* lib. i, p. 274.

If thou dost persevere in the study of the Holy Book with seriousness and faith, knock, and that which is now closed to thee will be opened by that porter[1] of whom Jesus speaketh in the Gospel according to St. John, in the tenth chapter and third verse. Still, it is not enough to seek and to knock; the most necessary thing for understanding divine things is *prayer*. The Lord exhorts us to pray when he says, not only, 'Seek, and ye shall find; knock, and it shall be opened unto you;' but also, 'Ask and it shall be given you.'"

This is the sixth voice.

Lord! make us to understand these words.

X. Sons of men, read the Book.

A bishop was filling Carthage, Africa, and the whole West with the knowledge of Christ. Persecution was raging in the empire. The bishop of Carthage was also to lay his venerable head upon the block. They wished to lead him to Utica, the birthplace of Cato. But he escaped from his persecutors; for he desired to die, if die he must, in the presence of his Church; before the men and the women, the aged and the young whom he had taught, that they might hear the last testimony which he would give by his words and his death to Jesus Christ. And when he learned that it was at Carthage, in the midst of his flock, that he was to bear the martyr's crown, he gave himself up to the proconsul. When the magistrate pronounced his condemnation to death, he cast a look of hope to heaven, and his lips uttered the simple words, "Blessed be God."

His name was St. Cyprian, a.d. 258.

Before thy head falls from the scaffold under the murderous sword, tell those who surround thee, O man of God! how they may find the path which leads to the eternal mansions to which thou lookest with hope and love!

He has spoken. He has spoken for all ages. O ye nations! listen to the voice of the martyr.

"God hath said many things through his servants the prophets;[3] but how much greater are those which the Son

---

[1] Jesus Christ himself.

[2] Letter from Origen to his former disciple Gregory Nazianzen. *Philocalia*, chap. xiii. (Collection of Origen's writings by St. Gregory and Basil.)

[3] Multa et per prophetas servos suos, etc.

hath uttered;[1] those which the Word of God, who inspired the prophets themselves, hath testified with his own voice? There he commands no longer that the path of him who is to come may be prepared. But he comes himself. He opens and points out the road to us; and we, who, imprudent and blind, were in the darkness of death, are enlightened by the light of grace, so that we may enter the way of life under the Lord's guidance."

And, again, the martyr says: "Beloved brethren, the teachings of the Gospel are God's instructions, the foundation upon which our faith must be built; the helm which guides us in our voyage;[2] the fort which defends our salvation. In instructing the obedient souls of believers on earth, these teachings will lead them to the mansions which are in heaven."

This is the seventh voice.

Lord! make us to understand these words.

XI. And the more heads of Christians fell beneath the sword, the more arose before the persecutors. The blood of the martyrs was the seed of the Church.

Then, Satan, whose spirit animated the princes and priests of paganism, inspired them with this new thought: "Let us burn," said they, "all the copies of the Book; let us destroy the word of God. Then the fountain from which this religion flows will be exhausted, Christianity will pass away from the earth, and will never reappear.

Truly this design came from the depths of hell; but Christ was watching in heaven. The priests of Jupiter and Bacchus called loudly for the Book. The proconsuls caused the houses to be searched. Alas! alas! there were cowards, who, fearing death, gave the cruel priests and satellites the Book of God. But others, faithful unto death, defended it; they asked that their lives should be taken rather than the Lord's word. The sacred Scriptures were heaped together on the public places and burned. From afar off the believers saw the flames arising. They stealthily crept at night to the places where the words which God had uttered had been burned, and tears

---

[1] Sed quanto majora sunt quæ filius loquitur.

[2] Gubernacula dirigendi itineris. St. Cyprian's works, De Oratione dominica, in initio, p. 217.

stole down their cheeks as they found nothing but ashes instead of the oracles of the Holy One of Israel.

It was the priests of the dissolute Jupiter, of the impure
Venus, of the staggering and drunken Bacchus, who burned
the New Testament in those days. Men of the nineteenth
century! who are those who burn it in our days?

Shame! shame! shame for ever, cried the Christians, on
those who gave up the sacred Scriptures to the priests. They
gave these cowards the name of *traitors*,[1] and drove them
from their meetings. Glory be for ever, cry the heavenly
spirits, to the witnesses and defenders of the word; they are
THE MARTYRS OF CHRIST.

"Hast thou the sacred Scriptures?" cried the barbarous
proconsuls to the martyrs.

"I have."

"Where are they?"

"In my heart."

And the defenders of the word of God were burned, so that
those living tablets upon which the finger of God has written
his word might be destroyed.[2]

This is the eighth voice.

Lord! make us to understand these words.

XII. Who is that man who stands like a rock in the bosom
of the sea, in the midst of the assembly of bishops, who si-
lences those who deny that he who hung upon the cross was
the true God, and who suffers frequent exile for defending the
Divinity of his Lord and my Lord? His name is ST. ATHANA-
SIUS, A.D. 325. What does he say? He says to Christians
whom error has misled: "If you wish to say any thing besides
what is written,[3] why do you dispute with us? We are determined to say and to know nothing save what is in the
Scriptures."[4]   Then addressing the heathen who were seeking
God, he said: "The sacred Scriptures, inspired by God, are
sufficient for the discovery of truth."[5]

This is the ninth voice.

Lord! make us to understand these words.

---

[1] Traditores.   [2] Deeds of Saturninus, Dativus, and others, in
Africa. See Ruinart, Du Pin, etc.

[3] Εἰ δὲ ἑτερὰ παρὰ τὰ γεγραμμενὰ λαλεῖν βούλεσθε.

[4] St. Athanasius's Works, De incarnatione Christi.

[5] Ibid., Oratio contra Gentes.

XIII. Who is that man who labours as a bishop among the Pictons on the banks of the Vienne, and who, from the walls of Poictiers, ravishes Gaul by his piety and his profound wisdom?

His name is ST. HILARY, A.D. 350. And what does he say? He turns to the East, to the city of Constantine, and, addressing the man who, seated upon an august throne, governs the world, he says: "O emperor! you seek faith; learn that you can find it, not in modern writings, but in the books of God."[1] Then, turning to the Christian people to teach them the way of life, he says: "Let us read what is written, and let us understand what we read, and our faith will be perfect."[2]

This is the tenth voice.

Lord! make us to understand these words.

XIV. Who is that young man who visits the flourishing schools of Athens, Alexandria, Constantinople, and Cæsarea, and having cultivated ancient sciences, displays as a bishop all the treasures of love, and seeks to re-establish peace between the divided East and West?

His name is ST. BASIL, A.D. 370. And what does he say? He says: "It is just and necessary that every one should learn from the Scriptures, inspired by God,[3] that which is useful in making them grow in piety; and that they should not become accustomed to human traditions."[4] And wishing still farther to turn the faithful away from the traditions and instructions of men, the holy bishop adds: "To attempt to take any thing away from the Scriptures, or to add any thing to them, is to fall from the faith, and is a most presumptuous crime."[5]

This is the eleventh voice.

Lord! make us to understand these words.

XV. Who is that man who stopped an emperor because his robe had been stained with blood, who refused to celebrate the

[1] Non de novis chartulis, sed de Dei libris. Works of St. Hilary, bishop of Poictiers. Ad Constantium Augustum, p. 244.

[2] Quæ scripta sunt legamus, etc. Ibid., De Trinitate, lib. viii.

[3] Ἕκαστον ἐκμανθανεῖν ἐκ τῆς θεοπνευστοῦ γράφης.

[4] Ὑπὲρ τοῦ μὴ προσεθνσθναῖ ἀνθρωπίναις παραδόσεσιν. Works of St. Basil, bishop of Cæsarea. Regulæ breviores, Responsio 95.

[5] Works of St. Basil, Sermo de fide, p. 244.

Lord's Supper in the presence of the man before whom Asia, Africa, and Europe trembled, because he had given up his subjects to the fury of his soldiers, and who, from the walls of Milan, summons the great Theodosius to humble himself before Him who alone is great and glorious? His name is St. Ambrose, a.d. 380. And what does he say? He directs the kings and the nations to the source of life. "Drink of the two cups of the Old and New Testaments," says he, "for in each of them you will drink Christ.[1] Drink Christ, that you may drink the blood by which you have been ransomed. Drink Christ, that you may drink his sayings. His sayings are the Old and New Testaments. A man drinks the sacred Scriptures when the sap of the eternal word descends into the veins of the soul and the strength of the mind.[2] For man shall not live by bread alone, but by every word of God."

This is the twelfth voice.

Lord! make us to understand these words.

XVI. Who is that hermit who sits in the place where the Lord was born, bending over the books of God; around whom a great number of disciples gather in the fields of Bethlehem to learn from him the meaning of the Scriptures, and who, from the city of David, spreads the knowledge of the word of God throughout the West? His name is St. Jerome, a.d. 390. And what does he say? Glancing from his solitude at the children of the world living in proud Rome, he writes to Læta, a Roman lady of high rank: "Accustom your daughter early to love the sacred Scriptures more than silk and precious stones.[3] Let her learn from Job's example of patience and courage, and, turning to the Gospels, let her always hold them in her hands."[4] Then, addressing those who say that the Bible can not be understood by all, the hermit of Bethlehem

---

[1] Utrumque poculum bibe Veteris et Novi Testamenti, quia ex utroque Christum bibis.

[2] Bibitur Scriptura divina, et devoratur Scriptura divina, cum in venas mentis ac vires animi succus verbi descendit æterni. Works of St. Ambrose, bishop of Milan. In Psalm., I, Enarratio.

[3] Pro gemmis et serico divinos codices amet.

[4] Ad Evangelia transeat, nunquam ea positura de manibus. Works of St. Jerome, author of the translation of the Scriptures called the Vulgate, used in the Roman Catholic church. Epistola, 107, sec. 12.

says: "The apostles have written, and our Lord himself has spoken, in the Gospels, not that a few merely, but that all should understand.[1] Plato wrote, but he wrote for a small number, and not for the nations. Scarcely three men understood him. But these, that is, the princes of the Church and of Christ, have written, not for a few, but for ALL MEN."[2]

This is the thirteenth voice.

Lord! make us to understand these words.

XVII. A young man, nineteen years of age, escapes from the pious instructions of his mother, and Carthage sees him enjoying with the heathen all the pleasures and vices of that great city. And the pious Monica exclaims in her prayers, "O God! convert my son!"

The young Numidian is seduced by the deceitful religion of Manes. Then Plato's philosophy takes possession of his soul, and kindles a devouring flame in his heart. And Monica cries in her prayars, "O God! convert my son!"

Soon he gave himself up with passion to the arts of rhetoric; the reputation of Ambrose strikes and attracts him. He enters the Christian temples of Milan in search of eloquence, and the words of the bishop beat against his heart as the mighty waves beat against the sea-shore. And Monica, with emotion, repeats in her prayers, "O God! convert my son!"

The son of Monica, full of anguish, ashamed of himself and his errors, one day entered his garden in great agitation; he knelt by a fig-tree; he wept abundantly, and cried unto the Lord out of the depths. And a voice as gentle as a child's said to him, "Take and read!" He arose; a Bible lay on a bench near him; he opened it, and his eyes fell on these words: "Put ye on the Lord Jesus Christ." Then peace flowed like a river in his soul, and a great light, like the Sun of Righteousness, enlightened his understanding. He had found the Saviour. He sat down in the Episcopal See of Hippo; he became the light of the West, and all ages have regarded him as the greatest doctor of the Church. His name was ST. AUGUSTINE, A.D. 396.

---

[1] Non ut pauci intelligerent, sed ut omnes.

[2] Non scripserunt paucis, sed universo populo. Ibid., Comment. S. Hieronymi in Psalm., 87.

In his days, all Christians, of both sexes, of every age and state, constantly meditated on the law of the Lord. What books are those men carrying in the highways and villages, in the squares and streets of cities, offering them to soldiers and to women, to young and old, to great and small? St. Augustine replies, with joy, "These are the holy Scriptures carried about publicly for sale."[1]

Many errors were springing up around. The doctrines of Pelagius, Priscillian, Arius, and the disciples of Donatus are mingling in the spiritual world like the lightning on a stormy night. The bishop of Hippo, firm as the planet which borrows its light from the sun, spreads a mild and constant light on the earth.

With what weapon do you resist these false teachers, O son of Monica; and to what authority do you appeal, O venerable bishop? He replies, "Who does not know that the canonical Scriptures of the Old and New Testaments are contained within certain limits, and that they should be preferred to all the posterior letters of bishops;[2] so that it is impossible to doubt or to question the uprightness and truth of that which is written?[3] These are certainly the books of the Lord, the authority of which we all acknowledge, believe, and obey. There let us seek the Church, there let us discuss our cause.[4] Let us reject all arguments derived from any other source than the canonical books. I do not want the Holy Church to be defended by human documents, but by God's oracles."

But tell us, O servant of God, What will those simple and peaceful souls, which do not love dispute, learn and find in the holy Scriptures?

He replies, "The spirit and object of all the holy Scriptures is the love of him who is supreme goodness, and the love of the beings who are capable of obtaining happiness through Him.[5] The holy Scripture ought first to lead the man who

---

[1] Scriptura venalis fertur per publicum. Works of St. Augustine, bishop of Hippo. In Psalm., 36.

[2] Omnibus posterioribus episcoporum litteris esse præponendum.

[3] Works of St. Augustine, bishop of Hippo. Epistola de baptismo contra Donatistos, t. ix, p. 98.

[4] Ibi discutiamus causam nostram.   [5] Ibid., De unitate ecclesiæ. p. 341.   [5] Works of St. Augustine, bishop of Hippo. De doctrina Christiana, l. i, c. 35.

reads it to acknowledge that he is a slave to the love of the world, and a stranger to that love of God and his neighbour which is prescribed in the word of God. The knowledge of the truth then vivifies him, and engenders in him humility and a holy contrition, instead of proud presumption. Filled with deep grief, he is then enabled, by constant prayer, to receive into his heart the consolation of God's grace. He does not fall into despair, but, on the contrary, he is seized with ardent hunger and thirst after righteousness. He then flees from the destructive charms of perishing things, and is filled with love for that which is eternal."[1]

This is the fourteenth voice.

Lord ! make us to understand these words.

XVIII. Sons of men, read the Book.

A hermit came down from the mountains near Antioch. He raised his voice in that metropolis of Asia, and the ears and hearts of all were ravished by his language. Soon the imperial courts rang with his name, and he was called to the patriarchal see of the new Rome, the capital of the world, Constantinople, on the banks of the Bosphorus. Who among the children of men ever spake like him ? A nation hung, as it were, upon his lips ; the poor were comforted, the great were astonished, and the Gospel was borne, by means of his efforts, to the barbarous countries of the Gentiles.

But suddenly a sound like the noise of a tempest was heard in the palace of the emperors ; a strong and wintery wind blew from the magnificent dwellings where the proud Eudoxia commanded ; it overthrew the patriarch from his seat, and drove him afar off into a desert ; and there, in exile, in a barbarous land, near the wild path along which the imperial satellites had dragged the servant of God, he died between two soldiers, exclaiming in triumph, " Glory be to God!" The nations, enchanted with his eloquence, called him ST. CHRYSOSTOM, A.D. 400, which means "the golden mouth."

O! if the patriarch of Constantinople could now address the old man at the door of his cottage, the young man in the field, the great in their palaces, the man of business in the midst of

[1] Works of St. Augustine, bishop of Hippo. De doctrina Christiana, l. i, c. 35.

his occupations, his buying and his selling, the priest in his
study, and the woman in the midst of her family! What would
he say to you, O rich men of this world! who have every thing
except the word of God, unless, perchance, it stands richly
bound on the shelves of your libraries?

Hear what "the golden mouth" spake: "We often see dice,
but never the Bible, unless among a few; and these are as well
off as though they had none, for they preserve it in cases, mag-
nificently bound, not for the purpose of deriving any useful
idea from it, but to display their opulence and splendour. It
was not to possess it in books that the sacred Scripture was
given to us, but to engrave it upon our hearts!"[1]

What would the Western patriarch say to you, O worldly
men, who exclaim, " How can we read the word of God? The
number of our public and private affairs does not leave us time
to do so. Hear what "the golden mouth" spake : " And is
it not a grave reproach that you are so absorbed in worldly
occupations that you have not a leisure moment for the most
necessary thing? But we have evidence that this is a false
pretext. This evidence is your social meetings with your
friends; your attendance at the theatre and other public places,
where you sometimes spend days together."[2]

What would the Western patriarch say to you, inhabitants
of the town and the country, who say, " We are poor; how
can we procure a Bible?" Hear what " the golden mouth "
spake : " I would ask you whether you have not all the tools
needed in your trade? And is it not very foolish to make
poverty a pretext, when an acquisition of such immense importance is concerned, if you do not advance such a pretext in
any other case?"

What would the holy patriarch reply to you who say, "The
study of the holy Scriptures belongs to the clergy—to the
priests; laymen should not attend to it!" Hear what " the
golden mouth" spake : " Let no one utter before me such cold
and reprehensible words as these : ' I am a man of the world;
I have a wife and children; it is not my business to read the
holy Scriptures; that is for those who have renounced the

---

[1] Works of St. Chrysostom, archbishop of Constantinople.   Homil. Johan., 32. Savil., ii, p. 686.   [2] Ibid., Homil. 9, in Johan.

world, and lead a solitary life with God.' What sayest thou,
O man? Is it not thy business to read the holy Scriptures,
because thou art disturbed by various cares? On the contrary,
it is much more thy business than that of those of whom thou
speakest.[1] Far from the battle-field, they do not receive many
wounds; but thou, who art always on the battle-field, art continually wounded, and therefore needest many more remedies
to heal thee. Let us not neglect, therefore, to procure Bibles,
lest we be mortally wounded. *Let us not heap up gold, but let
us collect Bibles.* The very sight of the Bible fills us with
horror for sin. What will it be when the assiduous study of
it shall have made our soul one of those living stones of which
the sanctuary of the Deity is built.[2]

What will the holy patriarch reply to you who say, "The
Bible can not be understood by all. It was written for the
priests and for men of great learning. But the people, the
mechanics, the labourers, can not know its meaning." Hear
what "the golden mouth" spake: "The grace of the Holy
Spirit caused these books to be written by publicans, by sinners,
by tent-makers, by shepherds, by herdsmen, by unlettered
persons, that no one might resort to this pretext; that the
contents of the Scriptures might be understood by all; that
the mechanic, the servant, the poor widow, the most ignorant
of men, might be profited by them.[3] As the teachers of all
ages, those holy writers who have been enlightened by the
grace of the Holy Spirit have explained every thing in *a clear
and distinct manner*, so that each may understand them, without resorting to any other person. 'And I, brethren,' says
St. Paul, 'came not with excellency of speech, or of wisdom.'
Take the Bible in thy hand; read it; remember carefully what
thou hast understood; read over frequently that which seems
obscure; if, after repeated study, thou dost not yet understand,

---

[1] Τὶ λεγεῖς ἄνθρωπε; οὐκ ἐστὶ σὸν ἐργὸν γράφαις προσέχειν, ἐπειδὴ μυρίαις
περιελκὴ φροντισὶ; σὸν μὲν οὖν μαλλὸν ἐστιν ἢ ἐκεῖνων.

[2] Works of St. Chrysostom, In Lazarum Conc., 3.

[3] Διὰ γὰρ τοῦτο ἢ πνεῦματος ᾠκονόμησι χαρὶς τελώνας, καὶ σκηνοποιοῦς,
καὶ ποιμένας, καὶ αἰπολοὺς, καὶ αγραμμάτους ταυτὰ συνθεῖναι τα βιβλία, ἵνα
μηδεὶς τῶν ἰδιωτῶν εἰς ταύτην ἐχῃ καταφευγεῖν τὴν προφασιν, ἵνα πασὶν εὐσυ-
νοπτὰ ἢ τὰ λεγόμενα, ἵνα, καὶ ὁ χειροτέχνης, καὶ οἰκἐτης, καὶ ἡ χηρὰ γυνὴ,
καὶ ὁ παντῶν ανθρώπων ἀμαθεστατὸς, κεφανὴ, etc.

8   X

ask a more enlightened brother or teacher.   And should no
man teach thee what thou seekest, God will explain it to thee
in some way or other.   Look at the eunuch of the queen of
the Ethiopians.   He was reading in his chariot on a journey.
There was nobody to explain what he was reading.   God
witnessed his zeal, and sent him a teacher.   It is true, there
is no Philip here, but the Holy Spirit which inspired Philip
is here.''

This is the last voice.

Lord! make us to understand these words.

XIX. Thus spoke these holy men, who were great servants
of God on earth, and who are now seated in the kingdom of
heaven with Abraham, Isaac, and Jacob.   Who will dare to
contradict what they said?   Who will cast reproach upon the
memory of the confessors of Christ, and pollute the ashes of
his martyrs?   Soldier, who standest in arms ready to fight in
order that thy people may eat the fruits of their labour in
peace; labourer, who leavest the fields at the approach of night
to return to thy cottage; mechanic, who remainest at home
when thy fellow-workmen are misled by foolish associates;
before thou goest to thy work; magistrate, before thou per-
formest thy daily duties; woman, in the tranquillity of the
domestic sanctuary; young man, who art led to wander by
the delusions of the world; monarch, who sittest on thy throne;
listen, all, to the counsels of the holy men of God; their wise
sayings come down to you through the lapse of ages.

O ye nations! read the word of God!

XX. Lord! if I hear another voice besides thine or those
of thy servants; if, though thou didst say unto me, when thou
wert here on earth, '*Search the Scriptures*,' other voices tell me,
'Shut them up, throw them aside, burn them:' Lord! what
must I do?''   And methought I heard sounds arising from
the leaves of the Holy Book before me, and unite in a voice
loud as the roar of the ocean, saying, "THOUGH AN ANGEL
FROM HEAVEN PREACH ANY OTHER GOSPEL UNTO YOU THAN THAT
WHICH WE HAVE RECEIVED, LET HIM BE ACCURSED."   And I
continued, "What, then, wilt thou say, O Lord! to those
who are opposed to having thy people read thy word, who forbid their purchasing it, and who require them to give it up if

they possess it, or command them to cast it into the fire? And methought I heard sounds arising from the leaves of the Holy Book before me, and unite in a voice loud as the roar of the ocean, saying, "Wo unto you, Scribes and Pharisees, hypocrites! for ye shut up the kingdom of heaven against men: for ye neither go in yourselves, neither suffer ye them that are entering, to go in."

XXI. There is a certain place, whether it be a city, a village, or a hamlet, I will not say, in a country which I will not name. Its inhabitants despised the word of God; they would not read it; they would not possess it; and all the books of God which were found there were either taken away, or torn up, or burned. And what happened to that place? The people spoke deceitfully; hatred incited to quarrels; they ate the bread of wickedness, and drank the wine of violence; the hand of the sluggard made them poor; want came on like an armed man.

"Take thou away from me the voice of thy songs," saith the Lord; "for I will not hear the melody of thy viols. But let judgment run down as waters, and righteousness as a mighty stream." This people are destroyed for lack of knowledge, and their way leadeth unto death.

There is another place, whether it be a city, a village, or a hamlet, I will not say, in a country which I will not name. Its young men sought the word of God, the full-grown men and the women read it, and the old men meditated on it. There was a man dressed in black; his appearance was venerable: there was great mildness in his countenance; he was called a *priest.* He said: "My children, take the Book; read it; it is God's word;" and they all took and read it. And my heart melted with joy when I beheld this. For I saw its inhabitants prosper, because the Lord blessed their dwellings. Their barns were full, and their wine-presses ran down with new wine. Their ways were ways of pleasantness, and all their paths were peace. The divine word had become a tree of life to all who had accepted it, and all who kept it had become very happy.

Why does that being, surrounded by the terrors of death, the sobs of a family filled with bitterness and mourning, and a glory which is fading away, preserve a peace so inexpressible, and seem in triumph to bear off the victory over the grave? Because he believed the word, which says, "Jesus is the Lamb of God which taketh away the sins of the world." Why is that soul borne in the arms of angels through the starry heaven to the bosom of God? Why does it see God face to face, and become like him? Because it believed the word of God, which says, "Jesus is the Way, and the Truth, and the Life; no man cometh unto the Father but by him." "Yea," saith the Spirit, "blessed is the man whose delight is in the law of the Lord; and in his law doth he meditate day and night." And all the saints and the blessed spirits answer, "He shall be like a tree planted by the rivers of water, that bringeth forth his fruit in his season; his leaf also shall not wither, and whatsoever he doeth shall prosper." And all the heavenly spirits said, "Amen." And all sang together, "Glory be unto the Father! glory be unto the Son! glory be unto the Holy Ghost! who was, who is, and who will be one God, blessed forever! Amen."

ESSAY III.[1]

THE MIRACLES; OR, TWO ERRORS.

" Illud nondum est vere credere, quum Dei virtutem mirantur, ut doctrinam simpliciter credant esse veram, non autem penitus se illi subjiciant."
                                                        CALVINUS.

GENEVA is still, in some respects, the city of the Reformation. It is aware of its primitive vocation, and, in spite
of the destructive influence of indifference and infidelity, no
religious subject is here investigated without causing a thrill
to run through the whole population.

This has lately been the case with regard to the question of
miracles. This city, which seems to be in a lukewarm state
when faith is concerned, regained something of its former sen-
sibility; it was aroused, when men asserted that the supernatural works of Christianity were here denied. We must acknowledge that it was a critical moment; and the cry of alarm,
uttered at that time by distinguished men, was justly re-echoed
within the walls of the city of Calvin, and pierced "even to
the dividing asunder of soul and spirit, and of the joints and
marrow." At present, it is true this feeling seems to have
passed away. But the opportunity of calmly examining the
subject of attack is on that account more favourable than it
was. We believe that both at Geneva and in France sincere
men who are seeking the truth feel the need of this. Doubtless, many true Christians have always believed in miracles
without much reflection. Now the Scriptures require of us an
intelligent faith. "We speak," say they, "as unto wise men;
judge ye what we say."

We are too deeply convinced of the uprightness and noble
sentiments of the author of the opinions to which we refer not
to believe that he will frankly and completely expose his doc-

[1] Read at the opening of the Summer Session of the Theological School
at Geneva, in 1840.

trines.   When he shall have done so, it will be time to decide
concerning them.   Meanwhile we shall consider, not a mere
local circumstance, but Rationalism in general, and more especially Rationalism in its bearing upon miracles.

There are two false views respecting the supernatural facts
of Christianity.   Some deny these facts altogether; they seek
by mythical interpretation, or by some other means, to reduce
the origin of our religion to proportions entirely natural; and
they assert that, during the time that Christ dwelt on the earth,
no event happened more extraordinary than those which are
daily taking place around us.   This is Rationalism.

By the other party a directly opposite position is taken.
There is a religion which consists, not in believing that "Christ
is the true God and eternal life," but essentially in believing in
miracles.   The sectaries of that religion, who are very numerous in our days, and are generally very highly esteemed in most
respects, are satisfied with admitting that there is a revelation,
but without believing the great truths which that revelation
teaches.   With them it matters little what doctrines are believed concerning man, salvation, or the person and work of
the Redeemer.   But are miracles spoken of?   That is their
sanctuary!   Filled with a zeal which is doubtless commenda-
ble, though unenlightened, in our opinion, they are eager to confess and defend them.   The supernatural character of religion
has so often been attacked, that they have directed their efforts
in resisting the attack to this point.   This was well enough;
but to go no farther was wrong.   These men are, frequently
at least, the friends of Christianity, and they have it in their
power to render, and do render valuable service to it; more than
one excellent defence of it has been made by them.[1]   But we
could wish, for their own good, that they knew the sacred
truths, that they possessed the rich blessings of that revelation
which they defend.   And it is to invite them into the interior
of the temple, whose entrances they are guarding, that we wish
to consecrate the second part of this Essay.

The two views which we have just described are equally false.
In one too little importance is given to miracles, since they are

---

[1] The admirable work of Paley may perhaps be adduced as an instance
of this.

denied; in the other, too much is given, since they are made the essential thing in religion, and the only point on which men are called to confess their faith.

To deny the existence of miracles is to fall into Rationalism; to separate miracles from the essence of Christianity is bordering on superstition.

It is true that the miracles of which we speak are real miracles; but it is a mistake in language to suppose that superstition must necessarily be a belief in that which is false. Superstition is a false opinion concerning certain facts or practices of religion, on which men rely with too much fear or with too much confidence. Such is the definition given to it in the French language. According to this definition, the falseness is not so much in the object concerned as in the opinion which is held concerning it and the importance attached to it. Now such is precisely the case with those who look upon miracles as the most important thing in religion. The term which we use is therefore grammatically correct.

Doubtless, superstition may have reference also to things which are false; and it is an evident advantage of that particular kind of superstition to which we allude, that it refers to things which are true. But the more true the object of faith, the more important it is that the faith we give it be sound and faultless. To mingle superstition with truth is an evil of great importance.

Desiring not to wound the feelings of any one, but at the same time to refute an error which we think very dangerous, we have not feared to use a word to designate it which most aptly expresses our idea, and which, at the same time, shows more clearly the importance of the evil which we wish to oppose. However, we care little for the name; it is the thing that is concerned.

No, it was not merely a religion of miracles that Jesus Christ came to found on earth. Such was the religion which the Jews sought after; "The Jews require a sign," says St. Paul. But as for us with the primitive Christians, we confess first of all "God manifest in the flesh, Christ crucified, the power of God and the wisdom of God."

We propose to set forth the true doctrine respecting miracles,

in opposition to Rationalism on the one hand, and to what we
think we may call a species of superstition on the other.

I. Christianity is a creation; it is the SECOND CREATION.

The entire nature and necessity of miracles are explained by
this important truth.

Religion is not a mere collection, like all the works of man;
it is not composed of systems artistically combined, prepared,
and arranged under a certain form, by one man or by several
men. The most powerful intellect, were it to range over the
whole earth, and to select in each place those things which it
thought the most excellent, and then to unite them, could not
have made Christianity. Christianity is a creation, and, consequently, it is a work beyond the capacity of man to achieve.
It were in vain for the most eminent naturalist to gather from
all sides the most beautiful branches and leaves; he could not
make a tree. A tree can be made only by the hands of God.
It is so with Christianity. It is, says Twesten, a plant come
down from heaven, and it receives its strength and life directly
from heaven.

After the first creation, *God rested*, we are told in the Scriptures. But God's repose is an eternal action. "Man," says
Melancthon, "imagines in his weakness that God, after having
created the world, left it to itself, as a ship-builder leaves the
vessel he has built to the care of the sailors." But it is not
so. God is continually present in the world, with the same
creating power with which he made heaven and earth. And
why should there not come a day when, if necessary, that God
who is ever present will do in the course of time, in history,
something similar to that which he did at the beginning in the
work of creation? "Our God is ever living," says an old pro-
verb of the Christian people.

The adversaries of miracles assert that we ought to admit
nothing that is out of the natural course of events. But we
require nothing more for Christianity than is required for the
works of nature. It is true that at present every thing in the
physical world is developed according to certain laws; things

---

¹ Ut faber discedit a navi exstructa et relinquit eam nautis.—(Loci Comm.
De Creatione.)

which do not exist proceed from those which exist already; the ear of corn grows out of the seed which was buried in the ground; that seed proceeded from another ear, which ear grew out of another seed; and so it is with all created things. But the time was when there was neither ear nor seed. If we go back for a certain space of time, we come to the first seed: who made it? We can not derive the first origin of things from these things themselves; else we would have to say that they existed before their existence. We must therefore resort to the source of all existence, to the supreme creating power, to God.

In the day of creation, "The things which are seen were not made of the things which appeared," but the universe was made by *the Word of God.* Then there was a great miracle, an immediate action of the supreme power; it created the heavens and the earth and all that in them is.

Now, we assert nothing more of Christianity than every wise philosopher says of nature. We do not say that miracles are performed now, although, of course, our God who is in heaven does whatsoever seems good unto him, and it were easy for him to work the most wonderful prodigies at present, if he chose to do so. In this second creation, which is called Christianity, we no more claim miracles for the ordinary course of the Church than the philosopher claims them for the ordinary course of nature. But, just as the philosopher must own that, at the origin of nature, God created, acted directly, and independently of all subsequent laws, to make that which was not: so we say that, in the origin of Christianity, God created, acted directly and independently of all subsequent laws; he then introduced into the world a supernatural work and power. At the moment when Christianity was first given, a great miracle took place; a miracle which is unequalled, and yet is displayed under a thousand different forms; just as the great miracle which God performed when, in the beginning, he created heaven and earth, is manifested under a thousand various aspects, through-out the whole of creation.

What happened at the commencement of our religion? *God was made manifest in the flesh.* "The eternal Word, which was .n the beginning, and which was God, by whom all things were made," came down from heaven to earth, and lived as a man in this world of sin. And shall this wonderful manifestation be accompanied by no sign? Shall he in whom was LIFE, and *that life the light of men*, come into the world, and yet no one observe it?

If a man of any peculiar capacity be charged with certain functions: if, for instance, he is, by the king's will, raised to a certain ministry men expect an immediate influence to be exerted, and important ameliorations to be made in the affairs of which he has the control. When a king visits a city, the ordinary course of business of its inhabitants is interrupted; something extraordinary is expected, and the people would be surprised if he did not give proofs of his presence, his munifi·cence, his majesty and power.

And yet men are astonished if, when God appeared in the world which we inhabit, he manifested his glory! While he went about from place to place here below as a man and a servant, they would have things follow their ordinary course, so that men should not perceive the presence of that God in the world! Ah! in this case, an ordinary state would have been most extraordinary, and an extraordinary state is simple, natural, and true.

What did he come to do here? "Behold, I come to make all things new." He came to create a new world, new heavens, and a new earth. He came to achieve a spiritual creation, no less wonderful than the visible creation. Who, then, will be astonished that God displayed his power when he came to create, and that he acted directly, and not according to certain laws which he had made, when he came to form something which was entirely new, and had not yet been subjected to any rule or law?

Yes, I see before me two creations: that described by Moses, and that related by the Evangelists; and the only thing which would astonish me would be not to find in one something similar to what I see in the other.

I am not astonished that at the first creation, God said, " Let there be light! and there was light." I am not astonished that, at the sound of his mighty voice, the earth produced its fountains, the trees sprang forth and bore fruit, and the waters, the earth, and the air produced living creatures in abundance.

Neither do I wonder that when, in the second creation, that voice which created the heavens and the earth was again heard, the blind recovered their sight, the maimed walked, the deaf heard, the winds and the waves were calmed, the water was turned into wine, and five barley loaves and two fishes, being multiplied in the hands of the Being who formed the world with all its productions and its treasures, were sufficient to nourish 5000 persons.

Invent, if you can, a creation without miracles; then I will yield the miracles of Jesus Christ. But as long as you can not do that, I will think it as natural that the power of God should be displayed when the creation which was to save my soul was concerned, as when that which was to form my body was effected.

Observe our answer to the Rationalists and infidels, whom the doctrine of miracles offends and scandalizes. We do not say to them, " These miracles are, we acknowledge, wholly incongruous, destitute of order, and contrary to every law ; for all that, whether you will or no, you must bow your head before them !"

We might say this; we would say so if the word of God required it; but we say, on the contrary, " In this case, the extraordinary event is order itself, and the transgression of the law is the law."

Is there a creature in existence which was produced by the very laws by which it is preserved ? Are not the creation of a being, on the one hand, and its development on the other, two distinct acts, subjected to very different laws ? You pre-serve a plant by cultivating it, watering it, and nourishing it; but do you suppose that by these means you would ever suc-ceed in creating it ? Why then are you astonished that some-thing different from what we witness now should have happen-ed at the origin of Christianity ? Why should the period when (as all acknowledge) the world received new life and underwent a new creation, be subjected to the daily course in which we are living ?

You have often been told in history that we must not judge

of past ages by the age in which we live; that it were unjust,
for instance, to measure the events of the days of the Crusades
by the narrow limits of the present manners; that different
times have different manners.   And must not this rule, which
is admitted in every case, be admitted on a much greater scale
when we are speaking of that epoch, unequalled in history,
when life and glory, when the God of heaven himself came down
to the earth?

It is true that miracles are supernatural facts; but in one
sense they are also natural facts.   They belong to a superior
order of things, to a superior world; and they are perfectly
conformed with the supreme law which governs them.   In that
world miracles are not miracles; they belong to the course of
nature.   At the establishment of Christianity, the superior
world acted upon the inferior world, conformably to the laws
which are peculiar to it; a miracle is nothing more than this.
What can be more necessary than this action?   And what can
be more natural than the manner in which it is accomplished?
Would you ask a soldier not to act like a soldier, or a learned
man not to talk like one?   How then can you ask God to act
and speak otherwise than as God?   It would be a miracle were
God to act like man; it is perfectly natural that God should
act like himself.

And is this idea of a superior law which modifies inferior
laws an unheard of thing?   Does not natural philosophy give
us similar instances?   Do we not constantly see the laws of
nature interrupted by the laws which are above them?   For
instance, there is a universal law of weight, in virtue of which
my arm falls down after it has been raised.   But the strength
of my will is sufficient to counteract that law, to constrain it
to yield, and to raise my arm again to the same height.   Just
so with miracles.   Laws and influences less elevated yield to
laws and influences which are superior.   Miracles are the right
of the strongest.

This extraordinary action of God is above all the laws of
nature with which we are acquainted; but it is connected with
the universal order of things.   It belongs to the vast plan of
God, which contains at once both the natural course of events
and these supernatural manifestations.   In the government of

an earthly king, according to the ideas of our modern nations, the king ought not, it is true, to appear in person habitually; every thing is accomplished through the medium of his ministers whom he has himself appointed; the responsibility, the counsel, and the action are theirs. This is the ordinary course of things. But there are circumstances in which the king must show himself to be superior to all his ministers; there are cases when he acts in opposition to them, when he degrades and dismisses them, and appoints others. How contracted would be the views of those who would pretend that this direct action of the king was contrary to the plan of the constitutional government! Not only is the royal action a part of the plan of that government, but it is its very perfection. Just so it is with the immediate interference of God in the government of the world by means of miracles. Those who would have God limit himself to permitting the laws which he has established to act, and then let these laws as it were, tie his hands, take a very narrow view of the plans of the Supreme Being. They must have a very mean idea of his greatness, and they do not even allow him the power of *veto*, which in the most democratic monarchies is granted to the king. Let us take a higher view of these things; and then that which appeared before to be the most shocking confusion will become the most beautiful harmony.

Take another example. True Christianity, true piety, may be thought very extraordinary in this selfish world; but as soon as Christianity has been recognized, men must no longer wonder at certain things which belong to its very nature, although they are wholly contrary to the common course of things in the world. To make oneself a slave is contrary to nature, for man loves liberty; he was born in it, and a man who is degraded enough to sell himself to another, deserves all the contempt of his fellows. Nevertheless, we are told that missionaries have become slaves among slaves, so that they might save some of them; and, far from exciting our contempt, they win our warmest admiration. As soon as Christianity is admitted, we call that a simple and even excellent deed which, a few moments before, we thought to be revolting.

So it was with miracles; that which in the ordinary course

of things would appear very extraordinary, becomes natural when the Supreme God reveals himself. When revelation is admitted, miracles are likewise admitted; as, when a Christian's charity is recognized, all the prodigies of devotion accompany it.

Without miracles, revelation would not reveal the power and divinity of him who speaks. Without them, instead of being a glorious and evident fact, it would be abstruse and obscure. Miracles alone give it real publicity. They alone can and do announce that the God of heaven makes known the mysteries of his charity to the earth.

To consider each of the miracles as an isolated fact is, as Neander remarks, a very erroneous manner of looking at them. Then, indeed, they would not be rational. Each miracle is a member of a vast whole, and is part of a union of manifestations of the Divine Creator. Suppose a man condemned by the laws sees his fetters suddenly unbound and the door of his prison opened, and hears these words: "Go, and save thyself!" I can then exclaim that the laws are broken. But if I consider this fact in its connection with other facts; if I learn that a great king has just returned to his capital, perhaps after a rebellion; that he resumes the throne; that he celebrates the marriage of his son, and that he wishes all his people even to the prisoner in his dungeon, to share the joy he feels: then this fact, which, when isolated, appeared extraordinary, seems perfectly natural in connection with this event. This is not the only fact of the same nature; other prisons have been opened, other debts have been paid, other misfortunes have been alleviated. And all these various events concentrate in one: "The king has returned, and he wishes to show his favour to his people."

It is even so with miracles; they unite in one single fact, the coming of God on earth, the restoration of union between the holy God and sinful humanity. This principal fact is the great miracle. It draws all the others along with it. Who will wonder at these lesser deliverances granted to the bodies of men when eternal deliverance of their souls appears? Are you surprised to see a beam of light entering your chamber when the glorious orb of the sun has risen in the skies? When once the principle is acknowledged, all the consequences must be submitted to.

Yes, the great miracle is CHRIST, the Eternal Word made

flesh. The great miracle is, the communion between God and guilty man restored by God himself; eternal life given back to the sinner. This is the miracle which the beloved disciple can not too highly exalt, when he exclaims, "That which was from the beginning, which we have heard, which we have seen with our eyes, which we have looked upon, and our hands have handled, of the Word of Life, declare we unto you; for THE LIFE WAS MANIFESTED, and we have seen it, and bear witness, and show unto you that eternal life which was with the Father, and was manifested unto us."

This miracle is the centre of all miracles; this prodigy called into being all the other prodigies which preceded, accompanied, and followed it. "He covereth himself with light as with a garment," says the prophet, and indeed that miraculous power which gleams throughout all nature, when the Eternal appears, is the glorious garment of God manifest in the flesh. It is not merely at the moment of his actual sojourn here below that this glory is resplendent on the earth. Ere the sun rises above the horizon, the dawn has intimated his approach, and after he has gone down a radiance remains to show he has been with us. Would we not expect the same thing of the Sun of Righteousness? He resembles not a tropical sun which rises without a dawn, and sets without a twilight; the splendours of his greatness precede him, and those of his power follow him.

Christ, the great miracle, once received,—"Christ the true God and eternal life,"—O, it is a small matter to admit the miracles which he wrought! But how can I disbelieve that great miracle? Can I, when the whole history of the world bears witness to it? Can I, when God himself reveals it in the Scriptures which he has inspired? Ah, Lord, sooner would we doubt of our own existence than of thine, of our own than of thy appearance in this world.

Is it needful to descend from these general considerations to particular facts? Is it needful to review all the miracles of the New Testament to justify them? No, the principles which we have already laid down are enough. We conceive that in defending miracles we should but dishonour them. At the same time, it may be that some minds require a few hints, and we are unwilling to refuse what may be useful. We shall, therefore, without going into details, indicate some applications of the principles which we have established.

It is the appearance of Christ that is the object of attack. This is the leading fact in Christianity, and it is sought to reduce it to the dimensions of an ordinary event. Christ is represented as a virtuous Israelite trained in the bosom of a pious family, who, finding the idea of the Messiah prevalent amongst the people and amongst his own relatives, appropriated it to himself, and made it the object of his life to realize it. The first miracle denied in this representation is, thus, that of the birth of the Redeemer; the Incarnation; the manifestation of God in the flesh; the sacred foundation of all our religion.[1] The Holy Scriptures declare to us that the birth of Christ did not spring from natural causes, and that the same immediately creative power which brought into existence the first Adam formed the second in his mother's womb. The narrative of the evangelists is so simple, so natural, so historical, that it is impossible to conceive it a myth framed by the imagination. Besides, such an idea as that of the incarnation was utterly foreign to Jewish monotheism which placed an impassable gulf betwixt God and the world. If in other religions, for example those of India, we find fabulous incarnations, this is explained by the peculiar character of the people. But ought we to be surprised to find in Christianity that, as truth actually realized, which existed elsewhere merely as conjectures and vain imaginings? If Christ is the Redeemer, if he is the author to humanity of a new and spiritual creation, we must, even if the sacred writers had kept silence, have taken for granted some such facts as they relate. If you wish to render foul water pure, will you do so by taking of that foul water itself? The author of a new creation must not himself come of the old creation which he is to change. The Regenerator of the human race must not himself be a polluted member of the corrupt body which he is going to purify. He who comes to bring a divine life into the world must himself emanate from that life and possess it in its fulness; for how, otherwise, can he communicate it? The first man of the new creation must issue from the hand of God, as did the first man of the old creation.

[1] See for this and other examples, the writings of various German Rationalists.

"No man putteth new wine into old bottles," said Christ himself, "but they put new wine into new bottles."

The birth of Christ, then, is the first of his miracles; it is the greatest miracle of humanity; and it is easily perceived how, around this miracle which brought heaven into so intimate a relation to earth, there should be clustered other supernatural facts—the rays of glory of that Dayspring from on high, which is to disperse the shadow of death.

No, Christ was not merely a virtuous man, reared by a pious family. It was not simply at Nazareth, at Jerusalem, amidst the conversations of the Pharisees and doctors, that his character was formed. "In him dwelt all the fulness of the Godhead bodily." And those who were about him "beheld his glory, a glory as of the only-begotten of the Father.

Shall we proceed now to the miracles of Jesus Christ themselves? It is said that he effected wonderful cures by virtue of his influence over the minds of men; and his almighty power is explained by comparing it to that of men whom we sometimes see, by a certain air of authority, oblige invalids to attempt that of which they thought themselves incapable; and by comparing it to that of the Mesmerists. Doubtless if the miracles of Jesus Christ had been performed only by the influence of his mind upon the minds of others, they would not have been supernatural acts; but this was not their character. On the contrary, the miracles of Christ were accomplished by the influence of his word upon physical nature—on the body. That mind should influence body is not an irrational idea, otherwise every human being would be an example of the irrational. Our minds have then an influence on our bodies: but it is on our own bodies only: whilst the mind of Jesus acted not only upon his own body, but upon the bodies of all creatures. He said to a dead man who had been four days in the grave, Arise! and in a moment the blood, the nerves, the muscles, all obeyed his word; just as in the healthy state the members of our body obey our will. Our volitions influence ourselves alone. Christ, the Lord of nature, gave commands to all nature. What more simple, more natural, more true?

But, on the other hand, what is more extraordinary and absurd than to seek to explain the miracles which Jesus Christ

S   Y wrought by his influence upon the mind—upon an excited and inflamed imagination? Let the imagination of a man born blind be excited ever so much, could it bestow on him the power of sight? Could the imagination of a dead man bring him to life? Do not we see Christ acting often upon the absent, the distant, persons with whom he had not and never had had any connexion whatever? Was it the operation of the mind of Jesus upon souls which had left the body, upon that of the daughter of the ruler of the synagogue, upon that of the young man of Nain, upon that of the brother of Martha and Mary whose remains had already begun to decay, which brought them back to life? Suppose this, however, to have been the case, would we not have had in this the greatest miracle?

Was it by the influence of his mind on other minds that, when Jesus commanded the winds and the waves, the winds and the waves ceased to rage, and there was a great calm?

Was it, in fine, by the operation of his soul upon other souls that Jesus fed five thousand men with five loaves and two fishes, producing by this miracle so great an impression upon these men themselves that, struck with the wonderful nature of that act of the Lord, they cried, "This is of a truth that Prophet that should come into the world," and they wished to take him by force *to make him a king?* No! Jesus manifested in this act his glory and his creating power; he displayed that power by which he ceases not throughout all ages to act, accomplishing the greatest things by the smallest means, and wonderfully compensating for the insignificance of the instrumentality by the greatness of that divine efficacy with which he invests it. Thus it was, to cite only one instance, that, fifteen hundred years afterwards he changed the face of the Church and the world by means of a monk the son of a miner at Mansfield, and a priest the son of a peasant at Tockenbourg.

And if, from the miracles of the Son of God, we go on to those which followed the effusion of the Holy Spirit on the day of Pentecost, what do we find? An attempt has been made to explain them according to the ordinary laws of nature. It is said that to men in the apostles' state of mind the smallest events would become invested with a character of solemnity: that, a *gust of wind* having happened, they believed they saw the answer to their prayer, and that the Jews who had come from the different countries of the earth were astonished at hearing each his own language spoken, because the idea did not occur to them that the apostles might have learned those different languages by travel.

But how is it possible to explain by a *gust of wind* the astonishing transformation which took place at the same moment in the apostles? How can it be thought that those disciples whom nothing had hitherto been able to inspire with courage,—whom nothing could draw out of their fear, their flight, their silence, —whom neither the remembrance of the words of Christ nor that of his miracles, nor even his resurrection—his resurrection from the dead—nor his ascension to heaven, could inspire with confidence, would be at once roused from their apathy, transformed, from being timid rendered courageous, from being silent filled with words of power, from being waverers rendered full of faith,—by a *gust of wind!* What was there, in so common a thing, which could appear to them so wonderful, and be enough to induce them to come out from their hiding place to face the Jews and the whole world?

Before the day of Pentecost, not one of the apostles taught publicly; immediately afterwards the Church is founded, it increases from day to day, from age to age; it subsists to eternity; and all this is brought about by a *gust of wind!* Still further, the apostles henceforth speak foreign languages, that gift of tongues remains for several ages in the Church, and it is a *gust of wind* by which that gift is bestowed!

No, it is said they had acquired these languages by travelling. And how had they learned the languages of Persia, Media, Parthia, in the east; of Mesopotamia, Cappadocia, Pontus, Asia, Phrygia, Pamphylia, on the north; of Arabia, Egypt, Lybia, Cyrene, in the south; of Crete and Rome in the west? How had they learned by travelling all these languages of the different people of the earth, those poor Galilean watermen who had only quitted their nets to follow Jesus into Judea, and who never had travelled, never appeared in any of the countries in which those languages were spoken.

Let us turn away from foolish words, which faith and reason equally reject. The Redeemer, raised to the right hand of the power of God, did not long try the patience of his disciples.

He opened the gates of heaven, and the heavens "dropped down from above, and the skies poured down righteousness." The fulness of the heavenly Spirit, who had disappeared from this earth on the sin of man, returned after the death and resurrection of the Son of God; and the kingdom of the Lord was anew founded here below. Human nature, divided and as it were broken by sin into many languages and many fragments, was anew brought together before God into one holy and glorious unity. To many nations succeeded one people only; to many races one race only—"the chosen generation, the holy nation, the peculiar people." And, as a sign and seal of that unity re-established on the earth, the division of languages, which was an effect of sin, was suspended. The Holy Spirit, the principle of love and of true communion of Spirit, removed all differences, and threw down all barriers. The charity which burned in the breasts of the apostles communicated itself to those who heard them, and the languages of those who heard them were spoken by the apostles. Thus were there, so to speak, but one language, one soul, and one heart. All the partition walls which separated brethren were cast down, and all were one in Jesus Christ. God loosed the tongues of his witnesses, and, in making them speak the languages of the people of the east, west, north, and south, manifested the universality of that Church which he was then establishing on the earth. A society it was at the time few in number, but within it were even already the languages of all the nations; and this miracle powerfully intimated that which after eighteen centuries we see coming to pass before our eyes, namely, that "Christ has redeemed by his blood men of every kindred, and tongue, and people, and nation." That was the birth-day of the new Church, the first day of the invitation of all nations to the supper of the Lamb.

Thus the most natural explanation of miracles is to see in them true miracles. To seek to deny them, far from assisting in their explanation, throws reason itself into inextricable difficulties.

Come, then, ye rash though doubtless upright men, who make it your pride to despoil Scripture of the great and the marvellous. See that true wisdom consists in observing and recognizing the great doings of God in the world, and not in reducing them to ordinary occurrences, by subtle and ingenious inventions. As all the prescriptions of empirics have disappeared before accurate observations on diseases and on the human body, as all the chimeras of the astrologers have been scattered by the study of the great laws of the heavenly bodies, so all the subtleties of scholastic theology must vanish before the reading and investigation of the word of God; so now, all the hypotheses of rationalism must be extinguished by the observation, study, and comprehension of that great fact, published by the Christian Scriptures, and which rules all the history of the world—GOD WAS MANIFEST IN THE FLESH. You know nothing of history truly so long as you know not this fact. Lay aside your ingenuities, your myths, and hypotheses; give your earnest study to the most glorious of all events that have ever taken place on earth for that human race to which you belong; rise to the height of that great miracle, and all the miracles which accompanied it will at once be explained to you.

II. To deny miracles is rationalism; to separate miracles from the very essence of Christianity is a sort of superstition. This last is the second of the false views which we pointed out.

There is often to be met with, at the present time, in the christian world, and amongst persons, in many respects, enlightened, an inclination to admit revelation and miracles without going further. The religion most common in our day is limited to a simple belief that a religion has been given by God, and that it is the religion of Jesus Christ.

Doubtless that is something; but the essence of this religion is the thing needful to be understood; above all, the thing needful to be possessed. But at the present time it is not even thought necessary to be known. If the minds, sincerely religious doubtless, which stop at that point, admit certain of the doctrines of revelation, they attach but little importance to them. They tell us that there must be great liberality of sentiment, that, on such subjects, either side may be taken indifferently. Orthodoxy, Arianism, Socinianism, are in their eyes only shades of distinction which do not exclude unity. Such individuals are ready at any time to confess their belief in miracles; but to profess faith in the doctrines of Christianity would be, in their estimation, an act of enslavement. They have a frame, but no picture; foundations, but no house raised on them for shelter; a pedestal, but no statue.   Miracles are their religion.

But the essential character of all superstitions is to suppose and multiply miracles, without revealing any thing which may subserve the glory of God or the salvation of man.

Indeed, true religion is composed of two elements: facts which surpass man, and truths which not less surpass him; facts and truths intimately united in a spirit of holiness and life.

Of these two elements the one, the miracles, can be easily invented; the other, the truths, it is impossible to invent.

A child may invent a miracle, and the more immature and infantine the human mind is, the more miracles will it suppose it has discerned.   But the truth of God, truth regarding eternity, regarding the salvation of man,—who shall discover it?

Thus all false religions are full of marvels, but destitute of doctrines.   They have miracles, they move heaven and earth, they keep in activity all the powers of creation; and all this to reveal nothing.   So that one may apply to them the celebrated verse of the Latin poet:—

Parturiunt montes; nascitur ridiculus mus.[1]

The superstitions of the Indians are full of miracles.   In China, the idols as soon as they are finished rise without assistance, and set themselves in the place they are designed to occupy.   The statue Amida in this way transported itself from Corea to Japan.

Habib, the son of Malek, cried, " Mahomet, it is noonday! if thou wishest us to believe in thee, cause darkness immediately to come on—stand upon Mount Abu-Kabai, and command the moon, which is now near the sun, for this is the fifteenth day of the month, to become full; then order it to place itself on Kaaba, to make the circuit of that holy building seven times, to lay itself prostrate before it, and to say to thee in good Arabic, so that all the inhabitants of the city and the country may understand it, " Peace to thee, true prophet of God!" After that, order it to enter by thy right sleeve, and to come out by thy left sleeve, then to divide itself into two parts, and go, one part to the west, the other to the east, and finally, with the light leap of a grasshopper, let the parts approach

---

[1] The mountain is in labour, and brings forth mouse.

and reunite." Mahomet replied, "I am not of those who draw back;" and immediately everything took place as the son of Malek had demanded—the moon spoke in excellent Arabic, and passed through the sleeves of the prophet.

The papacy has not invented fewer miracles than the superstitious heathen, or the disciples of Mahomet. Do not its legends, for example, tell us how Ignatius Loyola, the founder of the Jesuits, in the sixteenth century, walked often through the air; and how, entering a dark room at night, it was lighted by his presence alone, as if many torches had been brought thither? Two hundred miracles of Ignatius were presented to the auditors of the Rote, and to the congregation of Rites at Rome, as warrants for his canonization.

What is it that essentially distinguishes the miracles of Jesus Christ from those pretended miracles? Many things, doubtless; but the most important mark is this:—the miracles of Jesus Christ reveal a magnificent assemblage of truths, which are for the glory of God and the salvation of man, whilst all the miracles of superstition, Eastern, Romish, Mahometan, teach us nothing, reveal to us nothing.

But, it will be said, the miracles of Mahomet and of Rome were false miracles, and those of Christianity are true; it is impossible to compare them.

Doubtless there is a difference, and justice requires us to recognize it. But the doctrines of Christianity are so essential to the miracles of Christianity, that if they were separated from them, these last would cease to be the true miracles of the Gospel, and would acquire something of falsehood.

Ecclesiastical history informs us, that a pope—Stephen VI., caused to be exhumed the dead body of Formosus, one of his predecessors, who had been praised for his faith, knowledge of the Scriptures, and Christian virtues. He caused him to be arrayed in all the pontifical ornaments. A tiara was placed on his head, he was covered with the alb which hung down to his heels. The stole was put round his neck, with its crosses of lace and embroidery hanging on each side, and, above the whole, the cope, embroidered with gold, and clasped in front. He was then seated on the papal throne, and, according to Stephen, this was Formosus.

Then a council was assembled; and when all the fathers

were gathered in solemn state around the pontifical chair, Stephen advanced, and addressing Formosus, said, " Bishop of Oporto, wherefore didst thou suffer thyself to be drawn by thy ambition to usurp the See of Rome ?" The pope Formosus making no reply, a deacon was assigned to him as his counsel: but, in spite of the defence, Formosus was found and proclaimed guilty ; he was then deprived of his pontifical garments, the three fingers with which he was in the habit of giving his benediction were cut off, he was beheaded, and his body was thrown into the Tiber.[1]

Doubtless in some respects Stephen had reason on his side. This pope, invested with all the insignia of a sovereign pontiff, was certainly Formosus ; those were his hands, his fingers, that was his head. It was he whom the council judged, and whom his impious successor apostrophised.

And yet it was not he ; for his soul was awanting. Stephen deceived himself, and all the prelates did nothing but act an unworthy farce. Nothing of Formosus was there. The true Formosus had before this appeared before a higher tribunal, and was then in the presence of the Sovereign Judge.

And thus it is with miracles. Those who pretend to hold fast by the miracles of Christ, while they separate them from his doctrines, have without doubt, like Stephen, some show of reason. They have something, but it is a dead body. The life, the essential object of miracles—the doctrines of Christianity, is awanting to those miracles.

The miracles of Christ, apart from his doctrines, are not false, it is true ; but they are falsified, spoiled, inanimate, and powerless, and they can no longer be the objects of a pure faith.

The sacred doctrines of the Gospel are the essential thing. To attempt to make miracles the principal matter is not to profess Evangelical Christianity ; it is to reduce that religion to the level of contemptible superstitions, or at least to recall those times in the Middle Ages when, a corrupt Christianity being introduced among the unpolished nations, who were nevertheless full of that life and imagination that distinguish states which are still young, Christendom was seen forgetting the saving doctrine, viewing nothing but miracles in the Gospel,

[1] *Auxilius* de ordinationibus Formosi P. libb. II.—*Histoire Ecclesiastique* de l'abbé Fleury, livre 54.

imagining that they constantly saw the supernatural fact of primitive times renewed, and investing the *Saints*, even during their lives, with a strange halo of wonderful miracles.

Even then some lofty minds protested against this excessive love of miracles. The famous chancellor of the university of Paris, John Gerson, exclaimed with energy in the council of Constance, " In our days the Church is wanting in a fundamental knowledge of the Bible; and thus we see an increasing inclination for visions, revelations, and miracles. Let us beware of encouraging it." And the illustrious victim of that council, John Huss, replied to those who asked miracles of him, " It is by miracles that Antichrist will one day deceive the world. The confession of the truth and the sufferings endured for its sake are the surest proofs that a man is taught of God." " A true Christian," said he again, " does not look for miracles; but he holds fast to the promises of the word."

Thus, in those days as in ours, those who had not the sacred doctrines of the truth desired to fill their place by a love for miracles; and in our days, as in former times, those who possessed that truth considered it infinitely superior to all prodigies, and even to the true miracles of Jesus Christ.

To be contented with miracles is a characteristic of children; to proceed to the truths which they reveal is a characteristic of full-grown men.

Are the letters of credit which he carries with him the most important matters with an ambassador? Is it not rather the mission with which he is charged? What would men think of the ministers of a king if they were to amuse themselves in fumbling the parchment and the seals presented to them by an ambassador, and say that these are the principal things; that the message which he has received for them from his master matters but little; that it may be, in the opinion of one, a message of war, in that of another, a message of peace, and in that of a third, something else; that it is of little moment, provided they are certain that this man has been sent by the king? Would not the ambassador suppose that they were ridiculing him and his master? Would he not think that they were overgrown children: Would he not gather his credentials together and depart from such a cabinet?

Yet this is precisely what is now to be seen in the world;

in France, in Switzerland, and elsewhere, among Roman Catholics and among Protestants. It is enough, we are told, to
know there are miracles, which are the foundation of a revelation; and as to what that revelation may teach, it matters
little! According to one opinion, it may say that man is inclined to do evil, and according to another, that he is inclined
to do good. One may say that he is saved by grace, and another by works. One may believe that the Saviour is God, and
another that he is a man. It matters little; no one cares
about it; we have miracles; that is religion, that is salvation,
that is every thing; it is enough!

This is an unhappy superstition, which is but little better
than the infidelity which we refuted a little while ago.

This superstition deprives the miracles themselves of their
most divine characteristic. In truth, there is a negative and
a positive aspect in miracles. By their negative aspect, I mean
that which can not be explained by the laws with which we
are acquainted. By their positive aspect, I mean a manifestation of God for man's salvation. Now the negative aspect is
a mere indication, a sign[1] which directs me to the positive aspect, and invites me to look upon miracles as a new and glorious manifestation of the holy love of the Lord.

And it is not merely a vague love, an undetermined and vaporous manifestation of God that the finger of miracles points
us to; it is, in the language of the Scriptures, " the revelation
of the mystery which was kept secret since the world began;"
it is " the things which have not entered into the heart of man,
which God hath prepared for them that love him;" it is " the
great mystery of godliness, God manifest in the flesh," together with all that accompanies it.

It is this divine aspect of miracles that is despised by men,
when they look away from the truths which they display.

The facts of Christianity can not be separated from its doctrines. When the facts are preserved without the doctrines,
or the doctrines without the facts, not only one half of Christianity is taken away, but the other half is destroyed; just
as, in taking away the soul from the body, the body is killed.
God and God's word can not be separated.

If there are theologians in Switzerland, France, England,

---

[1] Such is the meaning of the Greek word translated *miracles: σημεῖα.*

and America, who, at the same time that they sacrificed the doctrines of Christianity, have pretended to preserve its miracles, there are others in Germany who, while they sacrifice miracles, pretend to preserve the doctrines, and who, in the name of pantheism, have spoken like the most pious Christians of the Trinity, the Fall, and Redemption.

But all these divisions only give us appearances, without the reality. The facts and doctrines of Christianity are not in their essence two distinct things placed side by side, but two circles with a common centre, two rays of light emanating from the same sun; the most intimate union exists between them. You will not thoroughly understand all the miracles until you have received the whole doctrine, and received it in your heart. Before he can view them in their real aspect, one operation must have taken place within man: that is an entire transformation of heart, understanding, and life, a new birth, a new creation. "Many," says Twesten, "will say, like Nicodemus, respecting the miracles, 'How can these things be?' But the believing Christian will reply, with his Master, 'We speak that which we do know, and testify that which we have seen.'"

It is true that the testimony of the word is sufficient to induce us to admit and believe these supernatural facts. God has said it; that ought to be enough. We present this testimony to every man, and require that he should believe it. But how much more easily will the Christian, "Who, being dead in trespasses and sins, hath been quickened by Christ." and hath, by regeneration, known "the exceeding greatness of the power of God to him-ward," understand "the working of His mighty power, which He wrought in Christ, when He raised Him from the dead!" Conversion is a miracle of God's grace, which makes it easy to understand all other miracles. How can I doubt that Christ should have caused a divine light to shine in the eyes of his apostle, and have spoken to him on the road to Damascus, since he has performed things less extraordinary in appearance, but no less wonderful for me, and "hath shined in my heart, to give the light of the knowledge of the glory of God in the face of Jesus Christ"? How can I doubt his having raised up the young man of Nain, or his friend at Bethany, when I myself have felt that "the Son quickeneth whom he will," and since he hath made me "pass from death unto life"?

Still further: not only does regeneration lead me to understand miracles, but it is a powerful demonstration of them. In the true Christian there is a new light and a new life. This is a fact of which every disciple of Christ is himself a proof. These gifts, which proceed from God, have nevertheless been communicated to him through certain men, who are the servants of God; just as the physical life which each individual possesses, and of which God alone is the author, has been communicated to him by his father and mother. But, in the same way that, rising in nature from generation to generation, we arrive at the first man, who, as the stock or father of the human race, received his existence directly from God by means of creation, so, in the order of grace, rising from epoch to epoch in the ages of the Church, we reach a primary, original, full, and immediate communication of life from God, which is a new creation. As in grace, so in nature; that which I see, and that which I am at present, necessarily leads me to a creation of what I see and am.

Now if the Spirit of God performs such great things, and works so powerfully for the conversion of souls, not only all around me but among all nations, from the ancient ones of India to the young tribes of Polynesia, from the wild hordes of New Zealand to the civilized inhabitants of London, Geneva, or Paris, this same Spirit must of course have wrought, in the primary and creating period, when the heavens were bowed down and brought salvation, with much more universal and wonderful power. "Then I see heaven open, and the angels of God ascending and descending upon the Son of man." The wonderful things of the present day make me admit all the miracles of the Gospel.

How can a man be satisfied with miracles, make them his religion, and despise the new birth and the new life? This would be the religion of Nicodemus, not that of Jesus Christ. That ruler among the Jews took precisely the same view as the persons of whom I speak. "The same came to Jesus by night, and said unto him, Rabbi, we know that thou art a teacher come from God: for no man can do *these miracles* that thou doest, except God be with him." This certainly was a confession of faith in miracles considered as the basis of revelation; it was a clear and solemn confession; but did it satisfy the Lord? We are told, a little while previous, that "Many believed in his name, when they saw the miracles which he did. But Jesus did not commit himself unto them." Jesus did not commit himself to any who made no further profession than that of belief in his miracles. The miracles ought to lead men to receive the spiritual gifts of Christ. Those men of whom St. John speaks did indeed perceive, from the wonderful works of Jesus, that he was the Messiah; but, destitute of a sense of internal wants, and possessing contracted, superficial, and undecided minds, they turned but partially unto him, and were ready to forsake him as soon as they might be required, by remaining faithful to him, to struggle against sin and the world. Perhaps some of them even desired to profit by the presence of the Messiah and his power to accomplish worldly objects, to procure their independence, or to distinguish themselves among their countrymen.

Jesus rejected this faith; "He did not commit himself unto them;" and seeing that Nicodemus had fallen into this error, but had a nobler and more profound mind than the rest, he placed the more important and glorious miracle which was to be accomplished in his heart in opposition to those external miracles which the ruler of the Jews acknowledged. "Jesus answered and said unto him, Verily, verily, I say unto thee, Except a man be born again, he can not see the kingdom of God. That which is born of the flesh is flesh; and that which is born of the Spirit is spirit. Marvel not that I said unto thee, Ye must be born again."

Thus it was that the Saviour taught "the man of miracles" the real nature of his religion and his kingdom. He showed him that while the law only cuts off the outward excrescences of sin, the Gospel gives a new heart, a new mind, and creates a new man, born of God. He showed the close connection which exists between outward miracles and inward regeneration, and placed the latter of these far above the former.

It is doubtless true that a man may simply have faith in miracles, and that that is better than no faith at all; but it is a human faith, which is often produced by false wonders, for which the Holy Spirit is not needed, and which, if it leads no farther, is useless. Christianity knows no real faith except that by which the Holy Spirit regenerates the heart and the life. That which does not produce in man a change which brings him near to God, scarcely deserves the name of faith in the view of the Gospel. "It is not really faith," says Calvin, "to admire the power of God in miracles, in such a way as to believe merely that the doctrine is true, without entirely submitting to it."[1] "There is a certain kind of faith," he says in another place, "which exists only in the mind, and which readily vanishes away, because it is not established in the heart; it is what St. James calls a dead faith. True faith is inseparable from the spirit of regeneration."[2]

We are now defending the religion of Jesus Christ against that of Nicodemus; we are requiring that Christianity be not reduced to such a superficial, powerless, outward, contracted system as that which that Pharisee admitted after having seen Jesus Christ; we are putting the doctrine of the new birth and new life in the highest place, as our Lord did. And if, among those who teach the doctrine of Nicodemus, there were any who wondered that we said, "Man must be born of the Spirit," we would only reply to such, as our Lord did, "Are ye masters in Israel, and know not these things?"

There is a great and eternal harmony between the miracles of Christianity and its doctrines. The harmonies of Christianity are found every where. There is harmony between Christianity and the world considered as a creation of God; to establish this truth, famous works on natural philosophy have been written in our own days. There is harmony between Christianity and the history of the human race. "The world," exclaims the greatest of modern historians, "seems to have been arranged solely to favour the advent and the doctrines of our Lord."[3] And while Christianity is in harmony with every thing that comes from God, shall it not be in harmony with itself? Yes; every where I meet with a striking harmony between the facts and the doctrines of the Gospel. The former lead me to the latter; the miracles possess no value unless they conduct me to the Christian truths; so that if, admitting the facts, I reject the dogmas, I refuse to follow the finger of God;

---

[1] Illud nondum est vere credere, quum Dei virtutem mirantur, ut doctrinam simpliciter credant esse veram, non autem penitus se illi subjiciant.— *In Johan.*, ii.　　[2] Vera fides spiritu regenerationis semper constat.—*Ibid.*
[3] John de Muller to Charles Bonnet.

I stop my ears to his powerful voice; I am blind and deaf. Let us hastily glance at these sublime harmonies, in which all the wisdom of the Lord shines forth.

FIRST HARMONY.—There is perfect identity of nature between miracles and the doctrine of *Inspiration,* as Christians ought to receive it. In truth, wherein consists the inspiration of the Scriptures? In the fact that the natural powers of the writer were withdrawn, while a virtue, which emanated from God, took their place, and dictated the sacred books which were to enlighten the world. Now, what is a miracle but a cessation of natural powers and an immediate intervention of God's power? The Bible itself is therefore a miracle, and all the wonders which surround it are but the accompaniments of this principal miracle. How can we admit the former and not admit the latter? What! shall I admit that God supposed it worth while to interfere directly when sight was to be restored to a poor blind man, or the command of his limbs to a poor paralytic; and shall I nevertheless imagine that he did not directly interfere when that Book of books, that code of laws for the human race, which was to remain on earth till the end of time, to enlighten the nations, to save souls, to found and preserve the eternal kingdom, was to be given to mankind? Shall I admit that God desired to act alone, without being assisted by any individual, when a dumb man was to be made to speak, or a dead man to be raised to life; but that when he is to make himself known to his creatures, to write those pages which are to point out to a fallen race the road to heaven, he only guides his servants, and that in such a way as not always to guard them from falling into error? No; I admit the miracle which produced the Bible before all others, and I treasure it up with adoration in my heart, as the word which the very mouth of my God has spoken.

SECOND HARMONY.—What is it that the miracles of Christ lead me to contemplate on earth? All manner of infirmities and suffering; the deaf, the blind, the leper, the dumb; fevers, bloody issues, the Wicked One violently tormenting souls and bodies; finally, death, fearful death. And what is the meaning of this mournful escort of humanity, which has never ceased to accompany it down to our times? These miseries speak to me of another misery, which is their source; of a rebellion and fall. They cry aloud to me, " Sin hath entered into the world, and death by sin." They declare to me that sin did not come into the world as a mere example, but as a beginning, a principle, the consequences of which extend to us. As St. Augustine has said, there are " several deaths," [1] but they all advance together in the train of sin, which is itself the first of them. If, at the sight of this troop of blind, paralytic, and dumb men who surround Jesus Christ, I say to myself, looking back upon the bodily beauty of Adam, God did not create man with such infirmities : I also say, in view of all the corruption which exists in our hearts, God did not create man such as He has forbidden that he should be ; God can not be the author of what is opposed to Himself ! He created man in a pure and normal state ; but, together with the physical evils from which Jesus delivered his contemporaries, there entered into the whole human race, as Melancthon says, a certain inclination which is agreeable to us, a certain attraction which leads us to sin, a vivacious plant, the fruits of which are miseries brought forth in all seasons—" original sin." [2] The miracles, then, reveal the fall and hereditary corruption of humanity.

THIRD HARMONY.—The miracles of Jesus Christ present him to us every where as promptly and powerfully delivering all who are in any kind of suffering or peril. Even though the unfortunate person belong to the lowest class of society, though he be at a great distance from Jesus, or even though he have merited his misfortune, nothing hinders Christ. He speaks, and his mighty voice is enough to drive away evil spirits and raise the dead. " He came to seek and to save that which was lost." But what is the object of these deliverances, other than to lead us to a still more admirable salvation, of which Christ is the author ? It is from condemnation, from sin and hell that he has come to save us ; and he delivers men from them, even though they be in the lowest degree of human corruption, and at the very gates of the eternal pit. Still more : in the same way that he drove away the evils with which those who surrounded him were struck, alone, and without the assistance of the sufferers, so he saves man alone, without any

---

[1] De civit. Dei, xiii, 12. Sicut universa terra ex multis terris, et universa ecclesia ex multis constat ecclesiis, sic universa mors ex omnibus.

[2] Vivax quædam ἐνέργεια peccatum originale.—Loci Comm. Theologici.

merit or assistance on the part of the latter.   The sufferings
of Christ, and his submission to God in his sufferings, his
death and the purity of his obedience in that death, his blood
which was shed, and the innocence of that blood—this is the
holy, the spotless, the only sacrifice, which alone expiates all
sins and is an equivalent for all sufferings.   What shall man
add to it ?   A perfect salvation, which has come down from
heaven, saves man, without the merits or the strength of man;
this is what the miracles announce, though feebly, and what the
Cross of redemption, raised on Golgotha, majestically proclaims.

And, far from viewing this way of salvation as irrational, I
see in it all the wisdom of God.   In truth, this righteousness
of Christ, which saves me, is not mine by nature : and thus I
learn deeply to humble myself before God; but it is mine to all
eternity, by a gift of grace : and thus I learn to know the
depths of that love of God which enriches me in my great poverty.   O blessed righteousness, which art not mine, and yet
art mine ! thou humblest and raisest me up in turn, and thou
preservest my soul in that sacred harmony of lowliness and
greatness, which makes it beautiful in the sight of God !

FOURTH HARMONY.—The faith of those whom Jesus healed
holds an important position in his miracles.   He desired to
show that it is in this way alone that he will save the souls of
men.   " The word is apprehended by means of faith alone,"
says Melancthon.[1]   Grace is as though it existed not for us,
if we do not believe that it exists.   Of what use would it be to
me that a wealthy and powerful man should have left his property to me, if I rejected every proof of it which was laid before me ?   But this faith, which is the instrument by means
of which I receive salvation, is not a meritorious condition of
it.   It is a great error (and is particularly the error of Rome)
to invent a faith of which love and good works are ingredients,
and by means of which man merits mercy.   I must be justified
before I can believe that I am ; and God must already have
adopted me as his son before I can know that he has done so.
It is not faith that produces this truth : it is this truth that
produces faith in me.   If the sick who were cured by Christ
had believed that it was they who, by means of their faith,
healed themselves, they would have done the very contrary of
what Jesus Christ required of them, and would have remained

8   Verbum tantum fide apprehenditur.   Z

in their wretchedness for ever.　Let us then understand in this too the harmony between the facts and the doctrines of Christianity.　"By grace are ye saved through faith."

FIFTH HARMONY.—Christ reveals himself in his miracles as communicating life.　The first act by which he displayed his glory at Cana shows, under an earthly figure, his power to give life, and to change the weakest things to the strongest. When he multiplied the loaves, he presented himself to the multitude as the Being who gave "that meat which endureth unto everlasting life."　When he raised the dead, he declared that he was "the resurrection and the life, and that he that believeth in him, though he were dead, yet shall he live."　The miracles of Jesus Christ, therefore, declare to all men that he communicates divine life.　Jesus is not satisfied with calling man; he creates something new within him.　Those learned men who analyze and discover every thing are ignorant of the most glorious life that exists in the world, unless they themselves have been "born of God."　What! when Jesus Christ gave life to a withered arm, to paralyzed limbs, to a dumb tongue, to a body lying in the tomb, shall he not give life to the soul of man, which is "dead in trespasses and sins"?　No; he who, believing in supernatural works, is satisfied with an ordinary, animal, intellectual, or even moral life, without receiving *divine life* in his heart, has not understood the miracles of the Redeemer, and has drawn no advantage from them.

SIXTH HARMONY.—The miracles show us the union which exists between God's free salvation and man's works.　Shall we say that, because Christ loosened the tongue of the dumb man, the dumb man will not speak? or that, because he straightened the limbs of the paralytic, the paralytic will not walk?　On the contrary, since these unfortunate men have been healed by Jesus Christ, they will act, speak, and walk now.　And yet this is what men deny respecting the doctrine of Christianity.　They constantly repeat, that to attribute salvation to Jesus Christ alone is to prevent a man from performing good works.　When the means of preventing a man from seeing shall be to restore his sight, then we shall understand how it can be, that to place the love of God in a man's heart is the means of hindering him from performing the will of God. "It is a base calumny," says Melancthon (for this is an old

accusation), " to say that we do not teach the doctrine of good
works; since we not only require works, but we also show they
can be performed." Yes, the doctrine of justification through
faith is the real doctrine of works. Far from impeding the
performance of them, it produces them. It takes away every
impure motive from our hearts—selfishness, pride, love of reward—and replaces them by the purest and most powerful
motives. If you tell me that this doctrine, by taking away
the intrinsic defect which naturally cleaves to all human actions,
even to those which have the best appearance, is opposed to
those actions, then I will maintain that the operation by means
of which a mortified limb is cut off kills the body instead of
saving it. The faith which I have in God's love to me produces God's love within me; and, instead of the discord of sin,
it establishes in my soul a sacred harmony with its Creator.
The moderns have discovered mechanical powers, by means of
which they multiply to an almost infinite extent the labour and
the products of man. Faith, in the spiritual world, is a more
wonderful power than all those of the material world. Steam
drives its cars and ships with great rapidity; faith draws from
their families those humble missionaries, who, forsaking all
things, go and raise the banner of Jesus Christ in the ends of
the earth, even among cannibals.

SEVENTH HARMONY.—Christ reveals himself in his miracles
as " God manifest in the flesh." If the standards of enemies,
carried before a triumphal car, display the glory of a conqueror,
and if bounty and mercy announce that a kind monarch is passing through his provinces, then the sick suddenly cured, the
evil spirits driven away, nature anew subjected to the power of
him who created it, the dead arising from their tombs, manifest
the glory of God made man.[1] The apostles did not possess
the constant gift of working miracles ; otherwise, would not
Paul have cured his friends Titus and Epaphroditus immediately? But Jesus possessed it continually, and he himself offers
this fact as a proof of his divinity. " My Father," said he,
" worketh hitherto, and I work." And the Jews understood
perfectly that by these words he " *made himself equal with God.*"
Jesus replied, to confirm them in this opinion, " What things
soever the Father doeth, these also doeth the Son likewise.

---

[1] Quæcumque enim miracula ostendit mundo, totidem Divinæ ejus poten-
tiæ testimonia fuerunt.—CALVIN.

The Son quickeneth whom he will; that all men should honour the Son, *even* as they honour the Father."

When, with the universal church, we believe in the great miracle of the divinity of Christ, the whole Scripture becomes clear to our minds. The miracles especially astonish us no longer; they are the natural works of his divinity, just as the ordinary labour of every day is to us. They are miracles, as Sartorius remarks, not for him, but for our inferior natures; in the same way that, on a lower scale, our actions are miraculous to the beasts, not because they are above nature in general, but because they are above their nature in particular. Listening to what the miracles proclaim, I therefore together with the apostles, worship in Jesus the Lord of heaven, the Word, the Author of all the manifestations of God, of all his creations, of all the works destined to prepare that redemption which the God of revelation has made for man.

Such are the harmonies which exist between the facts and the doctrines of Christianity. But the very effects of these doctrines present another relation to us. The miracles of Christ proved in the days of the Gospel that a power proceeding from God had entered into the world; the doctrines have never ceased during eighteen centuries to do likewise. The propagation of Christianity, and its effects around us and throughout the world, are a forcible demonstration of the divinity of the Gospel, which the inhabitants of Judea did not possess in the days of the Lord.

"Miracles," says John von Müller, "were performed for the purpose of awakening the contemporaries of Jesus; a greater miracle was reserved for our days, namely, the sight of the concatenation of all human affairs for the foundation and preservation of this doctrine." If the first acts of the Church were sufficient to lead the contemporaries of Jesus to believe, what shall take place now that this humble beginning has been changed into a magnificent triumph? Christianity is a perpetual miracle. "The ocular witnesses of Jesus Christ," says Lessing, "saw nothing but the foundation; but we have the building itself. And now that I see that building, which has lasted with such firmness for so many ages, I know that its foundations are good and true; and I know it more certainly than those could who saw those foundations laid."

Such are the intimate harmonies which exist between the facts and the doctrines of Christianity; and it is thus that the essence of the latter was already contained in the former.

Let men renounce then that fatal error through which they would fain separate the doctrines from the miracles, and receive one and reject the other. Let them understand that this is to sacrifice religion, and to compensate themselves with a vague and empty thing, which brings nothing to the soul. Let them forsake the religion of Nicodemus, and come to that of Jesus Christ. Let our Christianity be really distinct from all miraculous superstitions, whether past or present, as its foundation and essence is the great mystery of godliness.

I am not satisfied with hearing the trumpets whose loud voices proclaim the king's approach, but I hasten to behold him myself. I am not satisfied with hearing the bells which are rung in full chorus, but I enter into the sanctuary and worship. I am not satisfied with a religion of miracles; I must have *the true God and eternal life.*

O how much more beautiful do the miracles themselves appear to me, when I look upon them as living symbols, in which I find the image of all the truths which save me. Then they are not a dead body; they have a soul, a life, which is peculiar to them; and their existence has an object, for they lead me into the path of peace. These truths are what I want; for them my soul thirsts; to them I would hasten. I seize, I embrace, I grasp them, and exclaim, O my God! place them in my heart; and may I myself, quickened by them, like a corpse raised to life, be a miracle of thy love!

Having refuted, under the name of Rationalism, the doctrine which rejects miracles, we have opposed, under the name of superstition, that which makes miracles the essential part of religion.

This we have seen is a superstition very different from ordinary superstitions, and which is in many respects far superior to them, since it relates to truths, and not to fables. But, we repeat, there are certain truths, which, viewed in an exclusive manner, become errors. It is true, very true, that man has a body; but if nothing but the body be considered in man, and if the soul be regarded as a doubtful or unimportant thing, then we fall into an error which borders so closely on materialism, that that name may be applied to it. Just so it is with a Christian, or a church, that considers and professes nothing but miracles in Christianity. This is an error so similar to superstition that that name may justly be given to it.

But if in one aspect this superstition is preferable to ordinary superstitions, in another aspect it is less desirable. Indeed, the latter add, but do not diminish; whereas that to which I allude takes away the most essential doctrines of Christianity: the Trinity, the fall, and original, hereditary, and complete corruption of man, the incarnation of the Eternal Word, the real divinity of the Redeemer, the expiation by blood on the cross, regeneration by the Holy Spirit, justification by faith, creation of the new man unto good works, and election by grace. This particular kind of superstition, which is to be found in certain men who are enlightened by all the light of the age, savours greatly therefore of infidelity.

Hitherto there have been two kinds of infidelity in the Christian church. One of them (the preferable) is that of which we have just spoken, which is superstition in one aspect, and infidelity in another. The other is that more radical infidelity which denies both the doctrines and the facts. The former belongs peculiarly to the Western nations of Europe, and to America. It is the religion of the Unitarians in Switzerland, France, England, and the United States. The latter is found especially among the German races. Saxony is now its most powerful centre. These strong-minded nations do not stop half way, like our more enervated populations. Of what use, they have said, is it to keep a revelation, when there is no longer any thing to reveal; a pedestal, when there is no statue to place on it? And they have overthrown at once the dogmas and the facts. These are the Rationalists.

There is more consistency and candour in the Rationalist system, which rejects every thing, than in the mediate systems, which would unite truth with error. Nevertheless, in another aspect, Rationalism is a greater evil than Unitarianism. The latter preserves at least the great fact of a revelation; and this primary idea is a basis upon which a truly celestial doctrine might at some time arise. The pedestal without the statue is useless; but it witnesses that one is wanting, and calls for one.

The Rationalism of the German race has lately, we are informed, given the first token of its invasion of the country of the Gallic and British races. This doctrine, which has hitherto stopped at the limits of the German tongue, has now, we are told, crossed the frontier. We pass rapidly by this fact, as we are disposed to regard it, above all, as an act of sincerity; and we come to a reflection which is connected with it.

This commencement of invasion is an event in the Church. It was a great event for the world when, in the fourth, fifth, and sixth centuries, the invasion by the German race, in those same regions, then in a state of corrupt civilization, took place. It is true that, at that time, there was already reason to hope that the irruption of those barbarous nations which poured down upon an enervated people, would become an instrument, in the hand of God, to renovate the Roman people, and to establish throughout Europe a new nation and a new faith on the ruins of ancient Polytheism and the ancient nations. But it is no less true that these German tribes at first brought only desolation and death in their train, and seemed every where to destroy the little cultivation and religion which still existed.

Without wishing to make any comparison, the state of things is somewhat analogous. Unitarianism will perhaps be an easy conquest for German Rationalism. Long have these two doctrines advanced hand in hand. The crowd of Unitarians will not escape; they gravitate toward Rationalism. It is not the fathers but the children who will fall in; it is not the masters but the disciples.

Nevertheless, let us not fear! There is a vast difference between the invasion with which German Rationalism threatens us and that of the ancient Germans. Then those terrible nations met with no power capable of stopping them. Now, thanks be to God! there is in those Gallic and British races, and in the German races themselves, an energetic power, the power of the Christian's faith, which boldly rises and opposes that devastating torrent. This faith overcomes the world; and Unitarianism, Rationalism, and all anti-Christian powers must be sacrificed to it. Thanks be to God! all these human instructions are but isolated and ephemeral apparitions. The church of Christ in Germany, Switzerland, France, England, Holland, America, and the whole world, will arise, if need be, like one man, and, defending both doctrines and facts, will proclaim with one voice and heart "the great mystery of godliness—GOD MANIFEST IN THE FLESH.

Still further: the greatest excesses of Arianism, after Arius and Athanasius, alarmed the more religious semi-Arians, enlightened them, and, uniting them to the orthodox, brought them back to the sound doctrines of revelation.

May we not hope for the same victory in our day? Shall we not see noble and pious souls, which have indeed been drawn for some time into a mournful opposition to the truth, enlightened now by the evils which the invasion of Rationalism will bring in its train, casting themselves with grief, but with love, at the feet of the Saviour, exclaiming, like the disciple, for a short time unbelieving, "My Lord and my God"?

This would be the first good result which God would draw out of so great an evil; and then there would be great joy on earth and in heaven.

Nevertheless, let us be on our guard! A new error has appeared. To your tents, O Israel! Let us stand before the church of Jesus Christ, firm in our faith in his miracles, and firm in our faith in his mysteries; these are the two pillars upon which Christianity rests.

But let us remember that which these two pillars are called to sustain and to give to the world, namely, the perfume of a holy life, full of hope and love. A man may believe in the miracle, and admit the doctrine, and yet be nothing more than a tinkling cymbal. If the great wonder, in the days of the Gospel, was Christ manifest in the flesh, the great miracle in our days must be Christ manifest in us by a life of Christ, a life of heaven, a life of gentleness, meekness, righteousness, peace, and love. This is the object in the attainment of which all the miracles and the doctrines end. Without miracles and without doctrines, there can be no Christian life; but without Christian life, miracles and doctrines are nothing. O how beautiful is that miracle which can elicit from the world, as in the primitive ages, the exclamation, "See how they love one another."

Send thy church that miracle, Lord! It is the only one we ask. Clothed with that power thy redeemed will conquer the gates of the nations, and the cross will be planted on the walls of every people!

Wm. Collins & Co., Printers.

Other Solid Ground Titles

THE COMMUNICANT'S COMPANION by *Matthew Henry*

THE SECRET OF COMMUNION WITH GOD by *Matthew Henry*

THE MOTHER AT HOME by *John S.C. Abbott*

LECTURES ON THE ACTS OF THE APOSTLES by *John Dick*

THE FORGOTTEN HEROES OF LIBERTY by *J.T. Headley*

LET THE CANNON BLAZE AWAY by *Joseph P. Thompson*

THE STILL HOUR: *Communion with God in Prayer* by *Austin Phelps*

COLLECTED WORKS of James Henley Thornwell (4 vols.)

CALVINISM IN HISTORY by *Nathaniel S. McFetridge*

OPENING SCRIPTURE: *Hermeneutical Manual* by *Patrick Fairbairn*

THE ASSURANCE OF FAITH by *Louis Berkhof*

THE PASTOR IN THE SICK ROOM by *John D. Wells*

THE BUNYAN OF BROOKLYN: *Life & Sermons of I.S. Spencer*

THE NATIONAL PREACHER: *Sermons from 2nd Great Awakening*

FIRST THINGS: *First Lessons God Taught Mankind* *Gardiner Spring*

BIBLICAL & THEOLOGICAL STUDIES by *1912 Faculty of Princeton*

THE POWER OF GOD UNTO SALVATION by *B.B. Warfield*

THE LORD OF GLORY by *B.B. Warfield*

A GENTLEMAN & A SCHOLAR: *Memoir of J.P. Boyce* by *J. Broadus*

SERMONS TO THE NATURAL MAN by *W.G.T. Shedd*

SERMONS TO THE SPIRITUAL MAN by *W.G.T. Shedd*

HOMILETICS AND PASTORAL THEOLOGY by *W.G.T. Shedd*

A PASTOR'S SKETCHES 1 & 2 by *Ichabod S. Spencer*

THE PREACHER AND HIS MODELS by *James Stalker*

IMAGO CHRISTI: *The Example of Jesus Christ* by *James Stalker*

LECTURES ON THE HISTORY OF PREACHING by *J. A. Broadus*

THE SHORTER CATECHISM ILLUSTRATED by *John Whitecross*

THE CHURCH MEMBER'S GUIDE by *John Angell James*

THE SUNDAY SCHOOL TEACHER'S GUIDE by *John A. James*

CHRIST IN SONG: *Hymns of Immanuel from All Ages* by *Philip Schaff*

DEVOTIONAL LIFE OF THE S.S. TEACHER by *J.R. Miller*

Call us Toll Free at 1-877-666-9469

Send us an e-mail at sgcb@charter.net

Visit us on line at solid-ground-books.com

Uncovering Buried Treasure to the Glory of God

Printed in the United States
205849BV00002B/65/A

9 781599 250182